Roadside Networks for Vehicular Communications:

Architectures, Applications, and Test Fields

Robil Daher
University of Rostock, Germany

Alexey Vinel
Tampere University of Technology, Finland

Managing Director:	Lindsay Johnston
Editorial Director:	Joel Gamon
Book Production Manager:	Jennifer Romanchak
Publishing Systems Analyst:	Adrienne Freeland
Development Editor:	Austin DeMarco
Assistant Acquisitions Editor:	Kayla Wolfe
Typesetter:	Erin O'Dea
Cover Design:	Nick Newcomer

Published in the United States of America by
Information Science Reference (an imprint of IGI Global)
701 E. Chocolate Avenue
Hershey PA 17033
Tel: 717-533-8845
Fax: 717-533-8661
E-mail: cust@igi-global.com
Web site: http://www.igi-global.com

Library of Congress Cataloging-in-Publication Data

Roadside networks for vehicular communications: architectures, applications, and test fields / Robil Daher and Alexey Vinel, editor.
     pages cm
  Includes bibliographical references and index.
  Summary: "This book attempts to close the gap between science and technology in the field of roadside backbones for VCNs"-- Provided by publisher.
  ISBN 978-1-4666-2223-4 (hardcover) -- ISBN (invalid) 978-1-4666-2224-1 (ebook) -- ISBN 978-1-4666-2225-8 (print & perpetual access) 1. Vehicular ad hoc networks (Computer networks) 2. Intelligent transportation systems. I. Daher, Robil, 1973- II. Vinel, Alexey.
  TE228.37.R63 2013
  388.3'124--dc23
                             2012020189

British Cataloguing in Publication Data
A Cataloguing in Publication record for this book is available from the British Library.

Editorial Advisory Board

Table of Contents

Section 4
Information Dissemination

Detailed Table of Contents

Section 1
VANETs Enabling Technologies

Chapter 1

George Kadas, Alexander TEI of Thessaloniki, Greece
Periklis Chatzimisios, Alexander TEI of Thessaloniki, Greece

Vehicular Communication Networks is a subcategory of Mobile Communications Networks that has
the special characteristics of high node mobility and fast topology changes. In the current chapter, the
authors outline the basic characteristics and concepts of vehicular communications and present the
standardization and network deployment efforts carried out by the scientific community. In particular,
they focus their attention on the vehicle-to-infrastructure component of the network; moreover, the
authors specifically investigate security, quality of service, and routing, which constitute three of the
most challenging aspects in the field of Vehicular Networks. The authors further examine the ways that
infrastructure can provide efficient solutions to the problems that exist for each respective category and
review several proposed solutions.

Chapter 2

Matteo Petracca, National Interuniversity Consortium for Telecommunications, Italy
Paolo Pagano, National Interuniversity Consortium for Telecommunications, Italy
Riccardo Pelliccia, Scuola Superiore Sant'Anna, Italy
Marco Ghibaudi, Scuola Superiore Sant'Anna, Italy
Claudio Salvadori, Scuola Superiore Sant'Anna, Italy
Christian Nastasi, Scuola Superiore Sant'Anna, Italy

Intelligent Transport Systems (ITS) are a focus of public authorities and research communities in order
for them to provide effective solutions for improving citizens' security and lifestyle. The effectiveness
of such systems relies on the prompt processing of the acquired traffic- and vehicle-related information to react to congestion and dangerous situations. To obtain a dynamic and pervasive environment
where vehicles are fully integrated in the ITS, low cost technologies (capable of strongly penetrating
the market) must be made available by the effort of academic and industrial research. In this chapter,
the authors discuss the design and implementation of a prototype vehicular unit capable of interacting
with both roadside networks and in-vehicle electronic devices. More in detail, in order to scientifically

characterize the solution, the authors start from a clear statement of the requirements that the vehicle equipment should respond to. Then they detail the selection of the off-the-shelf components adopted in the prototyped on-board unit. In the last part of the chapter, the authors discuss several possible applications in which the developed device can be adopted, as well as open issues for future research activities.

Chapter 3

Claudio Cicconetti, Intecs S.p.A., Italy
Raffaella Mambrini, Intecs S.p.A., Italy
Alessandro Rossi, Intecs S.p.A., Italy

The deployment of more sustainable land transportation is a non-debatable global issue. It is generally agreed that Information and Communication Technology (ICT) will play the role of the main enabler to achieve the ambitious objective of improving transportation efficiency, thus reducing pollution, time and resource wastage, and accidents. In this chapter, after briefly introducing the general architecture of the ICT infrastructure for the new generation of Intelligent Transportation Systems (ITSs), the authors provide a survey of the wireless technologies available for implementing the data network required to transfer information between the peripheral devices, installed roadside and in the vehicles, and the data center where the actual storage and logic resides. Specifically, they consider the following alternatives: IEEE 802.11 in a Wireless Mesh Network (WMN) configuration, IEEE 802.16/WiMAX, Long Term Evolution (LTE), and HiperLAN/2. The latter is investigated in further details by providing results from preliminary laboratory trials carried out in the Italian project IPERMOB.

Section 2
Applications and RSU Deployment

Chapter 4

Alessandro Bazzi, National Research Council (CNR-IEIIT), Italy
Barbara M. Masini, National Research Council (CNR-IEIIT), Italy
Gianni Pasolini, University of Bologna, Italy

Many vehicles are currently equipped with On-Board Units (OBUs) that are in charge of collecting and processing data for some specific purposes (such as for travel monitoring, as requested by many insurance companies). These devices are connected to the cellular network by means of their Vehicle-to-Infrastructure (V2I) communication interface, and are thus able to transmit and receive information also related to real time traffic, pollution, local events, etc. Of course, as the number of OBU-equipped vehicles increases, the cost of this service increases as well, both in terms of network load and billing. In this chapter, the authors discuss the possibility of taking advantage of vehicle-to-vehicle (V2V) and Vehicle-to-Roadside (V2R) communications to save V2I resources, thus reducing the cellular network burden and, consequently, the service cost.

Chapter 5

Massimo Reineri, Politecnico di Torino, Italy
Claudio Casetti, Politecnico di Torino, Italy
Carla-Fabiana Chiasserini, Politecnico di Torino, Italy

Marco Fiore, INSA Lyon, INRIA, France

Oscar Trullols-Cruces, Universitat Politecnica de Catalunya, Spain

Jose M. Barcelo-Ordinas, Universitat Politecnica de Catalunya, Spain

The focus of this chapter is twofold: information dissemination from infrastructure nodes deployed along the roads, the so-called Road-Side Units (RSUs), to passing-by vehicles, and content downloading by vehicular users through nearby RSUs. In particular, in order to ensure good performance for both content dissemination and downloading, the presented study addresses the problem of RSU deployment and reviews previous work that has dealt with such an issue. The RSU deployment problem is then formulated as an optimization problem, where the number of vehicles that come in contact with any RSU is maximized, possibly considering a minimum contact time to be guaranteed. Since such optimization problems turn out to be NP-hard, heuristics are proposed to efficiently approximate the optimal solution. The RSU deployment obtained through such heuristics is then used to investigate the performance of content dissemination and downloading through ns2 simulations. Simulation tests are carried out under various real-world vehicular environments, including a realistic mobility model, and considering that the IEEE 802.11p standard is used at the physical and medium access control layers. The performance obtained in realistic conditions is discussed with respect to the results obtained under the same RSU deployment, but in ideal conditions and protocol message exchange. Based on the obtained results, some useful hints on the network system design are provided.

Chapter 6

Navin Kumar, University of Aveiro, Portugal

Luis Nero Alves, University of Aveiro, Portugal

Rui L. Aguiar, University of Aveiro, Portugal

There is great concern over growing road accidents and associated fatalities. In order to reduce accidents, improve congestion and offer smooth flow of traffic, several measures, such as providing intelligence to transport, providing communication infrastructure along the road, and vehicular communication, are being undertaken. Traffic safety information broadcast from traffic lights using Visible Light Communication (VLC) is a new cost effective technology which assists drivers in taking necessary safety measures. This chapter presents the VLC broadcast system considering LED-based traffic lights. It discusses the integration of traffic light Roadside Units (RSUs) with upcoming Intelligent Transportation Systems (ITS) architecture. Some of the offered services using this technology in vehicular environment together with future direction and challenges are discussed. A prototype demonstrator of the designed VLC systems is also presented.

Chapter 7

Mohamed Ahmed El-Dakroury, Ain Shams University, Egypt

Abdel Halim Zekry, Ain Shams University, Egypt

Hassanein H. Amer, American University, Egypt

Ramez M. Daoud, American University, Egypt

This chapter addresses the wireless communication aspect of traffic control in an urban vehicular environment. The IEEE 802.16e-2005 standard is used for Infrastructure to Vehicle communication. An architecture is developed with the target of minimizing overall data loss. Access Service Network Gateway (ASN-GW) is used to manage vehicle communication while roaming. OPNET simulations show that using ASN-GW gives good performance in mobility management. Simulations also show that introducing an interference source drastically degrades system performance. Using Dual Trigger HO (DTH) in a congested scenario improves system performance and reduces the impact of interference on the system.

Section 3
Quality of Service Provisioning

Chapter 8

Hamada Alshaer, Khalifa University, UAE

Thierry Ernst, l'Ecole des Mines Paristech, France

Arnaud de La Fortelle, l'Ecole des Mines Paristech, France

Resource availability in vehicular mobile networks fluctuates due to wireless channel fading and network mobility. Multi-homed mobile networks require a Quality-of-Service (QoS) control scheme that can select a routing path to guarantee high quality of communications with Correspondent Nodes (CNs) while using the maximum available bandwidth of wireless and radio communication technologies. In this chapter, the authors develop an intelligent distributed QoS control scheme which inter-operates between mobile routers, managing vehicular networks mobility, and Road Communication Gateways (RCGs). This proposed scheme manages Vehicle-to-Infrastructure (V2I) communications through enabling multi-homed vehicular networks to optimally distribute traffic among egress links of their mobile routers based on vehicular communication policies and available bandwidth and performance metrics of selected routing paths. This scheme considers the data control plane as a collaborative entity and specifies detailed operations to be performed in the mobile routers and RCGs. Simulation experiments show that the proposed scheme can improve the Congestion Window (CWND) of TCP and the e2e packet loss of video traffic, despite network mobility. It also guarantees the service parameter settings of uplink and downlink connections while achieving reasonable utilization efficiency of network resources and fairly sharing them.

Chapter 9

Zahra Taghikhaki, University of Twente, The Netherlands

Yang Zhang, University of Twente, The Netherlands

Nirvana Meratnia, University of Twente, The Netherlands

Paul J. M. Havinga, University of Twente, The Netherlands

Vehicular Communication Networks (VCNs) and Wireless Sensor Networks (WSNs) are emerging types of networks that have been extensively explored individually. However, their cooperation and exploring advantages offered by their integration are unexplored topics. Such integration help better investigate the impact of human mobility and transportation behaviours on the safety and the well-being of cities, their residents, their surrounding environments, and their ecology. In this chapter, the authors propose a quality-aware data aggregation technique for wireless sensor networks cooperating with vehicular communication networks, which quickly, reliably, and energy efficiently aggregate sensor data and send the aggregated value to roadside base stations, ensuring quality of service parameters has been put forward as an essential consideration for wireless sensor networks, which are often deployed in unattended and open environments and are characterized by their limited resources. To this end, in-network data aggregation is an efficient solution to save energy and bandwidth and to provide meaningful information to end-users.

Chapter 10

Fábio Pereira, Technical University Lisbon, Portugal
João Barreto, Technical University Lisbon, Portugal

Public transportation is becoming more and more importance in big urban centers, as it is a key ingredient to sustainable cities. Still, richer and more diverse public transport services imply increased complexity to the users of such services. In this chapter, the authors address the problem of journey planning for public transport users. This problem can be described as finding the best route between two given points in a city taking into account the available public transport services. The authors describe and compare traditional approaches that are already deployed in most cities. They then focus their attention on new and promising alternatives that become possible with the emergence of user-centric vehicular ad-hoc networks, complemented with roadside infrastructure. The authors discuss the benefits and challenges behind this new approach for journey planning in public transportation, and propose directions for possible solutions.

Section 4
Information Dissemination

Chapter 11

Mahabaleshwar S. Kakkasageri, Basaveshwar Engineering College, India
Sunilkumar S. Manvi, REVA Institute of Technology and Management, India

Vehicular Ad Hoc Network (VANET) has become an active area of research, standardization, and development because next generation vehicles will be capable of sensing, computing, and communicating. Different components in a vehicle constantly exchange available information with other vehicles on the road and cooperate to ensure safety and comfort of users using VANET. In VANET, information like navigation, cooperative collision avoidance, lane changing, speed limit, accident, obstacle, or road condition warnings, location awareness services, etc. play a significant role in safety-related applications. Safety related information dissemination is challenging due to the delay-sensitive nature of safety services. In this chapter, the authors survey some of the ongoing recent research efforts in information dissemination in VANETs. They also outline some of the research challenges that still need to be addressed to enable efficient information dissemination in VANET.

Chapter 12

Stefano Busanelli, Guglielmo Srl, Italy
Gianluigi Ferrari, University of Parma, Italy
Vito Andrea Giorgio, University of Parma, Italy
Nicola Iotti, Guglielmo Srl., Italy

In recent years, Vehicular Ad-hoc NETworks (VANETs) have experienced an intense development phase, driven by academia, industry, and public authorities. On the basis of the obtained results, it is reasonable to expect that VANETs will finally hit the market in the near future. In order to reach commercial success, VANETs must effectively operate during the first years of deployment, when the market penetration rate will be unavoidably low, and, consequently, only a small number of suitably equipped vehicles (VANET-enabled) will be present on the roads. Among the possible strategies to face the initial sparse VANET scenarios, the deployment of an auxiliary network constituted by fixed Road Side Units (RSUs), either Dissemination Points (DPs) or relays, is certainly one of the most promising. In order to maximize the benefits offered by this support infrastructure, the placement of RSUs needs to be carefully studied. In this chapter, the authors analyze, by means of numerical simulations, the performance of an application that leverages on a finite number of DPs for disseminating information to the transiting vehicles. The positions of the DPs are determined through a recently proposed family of optimal placement algorithms, on the basis of proper vehicular mobility traces. The analysis is carried out considering two realistic urban scenarios. In both cases, the performance improvement brought by the use of multi-hop broadcast protocols, with respect to classical single-hop communications with DPs, is investigated.

Chapter 13

Ayşegül Tüysüz Erman, University of Twente, The Netherlands
Ramon S. Schwartz, University of Twente, The Netherlands
Arta Dilo, University of Twente, The Netherlands
Hans Scholten, University of Twente, The Netherlands
Paul Havinga, University of Twente, The Netherlands

Vehicular Sensor Networks (VSNs) are an emerging area of research that combines technologies developed in the domains of Intelligent Transport Systems (ITS) and Wireless Sensor Networks. Data dissemination is an important aspect of these networks. It enables vehicles to share relevant sensor data about accidents, traffic load, or pollution. Several protocols are proposed for Vehicle to Vehicle (V2V) communication, but they are prone to intermittent connectivity. In this chapter, the authors propose a roadside infrastructure to ensure stable connectivity by adding vehicle to infrastructure to the V2V communication. They introduce a data dissemination protocol, Hexagonal Cell-Based Data Dissemination, adapting it for VSNs within a metropolitan area. The virtual architecture of the proposed data dissemination protocol exploits the typical radial configuration of main roads in a city, and uses them as the basis for the communication infrastructure where data and queries are stored. The design of the communication infrastructure in accordance with the road infrastructure distributes the network data in locations that are close or easily reachable by most of the vehicles. The protocol performs a geographical routing and is suitable for highly dynamic networks, supporting a high number of mobile sources and destinations of data. It ensures reliable data delivery and fast response. The authors evaluate the performance of the proposed protocol in terms of data delivery ratio and data delivery delay. The simulation results show that HexDD significantly improves the data packet delivery ratio in VANETs.

Preface

According to the reports of the United Nations, road traffic injuries are a major public health problem and a leading cause of death, injury, and disability around the world. Annually, nearly 1.3 million people die and more than 20 million are injured in road accidents. Nowadays, governmental, industrial, and research communities around the globe are working together to adopt new information and communication technologies, which will help to improve this sorrowful statistic.

A vehicular communication network is an example of such a new technology, which aims at improving the road safety and efficiency as well as driving comfort. It combines the up-to-date developments in wireless communications, embedded systems, automotive electronics, and human factors studies. Roadside telecommunication infrastructure, which allows moving vehicle exchanging the information with the fixed networks, being one of the key elements of future intelligent transportation systems, is a special focus of this book.

The book consists of 13 original contributions, dedicated to the architectures and applications of the roadside vehicular networks, written by the international team of experts and is organized as follows. Chapters 1 – 3 provide a general introduction into the concept of vehicular ad-hoc networks and the corresponding roadside infrastructure. Chapters 4 – 7 discuss existing and prospective roadside infrastructure enabled applications. In Chapters 8 – 10, the challenges and solutions for quality of service provisioning in vehicular networks are discussed. Finally, Chapters 11 – 13 explain the techniques of information dissemination in vehicular networks with and without road infrastructure.

The book will be interesting to the engineers and researchers whose professional interests include vehicular communications and automotive systems. The book can be also used as a supportive material for the master- and graduate-level students attending the university courses in wireless networking.

The editors would like to express their deep gratitude to all the authors for their contributions and cooperation, to all the members of advisory board and anonymous reviewers for their time and valuable suggestions. Last, but not the least, special thanks go to IGI Global and particularly to the editorial assistants Austin DeMarco and Hannah Abelbeck for their incredible help and patience during the preparation of the book.

Robil Daher
University of Rostock, Germany

Alexey Vinel
Tampere University of Technology, Finland

Tampere, Finland
31, August 2012

Section 1
VANETs Enabling Technologies

Chapter 1
The Role of Roadside Assistance in Vehicular Communication Networks:
Security, Quality of Service, and Routing Issues

George Kadas
Alexander TEI of Thessaloniki, Greece

Periklis Chatzimisios
Alexander TEI of Thessaloniki, Greece

ABSTRACT

Vehicular Communication Networks is a subcategory of Mobile Communications Networks that has the special characteristics of high node mobility and fast topology changes. In the current chapter, the authors outline the basic characteristics and concepts of vehicular communications and present the standardization and network deployment efforts carried out by the scientific community. In particular, they focus their attention on the vehicle-to-infrastructure component of the network; moreover, the authors specifically investigate security, quality of service, and routing, which constitute three of the most challenging aspects in the field of Vehicular Networks. The authors further examine the ways that infrastructure can provide efficient solutions to the problems that exist for each respective category and review several proposed solutions.

DOI: 10.4018/978-1-4666-2223-4.ch001

OVERVIEW AND BACKGROUND OF VANETS

Vehicular communications is an emerging part that has attracted much interest from academia and industry. In this chapter, we explore the aspects of vehicular communications and vehicular ad-hoc networks (VANET) to draw our attention on Vehicle-to-Infrastructure traffic model. In particular, we examine certain mechanisms to security-proofing a vehicular network, to provide quality of service according to certain needs and to route data traffic

What is a VANET?

A vehicular ad-hoc network (Hassnaa & Yan, 2009), acronymed VANET, is a special type of mobile ad-hoc network, utilizing vehicles as mobile nodes to create a network. This type of network can either be purely ad-hoc, meaning that all the traffic is being handled by the network nodes alone, or it may be assisted by the roadside network creating a vehicle-to-infrastructure relation in the network.

Inter-Vehicle Communications

Inter-vehicle communications allow a mobile vehicle to communicate with its surrounding environment, mobile or fixed networks. More specifically, vehicular nodes can communicate with their peers either via vehicle-to-vehicle communications or through the fixed roadside infrastructure. The communication and the delivery of information may range from motion data (speed, direction, location, etc.) to Internet media content, through the wide variety of supported applications that operate in a vehicular network.

The demands of the applications that operate in the vehicular environment, along with the properties and special traits of the vehicular access networks define the design and the requirements of the security provision, the quality of service provision, and the routing process within the network.

Inter-Vehicle Communication Challenges

The vehicular networks pose some serious challenges (Blum, Eskandarian, & Hoffmman, 2004) as the network's deployment is not an easy task. Moreover, the sparse deployment of the roadside infrastructure often plays key role to the smooth operation of the network.

Furthermore, we outline some of the major challenges that vehicular networks face and the possible ways that roadside equipment can help mitigate or even overcome those challenges.

- **Absence of central coordination:** While this is a major drawback of the purely ad-hoc part of the network, it poses no threat for the vehicle-to-infrastructure communication model, as the infrastructure assumes the role of the central coordinator for all the nodes that are in communication range with it.
- **Dynamic network:** One of the special traits of a vehicular network is its dynamic nature, which is a result of the mobile nodes and the high speed they develop considering the fact that they are vehicles. This results in a highly disconnected network, where the communication windows between nodes are often narrow. However, the deployment of the infrastructure and its use as an active part of the network comes from the need to solve the previously reported problem. Thus, infrastructure is employed to provide a level of stability to the dynamic network by coordinating the communication between its participants.
- **Security concerns:** Even though it will be analyzed later in chapter, it is really important to mention the issue of security that has risen with the VANET deployment. While the need for privacy and a secure environment is imperative to the deployment of a vehicular network, such environment cannot be guaranteed without the assistance of

roadside networks. In this case, a certain security policy is enforced on the network and the infrastructure is used to oversee it.

VANET Applications

In that regard, it is important to identify the four major categories (Kamini & Rakesh, 2010) of applications that exist in a VANET and provide numerous services:

- **Safety-oriented applications:** Examples include emergency break warning applications and lane-change warning applications. Safety-oriented applications are, as the name implies, applications that focus on providing the VANET nodes with the necessary mechanisms in order to maximize accident prevention and mitigate an accident's impact on the rest of the network.
- **Service-oriented applications:** Also known as infotainment applications, aim to provide the VANET participants with several services. They strive to make the driving experience of both driver and passengers more comfortable through various applications and services. That may include Internet access, media streaming, online gaming, etc.
- **Traffic efficiency applications:** Target at the improvement of traffic flow, reduction of road congestion, provision of alternate routes. This can be achieved in various ways such as electronic toll collection, rail intersection management, congestion awareness and information, real-time traffic conditions etc.
- **Driver assistance applications:** Aim to provide a secure and comfortable experience for the driver of the vehicle. Digital road maps downloading, navigation systems, parking assistance and automatic emergency call are only some of the services that can be provided and add up to

providing as much assistance as possible to the driver, without in any case compromising the driving experience.

It must be noted that this general taxonomy is affected by the vehicle-to-infrastructure relation. It is needless to say that certain applications could not achieve the required performance of delay, throughput and other network metrics if they were left to operate only in an ad-hoc manner (see Table 1).

Vehicular Communications: Vehicle-to-Infrastructure (V2I)

In this chapter, we specifically examine the V2I part of the vehicular communication model. V2I communications (Wiesbeck & Reichardt, 2010) refer to communication between road users and roadside equipment that is based on short or medium range communication technology. However, it must be noted that this architecture does not rely on the infrastructure in order to operate but rather exploits it to improve the network performance. Things that surely are essential for the existence of such a relation are:

1. A hybrid network meaning the existence of both vehicles and roadside equipment (in areas where the roadside equipment is either non existent or sparse, we cannot provide vehicle-to-infrastructure communications).
2. Protocols and mechanisms that support such a communication for both ends, vehicles and the infrastructure. Due to the special nature of the relation between vehicles and the roadside unit, the necessary interfaces are a pre-requisite. Routing protocols tailored for V2I communications are the most common example of this necessity.
3. Deployable penetration that means the existence of a sufficient number of roadside units placed alongside the highway or urban roads. We must note that another really important factor that shapes both the

Table 1. Characteristics and requirements of safety and infotainment applications in vehicular networks

	Safety Applications	Infotainment Applications
Reach	Local (1-hop neighbors)	Distant
Mode	Geocast/Multicast	Unicast/Multicast
Latency	Low	Various (application dependent)
Packet Delivery Ratio	High	Various (application dependent)
Connection Duration	Short	Long
Security	Yes	Yes

network penetration and deployment but also the service provision through protocol and mechanism design, is that the network operation must be efficient with a certain minimum of deployed infrastructure, at least for the early stages of its operation.

The IEEE 802.11p Standard

In the discussion about vehicular communications, one should not miss to mention the only (up to now) standard for this kind of communications. That is the IEEE 802.11p standard that has been developed to support both vehicle-to-vehicle and vehicle-to-infrastructure communications.

This standard utilizes the Dedicated Short Range Communication (DSRC) to complete wireless transactions and operates on the licensed band of 5.9 GHz for Intelligent Transportation Systems (ITS). The IEEE 802.11p standard supports vehicle-based communications and services such as toll collection, safety services and commercial transactions via vehicles. These services involve greatly the vehicle-to-infrastructure communication model.

The P1609 Standard Family

The P1609 standard family (IEEE Standard – P1609) also known as the upper layer WAVE standard is used to define the architecture, communication model and mechanisms of high-speed short range wireless low latency communications. Together with 802.11p, P1609 standard family comprises the base of the Wireless Access in Vehicular Environments (WAVE) architecture. Collectively the IEEE 1609 (1609.1, 1609.2, 1609.3, 1609.4, 1609.11) Family of Standards for WAVE describes wireless data exchange, security, and service advertisement between vehicles and roadside devices.

Work in Progress

Many initiatives across the world (Olariu & Weigle, 2009) have taken up the development of vehicular networks. The main objective of vehicular network deployment is to make transport safer and in particular to address issues and scenarios that are not addressed by the V2V component of vehicular communications. However, the stakeholders take interest in promoting service-oriented and infotainment applications to improve travel comfort. In many countries worldwide, the research for vehicular communications have been aggregated under an organization or initiative (Motsinger & Hubbing, 2007) and some of those have already deployed early stages of vehicular networks, while focusing on both V2I and V2V communications, in specific cities or regions around the world. Some of the most known initiatives that strive to improve vehicular communications are Japan's Smartway project (http://www.its.go.jp/ITS/topindex/topindex_sw2007.html) which has started its deployment in Tokyo and other regions in Japan and ITS Japan (http://www.its-jp.org/english) that strives to improve road transportation systems. Also, U.S.A's VII program (currently known as Research and Innovative Technology Administration, RITA – http://www.its.dot.gov), which also has deployed vehicular networks in certain regions across the country. Also ITS America (http://www.itsa.org) promotes ITS development in the USA.

There are numerous initiatives and R&D projects in Europe; we only refer those that are most relevant to the subject of this chapter.

- **NoW (Network-on-Wheels):** Is a German project, which mainly works on communication aspects for vehicle-to-vehicle and vehicle-to-roadside communication. The specific objective of the NoW project is the development of a communication system which integrates both safety and non-safety applications. The NoW project ended in May 2008 (http://www.network-on-wheels.de/).
- **SAFESPOT (Cooperative vehicles and road infrastructure for road safety):** Addresses co-operative systems for road safety, referred to as "smart vehicles on smart roads." In order to prevent road accidents, a "safety margin assistant" that detects potentially dangerous situations in advance, has been developed. This assistant represents an intelligent cooperative system utilizing vehicle-to-vehicle and vehicle-to infrastructure communication based on IEEE 802.11p for vehicular communications (http://www.safespot-eu.org/).
- **CVIS (Cooperative Vehicle Infrastructure Systems):** Aims at developing a communication system that is capable to use a wide range of wireless technologies, including cellular networks (GPRS, UMTS), wireless local area networks (802.11p), short-range microwave beacons (DSRC) and infra-red (IR). Additionally, A Framework for Open Application Management (FOAM) is defined that connects the in-vehicle systems, roadside infrastructure and back-end infrastructure that are necessary for cooperative transport management (http://www.cvis-project.org/).
- **PRESERVE (Preparing Secure Vehicle-to-X Communication Systems):** Is a project that mainly focuses on security concerns of the vehicular communications and aggregates and extends previous projects and their results. It aims to create an integrated V2X architecture, that is easy deployable, scalable, low-cost, and has no open deployment issues, and close-to-market. This project started 01/01/2011and is scheduled to have duration of 48 months, until 31/12/2014 (http://www.preserve-project.eu).
- **The European counterpart of ITS Japan and ITS America:** Known as ERTICO (http://www.ertico.com), joins together public (Ministries of Transport, European Commission) and private (European Industry) partners and work together to realize the development and deployment of ITS across Europe.

Finally, the international CALM (Communications Access for Land Mobiles - since 2007) initiative (http://en.wikipedia.org/wiki/Communications,_Air-interface,_Long_and_Medium_range) that has set its attention to setting the standards for vehicular communications and wireless technologies and comprises the base for several other initiatives that work on different areas of vehicular communications. The rapid and efficient spread of this type of networks is obvious across the globe in the recent years with only beneficial outcomes for the vehicular traffic.

Chapter Overview

The vehicular communications field and the vehicle-to-infrastructure component in particular have been debated for a long period by the research and scientific field. The majority of the research in vehicular communications has been directed in the purely ad-hoc part of the network in the vehicle-to-vehicle component.

At the same time, it is becoming increasingly clear that if we want to meaningfully contribute and make groundbreaking progress, we can no longer ignore the fact that the roadside network exploitation can offer vast improvement to the network performance in all its aspects and provide efficient solutions to matters where V2V architecture fails to address and solve.

Many key subjects that have to be resolved efficiently include quality of service provision, security proofing, and provision of a routing algorithm for the network and its participants.

This chapter overviews these three important aspects of the network, outline the current problems that they currently face and provide an aggregation of the proposed solutions in each respective field, always in relation with the vehicle-to-infrastructure architecture.

The reader is also introduced to the basic architecture, communication model, and characteristics of vehicular communications, in order to obtain a full understanding of vehicular networks.

SECURITY CHALLENGES IN VANETS AND PROPOSED SOLUTIONS

We cannot actually argue about a deployable VANET architecture without first concerning ourselves with the security aspects of this particular type of network. The need of finding efficient solutions to secure-proofing the vehicular environment is by all means imperative and the research on possible ways to fulfill the security requirements is continuous. In the following section, we try to aggregate and enumerate all these requirements and later on examine and present various solutions, in the form of targeted protocols, schemes, or mechanisms.

Mandatory Security Features for Vehicular Communications Networks

In this section, we investigate the security features (Yue, Jun, & Ju, 2009) that a VANET should have in order to be considered secure in all its aspects.

- **Authentication:** Authentication is a major requirement in VANET security because it ensures that the senders of messages are valid VANET members. However, the authentication process raises concerns about the privacy protecting of the vehicular nodes and this trade-off is investigated in detail later on.
- **Message Integrity:** This requirement ensures that the messages are not changed in transit and that the messages the driver receives are not false. This requirement falls under the non-cryptographic security of VANET and is explained later on.
- **Message Non-Repudiation:** This requirement ensures that a sender cannot deny having sent a message. Although this does not mean that the sender is identifiable. Only specific authorities should be allowed to identify vehicles by analyzing their sent messages.
- **Entity Authentication:** This requirement ensures that the sender of a message is an existing and authenticated vehicle of the network. This requirement can effectively thwart illusion attacks because the vehicles that participate in the network are real vehicles that have the necessary authorization.
- **Access Control:** Access control is required to ensure that all nodes that belong to the network, operate according to the roles and privileges authorized to them. Specifies what a node can do and what messages can generate in the network.
- **Message Confidentiality:** This is required when certain nodes want to communicate privately. This can only be performed by

the law enforcement authority vehicles that communicate with each other to convey private information.

- **Node Privacy:** This characteristic is used to ensure that the information is not leaked to unauthorized people that are not allowed to view the information. Therefore, a certain degree of anonymity should be available for messages and transactions of vehicles. Moreover, location privacy is a major issue in VANET security, so that a vehicle cannot be tracked by an outsider.

- **Real-Time Guarantees:** Because of the special nature of the VANET environment, that is high mobility and dynamic topology, the time windows for vehicular communications and especially Vehicle-to-Infrastructure are often narrow. Thus, it is essential in a VANET safety related applications that depend on strict time deadlines to be serviced efficiently.

- **Network Availability:** This requirement ensures that the network will be always available for its users at all times. While preventing attacks, such as Denial of Service that can compromise the availability of the network, this requirement provides all the needed bandwidth and network services to the applications so they can operate in an effective and secure manner.

The Problem

As it has already been mentioned, it is obligatory for VANET to have security provision for safety as well as infotainment applications. Due to the unique characteristics of VANETs, the aforementioned provision is not always guaranteed.

Some of the problems that have risen from the security requirements are being addressed by the solutions presented in this chapter as follows:

- Non-Repudiation
- Access Control

- Confidentiality
- Node Privacy
- Network Availability
- Message Integrity
- Message Authentication
- Entity Authentication
- Real-Time Guarantees

It is clear that researchers aim to a unified scheme that utilizes the necessary set of tools in order to supply VANET with an acceptable level of security. In the rest of this chapter, we outline and further analyze mechanisms, schemes and targeted protocols (proposed either in academia or in industry) that try to accomplish the general objective of securing VANETs. In most cases, many mechanisms and protocols are tied and work together to achieve that outcome.

Challenges and Problems in Vehicular Security

Being a special category of MANETs, VANETs have some unique characteristics that make their large scale deployment harder and pose some unique challenges (Stampoulis & Chai, 2007; Papadimitratos, Gligor, & Hubaux, 2006). For example, the information conveyed over a vehicular network may affect life-or-death decisions, making fail-safe security a necessity. However, providing strong security in vehicular networks raises important privacy concerns that should also be considered. The deployment of vehicular networks is rapidly approaching, and their success and safety will depend on viable security solutions acceptable to consumers, manufacturers, and governments.

Tradeoff between Authentication and Privacy

During authentication, all message transmissions need to be matched with their originating vehicles. On the other hand, personal information about vehicles should not be known to any other than the Trusted Authority (TA). In order to achieve efficient VANET security, these two completely opposite traits must come to equilibrium. This tradeoff is called resolvable anonymity. Therefore, a system needs to be introduced that enables vehicles to be anonymous to most participating nodes but also enables identification by central authorities in cases like accidents or malicious behavior.

Location Awareness

Certain location-based services are essential for most applications to be truly effective, so that reliance of the VANET system on GPS or other specific location based instruments can be increased as any error is likely to effect the supported applications.

High Mobility

Due to the high mobility of the nodes in VANETs, their topologies are highly dynamic and time windows are really narrow. This in itself is a major spatial and temporal constraint of the network. The proposed mechanisms, schemes or targeted protocols, should be able to perform all their operations concerning the secure-proofing of the network, while managing to satisfy these two constraints.

Privacy Problems and Proposed Solutions

It is clear from the previous contents of this section that preserving privacy plays a major role in securing VANETs in such a way that they would be deployable in large scale. Towards this direction, there has been great research efforts and many targeted protocols, novel schemes and mechanisms have been proposed to achieve this goal. Furthermore, we outline and investigate

proposed ways that make this privacy-preserving claim a reality.

Cryptographic Privacy

When we are referring to cryptographic privacy, we imply all the attributes that make a network secure using means of cryptography. In general, it is required that a message should be resilient against the compromise of its security as well as its sender's. Thus, it is important the privacy preserving of the nodes and messages of the network but at the same time, efficient authentication should be achievable to make sure that malicious nodes will not be part of the network.

Public Key Infrastructure (PKI): Role, Use, and Effectiveness

Public Key Infrastructure, also referred to as PKI, is one of the most popular ways used to secure VANET because it can meet most of the security requirements of a vehicular network environment such as anonymity, authentication, non-repudiation, etc. PKI is a set of hardware, software, people, policies, and procedures needed to create, manage, distribute, use, store, and revoke digital certificates. In cryptography, PKI is an arrangement that binds public keys with respective user identities by means of a Certificate Authority (CA). The role of PKI that assures this binding is called the Registration Authority (RA). The term Trusted Third Party (TTP) may also be used for the Certificate Authority (CA).

As mentioned before, PKI mechanisms use digital signatures to bind a public key with the real identity of a vehicle; in such a way that the certificate can be used to ascertain that a public key belongs to a certain vehicle, thus, eliminating the problems of data authentication and message non-repudiation. Pseudonymous certificates allow us to achieve both privacy and authentication.

Another element of the PKI architecture is the Certificate Authority. that is the entity that issues the digital certificates to the nodes (vehicles) of the network. A certificate is a vehicle's public key and identifier signed by the CA. The main function of the digital certificate is to certify that a certain vehicle (its identity is only known to the CA) is the owner of a public key. This allows vehicles or RSUs to trust the signatures or assertions that are made by the private key that corresponds to the public key (private/public key pair) that has been certified by the CA.

It is well understood from the aforementioned definition of PKI that it comprises a set of elements that all together create a security net over VANET. In this regard, we review all the elements one-by-one and all together to have a complete picture of the way public key infrastructure secures VANETs.

Pseudonyms

The (long-term) root certificate provided by the CA and the pseudonym certificates (short-term) with corresponding key pairs (public keys-private keys) are assumed to be able to protect the vehicle's privacy by not linking the certificates directly to vehicles.

Dötzer (2005) proposes a system for pseudonym security. The system operates under the assumptions that every vehicle is equipped with a tamper-resistant device, which offers secure memory to store secrets and secure computation as well as that the vehicle is able to execute small programs and cryptographic algorithms. It is further assumed that during production of the vehicle, a secure connection between this device and authority A is available, using Hardware Security Module (HSM). There are three operating phases in this system; the initializing phase (during which the systems of the vehicles are set up), the operational phase as the major mode of operation (during which vehicles can send messages signed according to a chosen pseudonym), and the credential revocation phase (during which predefined situations can lead to the disclosure of a

vehicle's real ID and the shutdown of its system). Protection against misuse of the credentials is provided by the tamper-resistant device and the revocation mechanism provides robust network availability.

The main reason to maintain privacy in vehicular networks is to thwart any adversary that tries to compromise the network and its participants. In Sampigethaya et al. (2005), the authors provide a solution to the problem of privacy preservation by allowing any vehicle to be able to achieve unlinkability between two or more of its locations in the presence of tracking by an adversary. The proposed scheme combines group navigation and a random silent period enhancement technique to provide user privacy and mitigate vehicle tracking. The assumptions of this scheme are a trusted authority and the ability for the authority to track a vehicle based on the strength of its signal. Between the pseudonym changes, the vehicle stays silent for a random period of time so the adversary cannot track it using temporal and spatial relation as observed in Leping, Matsuura, Yamane, and Sezaki (2005).

The certificate authorities play an important role to the preservation of privacy in vehicular networks; not only to provide the legitimate nodes with the necessary certificates but also to prevent malicious nodes from harming the network. Papadimitratos et al. (2007) propose a system architecture in Papadimitratos, Buttyan, Hubaux, Kargl, Kung, and Raya (2007) that supports privacy protection and secure communication among others. One basic aspect of this system is the crosschecking of the vehicles between CAs so that security can be achieved in regional scale. Each node, being either a vehicle or an RSU, holds a unique id and a pair of public/private keys. The CA that manages the long-term certificates is responsible for their replacement once the old ones expire. To achieve privacy protection, each node is equipped with a set of distinct certified public keys known as pseudonyms and they are used to sign the outgoing messages of the vehicle. Frequent changes on these pseudonyms, issued by a trusted pseudonym provider, make tracking of vehicles extremely hard. Because of the variable rate of pseudonym switch depending mostly on network parameters (velocity, policy, number of nodes), the concept of pseudonym refill is also explained in which a node requests an (i+1) set of pseudonyms before his i set depletes.

In Freudiger et al. (2007), the authors propose a scheme utilizing a protocol that both aim to provide unlinkability between the vehicle and its transmitted messages and provide location privacy for the driver. For this purpose, pseudonyms are utilized to disclose the driver's private information However, updating pseudonyms in a monitored area has been proven ineffective because the location information of the messages can still be used to exploit temporal and spatial tracking on the vehicle. This chapter assumes that the vehicles have a tamper-proof device and that before entering the network a vehicle registers with the CA and receives a set of pseudonyms. The authors also proposed the creation of anonymizing regions known as mix-zones in order to force pseudonym change to take place there. Because the effectiveness of the proposed approach lies mainly on the number of vehicles and the randomness of the zone's whereabouts, the authors also proposed the placement of these regions at road intersections where vehicles mix all together and their velocity and direction usually change. However, if the mix-zones have fixed or expected locations, the adversary may know where and when to launch an attack. For this reason, a protocol named CMIX is introduced that creates cryptographic mix zones, in which every vehicle uses a symmetric key to encrypt their sending data throughout the pseudonym change process and to keep it secure the RSU, which provides that symmetric key, changes it during the update process.

Building blocks of the VANET's privacy preservation are the vehicle's credentials and keys. This information should remain private from the rest of the network. Towards this direction, Papadimitratos et al. (2008) propose a system architecture addressing the privacy preserving of identity, credentials, key management and secure communications. This particular architecture assumes the existence of several CAs to service multiple regions as well as the ability to cross-certify vehicles when entering new regions. Every vehicle is registered with only one CA, and it has a long-term identity along with a pair of public/ private keys and a long-term certificate issued by the CA (which is later renewed upon expiration) that contains attributes of the node (mostly used for access control) and lifetime of the certificate. In order to satisfy the privacy requirement, this architecture uses pseudonyms that are switched frequently so the messages signed by these pseudonyms cannot be linked back to the originating vehicle. In order to obtain certificates, a vehicle issues a message to the CA over a secure channel, identifying itself and registering to the CA (via public key). After authentication, the vehicle sends a set of pseudonyms that contain an identifier of the CA, the lifetime of the pseudonyms, the public key and the signature of the CA, covering all the private information about the vehicle. This architecture also utilizes the aforementioned pseudonym refill mechanism.

Key factor to the non-traceability of the vehicular nodes and therefore the protection of their privacy, is for the use of pseudonyms for a short period of time. This concern is being addressed by Calandrielo et al. (2007). The authors propose a scheme in which every node is equipped with a set of pseudonyms. Each pseudonym is used for limited period of time. The combination of pseudonyms and group signatures is the basic element of the proposed scheme. Every node is equipped with a group signature key and instead it generates its own set of pseudonyms and with the group signature key it generates a group signature on each pseudonym. In this scheme, the nodes can generate and self-certify their own pseudonyms.

Certificate Revocation

Due to the numerous threats in VANET, it is possible to revoke a certificate for one of the following reasons:

- **Key Compromise:** The private key of the vehicle or the RSU is suspected to be or is compromised.
- **Change of affiliation:** Some information about the certificate of the vehicle or the RSU or any other information is no longer valid.
- **Suspended:** The certificate is suspended.
- **Cessation of operation:** The certificate is no longer needed for its assigned purpose.
- **Change of Policy:** The CA no longer operates under the certain security policy and no longer service certificates.

The most common way to revoke a certificate is by using Certificate Revocation Lists (CRLs) that contain the certificate identities of misbehaving nodes, are used to inform the nodes of the network about misbehaving nodes with revoked privileges in an attempt to exclude those nodes from the network. However, a challenge that remains is the distribution of this list to the vehicles, because due to the size of the network in can grow exponentially. Thus, the vehicular nodes before verifying any received message, each node checks whether or not the sender is included in the up-to-date CRL. The real problem that rises with CRLs is their distribution, which is prone to long delays and might not always be an easy task because of the real-time nature of the mechanism, but also their creation because of their rapidly growing size due to the fast-changing pseudonyms of the network nodes. In the case of group signatures, the group manager is responsible to reveal the credentials of the suspicious vehicle for the CA to revoke its privileges.

In place of the CRL, due to its hard distribution to the vehicles, some other approaches have been proposed for the revocation of the misbehaving vehicles. Towards that direction, Wohmacher (2000) proposes the Online Certificate Status Protocol (OCSP), which can verify the current validity of a certificate online. If a more timely reaction is required, the proposed protocol can be employed instead of CRLs. The protocol is utilized between a client and a server where the client queries the server for a set of certificates in order to check their validity and the server after executing the necessary checks on its part, responds with the certificate validity status to the client. A certificate response from the server can be unknown, revoked, or good. Unknown means that the server has no information about the queried certificate, revoked means that the certificate has been revoked or is on hold and good may mean that the certificate has not been revoked, it has not been issued yet or the time the response was produced it was out of its validity. The OCS protocol is especially effective for attribute certificates (used to manage access control) in which the status information need to be up-to-date.

An almost certain pre-requisite to achieve privacy in vehicular networks is the existence of TPD units (Tamper-Proof Devices) on vehicles. Raya et al. (2007) take advantage of this and propose a protocol that leverages the presence of a TPD unit on board the vehicle. If the CA determines that a vehicle must be revoked, with the help of the roadside infrastructure, initiates a two-party end-to-end protocol with the tamper-proof device of the vehicle during which the CA instructs the TPD to erase all cryptographic material it stores and halt its operation upon completion of the protocol. The protocol actually "kills" the TPD, depriving the misbehaving node from its cryptographic keys and, thus, ensuring that all its messages are ignored by all other correct nodes.

Also in Raya et al. (2007), the use of the RC²RL protocol is proposed that targets to the dramatic decrease of the time in which the nodes of a VANET can obtain an updated CRL. It is utilized when the CA (which is responsible for the revocation) wants to revoke only a subset of the vehicle's keys or when its tamper-proof device is unreachable. Given the large size of the CRL in VANETs, the protocol utilizes bloom filters (a probabilistic data structure used to test whether an element is a member of a set),thus, decreasing the CRL size to only a few KB and making it possible for it to be transmitted via radio frequency. This protocol relies on the infrastructure to broadcast the compressed CRL in frequent intervals.

Additionally in Raya et al. (2007), the LEAVE warning system is proposed that relies on the collective information gathered from a vehicle's neighborhood. Due to the fact that LEAVE cannot sense or collect the necessary information on its own, it relies on a mechanism named MDS (Misbehavior Detection System). Since all vehicles can be attackers with the same probability, the warning messages may contain correct or wrong accusations. Given the limited amount of available evidence, vehicles rely on the assumption of honest majority and crosscheck all received accusations. An accusation issued by a node has a lower weight when this node is already accused by other participants. If the sum of weighted accusations (the eviction quotient) against a vehicle exceeds a defined threshold, it is locally evicted by LEAVE until the evicted node gets in the region of a CA and has his certificate revoked. More precisely, warning messages are transformed into disregard messages that instruct all the neighbors of the attacker to ignore its messages.

Group Signatures: Requirements, Effectiveness, and Proposed Solutions

Group signatures address the privacy requirement by providing anonymity within a certain set of nodes, namely a group. A group consists of several group members and one Group Manager (GM). A group signature is produced by using the message to be signed, the secret signing key of the sending node and the group public key. A Group Signature scheme lets the members of a group to sign messages on behalf of the group. Signatures can be verified with respect to a single group public key, but at the same time, they do not reveal the identity of the signer.

In general, a secure group signature scheme should fulfill the following requirements:

- **Unforgeability:** Only group members are able to sign messages on behalf of the group.
- **Anonymity:** Given a valid signature of a message, identifying the actual signer is computationally hard for everyone but the group manager.
- **Unlinkability:** Deciding whether two different valid signatures were computed by the same group member is computationally hard.
- **Excludability:** Neither a group member nor the group manager can sign on behalf of other group members.
- **Traceability:** The group manager is always able to open a valid signature and identify the actual signer.

Group signature-based mechanism is another proposed way that can preserve the vehicles' privacy in vehicular networks. Jinhua et al. (2007) propose a security framework to preserve VANETs using group signatures. In this framework, members of the network maintain only a small set of group public/secret key pairs and they are anonymous within the group from which they sign. This framework assumes that all the messages that exist in the network are authenticated.

Another group signature-based approach is proposed by Boneh et al. (2004). In this approach, the authors propose a group signature-based scheme that is based on the Strong Diffie-Hellman (SDH) assumption as it is explained in Boneh and Boyen (2004). The scheme is based on a zero knowledge protocol for SDH in which the Fiat-Shamir heuristic is applied.

Xiaoting et al. (2007) propose among others a scheme for OBU-to-RSU communication based on ID-based group signatures. An identity string is used as a public key to sign the messages. That way, the workload caused by the certificate management process can be avoided, and the public key updating and revocation operations can become rather simple.

Privacy in Terms of Trustworthiness and Data Integrity

When we are referring to trustworthiness and data integrity in order to ensure privacy, we should discuss all the attributes that make a network secure, without using means of cryptography to conceal the node's information but rather to ensure the integrity and trusted origin of messages. In general, it is required that a message that exists in the network to be trustworthy and to maintain data integrity. The concepts of trustworthiness and data integrity have risen and several trust systems have been developed to fulfill them.

Dhurandher et al. (2010) propose a robust algorithm to provide trustworthiness in VANET environment, namely VSRP. The algorithm provides trustworthiness by running reputation and plausibility checks. The algorithm takes into consideration three types of messages: application of brakes, traffic jam, and accident. These messages can highly affect the network if compromised. The algorithm uses a trust table in order to maintain the trust levels of its neighborhood; this table holds values from 0 to 4, 0 being the lowest trust value assigned to a malicious node. In order to manage the reputation slots for each neighbor (if a suspicious behavior is detected), the vehicle increases the counter assigned to that behavior and if it reaches a certain threshold, the general reputation counter for this vehicle drops by 1 unit.

Trustworthiness does not only reside in message trustworthiness but also to the regions in which the vehicles are moving. To ensure that the vehicles will be moving into trusted regions, Serna et al. (2008) describe a scheme to provide trust condition for the vehicle participating in VANETs, while being in a untrusted area (meaning a region that is serviced by a different CA). This scheme enables CA interoperability with no explicit agreements. Moreover, the concept of CA Federations is proposed in which an agreement is made between the different CAs on a security minimum for all of them to inter-operate and thus, eliminating untrusted territories. In this approach, instead of distributing new sets of "compatible" certificates to the VANET nodes, the only requirement is to give them access to the trusted repository of the CA Federation to update their local certificates.

Most of the schemes, mechanisms, and targeted protocols that aim to deem a network, message, or region trustworthy for its participants make use of infrastructure-assistance to achieve that goal. We are examining the Kerberos approach, included in the paper by Wex et al. (2008), which is a successor of the Needham-Schroeder protocol. It relies on an online interaction with a central Key Distribution Center (KDC) for authentication in order to get a valid "trust" token for a service (contains a session key, a validity period and the requesting node's identity encrypted with the server's secret key). The authorization information is kept at the services locally. Due to scalability problems in large environments, newer versions of Kerberos also allow the central management of authorization information and their integration in the issued tokens.

Gomez et al. (2011) assume the existence of fixed elements of the infrastructure with Internet connectivity and certain processing capabilities that also communicate with all vehicles that pass close to them. The infrastructure elements used in this approach are Road Side Units that communicate with the vehicles, with other RSUs and with the Base Stations that connect to the Internet through backbone networks. An honest majority policy is applied, but the case of malicious node is not excluded entirely. The main focus of this approach is to identify and isolate such malicious users by means of an accurate trust and reputation management mechanism application. The proposed approach defines that every time it receives a message, it first checks the reputation of the sender in order to decide whether to drop, accept or accept and forward the message. These three actions represent the three levels of trust used in this approach, so a node can be not trusted (reject), more or less trustworthy (accept but not forward) and fully trusted (accept and forward). Each message has a corresponding severity to the sender's reputation with a severity maximum for each trust level depending on the message. Additionally, a reputation score will be computed for each node taking into account three different sources of information, namely: direct previous experiences with the targeting node, recommendations from other surrounding vehicles and, when available, the recommendation provided by a central authority through Road Side Units. Concerning the recommendations provided by the infrastructure (when available), they are used to identify and isolate malicious nodes travelling throughout the country. The central authority controlling RSUs can manage a database containing all those users who have been deemed malicious.

Authentication Problems and Proposed Solutions

Although in the previous section we described the significance of privacy in order to maintain a secure Vehicular Network, we should not perceive it to be the only goal. A vehicular network must provide in any case and at all times robust authentication for its participants while preserving their privacy. Authentication can and should be achieved in all the privacy schemes, either PKI-based or group signature-based, that have been developed for vehicular networks, as it is an integral part of the VANET security.

Subsequently, we present and examine several authentication architectures for VANET environment, in which Road-Side Units play an important role:

Chenxi et al. (2008) propose an RSU-aided message authentication scheme, called RAISE. In particular, when an RSU is detected, nearby vehicles start to associate with it. The RSU assigns a unique shared symmetric secret key and a pseudo ID that is shared among the vehicles. With the symmetric key, each vehicle generates a symmetric keyed-Hash Message Authentication Code (HMAC) and then broadcasts a message signed with this symmetric HMAC code instead. Receiving vehicles are able to verify the message by using the notice about the authenticity of the message disseminated by the RSU. The RSU knows the authenticity of the messages because it shares HMAC encryption keys vehicles they were disseminated to. In any circumstance that a vehicle cannot verify a received message, it will use the PKI-based scheme to do so.

In vehicular networks, message authentication must happen in such way that the receiver of the message knows for sure that the message is trusted. Studer et al. (2009) propose a mechanism that makes use of the public key infrastructure along with the roadside network to authenticate messages in the network. The sender signs its messages with TACK's private key and from time to time broadcasts its RA-signed certificate. The receivers can use these two pieces of information to verify the sender's validity.

Wasef et al. (2009) propose a protocol that accelerates the authentication (revocation check) process. A general PKI scheme is deployed and by utilizing it the authentication enhancement happens. Bilinear pairing and hash chains are used as tools to achieve this fastening in the authentication process. The sender calculates his revocation check and appends it in the message along with his public key, the OBU's ID, a timestamp and a HMAC which plays the role of the authentication code. The receiver checks the validity of that information and either verifies the sender or drops the message and updates the CRL adding the non-valid node.

A certain example where PKI-based and group signature-based solutions co-exist and operate in the same environment is proposed by Wasef et al. (2009). The ASIC verification scheme supports stand-alone aggregate signatures verification and aggregate certificates verification. Furthermore, it supports simultaneous aggregate signatures and certificates verification.

Perrig et al. (2002) propose an authentication protocol, named Timed Efficient Stream Loss-tolerant Authentication (TESLA). TESLA, according to its creators has low communication and computation overhead, tolerates packet loss, and scales to a large number of nodes, characteristics that make it ideal for vehicular environments. TESLA also works under the assumption that all sender and receiver(s) loosely time-synchronized and on the precondition that either the sender or the receiver must buffer some messages. TESLA uses one-way hash chains to authenticate keys at the receivers. The main idea of TESLA is that the sender attaches to each packet a MAC (Message Authentication Code) computed with a key known only by the sender. The receiver buffers the received packet without being able to authenticate it. In subsequent event, the sender reveals the key to the receiver rendering him able to authenticate the packet.

While TESLA is vulnerable to Denial of Service (DoS) attacks as the sender can be flooded with time-synchronization requests to compromise its security, TESLA++, investigated in Studer, Bai, Bellur, and Perrig (2008) addresses exactly that particular weakness. In TESLA++, the receiver only stores a self-generated MAC to reduce the memory requirements. Since the receiver only stores a shortened version of the sent data, the sender firstly sends the MAC and then the message with its corresponding key. In TESLA++ authentication, the sender first sends the MAC to the receiver, which in turn checks to see if there

is a corresponding key to it (checking to see if the message key has been broadcasted yet); if there is, the MAC is dropped. Once the key can be disclosed, the sender will send any messages and the key that is used to calculate their MACs.' To verify a message, the receiver first verifies the validity of the key by following the one-way key chain back to a trusted key. The receiver then calculates the shortened MAC of the message and compares it with the MAC and index stored in his memory. If the receiver has a matching MAC/key index pair in memory, the receiver considers the message authentic. In any other case, the receiver considers the message unauthentic and discards the message.

The contribution of Studer et al. (2008) is a framework for message authentication using a combination of Elliptic Curves Digital Signature Algorithm (ECDSA) signatures and TESLA++. Once an OBU verifies a message using TESLA++, it can verify the ECDSA signature if non-repudiation is required. The ECDSA component also provides authentication in multi-hop communications if the OBU has no memory of the TESLA++ MAC. Due to that versatility of multiple verifications, this framework can meet many of the security needs of VANET.

Adversaries in VANETs

We term as an adversary or attacker any node that tries to compromise the security of the vehicular network. Such nodes can achieve that either by launching various attacks in the network, depending on what they are trying to achieve or by operating in a totally different way, than the one defined from the network policy, causing problems for the other legitimate nodes.

Greedy Driver

Following the honest majority rule, a greedy driver that is a member of the VANET will try to mislead his fellow drivers for personal gain. For example, misleading the other members of the VANET to believe that there is congestion in the road ahead while there is not, would create much better driving conditions for him.

Eavesdropper

This kind of adversary tries to obtain others' personal information and credentials and causes a serious breach in the privacy of the network. The eavesdropper may use illusion attack to impersonate another vehicle in order to gain access to certain privileges or its personal information. A very effective way to minimize this adversary's effect on the network is using cryptographic privacy and to manage the sensitive data in tamper-proof devices.

Pranksters

They are adversaries that will attempt to cause problems in the network to have fun. A prankster could also abuse the security vulnerability to Denial of Service (DoS) attacks to disable applications or prevent critical information from reaching another vehicle.

Malicious Attacker

This kind of adversary deliberately attempts to cause harm on the vehicular network. Normally, this adversary has specific targets and has access to more resources than other adversaries. In general, such kind of adversaries will be less in numbers than other kinds; they pose probably the most serious threat for the VANET security provision system.

Security Attacks against VANET

In this section, we aim to categorize the major security attacks that have been launched on VANET and we attempt to summarize some of the solutions that have been proposed in order to

diffuse or minimize the effect of those attacks on the network.

The most active fields of interest when it comes to security attacks in VANET are: anonymity, key management, privacy, reputation, location.

Anonymity

While VANET security tries to preserve the anonymity of its members, attackers may aim to discover the physical identity of a vehicle, in most cases with malicious intent.

Malicious Vehicle

One of the most important security requirements of VANETs is privacy. To avoid being tracked, the use of randomly changing pseudonyms is suggested. This can lead to a situation where a malicious vehicle M can easily change its identity to node N without being punished.

Key Management

Key management deals with the secure generation, distribution, and storage of keys. There are three main approaches for key management: key exchange, key agreement, and key management infrastructure.

Brute Force Attack

This attack in the form of exhaustive search for all the possible keys can pose a really serious threat against the members of the VANET, since the distribution of safety-related information should not be tampered with and is of crucial importance to the ITS system.

A proposed solution to this kind of attacks as proposed in Langley, Lucas, and Huirong (2008) operates under the condition that there is a unique identifier for each vehicle, such that one can learn if a vehicle is an authorized VANET participant. Because uniqueness in VANETs raises privacy issues, it has been decided to use Vehicle Identification

Number (VIN), which is a piece of information unique to every vehicle., The process specifies calculating really large number, appending the VIN to that number and then hashing it with a hashing algorithm. Because of the uniqueness of the VIN in each vehicle and the use of random large numbers to generate the unique identifier, the probability of a security compromise from a brute force attack is dramatically decreased because not only the attacker would have to know the VIN of the vehicle, but also to guess correctly the random large number used and the hashing algorithm used to generate it.

Misbehaving and Faulty Nodes

While there is an honest majority policy in VANETs, none can guarantee that a certified node will not develop malicious behavior. Although, the default reaction of the network to such events is known, certificate revocation is not always applicable because it requires infrastructure support and the misbehaving of the suspicious node may not always hold reason for revocation by the CA. In this regard, many solutions have been developed and proposed in order to protect the members of the VANET from such malicious behavior. However, it must be noted that not all suspicious behaviors must be considered malicious but there should be a malfunction threshold.

A really efficient solution to this security compromise is a known scheme examined earlier in the certificate revocation section. The LEAVE scheme along with MDS that are proposed in Studer, Bai, Bellur, and Perrig (2008) but also C^{2}RL are used to make certain that the misbehaving and faulty nodes will be dealt with in a fast and effective manner. In LEAVE scheme, we have a cooperation of the LEAVE protocol with the MDS mechanism to detect and locally isolate any misbehaving node until a CA comes in range to revoke the certificate of the misbehaving node. On top of that, what C^{2}RL does is that is ensures a fast and efficient distribution time for the most

up-to-date CRL from the infrastructure towards the vehicular nodes so that they have the knowledge to ignore messages of revoked nodes and avoid a possible security compromise.

Privacy

Privacy is a key aspect in VANET and refers to the ability of the drivers to protect sensitive information about them and their vehicles against unauthorized observers or malicious attackers.

Malicious User

In vehicular networks, privacy preservation is a key aspect for them to be deemed secure. Thus, keeping private the credentials and other valued information of the vehicle and the driver, from malicious users (in most cases, outsiders to the network) that have as a goal to cause damage by exploiting network vulnerabilities, is obligatory.

One solution to overcome the problem of malicious users involves the use of shared keys (Haas, Jason, Hu, Yih-Chun, Laberteaux, & Kenneth, 2010), issued and certified by a trusted third party, between a set of vehicles in the authentication process, that way when a message cannot be traced back to a single vehicle because of the sharing of the same key between a set of vehicles. Moreover, during the authentication process many keys are used by the vehicles because one key may belong to different vehicles. This also helps to the detection of a malicious node, because the RSU is able to trace back the set of keys to the misbehaving vehicle.

Traffic Analysis Attacks

This category of attacks is one of the most serious threats against the privacy of VANETs and it aims to compromise the anonymity of communications. There are many attacks under this category, such as message coding attack, message volume, etc.

A robust solution against these kinds of attacks is a proposed protocol, namely VIPER (Cencioni

& Di Pietro, 2007). The proposed VIPER protocol defines that the vehicles in a group (a group is defined as all the vehicles that are registered with the same RSU) will act as mixes for the outgoing messages. In particular, the messages are being re-encrypted via public key algorithm. Additionally, in order to prevent eavesdropper attacks, every message is encrypted using the node's secret encryption factor and the public key of the RSU. Subsequently, every relay node re-encrypts the message using its own encryption factor. The RSU is the only VANET's component in this architecture that can decrypt the message using its own private key and that is what deems VIPER resilient against traffic analysis attacks.

Reputation

Reputation is usually defined as the amount of trust inspired by a particular member of a community, for the particular purposes of this chapter, a vehicular network. Reputation systems are used to trust and encourage trustworthy behavior and work under the assumption that the majority of the network nodes are honest. In VANETs, these kinds of systems can be used to defend against compromised nodes, and malicious ones.

Malicious Nodes

The distribution of information about local traffic or road conditions is one of the emerging VANET applications, since it can increase traffic safety and improve mobility. However, one of the main challenges is to forward event-related messages in such a way that the information can be trusted by receiving nodes. Malicious nodes exploit exactly that by forwarding false traffic information.

While an honest majority policy is being followed in VANET environment, there are always nodes that attempt to compromise the network security. A very effective to halt the operations of pranksters, greedy drivers or malicious attackers is a trust-based system that dramatically reduces the

effect of their actions. Using reputation systems (Wex, Breuer, Held, Leinmuller, & Delgrossi, 2008), it is feasible for the valid or honest participants of the network to ignore messages or warnings from these nodes and maintain security.

Illusion Attack

Illusion attack is a new security threat on VANET applications in which the adversary intentionally deceives sensors of his own vehicle to produce wrong sensor readings. As a result, the corresponding system reaction is invoked and incorrect traffic warning messages are broadcasted to neighbors, creating an illusion condition on VANET.

A really effective solution against illusion attacks is plausibility checks (Dhurandher, Obaidat, Jaiswal, Tiwari, & Tyagi, 2010; Nai-Wei & Hsiao-Chien, 2007). In a plausibility check, a node can calculate if a message he received is fake or real (trustworthy), based on measurements from its own sensor data or from data transmitted by other vehicles or even the local RSU. Based on these measurements and a set of rules to examine and filter the data, the node can make a judgment to either trust or drop the message.

Another proposal that attempts to thwart illusion attacks in vehicular communications is Trust and Reputation Infrastructure-based Proposal, in short TRIP (Marmol & Perez, 2012). In TRIP, whenever a vehicle receives a message or warning from another vehicle it first checks the other vehicle's reputation in order to decide whether to drop or accept the message. Depending on the sender's reputation level, the receiving vehicle can drop the packet, receive but not forward it, or receive and forward it. In order for the receiving node to take this decision, a reputation score will be computed taking into account, direct experiences, recommendations from neighboring vehicles and recommendations from the central authority (through the RSUs). The RSU-provided recommendations are extremely useful as the central authority can provide information about the malicious nodes in the network. Due to the different set of recommenders, there are concerns about the accuracy of the system. However, with the contribution of RSU-acquired reputation information, there is an increased accuracy and resilience of the system.

Location

Location refers to vehicle position in a vehicular ad-hoc network. It is one of the most valuable pieces of information (used in geographic routing) and is often readily available through positioning services such as Global Positioning System (GPS).

Forging Positions and Sybil Attack

Position attacks can occur when the line of sight of the vehicle's sensors is blocked. An attacker can launch a position attack by modifying position packets, replaying false position packets and dropping critical position packets.

The Sybil attack is a well-known harmful attack in VANETs whereby a vehicle claims to be several vehicles either at the same time or in succession. In addition, a Sybil attack refers to an attack where the vehicle's identity masquerades as multiple simultaneous identities. The Sybil attack is harmful to network topologies, connections, network bandwidth consumption.

A solution that has been proposed in Hubaux, Capkun, and Jun (2004) involves the existence of tamper-proof GPS devices that can transmit the location information of the vehicle to the neighborhood of the vehicle or to an infrastructure. However, this approach has many limitations due to the existence of the tamper-proof GPS device and its known weaknesses.

Another solution to this attack has been proposed in Soyoung, Aslam, Turgut, and Zou (2009) where an approach called "timestamps series" is being proposed. This approach specifies that vehicles obtain certified timestamps, signed and issued by RSUs. An outgoing message contains a series of the most recently obtained timestamp certificates and "shows" them when it passes from RSU regions. The proposed approach takes advantage of the spatial and temporal correlation between vehicles and RSUs and assumes that is rather rare or impossible for two or more vehicles to pass from an RSU at the same time. Based on this, Sybil attacks can be detected and thus avoided when a vehicle receives multiple messages with very similar timestamp series.

An effective infrastructure-aided solution that can thwart a Sybil attack is an infrastructure-based architecture, namely NOTICE proposed in Rawat, Treeumnuk, Popescu, Abuelela, and Olariu (2008). In NOTICE, sensor belts (infrastructure) are embedded in the highway itself. Pressure sensors that are placed in each belt allow every message to be associated with a physical vehicle passing over the belt. Thus, a vehicle cannot pretend to be multiple vehicles and there is no need for an ID to be assigned to vehicles. The placement of belts for the detection of passing vehicles is more effective than roadside infrastructure and the interaction is performed in a simple and secure fashion.

Position Cheating and False Position Disseminating

The position of a node is periodically broadcasted in beacon packets so that every node within the wireless transmission range is able to build up a table of neighboring nodes including their positions. When a node disseminates wrong position data many, if not all the services of the VANET are affected. Wrong position information could be the result of malfunction in the positioning hardware or may be falsified intentionally by attackers to reroute data. Malfunctioning nodes may degrade the performance of a system to some extent while rerouting of data through malicious nodes violates basic security goals such as confidentiality, authenticity, integrity, or accountability.

Most solutions for the mentioned attacks are decentralized without the assistance of the roadside network. However, the solution proposed in Yan, Olariu, and Weigle (2008) involves a V2I component. In particular, all vehicles are equipped with GPS devices and numerous sensors; based on these sensors, the vehicle can make judgments for itself on the authenticity of the position information it receives from its neighborhood. For the operation of the protocol it is essentially to assign a unique ID to the vehicle that can only be issued by the central CA since the vehicle's ID can be changed by the attacker to launch an attack.

Availability

Availability is defined as the ability of a user to access the network and its resources in order to service his request. When considering life critical information, unavailability of the network should not be a case. In general, unavailability of the network resources is a network state that we do want to anticipate.

Denial of Service

A Denial-of-Service (DoS) attack is an attempt to make the resources of a network unavailable to its authorized users. Considering VANETs, this attack may be a serious threat to the network because of the safety and life-critical messages disseminated in the network.

An effective solution against DoS attacks in VANETs is proposed in Rawat, Treeumnuk, Popescu, Abuelela, and Olariu (2008), where the NOTICE architecture dictates that a road belt will not react to a single incident reported by a vehicle. On the contrary, the belt will wait for subsequent corroborations of the reported incident before deciding to propagate the information to the other participants in the network. Thus, injecting false information into the belt (targeting to denial of service) is thwarted by this mechanism of NOTICE.

Concluding this section, we have extensively analyzed vehicular communications, and espe-

cially vehicle-to-infrastructure communications that is one of the most challenging tasks. We have introduced the basic requirements for secure vehicular networks and how these requirements can be fulfilled in order to have an efficient security provision of vehicular networks. We have also outlined the main challenges and trade-off that the researchers currently face towards this direction. Moreover, we have overviewed several works on privacy preservation, authentication efficiency and security attacks against vehicular networks. We have also performed a survey of vehicle-to-infrastructure security schemes, mechanisms, and targeted protocols and categorized them into a detailed taxonomy. This approach allowed us to identify the current problems to that particular field of vehicular communications and discuss various proposed solutions.

HETEROGENEOUS QUALITY OF SERVICE (QOS) IN VANETS

Quality of Service Provision: Definition, Metrics, and VANET Implementation

Quality of Service (QoS): the term refers to resource reservation control mechanisms. Basically, it enables the provision of different priorities for different applications, users or data flows.

In order to define and fully comprehend Quality of Service, there are some terms that need to be explained.

- **Bit rate:** Also referred to as data rate, is the number of bits that are conveyed per unit of time.
- **Communication duration:** Is the time during which there is an established connection between two elements of the VANET. Due to the network's highly dy-

namic nature, we usually attempt to increase the connection's duration, maximize data throughput during that time, or even both.

- **Delay/Latency:** The time it takes for data to travel across the network from the sender to the receiver.
- **Jitter:** Packets from the source will reach the destination with different delays. A packet's delay varies with its position in the queues of the routers along the path between source and destination and this position can vary unpredictably. This delay variation is known as jitter and can seriously affect the quality of streaming audio and/or video.
- **Packet loss/Dropped Packets:** The routers might fail to deliver some packets if their data is corrupted or they arrive when their buffers are already full. The receiving application may ask for this information to be retransmitted, possibly causing severe delays in the overall transmission.
- **Bit Error Rate (BER):** Is the number of bit errors divided by the total number of bits transmitted during a certain amount of time.
- **Voice over IP (VoIP):** Is the widely used technology used to deliver voice communication over the Internet Protocol (IP).

Quality of Service provision guarantees a certain level of performance to a data flow, by meeting a required bit rate, delay, jitter, packet loss probability, Bit Error Rate, and communication duration.

Depending on the needs of applications and the transmitted data, such as life critical information, it is understandable that relaying messages over a large area without infrastructure support would have a negative effect on the delay and delivery ratio of messages and thus affecting negatively the quality of service provision in vehicular networks.

If we can improve QoS of VANETs in terms of delay, response time, and throughput, we could in many ways improve both safety and comfort of the driver and passengers of any vehicle.

Quality of Service Challenges in Vehicular Environment

Quality of service is a very important feature for safety-related applications (real-time) such as emergency break warning, congestion warning, etc. Service-oriented applications such as VoIP, streaming multimedia and online gaming are also affected by quality of service requirements. Due to the fast-changing environment of VANETs, the fulfillment of those requirements per application is a challenging task.

There are two major categories of applications in vehicular communications that require QoS provision and their requirements are totally different:

- Safety-Oriented Applications (time-sensitive)
- Service-Oriented Applications (not time-sensitive)

Safety-related applications, deliver critical life-or-death messages. This means that the data packets are small, compared to service-oriented messages but the network must be able to deliver those small data packets with short delays and high reliability.

Unlike safety-related services, in service-oriented services the main objective is to maximize the amount of data that each vehicle receives, especially in the case of vehicle-to-infrastructure communications since this should happen before the vehicle leaves the coverage area of the roadside beacon.

Based on the above, we can safely assume that in VANETs, the real QoS challenges are packet delivery ratio and connection duration rather than typical QoS metrics such as end-to-end delay and jitter.

Vehicular Network Characteristics that Limit Quality of Service Provision

Due to the special nature of the VANET environment, there are some limitations imposed either by the network itself or by the vehicles participating in it (Cheng, Shan, & Zhuang, 2012). These restrictions make the quality of service provision in VANETs a rather challenging task. Such limiting characteristics are:

- **Dynamic Network Topology:** Since the nodes participate in an ad-hoc wireless network, they do not have any restriction on mobility and the network topology changes dynamically. Hence, the admitted QoS sessions may suffer due to frequent path breaks, thereby requiring such sessions to be reestablished over new paths.
- **Lack of Central Coordination:** Unlike wireless LANs and cellular networks, ad-hoc networks do not have central controllers to coordinate the activity of nodes. This further complicates QoS provisioning in network.
- **Physical Level Restrictions:** In a broadcast medium, usually the radio waves suffer from several impairments such as attenuation, multi-path propagation, and interference during propagation of the messages.
- **Limited Resource Availability:** Network resources such as bandwidth, battery life, storage space, and processing capability are limited in the network.
- **Operational Factors:** Due to the possibility of vehicle malfunction, the position information disseminated in the network might be false. This can greatly affect the QoS provision in VANETs, as safety or data packets cannot arrive to their intended recipients inside the time limits set by their respective services.
- **Security Concerns:** Due to the possible insecurity of the network and under the threat of a potential attack, the information disseminated by the vehicle might not be trusted and be false. This can greatly affect the QoS provision of the network, as data packets cannot reach their destination either in a certain time limit or even not at all.

In the following subsections, we examine several proposed ways to completely nullify or mitigate the effect of those VANET traits on the quality of service provision.

Heterogeneous QoS in VANET

Many different categorizations have been proposed to distinguish the individual needs of VANET's applications, with each one focusing on a different angle of the network.

Thus, depending on the type of traffic, there are three classes of services and the associated QoS requirements (Wang, Giannakis, and Marques, 2007):

- **Best effort services:** Entail applications such as e-mail and http Web browsing. They come with a prescribed maximum allowable bit-error rate but pose no requirements on delay guarantees.
- **Non-real-time services:** Involve mission-critical but delay-tolerant applications such as file transfers. They often require minimum rate (i.e., throughput) guarantees but do not impose any delay bounds.
- **Real-time services:** Such as safety-related applications, video conferencing

and streaming entail guarantees on BER, throughput, and latency.

Another categorization focuses on the QoS provision depending on the application type (Sichitiu & Kihl, 2008):

- **Traffic Management:** This category of applications target to improve traffic flow by the means of traffic light scheduling, emergency vehicle assistance, and traffic monitoring.
- **Safety-Related Applications:** This category focuses on enabling the vehicles to be able to avoid or mitigate to a minimum the damage caused by an accident.
- **Traveler Information:** This category aims to provide the driver with all the necessary information to assist him such as downloading maps, navigation provision, road signs, local rest areas, etc. Moreover, the locality of this particular application category makes it even easier for it to be deployable through means of infrastructure.
- **Comfort-Related Applications:** This category focuses on providing the passengers of the car with comfort by means of Internet connection, video and sound streaming, games, and others means of entertainment.
- **Traffic Coordination and Assistance:** This category provides services such as passing and lane change. Clearly, these applications require close-range inter-vehicle communications with tight real-time constraints and can be implemented in either sparse roadside equipment environment or a ubiquitous roadside equipment environment. These applications also take into account the ZOR (Zone of Relevance) concept.

QoS Provision in Vehicular Environment and Proposed Solutions

Very few works focused on data transmission scheduling in roadside-to-vehicle systems so far. In this section, we survey vehicle-to-infrastructure architectures that have been developed to enable QoS provision for VANET applications.

Possible Modes of QoS Provision

QoS through Link-Reliability

A wide variety of applications is expected to be developed for VANETs. These applications have different requirements for properties such as delay, jitter, bandwidth, throughput and security. Most of these properties are strongly influenced by the successful transmission rates between intermediary nodes. Therefore, a mechanism that offers a way of choosing among options with distinguished successful transmission rates expectations can be used to support policies that provide different levels of end-to-end quality for distinct applications.

QoS via Throughput Maximization

Another network metric that plays an important role in QoS provision is network throughput. Taking into account the dynamic nature of the VANET and short time-frame that exists for Vehicle-to-Vehicle and Vehicle-to-Infrastructure communications, it is imperative that a mechanism that can maximize the data throughput during that sort duration is a must. This mechanism applies mostly on service-oriented applications where a large amount of data must be transferred in short time.

QoS through End-to-End Delay Minimization

An attribute that is really important to safety-oriented applications is minimum delay. Due to the real time nature of all safety-oriented applications as well as the critical life-or-death information that are being disseminated, the delay of the messages must be kept to a minimum. Thus, bandwidth of the network is often reserved to service only this kind of messages, in order to fulfill the minimum delay requirement. This kind of QoS provision is tied to the VANET large-scale deployment and must be serviced at all times.

The above are only a few of the ways that quality of service can be provided in vehicular networks. As previously mentioned, we considered high throughput and link-reliability, which in turn grants higher connection duration, to be of key importance to the vehicular quality of service provision.

QoS Provision: Proposed Solutions for Vehicle-to-Infrastructure Environment

Subsequently, we outline several proposed solutions for quality of service provision for the vehicular environment and in particular for the vehicle-to-infrastructure communication model, which plays an important role in achieving this goal.

As found in Saleet et al. (2009) presented a protocol to provide quality of service in VANET routing, called AMR. This protocol ensures minimum end-to-end delay while maintaining a threshold for the connectivity probability and the hop count through each selected path. In the center of the cell there is a fixed infrastructure which is a Road Side Unit. This RSU is responsible of aggregating the location information about all vehicles within its cell. In AMR, the RSU located in the center of each cell acts as a location server. Therefore, the RSU is responsible for saving current location information about all the vehicles that belong to that cell. Each vehicle updates its location information to the RSU each time it moves one transmission range far from its previous location. This enables the local RSU to have a local view of the network composed by the vehicles it manages. Therefore, a map of

routes will be constructed between the RSU and the vehicles.

A routing protocol is proposed by Ksentini et al. (2010), that strives to achieve QoS in routing via RSU-assistance and proxy vehicle use, namely PVR. In PVR, a mechanism based on IEEE 802.11 is utilized, where the vehicular networks use the "cooperative and opportunistic" concept to shorten the access delay and to reduce the interference problem within the range of a RSU in a highway environment. In fact, vehicles which are located far apart of the gateway send data, by greedy forwarding, to some particular vehicles called proxies during the long disconnection period. When vehicles enter the RSU transmission range, only the proxy vehicle is allowed to transmit data to the RSU.

Exploiting travel information is a really efficient way to improve quality of service. Sun et al. (2006) propose a QoS-enabled routing protocol using travel information to a large extent, namely GVGrid. This protocol assumes that every node (vehicle) has a short-range wireless device that has the same transmission range across the network nodes. GVGrid partitions the geographic region into squares of equal-size called grids. During route discovery, GVGrid attempts to find the route that is expected to have long lifetime, based on the position of each vehicle. This expected lifetime of a route is determined by the vehicles' movement on that route and characteristics (such as traffic signals and stop signs) of the roads on which the route is based.

There have been many proposals as to how to provide quality of service through infrastructure exploitation. A particular architecture proposed by Zhang et al. (2007) operates under the assumption that the vehicles know the service deadlines of their requests. Thus, the RSU knows the deadline (duration) of the communication since the vehicles send the relevant information to the RSU when they enter its range. Due to the high mobility of the network, when a vehicle's request has not been serviced yet and the vehicle exits the regions of the RSU, the request is automatically dropped. With the aforementioned as a given, there have been proposed two scheduling schemes based on the parameters of data size and deadline. In the data size scheme, if the vehicle can communicate with the RSU at the same transmission rate, the data size can decide the duration of the communication. In the deadline scheme, if a request cannot be serviced by the RSU by its deadline it is automatically dropped.

Another approach is the proposal of a routing protocol to provide quality of service in vehicular environment. In their proposal, Korkmaz et al. (2006) assume the existence of roadside gateways that have two interfaces that the vehicles are connected to access Internet services, one for the wireless traffic, and one for the wired (Internet) traffic. It is also assumed that the transmission range of the RSU can be extended via multi-hop communication, but also that the downlink and the uplink packets have separate channels so there is no contention over the same medium. Another assumption made is that all the vehicles are equipped with GPS devices and the position information is exchanged via one-hop neighbors, therefore an access point to the wireless medium is also assumed to be equipped on the vehicles. CVIA-QoS protocol is designed to provide throughput guarantees and fixed delay bound to soft real-time applications like safety-related applications, voice, and video streaming in linear vehicular networks. The best effort traffic is handled with the remaining bandwidth after allocating resources for real-time traffic. In CVIA-QoS, one time slot is divided into two periods, the High Priority Period (HPP) and Low Priority Period (LPP), respectively. In CVIA-QoS, packets admitted to HPP are delivered to the gateway in one time slot. Furthermore, an admission control mechanism is introduced where admission decisions are made by the gateways and executed by the temporary routers.

Alcaraz et al. (2009) propose a mechanism to enhance the quality of service provision. The proposed mechanism attempts to minimize the backlog of data, meaning unprocessed requests/ data, which is equivalent of maximizing the throughput. This is being achieved by this particular mechanism by assigning different weights (relative importance factor) to vehicles according to their estimated connection lifetime.

Despite its numerous advantages, QoS provision via RSU assistance has some drawbacks, one of these being its ineffectiveness in sparse or no RSU environment. Ramirez et al. (2007), propose a QoS-enabled routing protocol, namely AODVM that aims to connect the two network segments that comprise a vehicular network that is the mobile network and the fixed infrastructure respectively. The gateway discovery process, by the vehicles that need to communicate can happen in three different ways—proactively, reactively, and in hybrid manner—and in every way the existence of infrastructure is mandatory, so in sparse infrastructure environment this protocol would face several issues.

Unlike rural areas where the traffic load might be low, in urban areas where the traffic is dense, message relay may face unavoidable delays. To that end, a routing protocol, namely DTRP, is proposed by Saleet et al. (2010). In DTRP, the gateway constructs a set of routes between itself and the mobile nodes based on its view about the local network topology. Nevertheless, one should note that if these routes consist of intermediate mobile nodes, they cannot be considered to be stable due to intermediate nodes' mobility. To increase their stability, DTRP builds routes based on intermediate and adjacent road intersections towards the gateway. These routes are called backbone routes. In order to meet the end-to-end delay requirement, the selected backbone routes should have high connectivity probability. In low-density roads, one way to increase the connectivity probability is to increase the road density increases, the transmission range should be reduced to avoid high interference, but the transmission range should still guarantee high connectivity. Hence, in DTRP, the gateway will decide on the transmission range that each vehicle should use in order to achieve high route connectivity. It is worth noting that VANETs exhibit different behaviors depending on the traffic volume. This implies a variation in the traffic patterns, which DTRP aims to mitigate.

In many of the proposed architectures, the authors also take into account the absence of fixed roadside network providing the VANET participants with mobile gateways. A multi-layer cooperation framework is proposed by Iera et al. (2007) that explores exactly this possibility. In this architecture the gateway, which can be either fixed roadside equipment or a mobile node, has a central role. The gateway must have the ability of both the external network and the vehicular network to match user preferences and QoS requirements. Furthermore, the gateway has to be provided with communication and negotiation capability towards the external network and also the VANET nodes. The roadside (fixed) gateways are more prone to route Internet traffic, but there is no limitation since the "best" route is always chosen based on certain criteria. What is innovative in this approach is that while searching for the most efficient route the packets exchanged between the gateway and the sender node contain network information concerning delay, throughput, link lifetime, etc. The gateway, which is capable of interpreting that information, uses them additionally to make a decision about the best possible route (see Table 2).

Table 2. Characteristics of the reviewed QoS-enabled protocols for vehicular networks

	Link-Reliability	Maximization Throughput	End-to-End Delay Minimization
AMR	YES	N/A	YES
PVR	N/A	YES	YES
GVGrid	YES	N/A	N/A
CVIA-QoS	N/A	YES	YES
AODVM	N/A	N/A	YES
DTRP	YES	NO	NO

In this section, we have investigated vehicle-to-infrastructure communications, and the challenges that they pose to efficient QoS provision in vehicular environment. We explored the trade-offs that can greatly affect the quality of service provision in vehicular networks and presented additional detail on the weaknesses and strengths of the current research. We have also overviewed several vehicle-to-infrastructure quality of service provision schemes, mechanisms and targeted protocols and categorized them by employing various criteria. This categorization allowed us to identify the current problems of QoS provision in vehicular-to-infrastructure communications. We carefully reviewed these issues and illuminated the proposed solutions for each of them.

ROUTING AND MESSAGE FORWARDING ISSUES

Routing is one of the key research issues in vehicular networks as long as it supports most emerging applications. Vehicular communications require fast and reliable communication between cars (vehicle-to-vehicle) or between a car and a roadside unit (vehicle-to-infrastructure). In the context of this chapter, we only examine the vehicle-to-infrastructure side of the vehicular communication routing process. The greatest advantage of infrastructure-based communication is the fact that the density of the equipped cars needed for a working application is much smaller than in the case of a VANET.

Characteristics of Infrastructure-Assisted Routing in Vehicular Networks

In this section of the chapter, we explore the case of infrastructure exploitation by routing protocols in order to improve the routing process in vehicular networks. Due to the fact that the improvement in routing achieved by infrastructure exploitation in vehicular networks is great, there has been an emerging set of routing protocols tailored specifically for vehicle-to-infrastructure environment.

Summarizing the above, the definitive characteristic of V2I communications in order to maximize the routing performance of the network is:

- **Infrastructure exploitation:** A situation that many protocols neglect is the existence of previous infrastructure along the roads. Such infrastructure consists of devices deployed by road operators and private telecommunications companies. Routing protocols could benefit a lot from those devices, which could act as relays, buffers, and so on. Moreover, useful information about the traffic state could be obtained from them, helping algorithms to make more intelligent decisions.

Several characteristics (Toor, Muhlethaler, & Laouiti, 2008) of the vehicular environment that make routing a challenging task, are:

- **Highly Dynamic Topology:** Since vehicles are moving at high speed, the topology formed by VANETs is changing fast and dynamically.
- **Frequently Disconnected Network (Intermittent Connectivity):** The highly dynamic topology results in frequently disconnected network since the link between two vehicles can quickly disappear while the two nodes are transmitting information. The problem is further exacerbated by heterogeneous node density where frequently traveled roads have more cars than non-frequently traveled roads. A robust routing protocol needs to recognize the frequent dis-connectivity and provides an alternative link quickly to ensure uninterrupted communication.
- **Propagation Model:** In VANETs, the propagation model is usually not assumed

to be free space because of the presence of buildings, trees, and other vehicles. A VANET propagation model should well consider the effects of free standing objects as well as potential interference of wireless communication from other vehicles or widely deployed access points.

- **Network Penetration:** In vehicular networks, especially in vehicle-to-infrastructure communication, network penetration plays a really important role. In sparse or no infrastructure environments, the routing process might be halted by factors such as roadside equipment absence or thin vehicle density. This can severely affect safety-related (life critical information) or infotainment-related applications and services. In that regard, we consider that network penetration is a key factor for the success of the routing, as of any other process or service in vehicular environment.

However, there are also disadvantages in the use of infrastructure in the routing process. This could seem as no surprise that avoiding the use of single point message aggregating equipment.

Due to the high degree of the centralization, the server can become a bottleneck or even a single point of failure. However, the main reason not to use a centralized system for managing traffic information could very well be non-technical; it simply does not seem to be desirable to hand the control of this data over to one central authority, potentially limiting the access to data collected jointly by all traffic participants.

On the other hand, there are some special traits to vehicular networks and their participants that help in making the routing process more efficient and improve the network performance in overall. Such traits are (Nekovee, 2005):

- **Patterned Mobility:** Vehicles follow a certain mobility pattern that is a function of the underlying roads, the traffic lights, the speed limit, traffic condition, and drivers' driving behaviors. Because of the particular mobility pattern, we can predict vehicle movement and design routing protocols exploiting this particular fact to make data dissemination in vehicular environment less challenging.

- **Unlimited Battery Power and Storage:** Nodes in VANETs are not subject to power and storage limitation as in sensor networks, another class of ad hoc networks where nodes are mostly static. Nodes are assumed to have ample energy and computing power. Therefore, optimizing duty cycle is not as relevant as it is in sensor networks.
- **On-board Sensors:** Nodes are assumed to be equipped with sensors to provide information useful for routing purposes. Many VANET routing protocols have assumed the availability of GPS unit from on-board Navigation system. Location information from GPS unit and speed from speedometer provides good examples for plethora of information that can possibly be obtained by sensors to be utilized to enhance routing decisions.

Routing Modes in Vehicular Communications: Vehicle-to-Infrastructure Broadcast

Data broadcast is an attractive solution for large-scale data dissemination. In contrast to unicast, where a data item must be transmitted many times to answer multiple requests, broadcast has the potential to satisfy all outstanding requests for the same data item with a single response. The participation of RSU in the routing process involves broadcast techniques from the RSU to the participants of the network. The two most common ways, are the pull-based approach and the push-based approach. We then outline the basics about these two concepts (Vishal & Narottam, 2010).

Pull-Based Broadcast Dissemination

In pull-based broadcast, commonly known as on demand broadcast, the RSU disseminates data items in response to explicit requests submitted by vehicles. Compared to its push-based counterpart, pull based is more scalable to large size databases. This broadcast model is reactive.

Push-Based Data Dissemination

In push-based broadcast, the Road Side Unit broadcasts the whole or part of the database periodically according to a static broadcast program. All vehicles listen passively to the broadcast channel to retrieve data items of interest without sending any request. This broadcast model is proactive.

Infrastructure-Assisted Routing: Proposed Solutions

In this subsection, we study several proposed solutions for VANET routing that improve the performance of the network by utilizing the roadside network. As mentioned in the quality of service subchapter, several routing protocols make use of the roadside network to provide quality of service in it, so we also explore these scenarios from the routing scope.

A protocol that we studied under a different scope in the quality of service subchapter is also examined here. Sun et al. (2006) propose the GVGrid routing protocol, namely. This protocol assumes that every node (vehicle) has a short-range wireless device that has the same transmission range across the network nodes. GVGrid partitions the geographic region into squares of equal-size called grids. During route discovery, GVGrid attempts to find the route that is expected to have long lifetime, based on the position of each vehicle.

This expected lifetime of a route is determined by the vehicles' movement on that route and characteristics (such as traffic signals and stop signs) of the roads on which the route is based.

In dense urban areas, where the traffic load grows exponentially, it is expected to have certain unavoidable delays in the routing of the messages. To mitigate the effect of those delays to the network's performance, Saleet et al. (2010) propose a delay tolerant routing protocol, namely DTRP. In DTRP, the gateway constructs a set of routes between itself and the mobile nodes based on its view about the local network topology. Nevertheless, one should note that if these routes consist of intermediate mobile nodes, these routes cannot be considered to be stable due to intermediate nodes' mobility. Hence, in DTRP, the gateway will decide on the transmission range that each vehicle should use in order to achieve high route connectivity. It is worth noting that VANETs exhibit different behaviors depending on the traffic volume. This implies a variation in the traffic patterns, which DTRP aims to mitigate.

In the standardized (IEEE 802.11p) communication architecture for vehicular networks, a channel is always dedicated to safety messages. Based on that, Ferreira et al. (2009) proposed an infrastructure-based solution found in Ferreira, Meireles, and Fonseca (2009), where the RSU play a major role in rebroadcasting warning messages in the network. In this approach there exists a control channel, which is dedicated to service safety messages, along with a service channel to be used for the rest services. Every CCH interval will be divided into an Infrastructure Period (IP) and a Slotted Period (SloP). The IP is reserved for RSUs coordination and for beacon transmission by RSUs, where all vehicles should listen to the channel. The beacon contains information about the SloP. By using beacons, the RSU will know the time the event was triggered and, in the next beacon, will inform that a specific slot will be used to rebroadcast the message.

The TRAFIC Initiative

In Brahmi et al. (2010), the TRAFIC initiative is explored, that utilizes the roadside infrastructure to improve routing in vehicular environment.

The TRAFIC project is a research and industrial initiative which aims to contribute to the global academic and industry effort to develop ITS systems. More specifically, TRAFIC defines a hybrid communication infrastructure that exploits the offered opportunities of inter-vehicle cooperation, as well as the advanced capabilities of communicating devices deployed along the roads. TRAFIC hybrid infrastructure gathers several communication components: a network infrastructure and a vehicular network. In particular, the network infrastructure consists of a wired/wireless access network (such as Wi-Fi/DSRC access points, WiMAX access, 2G/3G access, etc.), a backbone, and a sensor network. The access network ensures connectivity between the vehicular network and the backbone. The sensor network helps in detecting fine granularity traffic and security statistics related to roads and vehicles conditions while the backbone ensures the IP connectivity and houses the value-added services offered to vehicle users.

Based on this initiative and what it offers, Brahmi et al. (2010) propose the TRAFIC Efficient Routing Protocol (TERP) that uses the hybrid communication infrastructure proposed in TRAFIC. It defines an end-to-end efficient routing policy based on using two routing approaches: trajectory-based using SIFTv2 (Simple Forwarding over trajectory Version 2) protocol and dynamic decision-based routing using LoP (LTT over Progress) which targeted for V2I routing. Depending on the role of the packet forwarder (source or intermediate nodes) and applications requirements, TERP selects the appropriate routing approach. However, we only examine the V2I case of the operating scenario. LoP relies on TRAFIC communication infrastructure and more specifically the Road Side Units (RSUs) deployed at road intersections. The RSUs can communicate with the vehicles within their coverage range and have knowledge of their local road topology (each RSU knows the neighboring RSUs).

Geographic routing also known as geocast has been one of the most popular approaches in infrastructure-aided routing. Borsetti et al. (2010) propose a routing scheme, based on geographic routing, to increase the reliability and range of multi-hop communications. The proposed approach works under the assumption that all the RSU components of the network have no delays to their inter-communications, and they can be thought of as one node in a network graph. Using this graph representation, topology-aware routing protocols would be able to compute more optimal routes and, when it is the case, efficiently route packets through the infrastructure.

In most cases, what infrastructure assistance can offer and which is difficult to achieve in a purely ad-hoc environment, is traffic comfort and traffic efficiency services (i.e. digital map download, paid services, etc.). Shen et al. (2008) propose a routing protocol with RSU-assistance for vehicular environment and especially for Internet access. The authors consider a hybrid VANET composed of vehicles constrained to move on roadways and sparse RSU deployment. This protocol works under the assumptions that every vehicle is equipped with a radio transceiver and a GPS receiver and have location awareness. Each RSU is directly connected to the Internet by high capacity cables, thus assuming that information can be exchanged among RSUs via the wired network with minimal delay. Additionally, both RSUs and vehicles are assumed to transmit at the same fixed power level. When a vehicle is out of transmission range of an RSU or physical obstacle block their communications, other vehicles will be used to relay the data traffic. Whenever a vehicle sends or relays a packet, it piggybacks its current location and mobility information, and the corresponding timestamp in the packet. This way, an RSU can obtain location and mobility information of all vehicles in the area

In both ad-hoc and hybrid vehicular environment, a factor of outmost importance for the success of the routing process is vehicular density. Gupta et al. (2010) recognizing exactly this important parameter proposed an RSU-assisted routing algorithm, namely VD4. In VD4, every time a vehicle passes an RSU, the following information is sent to it; the time of arrival of the vehicle (as a timestamp), the speed of the vehicle, the direction of movement, the data packets (if it has any). The data packets that are received by the RSU are marked with a unique sequence number, which is used to check for duplicity of the packet. If the packet is already present at the RSU, it is dropped otherwise it is forwarded to the farthest in range vehicle on the most optimal path as has been calculated by the delay model. However, it must be noted that this algorithm operates in a network under several assumptions. It is assumed that, the vehicles are sufficiently equipped with wireless transmitters that can transmit in a short range (100 m – 200 m) for transmitting data packet whenever a vehicle reaches the vicinity of the original data packet carrying vehicle or to the RSU. In addition, every roadside intersection is equipped with a RSU, which is capable of storing data packets sent by vehicles as and when required. The information necessary for the proper routing is included by the source in the packet at the time of transmission. Each vehicle and RSU knows its present location using GPS. The RSU maintains the information of vehicles such as the speed, direction etc. that passed it and also an estimate of total number of vehicles present on each path at a given point in time. This information is periodically updated so that the evaluation of the optimal path may be done with the latest information. The vehicles are assumed to move with uniform speed on a path.

A representative example of infrastructure-assisted routing and how it can improve the network's performance is presented by Yanlin et al. (2006). The authors propose an RSU-assisted routing protocol. The RAR protocol is based on three concepts: sectors, advertisements, affiliations. A sector is the road surface between several RSUs. Advertisements are used to advertise new services and are broadcasted by the RSUs. When a vehicle receives an advertisement, it must decide if it will enter the new sector. If and when a vehicle changes sector, it must also change its affiliation. This change is mandatory for the RSU to be able to locate the vehicle within the sector and forward any packages to it via wireless means. In this protocol, the routing is singled-phased and involves discovering the best routes and using the RSUs as shortcuts. The infrastructure network is assumed to be a special sector and can decide based on the destination's address whether it is in the infrastructure network or in VANET. If the destination is in VANET, RSUs know the destination sector by querying other RSUs. At the end of this phase, the best route is discovered and routing performance is improved by limiting ad-hoc routing in a small scope (sectors) and utilizing backbone networks.

Many of the proposed routing protocols support both ad-hoc and hybrid routing for vehicular networks. This happens mainly because of the indistinguishable nature of the vehicular networks and because it would be costly to develop a protocol for a single type of communication. Rongxi et al. (2008) propose a routing scheme for hybrid vehicular environment. In the context of this chapter, we only examine the vehicle-to-infrastructure part of this scheme. The basic concept is that, upon receiving a route request from a vehicle wanting to transmit data looks into its records to find out in which local peer group the destination belongs to. If the sender and the receiver move into the same group, the RSU update the corresponding fields in the received request and broadcasts the message to one-hop neighbors but also the neighboring RSUs. In the case that the sender and the destination moving in different local peer groups, the sender's RSU

forwards the message to the destination's local peer group in an attempt to find a reliable RSU close to the destination and identify the actual destination vehicle. Once all these preconditions have been met, the destination's RSU sends a message to the corresponding RSU on sender's side which in turn informs the sender vehicle to start transmitting data that are routed via the two RSUs to the destination.

In this subchapter, we have overviewed vehicle-to-infrastructure routing, which is one of the most challenging tasks for vehicular communications. We have presented the advantages and disadvantages of the infrastructure utilization to assist vehicular communications and particularly the routing process. We have examined in what degree the infrastructure penetration in the network affects the performance of the network and what effects this might have on safety or infotainment message dissemination. We have identified and analyzed the current problems that vehicular routing faces. Furthermore, we have aggregated and categorized several proposed solutions, which include mechanisms, schemes, and targeted protocols for this matter.

THE FUTURE OF VEHICLE-TO-INFRASTRUCTURE COMMUNICATIONS

It is a fact that the V2I communication model is more expensive compared to its ad-hoc counterpart; however, it is also a fact that the V2I communications have much yet to offer in all aspects of the vehicular environment, from active safety to infotainment services. Vehicular communications are becoming a reality because the market has recognized the significance that they will have in the near future. This alone gives a promising development for the proposed technologies. Market penetration will play an important role in this particular field due to the funds that will push its development. However, the penetration of vehicular network technology is still weak, hence there is a need for a minimum of infrastructure support to increase the penetration by the provision of helpful services. At the same time, deploying new infrastructure for these networks necessitate a lot of investment and at a high cost. The main conclusion of the current chapter is that Vehicle-to-Infrastructure Communications will help towards the improvement of the active and passive road safety on the road.

CONCLUSION

Concluding this chapter, we have discussed extensively about vehicular communications networks. In particular, we have analyzed the vehicle-to-infrastructure component of this hybrid network. We have also performed a survey on some of the most challenging tasks for V2I communications, such as security and privacy, quality of service provision and routing issues. We have investigated occasions in which the infrastructure element assisted in overcoming several problems, but also when it worsened the performance of the network. In each subchapter, we have provided a detailed categorization of the problems and challenges that exist in each respective field of interest, and presented several proposed solutions that make use of the infrastructure element to provide a solution for the studied problems. However, the realization for many of those scenarios still demands heavy deployment of the roadside infrastructure to support the network and the desired needs and applications.

REFERENCES

Alcaraz, J., Vales-Alonso, J., & Garcia-Haro, J. (2009). Control-based scheduling with QoS support for vehicle to infrastructure communications. *Wireless Communications*, *16*, 32–39. doi:10.1109/MWC.2009.5361176

Blum, J., Eskandarian, A., & Hoffmman, L. (2004). Challenges of inter-vehicle ad-hoc networks. *IEEE Transactions on Intelligent Transportation Systems*, *5*(4), 347–351. doi:10.1109/TITS.2004.838218

Boneh, D., & Boyen, X. (2004). Short signatures without random oracles. In C. Cachin & J. Camenisch (Eds.), *Eurocrypt 2004 Conference*, (pp. 56–73). Eurocrypt.

Boneh, D., Boyen, X., & Shacham, H. (2004). Short group signatures. *Lecture Notes in Computer Science*, *3152*, 41–55. doi:10.1007/978-3-540-28628-8_3

Borsetti, D., & Gozalvez, J. (2010). Infrastructure-assisted geo-routing for cooperative vehicular networks. In *Proceedings of the Vehicular Networking Conference*, (pp. 255-262). IEEE.

Brahmi, N., Boukhatem, L., Boukhatem, N., Boussedjra, M., Nuy, N., Dau Labiod, H., & Mouzna, J. (2010). End-to-end routing through a hybrid ad hoc architecture for V2V and V2I communications. In *Proceedings of the 9th IFIP Annual Mediterranean Ad Hoc Networking Workshop*, (pp. 1-8). IFIP.

Calandriello, G., Papadimitratos, P., Hubaux, J.-P., & Lioy, A. (2007). Efficient and robust pseudonymous authentication in VANET. In *Proceedings of the Fourth ACM International Workshop on Vehicular Ad Hoc Networks*, (pp. 19–28). ACM.

Cencioni, P., & Di Pietro, R. (2007). VIPER: A vehicle-to-infrastructure communication privacy enforcement protocol. In *Proceedings of the IEEE International Conference on Mobile Adhoc and Sensor Systems*, (pp. 1-6). IEEE.

Cheng, H. T., Shan, H., & Zhuang, W. (2012). Infotainment and road safety service support in vehicular networking: From a communication perspective. *Mechanical Systems and Signal Processing Journal*. Retrieved from http://bbcr.uwaterloo.ca/~wzhuang/papers/MSSP_vanet_survey_2010.pdf

Dhurandher, S. K., Obaidat, M. S., Jaiswal, A., Tiwari, A., & Tyagi, A. (2010). Securing vehicular networks: A reputation and plausibility checks-based approach. In *Proceedings of the GLOBECOM Workshops*, (pp. 1550-1554). GLOBECOM.

Dötzer, F. (2005). Privacy issues in vehicular ad hoc networks. In *Proceedings of the Workshop on Privacy Enhancing Technologies (PET)*. ACM Press.

Ferreira, N., Meireles, T., & Fonseca, J. A. (2009). An RSU coordination scheme for WAVE safety services support. In *Proceedings of the IEEE Conference on Emerging Technologies & Factory Automation*, (pp. 1-4). IEEE.

Freudiger, J., Raya, M., Félegyházi, M., Papadimitratos, P., & Hubaux, J.-P. (2007). *Mix-zones for location privacy in vehicular networks*. Paper presented at the 1st International Workshop on Wireless Networking for Intelligent Transportation Systems. Vancouver, Canada.

Gomez Marmol, F., & Martinez Perez, G. (2011). TRIP: A trust and reputation infrastructure-based proposal for vehicular ad hoc networks. *Network and Computer Applications Journal*. Retrieved from http://people.stfx.ca/x2010/x2010qfo/ HONOR_THESIS/TRMSIM_RESOURCES/ TRIP,%20a%20trust%20and%20reputation%20 infrastructure-based%20proposal%20for%20ve-hicular%20and%20Ad%20Hoc%20Network.pdf

Guo, J., Baugh, J. P., & Wang, S. (2007). A group signature based secure and privacy-preserving vehicular communication framework. In *Proceedings of the Mobile Networking for Vehicular Environments Conference*, (pp. 103-108). IEEE.

Gupta, A., Chaudhary, V., Kumar, V., Nishad, B., & Tapaswi, S. (2010). VD4: Vehicular density-dependent data delivery model in vehicular ad hoc networks. In *Proceedings of the Sixth Advanced International Conference on Telecommunications*, (pp. 286-291). IEEE.

Haas, J. J., Hu, Y.-C., & Laberteaux, K. P. (2010). The impact of key assignment on VANET privacy. In *Proceedings of 1st International Workshop on Security and Communication Networks*, (vol 3, pp. 233-249). New York, NY: John Wiley & Sons, Ltd.

He, R., Rutagemwa, H., & Shen, X. (2008). Differentiated reliable routing in hybrid vehicular ad hoc networks. In *Proceedings of the IEEE International Conference on Communications*, (pp. 2353-2358). IEEE.

Huang, L., Matsuura, K., Yamane, H., & Sezaki, K. (2005). Enhancing wireless location privacy using silent period. In *Proceedings of the Wireless Communications and Networking Conference*, (pp. 1187-1192). IEEE.

Hubaux, J. P., Capkun, S., & Luo, J. (2004). The security and privacy of smart vehicles. *IEEE Security & Privacy*, 2, 49–55. doi:10.1109/ MSP.2004.26

IEEE. (2007). *IEEE standards association, IEEE P1609.1—Standard for wireless access in vehicular environments (WAVE)—Resource manager, IEEE P1609.2—Standard for wireless access in vehicular environments (WAVE)—Security services for applications and management messages, IEEE P1609.3—Standard for wireless access in vehicular environments (WAVE)—Networking services, IEEE P1609.4— Standard for wireless access in vehicular environments (WAVE)—Multi-channel operations, adopted for trial-use in 2007.* Piscataway, NJ: IEEE Press.

IEEE. (2010). IEEE standard for information technology--Telecommunications and information exchange between systems--Local and metropolitan area networks--Specific requirements part 11: Wireless LAN medium access control (MAC) and physical layer (PHY) specifications amendment 6: Wireless access in vehicular environments. In *IEEE Std 802.11p-2010 (Amendment to IEEE Std 802.11-2007 as amended by IEEE Std 802.11k-2008, IEEE Std 802.11r-2008, IEEE Std 802.11y-2008, IEEE Std 802.11n-2009, and IEEE Std 802.11w-2009)*, (pp. 1-51). Washington, DC: IEEE Press.

Iera, A., Molinaro, A., Polito, S., & Ruggeri, G. (2008). A multi-layer cooperation framework for QoS-aware internet access in Vanets. *Ubiquitous Computing and Communication Journal, 10*(4), 10–19.

Japan Ministry of Land. (2007). *Infrastructure and transport, road bureau, smartway 2007 public road test*. Retrieved from http://www.its.go.jp/ITS/topindex/topindex_sw2007.html

Kamini, & Kumar, R. (2010). VANET parameters and applications: A review. *Global Journal of Computer Science and Technology, 10*(7), 72-77.

Korkmaz, G., Ekici, E., & Ozguner, F. (2006). Internet access protocol providing QoS in vehicular networks with infrastructure support. In *Proceedings of the Intelligent Transportation Systems Conference ITSC*, (pp. 1412-1417). IEEE.

Ksentini, A., Tounsi, H., & Frikha, M. (2010). A proxy-based framework for QoS-enabled internet access in VANETS. In *Proceedings of the Second International Conference on Communications and Networking*, (pp. 1-8). IEEE.

Kumar, V., & Chand, N. (2010). Data scheduling in VANETs: A review. *International Journal of Computer Science & Communication, 1*(2), 399–403.

Langley, C., Lucas, R., & Fu, H. (2008). Key management in vehicular ad-hoc networks. In *Proceedings of International Conference on Electro/Information Technology*, (pp. 223-226). IEEE.

Liu, B., Zhong, Y., & Zhang, S. (2007). Probabilistic isolation of malicious vehicles in pseudonym changing VANETs. In *Proceedings of the 7th IEEE International Conference on Computer and Information Technology*, (pp. 967-972). IEEE.

Liu, Y., Bi, J., & Yang, J. (2009). Research on vehicular ad hoc networks. In *Proceedings of the Control and Decision Conference, CCDC 2009*, (pp. 4430-4435). CCDC.

Lo, N.-W., & Tsai, H.-C. (2007). Illusion attack on VANET applications - A message plausibility problem. In *Proceedings of the 2nd IEEE Workshop on Automotive Networking and Applications (AutoNet 2007)*, (pp. 1-8, 26-30). IEEE.

Motsinger, C., & Hubbing, T. (2007). *A review of vehicle-to-vehicle and vehicle-to-infrastructure initiatives*. Clemson, SC: University of Clemson.

Moustafa, H., & Zhang, Y. (Eds.). (2009). *Vehicular networks techniques: Standards and applications*. Boca Raton, FL: CRC Press. doi:10.1201/9781420085723

Nekovee, M. (2005). *Sensor networks on the road: The promises and challenges of vehicular adhoc networks and vehicular grids*. Paper presented at the Workshop on Ubiquitous Computing and e-Research. Edinburgh, UK.

Olariu, S., & Weigle, C. M. (Eds.). (2009). *Vehicular networks from theory to practice*. Boca Raton, FL: CRC Press. doi:10.1201/9781420085891

Papadimitratos, P., Buttyan, L., Holczer, T., Schoch, E., Freudiger, J., & Raya, M. (2008). Secure vehicular communication systems: Design and architecture. *IEEE Communications, 46*, 100–109. doi:10.1109/MCOM.2008.4689252

Papadimitratos, P., Buttyan, L., Hubaux, J.-P., Kargl, F., Kung, A., & Raya, M. (2007). Architecture for secure and private vehicular communications. In *Proceedings of ITST 2007, 7th International Conference on ITS Telecommunications*, (pp. 1-6). ITST.

Papadimitratos, P., Gligor, V., & Hubaux, J.-P. (2006). Securing vehicular communications - Assumptions, requirements, and principles. In *Proccedings of Workshop on Embedded Security in Cars*. IEEE.

Park, S., Aslam, B., Turgut, D., & Zou, C. C. (2009). Defense against Sybil attack in vehicular ad hoc network based on roadside unit support. In *Proceedings of the Military Communications Conference*, (pp. 1-7). IEEE.

Peng, Y., Abichar, Z., & Chang, J. M. (2006). Roadside-aided routing (RAR) in vehicular networks. In *Proceedings of the IEEE International Conference on Communications*, (pp. 3602-3607). IEEE.

Perrig, A., Canetti, R., Tygar, J., & Song, D. (2002). The TESLA broadcast authentication protocol. *RSA CryptoBytes Newsletter*, *5*, 2–13.

Ramirez, C. L., & Veiga, M. F. (2007). QoS in vehicular and intelligent transport networks using multicast routing. In *Proceedings of the IEEE International Symposium on Industrial Electronics*, (pp. 2556–2561). IEEE.

Rawat, D. B. Treeumnuk, D., Popescu, D. C., Abuelela, M., & Olariu, S. (2008). Challenges and perspectives in the implementation of NOTICE architecture for vehicular communications. In *Proceedings of the 5ᵗʰ IEEE International Conference on Mobile Ad Hoc and Sensor Systems*, (pp. 707-711). IEEE.

Raya, M., Papadimitratos, P., Aad, I., Jungels, D., & Hubaux, J.-P. (2007). Eviction of misbehaving and faulty nodes in vehicular networks. *IEEE Journal on Selected Areas in Communications*, *25*(8), 1557–1568. doi:10.1109/JSAC.2007.071006

Saleet, H., Langar, R., Basir, O., & Boutaba, R. (2009). Adaptive message routing with QoS support in vehicular ad hoc networks. In *Proceedings of the Global Telecommunications Conference*, (pp. 1-6). IEEE.

Saleet, H., Langar, R., Naik, S., Boutaba, R., Nayak, A., & Goel, N. (2010). QoS support in delay tolerant vehicular ad hoc networks. In *Proceedings of the IEEE Global Telecommunications Conference*, (pp. 1-10). IEEE.

Sampigethaya, K., Huang, L., Li, M., Poovendran, R., Matsuura, K., & Sezaki, K. (2005). CARAVAN: Providing location privacy for VANET. In *Proceedings of the Workshop on Embedded Security in Cars*. Embedded Security in Cars.

Serna, J., Luna, J., & Medina, M. (2008). Geolocation-based trust for VANET'S privacy. In *Proceedings of the Fourth International Conference on Information Assurance and Security*, (pp. 287-290). IEEE.

Sichitiu, M. L., & Kihl, M. (2008). Inter-vehicle communication systems: A survey. *Communications Surveys & Tutorials*, *10*(2), 88–105. doi:10.1109/COMST.2008.4564481

Stampoulis, A., & Chai, Z. (2007). *Survey of security in vehicular networks*. Project CPSC 534. Retrieved from http://zoo.cs.yale.edu/~ams257/projects/wireless-survey.pdf

Studer, A., Bai, F., Bellur, B., & Perrig, A. (2008). Flexible, extensible, and efficient VANET authentication. In *Proceedings of 6th Annual Conference on Embedded Security in Cars*. Embedded Security in Cars.

Studer, A., Shi, E., Fan, B., & Perrig, A. (2009). TACKing together efficient authentication, revocation, and privacy in VANETs. In *Proceedings of 6th Annual IEEE Communications Society Conference on Sensor, Mesh and Ad Hoc Communications and Networks*, (pp. 1-9). IEEE.

Sun, W., Yamaguchi, H., Yukimasa, K., & Kusumoto, S. (2006). GVGrid: A QoS routing protocol for vehicular ad hoc networks. In *Proceedings of the 14th IEEE International Workshop on Quality of Service*, (pp. 130-139). IEEE.

Sun, X., Lin, X., & Ho, P.-H. (2007). Secure vehicular communications based on group signature and ID-based signature scheme. In *Proceedings of the IEEE International Conference on Communications,* (pp. 1539-1545). IEEE Press.

Tamer, N., Pravin, S., & Liviu, I. (2006). A comparative study of data dissemination models for VANETs. In *Proceedings of the Third Annual International Conference on Mobile and Ubiquitous Systems: Networking & Services*, (pp. 1-10). IEEE.

Toor, Y., Muhlethaler, P., & Laouiti, A. (2008). Vehicle ad hoc networks: Applications and related technical issues. *IEEE Communications Surveys & Tutorials*, *10*, 74–88. doi:10.1109/COMST.2008.4625806

Tsugawa, S. (2005). Issues and recent trends in vehicle safety communication systems: IATSS research. *Journal of International Association of Traffic and Safety Sciences*, *29*(1), 7–15.

Wan, S., Tang, J., & Wolff, R. S. (2008). Reliable routing for roadside to vehicle communications in rural areas. In *Proceedings of the IEEE International Conference on Communications*, (pp. 3017-3021). IEEE.

Wang, X., Georgios, B., Giannakis, A., & Marques, G. (2007). A unified approach to QoS guaranteed scheduling for channel-adaptive wireless networks. *Proceedings of the IEEE Journal*, *95*(12), 2410–2431. doi:10.1109/JPROC.2007.907120

Wasef, A., & Shen, X. (2009). MAAC: Message authentication acceleration protocol for vehicular ad hoc networks. In *Proceedings of Global Telecommunications Conference*, (pp. 1-6). IEEE.

Wasef, A., & Shen, X. (2009). ASIC: Aggregate signatures and certificates verification scheme for vehicular networks. In *Proceedings of Global Telecommunications Conference*, (pp. 1-6). IEEE.

Werner, W., & Lars, R. (2010). C2X communications overview. In *Proceedings of the URSI International Symposium on Electromagnetic Theory*, (pp. 868-871). URSI.

Wex, P., Breuer, J., Held, A., Leinmuller, T., & Delgrossi, L. (2008). Trust issues for vehicular ad hoc networks. In *Proceedings of the Vehicular Technology Conference*, (pp. 2800-2804). IEEE.

Wohlmacher, P. (2000). Digital certificates: A survey of revocation methods. In *Proceedings of the ACM Workshop*, (pp. 111–114). ACM Press.

Yan, G., Olariu, S., & Weigle, M. C. (2008). Providing VANET security through active position detection. *Computer Communications*, *31*, 2883–2897. doi:10.1016/j.comcom.2008.01.009

Zhang, C., Lin, X., Lu, R., & Ho, P.-H. (2008). RAISE: An efficient RSU-aided message authentication scheme in vehicular communication networks. In *Proceedings of the IEEE International Conference on Communications*, (pp. 1451-1457). IEEE.

Zhang, Y., Zhao, J., & Cao, G. (2007). On scheduling vehicle-roadside data access. *ACM International Workshop on VehiculAr Inter-NETworking ACM VANET*, (pp. 10–19). ACM Press.

KEY TERMS AND DEFINITIONS

Dedicated Short Range Communication (DSRC): Is a short to medium range wireless protocol specifically designed for automotive use.

IEEE 802.11p: Is the standard that specifies the technologies for vehicular communications.

Intelligent Transportation Systems (ITS): Is a worldwide initiative to add information and communications technology to transport infrastructure and vehicles.

Mobile Ad-Hoc Network (MANET): Is a type of ad hoc network that can change locations and configure itself on the fly.

Vehicle-To-Infrastructure Communications (V2I): Wireless communication between a vehicle and an infrastructure (also termed as vehicle-to-roadside [V2R]).

Vehicle-To-Vehicle Communication (V2V): Wireless communication between two vehicles equipped with short and medium range wireless communication capabilities.

Vehicular Ad-Hoc Network (VANET): Is a form of Mobile Ad-Hoc Network (MANET), to provide communications among nearby vehicles.

Wireless Local Area Network (WLAN): A type of network in which a mobile user can connect to a Local Area Network (LAN) through a wireless (radio) connection.

Chapter 2
On–Board Unit Hardware and Software Design for Vehicular Ad–Hoc Networks

Matteo Petracca
National Interuniversity Consortium for Telecommunications, Italy

Paolo Pagano
National Interuniversity Consortium for Telecommunications, Italy

Riccardo Pelliccia
Scuola Superiore Sant'Anna, Italy

Marco Ghibaudi
Scuola Superiore Sant'Anna, Italy

Claudio Salvadori
Scuola Superiore Sant'Anna, Italy

Christian Nastasi
Scuola Superiore Sant'Anna, Italy

ABSTRACT

Intelligent Transport Systems (ITS) are a focus of public authorities and research communities in order for them to provide effective solutions for improving citizens' security and lifestyle. The effectiveness of such systems relies on the prompt processing of the acquired traffic- and vehicle-related information to react to congestion and dangerous situations. To obtain a dynamic and pervasive environment where vehicles are fully integrated in the ITS, low cost technologies (capable of strongly penetrating the market) must be made available by the effort of academic and industrial research. In this chapter, the authors discuss the design and implementation of a prototype vehicular unit capable of interacting with both roadside networks and in-vehicle electronic devices. More in detail, in order to scientifically characterize the solution, the authors start from a clear statement of the requirements that the vehicle equipment should respond to. Then they detail the selection of the off-the-shelf components adopted in the prototyped on-board unit. In the last part of the chapter, the authors discuss several possible applications in which the developed device can be adopted, as well as open issues for future research activities.

DOI: 10.4018/978-1-4666-2223-4.ch002

INTRODUCTION

In recent years, Intelligent Transport Systems (ITS) have gained a considerable interest from both public authorities and research community. By integrating computers, electronics, satellites, and sensors in the transport systems, ITS can make every transport mode more efficient, safe and energy saving, thus improving citizens' lifestyle and drivers' security. The new generation of ITS will include an integrated approach for travel planning, transport demand, traffic management, emergency management, road pricing, and the use of parking and public transport facilities, while requiring scalable installations (in terms of costs and communication capabilities) and limited interventions of civil infrastructures (Pagano, Petracca, Alessandrelli, & Nastasi, 2011).

Due to the high importance and relative difficulties in developing new interoperable and scalable ITS, the European Parliament published in July 2010 the Directive 2010/40/EU "On the framework for the deployment of Intelligent Transport Systems in the field of road transport and for interfaces with other modes of transport" (European Parliament, 2010). Together with objectives and benefits of ITS, in the Directive it is pointed out the necessity of an integrated approach among telecommunications, electronics, and information technologies with transport engineering to successfully plan, design, operate, maintain and manage transport systems. Moreover, it is underlined the necessity of adopting standards to provide interoperability, compatibility and continuity for the development and operational use of ITS. To the end of fulfilling such requirements four priority areas for the development of effective ITS have been identified:

1. Optimal use of road, traffic and travel data;
2. Continuity of traffic and freight management ITS services;
3. ITS road safety and security applications;
4. Linking the vehicle with the transport infrastructure.

The four reported priority areas identified by the European Union (EU) establish a first step towards the development of an EU-wide ITS system, and they must be considered of equal importance. However, from a research point of view, the latter point can be considered one of the most promising, but at the same time the most challenging, for an effective deployment of new ITS. In order to link vehicles with the transport infrastructure new plug-and-play measures to integrate ITS applications on an open in-vehicle platform must be considered (European Parliament, 2010), as well as the development and implementation of Vehicle-to-Vehicle (V2V), Vehicle-to-Infrastructure (V2I) and Infrastructure-to-Infrastructure (I2I) cooperative systems (European Parliament, 2010). As a consequence, in-vehicle plug-and-play ITS-related solutions and roadside networks for vehicular communications must be considered as key building blocks of new generation ITS.

The possibility of establishing network communications among vehicles, and between vehicles and roadside devices (Figure 1), opens new interesting and challenging application scenarios in the ITS research field. Traffic-related data can be sent in real-time from ITS control rooms to in-vehicle equipments to the end of communicating road congestions, car accidents, alternative routes, etc., to the driver. At the same time crucial vehicle-related data, such as fuel level, break alarms, etc., coming from in-vehicle electronic devices can be sent from the vehicle to the control room, in charge of helping the driver in finding a solution (e.g., calling the closer tow truck). Two features are required to effectively integrate roadside networks in ITS: the pervasiveness of the developed hardware technologies (for both on-board and roadside units) and the use of standard interfaces and protocols. If from one hand the pervasiveness can be easily reached by developing low-cost devices, on the other hand the use of standard interfaces and protocols permit to fulfill the EU directives for creating interoperable and scalable ITS.

In this chapter, we present a low-cost vehicular device, hardware, and software in-house designed and targeted to allow for a full interoperability of roadside networks and in-vehicle intelligence. Leveraging on the most widely accepted ITS architectures and communication standards we developed our in-vehicle device aiming at fulfilling the two main requirements mentioned above: pervasiveness and use of standard interfaces and protocols. The rest of the chapter is organized as follow: in the next section, we present state-of-the-art standards and communication architectures for both linking vehicles to roadside networks and acquiring vehicle-related data. Moreover, state-of-the-art vehicular devices are presented and their features analyzed in respect of standard solutions. In the following section, we present our on-board unit device starting from a high-level system requirements analysis. In the OBU Device Applications and Performance Analysis section, a set of applications in which the developed device can be adopted are discussed and a delay time analysis in sending

in-vehicle data to roadside networks is presented. Open issues for future research activities and conclusions are presented in the last two sections.

STATE-OF-THE-ART

Standard Solutions for In-Vehicle to Roadside Data Transmission in ITS

In this section state-of-the-art standards and architectures for linking vehicles to roadside networks by means of wireless communications in ITS are presented, as well as standard solutions for in-vehicle data acquisition.

Standards and Architectures for Wireless Communications in ITS

The first attempt to propose standardized wireless solutions for ITS systems date back to the year 2001 when the Technical Committee 204, Working Group 16 of the International Organization for Standardization (ISO) started to develop a basic set of ITS communication standards under the name Communications Access for Land Mobiles

Figure 1. Reference scenario vehicle-to-vehicle and vehicle-to-infrastructure communications in ITS

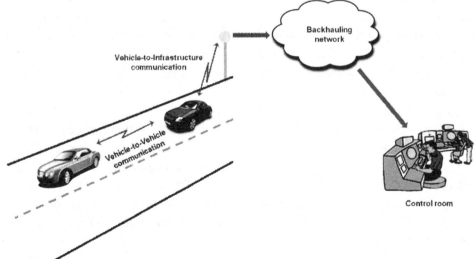

(CALM) (ISO TC 204 WG 16, 2011). The main goal of the Working Group 16, according to the CALM concept, is to define a family of international standards for a common architecture, protocols, and interface definitions related to wireless-based, interoperable access technologies for ITS applications and services. The CALM standard establishes three possible communication modes for ITS: vehicle-to-vehicle, vehicle-to-infrastructure and infrastructure-to-infrastructure, while considering a large set of wireless communication standards (WLAN, LTE, WiMAX, UMTS, EDGE, GPRS) in its reference system architecture (Figure 2) (CALM Forum Ltd., 2006). The CALM concept has been adopted in research and development projects such as SAFESPOT (Vivo, Dalmasso, & Vernacchia, 2007) and CVIS (Ernst, Nebehaj, & Srasen, 2009).

In 2007, in Europe, a process for the development of a set of standards for cooperative ITS with inter-vehicle communication systems started with the first official release of the Car 2 Car Communication Consortium (C2C-CC) manifesto (Car 2 Car Communication Consortium, 2007). The C2C-CC is a non-profit industrial driven organization initiated by European vehicle manufacturers and mainly supported by equipment suppliers and research organizations. The consortium mainly aims at increasing road traffic safety and efficiency by means of cooperative intelligent transport systems with inter-vehicle communications supported by vehicle-to-roadside communications. Moreover, it works in close cooperation with European and international standardization organizations, in particular ETSI TC ITS (Etsi, 2011), in order to achieve common European standards for ITS. The first draft system architecture proposed by the consortium is depicted in Figure 3, and it comprises three distinct domains: in-vehicle, ad-hoc, and infra-structure. Regarding the technologies adopted in the various segments, these are mainly based on Wireless LAN (WLAN) standards (IEEE 802.11a/b/g/p), though other radio technologies (GPRS, EDGE, UMTS,

WIMAX) have been considered in the protocol architecture of the Car 2 Car communication system (depicted in Figure 4).

Although the two standardization initiatives come from different organizations, a convergent architecture is auspicated in the next future years (Villeforceix & Petti, 2011).

Vehicle-to-Infrastructure Communications

In both standardization initiatives introduced in the previous section, the key wireless technologies for enabling data transmission from vehicles to roadside networks, and vice versa, are: GPRS, UMTS, WiMAX, LTE, and WLAN. Considering their use in ITS applications targeted to the vehicular environment each one of them shows advantages and drawbacks.

One of the main problems in connecting vehicles to the network infrastructure is the high mobility degree of the network nodes (vehicles). This problem can be mitigated by adopting technological solutions developed for the second, third and fourth generation of cellular networks (Ohmori, Yamao, & Nakajima, 2000). Nevertheless, the use of such kind of technologies in vehicle-to-vehicle and vehicle-to-infrastructure communications is strongly limited by the additional cost, which ITS users should pay to Telco operators. Regarding approaches based on "classic" IEEE802.11 standards (a/b/g/n) more considerations must be made. In fact, if from one hand they are able to guarantee a free service to ITS users, thus enforcing technology pervasiveness, on the other hand their use is not recommended in such a scenario because of the strong limitations in vehicle relative speed (Cottingham, Wassell, & Harle, 2007).

To address the lack of an open WLAN standard for V2V and V2I communications, the IEEE Working Group 1609, established in 2006, started the development of the Wireless Access in Vehicular Environment (WAVE) standard (IEEE Computer Society, 2010). In the suite of WAVE protocols,

Figure 2. CALM system architecture (from CALM Forum Ltd., 2006)

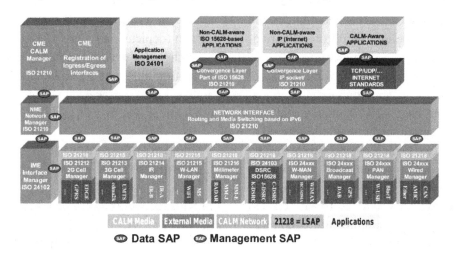

the IEEE 802.11p standard for Physical and Data Link layers, is derived from IEEE 802.11a, aiming at conforming the WLAN specifications with the vehicular environment: it guarantees a seamless communication between two network nodes with a relative speed up to 200 km/h (Qian & Moayery, 2009) in the 5.9 GHz frequency band. Although the standard definition started in 2006, the first official document has been released in July 2010 only; today several wireless transceivers compliant with IEEE 802.11p are available on the market. In any case, their full utilization in ITS applications is still not affordable for the research community due to the lack of IEEE802.11p driver implementations fully supporting the Medium Access Control (MAC) layer of the standard released in 2010. For

Figure 3. Car 2 car draft system architecture (from Car 2 Car Communication Consortium, 2007)

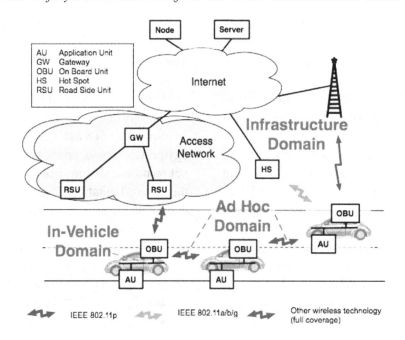

Figure 4. Protocol architecture of the car 2 car communication system (from Car 2 Car Communication Consortium, 2007)

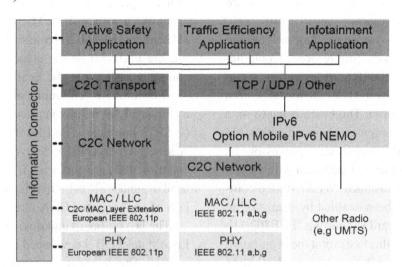

this reason, almost all the current implementations, running on off-the-shelf hardware equipment, adopt the popular IEEE 802.11a standard (Annese, Casetti, Chiasserini, Di Maio, Ghittino, & Reineri, 2011). Furthermore, the "a" version of the IEEE 802.11 standard makes use of a larger number of communication channels and it is implemented by a large set of commercial transceivers.

In-Vehicle Data Acquisition

Since the introduction of the first on-board vehicle computers, in the early 1980s, the importance of on-board diagnosis systems has increased over time. Ever since, the quality of the diagnostic information they can provide has improved, passing from malfunction indication lights to standardized real-time digital interfaces. The Assembly Line Diagnostic Link (ALDL) (Boynton, 2006) is the first proprietary implementation of an on-board diagnostic interface. This was proposed by General Motors and it was mainly used by proprietary maintenance facilities. ALDL quickly became the first On-Board Diagnostics (OBD-I) standard adopted in the USA for vehicle emission testing. However, it was only with the OBD-II (California

Air Resources Board, 1992) that full diagnosis capabilities and standardization were achieved. Topics of the standard are: structure of the diagnosis connector, protocols for the electrical signals, messages format, and a list of readable vehicle parameters. The equivalent European standard, published in 2001, is known as EOBD, while the JOBD is the equivalent version in Japan.

Since 2008, OBD-II compliant parameters are acquired by in-car Electronic Control Unit (ECU) and sent to OBD-computers adopting the Controller Area Network (CAN) communication protocol (Farsi, Ratcliff, & Barbosa, 1999). The basic features of the CAN standard are: high-speed data rate, low-cost physical medium, fast reaction times and error detection and correction capabilities. The communication among in-vehicle electronic devices imposes the use of CAN compliant interfaces implementing the transmission physical layer, form which useful vehicle-related data can be acquired.

WLAN-Based On-Board Unit for ITS

In this section state-of-the-art WLAN-based on-board unit devices coming from both research and industrial activities are presented and their main feature discussed in respect of standard communication solutions.

A first solution for connecting vehicles to roadside network is the Single Board Computer (SBC) (Guo & Wu, 2009) based device prototyped in December 2009 by the Institute for Infocomm Research in Singapore. The board is based on a Soekris Net4801 computer, equipped with a 233 MHz NSC SC1100 single chip processor, on which a developed embedded board with a CAN interface has been installed. WLAN-based communications have been enabled by means of an installed wireless card supporting IEEE802.11b standard. Although this first prototype of on-board device adopts standard interfaces from the CALM architecture, it lacks an integrated approach among components since it uses several interconnected peripherals in different boards.

The C-VeT mobile node (Cesana, Fratta, Gerla, Giordano, & Pau, 2010) developed by the University of California in Los Angeles in 2010 is another example of on-board unit for V2V and V2I communications targeted to ITS. The device is a strong PC equipped with an Intel Dual Core Duo processor at 2.5 GHz and an IEEE802.11a/b/g/n wireless card. Moreover, an IEEE802.11p interface based on a Daimler-Benz customized chipset is present on the on-board unit. The C-Vet device is a first example in which wireless communication adopting the WAVE standard has been enabled, even if a customized driver not publicly available is used. The board in its current version can be used for I2V communication only because of the lack of CAN-based communications to send vehicle-related data.

Due to the increasing perspectives in connecting vehicles to roadside networks several prototypes of on-board units for vehicular communications are nowadays provided by private companies. A first example is the NEC LinkBird-MX public available since 2010 and widely adopted by the research community to evaluate IEEE802.11p performance through real experiments (Festag,

Hessler, Baldessari, Le, Zhang, & Westhoff, 2008; Martelli, Renda, & Santi, 2011). The LinkBird is equipped with a MIPS Microprocessor at 266 MHz and a IEEE802.11p wireless card supporting the draft 3.0 of the standard. CAN based communications can be enabled by installing external modules communicating by means of a Universal Asynchronous Receiver/Transmitter (UART) interface. The LinkBird on-board unit is an effective solution for vehicular networks experimental purposes, even if it cannot be easily used to send V2X vehicle-related data due to the lack of an integrated CAN interface.

The last on-board unit device presented is the LocoMate™ OBU developed by Arada Systems in 2010. The device is equipped with a 680 MHz CPU and integrates GPS, IEEE802.11p, and Bluetooth peripherals. The IEEE802.11p based communications are supported by a draft implementation of the full standard, no public available, while no CAN communications are supported, even if a CAN interface is mentioned without more details in the device datasheet, underlining again the high potential and the strong necessity in enabling V2X transmission of data gathered from ECUs through the CAN.

The four presented devices, depicted in Figure 5, establish a first step towards the creation of low-cost and integrated on-board unit solutions able to fully connect vehicles to roadside networks and strongly penetrating the market to reach a real pervasiveness of ITS.

ON-BOARD UNIT SYSTEM DESIGN

In this section, we present the hardware and the software solutions developed to deploy a low-cost on-board unit device, integrated combining off-the-shelf hardware modules from the consumer electronics market, able to effectively link vehicles and roadside networks. Before presenting the final device architecture a high-level system requirements analysis is performed. The section

Figure 5. On-board unit devices

a. SBC   b. C-Vet

c. NEC LinkBird   d. LocoMate™

ends with an analysis of the developed OBU device capabilities. An optinal board configuration is considered as an RSU solution, suitable for roadside networks.

System Requirements

In order to clearly define high-level system requirements a careful analysis regarding on-board unit device objectives must be performed. To such a device is mainly demanded to enable vehicle-to-roadside communications in ITS while providing the possibility to acquire vehicle-related data. Moreover, to the device is requested a full compatibility with standard solutions suggested by established ITS Standardization Committees as well as proposed next generation ITS. Flexibility, extendibility, and cost-effective hardware and software solutions are additional characteristics to be considered looking at technology pervasiveness and future applications support.

To deeply analyze the requirements related to the main objective briefly introduced above, three main topics will be discussed in the following: OBU design in respect of ITS integrations, OBU design in respect of vehicle-related data acquisition, and OBU hardware and software components in respect of technology pervasiveness and future applications support. The whole set of high-level system requirements identified in the three mentioned topics is reported at the end of the section.

In respect to the ITS integration, the definition of the system requirements starts by analyzing a general ITS architecture while understanding at which level on-board unit devices play an effective role. Considering a recently ITS vision proposed in 2011 (Pagano, Petracca, Alessandrelli, & Nastasi, 2011), and depicted at high-level in Figure 6, an ITS system can be easily instantiated in separated and interconnected tiers. The suggested architecture is composed by four tiers: data collection, network, calculus and application. Each layer is devoted to a specific function and could be theoretically changed or upgraded without effects on the connected layers if standard connections among tiers (e.g., based on Web services transactions) are adopted. The data collection layer is in charge of collecting mobility data and it is composed by vehicular networks and road-side networks, possibly organized through ad-hoc segments. While the former represents the ad-hoc segment reported in the C2C-CC manifesto, the latter can be seen as an extension towards the definition of a resident sensing segment. In case of Wireless Sensor Networks (WSN), they are part of the data collection layer, in the shape of special devices, as in Ceriotti et al. (2011) and Mambrini et al. (2011), where low-cost embedded systems are adopted to provide automatic adaptive lighting in road tunnels and collect traffic related information with the aim of improving road safety and efficiency. When the data are collected, they are sent trough a backhauling network (connecting the roadside networks) to the calculus infrastructure (either a data grid or a computer cloud), where they are analyzed, and events are detected. Composed events are sent to the application layer, which is in charge of reacting to the detected event (e.g., sending an ambulance in case of accidents, providing mobility information upon request). As previously introduced, vehicular networks work at the data collection layer of the system, where the collection and transmission of huge amount of data is mandatory for enabling effective ITS applications. Regarding the OBU, the device is requested to support several wireless communication technologies to ensure connection reliability, though no simultaneous connections must be necessarily supported due to possible handovers among device interfaces (Giordano, Lenzarini, Puiatti, Kulig, Nguyen, & Vanini, 2006) which guarantee to have only one active connection, thus avoiding to pay several Telco providers at the same time. Moreover, the device computational power must be suited to locally elaborate the gathered data, as well as enough storage memory must be available in the device to keep record of locally processed and geo-located notified events.

In respect to the in-car integration for acquiring vehicle-related data, the system requirements must be analyzed starting from the complexity and specificity in the Electronic Control Units (ECU) installed by car vendors in last generation

vehicles. Nowadays cars are equipped with dozens of microprocessors running up to hundred million lines of code (Charette, 2009). As a consequence, the integration of the typical on-board unit device function in existing car ECUs is completely unfeasible, due to the high costs associated with the redesign of the electronic car system and the subsequent development of new software. A more viable approach is that of effectively gathering data from car ECUs implementing plug-and-play solutions (e.g. enabled in our board) based on established in-car communication standards. Following this rational, to fulfill in-car integration of new functionality, the developed device is requested to support CAN-based communications in order to acquire vehicle-related data, shared by ECUs in compliance with the OBD-II protocol.

A prominent topic for this requirement analysis is related to pervasiveness and future application support. The pervasiveness of a vehicular on-board unit mainly depends on its costs, as only low-cost devices will be able to strongly penetrate the market; a god feature would be backward compatibility with old vehicles. The low-cost objective can be reached by adopting off-the-shelf consumer electronics hardware components and open-source software, while mandatorily adopting free of charge wireless communications (e.g., WAVE) and optionally licensed 2G, 3G and 4G. Regarding the future application support, this can be reached adopting both high computational capabilities processors and open-source software for open and free of charge ITS applications.

Starting from the high-level system requirements analysis performed, and taking into account the proposed wireless standards and system architectures for vehicular networks, the following set of system requirements can be detailed:

- **Computational power:** The main core of the system must permit a local elaboration of the data gathered from the infrastructure and from the car electronics within strin-

Figure 6. A multi-tier intelligent transport system architecture (from Pagano, Petracca, Alessandrelli, and Nastasi, 2011)

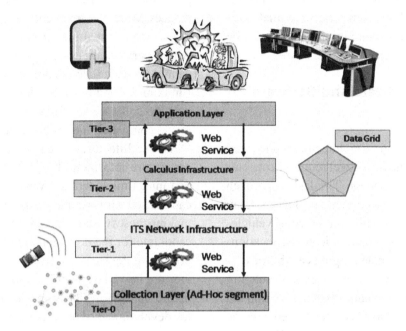

gent timing constraints so that real-time applications can be executed by the embedded device;

- **Storage memory:** The system must permit to maintain record on the events processed, notified, and communicated to the OBU (as the flight recorder does in airplanes) both from RSU and ECU devices;
- **GPS equipment:** The system must be able to communicate its own position to perform geo-located based services;
- **Wireless communication:** The system must be equipped with one or more wireless transceivers to allow the communication with the road infrastructure (V2I communications) and with other vehicles (V2V communications). The adoption of a RF adapter able to communicate through unlicensed wireless network is mandatory;
- **In-vehicle data acquisition:** The system must be able to acquire data, in a plug-and-play manner, from the car electronic control unit by means of a CAN-based com-

munications compliant with the OBD-II protocol;
- **Low-cost hardware solutions:** The OBU is targeted to low/middle class vehicles; in such respect a good approach is the integration of off-the-shelf hardware components (including a programmable and versatile computing unit) instead of the design of a fully specific device;
- **Operating system:** The system must adopt open-source software solutions, such as Linux Embedded, as operating system to follow a low-cost, open, flexible, and modular approach;
- **Communication reliability:** The device must be able to manage handovers through its network adapters.

From the reported high-level system requirements, the on-board unit functional block diagram, with its logical connections, can be easily depicted. The diagram is proposed in Figure 7, and it is mainly composed by a process unit connected to storage memories, wireless communication interfaces, vehicle controller interfaces, and GPS unit. On the local bus connection eventual additional interfaces for future improvements can be installed in future releases of the board.

Proposed Hardware and Software Architecture

In Figure 7, our proposed architecture is presented as a response to the high-level requirements outlined in the previous section. The design approach aims at permitting an in-vehicle plug-and-play seamless integration, while guaranteeing vehicle-to-roadside wireless communications, location-aware services, and data logging capabilities.

To select the device components responding to the system requirements a first analysis on the device architecture have been performed with the objective of achieving the right trade-off between computational capabilities and costs. In the system design, three main architectures based respectively on microcontrollers, ARM processors, and x86 processors have been considered, and their advantages and drawbacks identified. Regarding the microcontroller based architecture the solution has been mainly considered due to the extreme low-cost of such peripherals, cheaper than 15$, and their clock frequencies had recently upgraded to figures close to 100 MHz. Although the cost of the single microcontroller is a great advantage to keep the final OBU cost extremely low, the relative low working frequencies do not allow the real-time processing of a substantial amount of data gathered from both ITS and in-vehicle electronic devices. Moreover, microcontroller-based systems require to adopt minimal operating systems in which peripherals drivers provided by vendors cannot be used (drivers are usually released for Linux and Windows OS), thus requiring an expensive software re-engineering process which makes completely unfeasible such kind of solution. Device architectures based on ARM and x86 processors are not affected by this last issue, high-end or Linux Embedded and Windows distributions can be used with original peripherals drivers, thus making these two considered architectures a good candidate for the development of a low-cost on-board unit device. Concerning ARM processors, they are nowadays widely adopted in the mobile phone industry which from one hand promoted the development of processing units of increased computational capabilities, finally reaching 1 GHz speed, and on the other hand fostered a reduction in the devices cost. ARM processors are nowadays available at a price lower than 50$. Similar or bigger computational capabilities can be reached by x86 processors, while requiring higher costs. Following these considerations, we decided to adopt for our platform an ARM-based architecture. More in detail, the Atmel AT91SAM9G20, a 30$, 400 MHz, 32-bit architecture has been chosen as core of our system.

Once the device architecture has been chosen the data logging capabilities of the device have been analyzed aiming at developing a solution

Figure 7. Logical block design for a fully integrable OBU device

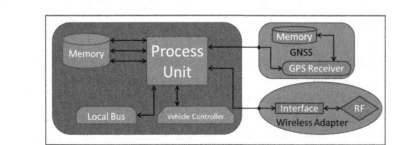

based on removable storage units. Advantages and drawbacks of both Secure Digital (SD) and Compact Flash (CF) memories have been analyzed in respect of memory capacity, device cost, and Printed Circuit Board (PCB) cost due to memory size. Although the first two points can be considered negligible due to storage capacities enhancements and cost reduction of both technologies, the last suggests to adopt SD memories due to their smaller size permitting to reduce the size of the final device with a cost reduction for the PCB printing.

The requirement of enabling geo-located based services has been addressed analyzing off-the-shelf GPS units integrating a receiver antenna and showing a reduced size. Due to such selecting criteria commercial USB-based GPS devices have been discarded, favoring much more compact devices in the same range of price, such as embedded GPS unit. The final equipment selected and installed on the board is the SPK Electronics GS405, a GPS receiver with a compact size and able to provide location data compliant with the NMEA0183 protocol (National Marine Electronics Association, 1993).

Regarding the wireless communication peripherals to be installed on the OBU device only WLAN based transceivers have been considered due to the mandatory nature of such a requirement. The possibility of adding more transceiver devices implementing GPRS, EDGE, UMTS, and WIMAX technologies has been enabled by adding General Purpose Input Output (GPIO) interfaces to the OBU design. Concerning WLAN-based communications, off-the-shelf transceivers implementing IEEE802.11p standard have been considered in a first stage. Although several mini-pci based devices implementing the physical layer of the standard have been found, open-source drivers implementing the MAC layer are not yet available. For this reason, we decided to install in our board an IEEE802.11a/b/g/n transceiver connected through a USB interface. The selected

device is the Ralink WUBR-506N, which has driver support both for Linux and Windows OS. The future use of off-the-shelf IEEE802.11p compliant transceivers in the developed board is extremely simple due to both possibilities of directly changing the mounted WLAN transceiver or adding a new interface connected to the installed GPIO interfaces.

The in-vehicle data acquisition requirement has been addressed integrating a CAN bus transceiver in the OBU device. The transceiver has been selected according to two main criteria: driver availability and cost. Looking at already developed embedded systems designed for the automotive industry several peripherals have been founded, and among them the one responding to the selection criteria has been chosen. CAN-based communications in the developed device are provided by the Microchip MCP2515 transceiver connected to the system main core trough a Serial Peripheral Interface (SPI).

The whole set of peripherals chosen as components of the developed off-the-shelf based OBU device can be easily purchased at low costs by vendors, nevertheless a low-cost approach in selecting the hardware components results completely negligible if the selected software to be run on the device must be bought. To avoid extra costs due to software licenses we selected as operating system Emdebian, an embedded version of Linux OS in which the Linux kernel 2.6.37 has been properly modified to connect all the peripherals to the ARM processor, and in which the basic drivers to enable communication with the vehicle network (through the CAN bus) and the infrastructure (through the wireless channel) have been enabled starting from original vendors drivers. The choice of using an open-source operating system on one hand guarantees the openness, flexibility, and modularity of the developed solutions, while on the other hand leaves to the stakeholders the possibility of protecting their software at the application layer (see Figure 8).

The presented hardware and software components adopted to develop the low-cost off-the-shelf OBU are summarized in the following:

- **System core:** Atmel AT91SAM9G20, a 32-bit Atmel ARM processor having 400 MHz clock speed and directly connected to non-volatile storage modules hosting the operating system;
- **Storage memory:** Non-volatile storage memories based on SD cards;
- **GPS localization:** SPK Electronics GS405, an embedded GPS device compliant with the NMEA0183 protocol and connected through a serial communication to the system core;
- **Wireless communication:** Ralink WUBR-506N, a USB-based transceiver supporting the IEEE802.11a/b/g/n standards;

- **In-vehicle data acquisition:** Microchip MCP2515, a CAN bus transceiver connected to the system core trough a SPI bus;
- **General Purpose Input Output:** Several GPIO devices have been installed in the board for supporting additional peripherals and for enabling debugging purposes;
- **Operating system:** Emdebian, a Linux embedded OS in which the Linux kernel 2.6.37 has been properly modified to connect all the peripherals to the system core.

In Figure 9 a picture of the developed device, with all the components listed above, is shown. The final size of this first release of the board has been kept larger than the necessary due to debugging purposes, and it can be significantly reduced. Regarding the price of the full board, with both PCB printing and peripherals costs, this is lower

Figure 8. OBU device schematic diagram

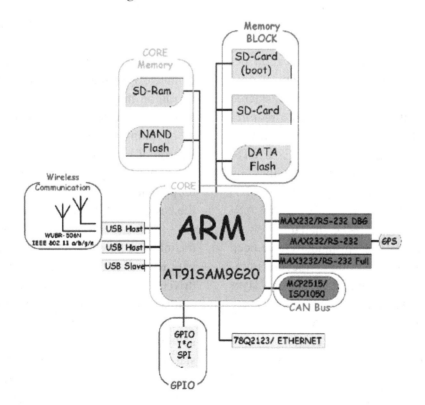

Figure 9. The developed OBU device

than $300 per unit with the possibility of a greater reduction in case of a large scale production.

Considering the OBU devices presented in the WLAN-based on-board unit for ITS section, the developed board can be considered an effective solution based on off-the-shelf components in which in-vehicle data acquisition and vehicular based communications capabilities have been integrated into a single device. Although a WAVE compliant transceiver is not still present on the board it can be easily installed in a future release thanks to the installed GPIO interfaces, thus reaching state-of-the-art vehicular communication capabilities provided in an early stage by C-Vet, NEC LinkBird, and Locomate™.

The Developed Device as OBU Counterpart: RSU Capabilities

The embedded device described in the previous section has been developed with the main objective of being installed into low/middle class vehicles as on-board unit for vehicular communications with in-vehicle data acquisition capabilities. Indeed, in answering to the wireless communication requirement, road-side-unit capabilities have been enabled thanks to the installed GPIO interfaces. In fact, although no CAN bus based communications

are still necessaries more wireless transceivers can be installed, thus creating an off-the-shelf based road-side-unit to be used in the data collection layer of future ITS (as discussed in the System Requirements section). From one hand GPRS, EDGE, UMTS, and WIMAX transceiver could enable data communications towards backhauling networks access points, while on the other hand the use of transceivers implementing the IEEE802.15.4 (IEEE Computer Society, 2003) standard could enable interoperability with wireless sensor networks collecting traffic related data for traffic management and logistics purposes.

Even if the board design guarantees a simple integration of wireless peripherals some considerations must be done on the device system core. The Atmel AT91SAM9G20 has been chosen due to its capabilities in managing different interfaces while providing a real-time processing of a considerable amount of data gathered from both ITS and in-vehicle electronic devices. In case of a RSU device the amount of data gathered from vehicles and other network devices could be quite large, thus requiring a system core with enhanced capabilities such as the Texas Instruments Sitara ARM Cortex™-A8, a 32-bit based processor working at up to 1.5 GHz of speed and available on the market for a price of $50.

OBU DEVICE APPLICATIONS AND PERFORMANCE ANALYSIS

In this section of the chapter, we propose two sample applications for our OBU device. The first application can be included in the set of driver safety and assistance ones. In this case in-vehicle data must be sent within a constrained time to a control room, the effectiveness of the develop OBU device in such a scenario has been proven by means a delay time analysis in sending in-vehicle data to roadside networks. The second application belongs to the resource efficiency set, and the use of an OBU device able to gather car-

Figure 10. Communication scenario for in-vehicle to roadside networks data transmission

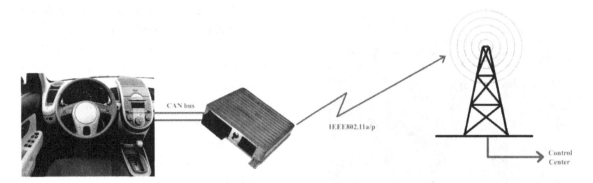

related parameters is discussed in respect of the fuel level estimation problem. The classification of both presented applications is according to the taxonomy reported in Popescu-Zeletin, Radusch, and Rigani (2010).

Driver Safety and Assistance

The possibility to send in-vehicle data through a roadside network to a control center permits to enhance proactive driver safety applications, as well as to better assist a driver in case of dangerous events. As matter of example it is possible to consider a scenario in which alarms regarding wheels and brakes are detected inside the car and sent through a V2I communication to a control room which in turn can send an alert message to other cars in the same route, while providing in-route assistance to the damaged car. The communication scenario of the reported example is depicted in Figure 10.

In such a scenario, once the dangerous event is detected the alarm must reach the control center as soon as possible to promptly react to the new situation. The total end-to-end delay from the ECU devices installed inside the car to the control center must be as low as possible. To evaluate the transmission end-to-end delay making use of our OBU, a realistic testbed, similar to the real scenario depicted in Figure 10, has been set up as shown in Figure 11.

The alarm signal is generated by a laptop where a Graphical User Interface (GUI) can be used to "simulate" brakes and wheels problems. The signal is then propagated via the serial port to the car ECU, which is emulated by a version of the developed device without wireless connectivity. The on-board unit is connected to the ECU with the CAN bus and communicates in wireless with a laptop that acts as a control center. The adopted scenario permits to evaluate the end-to-end delay as the sum of the delays introduced by the CAN

Figure 11. Adopted scenario for the end-to-end delay evaluation

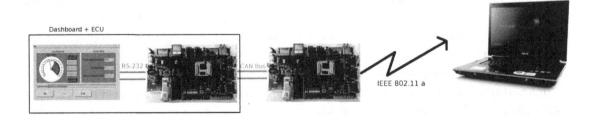

bus, the device communication stack and a one-hop wireless link. The evaluation of end-to-end delays in case of a backhauling network and a calculus infrastructure between the road-side unit and the control center is straightforward and it results in an increased final end-to-end delay due to not negligible travel times in both ITS layers. The end-to-end delay distribution for the developed testbed is depicted in Figure 12. The results have been obtained in an indoor scenario with a wireless transmission compliant with the IEEE802.11a standard and placing the OBU and the control center at a distance of 20 meters. The probability density function (pdf) shows a peak at 5 ms, while the 98% of the experienced end-to-end delays are lower than 38 ms. The highest experienced delays are mainly due to packet re-transmission at the Medium Access Control (MAC) layer in the wireless segment. The developed device guarantees the communication of in-vehicle data to the roadside network for a large part of the occurrences in a bounded delay. Furthermore, the time overhead introduced by the adopted communication stack is minimal and likely to be reduced by optimization on the kernel scheduling policy.

Advanced Driver Assistance Services

The possibility for car navigation systems of receiving ITS related data from a roadside network permits to better assist the driver during all his/her travel. For example, information of possible queues and average travel time along the followed path can be showed on the car dashboard and used to calculate the optimal route, thus avoiding traffic congestions and giving to the driver a better driving experience. Moreover, the same traffic-related data can be used to integrate in-vehicle information to provide advanced driver assistance services, as in case of the residual vehicle autonomy notification application provided by new generation cars.

Nowadays in all vehicles the residual fuel level and its consumption estimation (e.g. the time before the fuel level goes beyond a certain amount) is calculated by internal parameters, such as instantaneous speed and acceleration levels (Ahn, Rakha, Trani, & van Aerde, 2002). The use of the above-mentioned parameters does not take into account any external factor, such as traffic behavior, which instead heavy influences the fuel consumption (van Mierlo, Maggetto, van de Burg-

Figure 12. End-to-end delay distribution

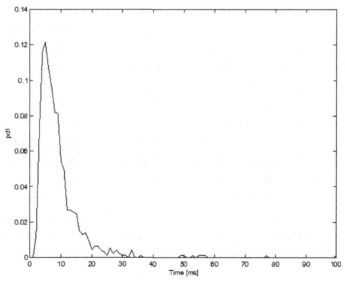

wal, & Gense, 2004). This simplification results in the impossibility for the drivers to effectively plan when to stop in a gas station to refill. Linking the vehicles with the transport infrastructure while enabling the transmission of traffic-related data results in helping the drivers to travel in a much more comfortable way while saving money and reducing environmental pollution.

OPEN ISSUES FOR FUTURE RESEARCH

The approach followed throughout this work was that of integrating consumer electronics modules into a single low-cost embedded system operated as OBU in vehicular networks. Following the general trend observed in technological development, these components are expected to lower their costs in the future; an open architecture will therefore permit to release future versions of our OBU, just by upgrading some of the modules, which show lower costs or added-value. For instance, new IEEE802.11p-compliant transceivers will be commercialized as soon as vehicular communications technologies will be transferred to industry; at that time, it will be easy to replace the installed IEEE802.11a transceiver with the new one without re-engineering our board. The other key approach is that of closely follow the Linux community, very actively supporting new peripherals contributing with new drivers; in a wide range of cases the applications developed for Linux Embedded Operating Systems show acceptable performances in terms of communication reliability and time overhead, and task latency at the user level.

A main research issue for future research activities in this area is that of keeping separated hardware capabilities from the specific functionality required to the board at application level; in other words, it will be of great interest to design high level ITS applications from the functional perspective, by adopting a Model Driven Engineering approach, instead of developing specific applications targeted to a specific device. This would permit to host in our OBU, or in other commercial devices, a set of ITS applications, defined at design level, and functionally compatible with the local available resources (notably memory, peripherals, and computing capabilities), thus avoiding a strong dependence on hardware components.

CONCLUSION

In this chapter we presented an off-the-shelf, consumer electronics-based, on-board unit device for linking vehicles to roadside networks in ITS. The OBU hardware design process has been mainly based on high-level systems requirements highlighted in three main topics: OBU design in respect of ITS integrations, OBU design in respect of in-car integration, and OBU hardware components in respect of technology pervasiveness and future applications support. According to the system requirements, commercial off-the-shelf components have been identified while considering standardization efforts and already existing standard solutions. The final developed device can be considered an effective low-cost solution in which in-vehicle data acquisition and vehicular-based communications capabilities have been integrated into a single device. Performance evaluation in a real testbed representing a driver safety and assistance application shows the effectiveness of the developed OBU device in managing CAN and WLAN-based communications, which are able to guarantee an end-to-end delay lower than 38 ms in 98% of cases. Due to the low-cost and plug-and-play capabilities, the developed device is an effective solution in enabling advanced driver safety and assistance services by means of in-vehicle and roadside communications.

REFERENCES

Ahn, K., Rakha, H., Trani, A., & Van Aerde, M. (2002). Estimating vehicle fuel consumption and emissions based on instantaneous speed and acceleration levels. *Journal of Transportation Engineering, 128*(2), 182–190. doi:10.1061/(ASCE)0733-947X(2002)128:2(182)

Annese, S., Casetti, C., Chiasserini, C. F., Di Maio, N., Ghittino, A., & Reineri, M. (2011). Seamless connectivity and routing in vehicular networks with infrastructure. *IEEE Journal on Selected Areas in Communications, 29*(3), 501–514. doi:10.1109/JSAC.2011.110302

Boynton, T. (2006). *General motors computerized vehicle control systems: A short history*. Retrieved from http://tomboynton.com/GMnetworks.pdf

California Air Resources Board. (1992). *On-board diagnostics (OBD-II)*. Sacramento, CA: California Air Resources Board.

CALM Forum Ltd. (2006). *The CALM handbook*. Retrieved from http://www.isotc204wg16.org/pubdocs

Car 2 Car Communication Consortium. (2007). *The car 2 car communication consortium manifesto*. Retrieved from http://www.car-to-car.org

Ceriotti, M., Corrà, M., Orazio, L. D., Doriguzzi, R., Facchin, D., & Jesi, G. P. ... Torghele, C. (2011). Is there light at the ends of the tunnel? Wireless sensor networks for adaptive lighting in road tunnels. In *Proceedings of ACM/IEEE International Conference on Information Processing in Sensor Networks*. Chicago, IL: ACM/IEEE.

Cesana, M., Fratta, L., Gerla, M., Giordano, E., & Pau, G. (2010). C-VeT the UCLA campus vehicular testbed: Integration of VANET and mesh networks. In *Proceedings of European Wireless Conference*. Lucca, Italy: IEEE.

Charette, R. N. (2009). This car runs on code. *IEEE Spectrum*. Retrieved from http://spectrum.ieee.org/green-tech/advanced-cars/this-car-runs-on-code/0

Cottingham, D. N., Wassell, I. J., & Harle, R. K. (2007). Performance of IEEE 802.11a in vehicular contexts. In *Proceedings of IEEE Vehicular Technology Conference*. Dublin, Ireland: IEEE Press.

Ernst, T., Nebehaj, V., & Srasen, R. (2009). CVIS: CALM proof of concept preliminary results. In *Proceedings of International Conference on Intelligent Transport Systems Telecommunications*. Lille, France: IEEE.

ETSI. (2011). *ETSI technical committee on intelligent transport systems*. Retrieved from http://www.etsi.org/website/Technologies/Intelligent-TransportSystems.asp

European Parliament. (2010). Directive 2010/40/EU on the framework for the deployment of intelligent transport systems in the field of road transport and for interfaces with other modes of transport. *Official Journal of European Union*. Lyon, France: European Parliament.

Farsi, M., Ratcliff, K., & Barbosa, M. (1999). An overview of controller area network. *Computing & Control Engineering Journal, 10*(3), 113–120. doi:10.1049/cce:19990304

Festag, A., Hessler, A., Baldessari, R., Le, L., Zhang, W., & Westhoff, D. (2008). Vehicle-to-vehicle and road-side sensor communication for enhanced road safety. In *Proceedings of European International Conference on Intelligent Tutoring Systems*. Montréal, Canada: IEEE.

Giordano, S., Lenzarini, D., Puiatti, A., Kulig, M., Nguyen, H. A., & Vanini, S. (2006). Demonstrating seamless handover of multi-hop networks. In *Proceedings of International Workshop on Multi-Hop Ad Hoc Networks: From Theory to Reality.* Florence, Italy: IEEE.

Guo, H., & Wu, Y. (2009). An integrated embedded solution for vehicle communication & control. In *Proceedings of International Conference on Robotics, Informatics, Intelligence Control System Technologies.* Bangkok, Thailand: IEEE.

IEEE. Computer Society. (2003). *Wireless medium access control (MAC) and physical layer (PHY) specifications for low-rate wireless personal area networks (LR- WPAN).* Washington, DC: IEEE Computer Society.

IEEE. Computer Society. (2010). *802.11p-2010 - IEEE standard for local and metropolitan area networks - Specific requirements part 11: Wireless LAN medium access control (MAC) and physical layer (PHY) specifications amendment 6: Wireless access in vehicular environments.* Washington, DC: IEEE Computer Society.

ISO TC 204 WG 16. (2011). *Communications access for land mobiles (CALM).* Retrieved from http://www.isotc204wg16.org

Mambrini, R., Rossi, A., Pagano, P., Ancilotti, P., Salvetti, O., & Bertolino, A. ... Costalli, L. (2011). IPERMOB: Towards an information system to handle urban mobility data. In *Proceedings of Models and Technologies for ITS.* Leuven, Belgium: ITS.

Martelli, F., Renda, M. E., & Santi, P. (2011). Measuring IEEE 802.11p performance for active safety applications in cooperative vehicular systems. In *Proceedings of IEEE Vehicular Technology Conference.* Budapest, Hungary: IEEE Press.

National Marine Electronics Association. (1993). *NMEA 0183: Standard for interfacing marine eletronic devices.* Severna Park, MD: NMEA.

Ohmori, S., Yamao, Y., & Nakajima, N. (2000). The future generations of mobile communications based on broadband access technologies. *IEEE Communications Magazine, 38*(12), 134–142. doi:10.1109/35.888267

Pagano, P., Petracca, M., Alessandrelli, D., & Nastasi, C. (2011). Enabling technologies and reference architecture for a EU-wide distributed intelligent transport system. In *Proceedings of ITS European Congress.* Lyon, France: ITS.

Popescu-Zeletin, R., Radusch, I., & Rigani, M. A. (2010). *Vehicular-2-X communication.* Berlin, Germany: Springer. doi:10.1007/978-3-540-77143-2

Qian, Y., & Moayery, N. (2009). Medium access control protocols for vehicular networks. In Moustafa, H., & Zhang, Y. (Eds.), *Vehicular Networks Techniques, Standards, and Applications* (pp. 41–62). Boca Raton, FL: CRC Press. doi:10.1201/9781420085723.ch3

Van Mierlo, J., Maggetto, G., Van de Burgwal, E., & Gense, R. (2004). Driving style and traffic measures-influence on vehicle emissions and fuel consumption. *Journal of Automobile Engineering, 218*(1), 43–50. doi:10.1243/095440704322829155

Villeforceix, B., & Petti, S. (2011). Communications in ITS for cooperative systems deployment. In *Proceedings of the Fully Networked Car Workshop.* Geneva, Switzerland: IEEE.

Vivo, G., Dalmasso, P., & Vernacchia, F. (2007). The European integrated project SAFESPOT: How ADAS applications co-operate for the driving safety. In *Proceedings of Intelligent Transportation Systems Conference.* Seattle, WA: IEEE.

Chapter 3
A Survey of Wireless Backhauling Solutions for ITS

Claudio Cicconetti
Intecs S.p.A., Italy

Raffaella Mambrini
Intecs S.p.A., Italy

Alessandro Rossi
Intecs S.p.A., Italy

ABSTRACT

The deployment of more sustainable land transportation is a non-debatable global issue. It is generally agreed that Information and Communication Technology (ICT) will play the role of the main enabler to achieve the ambitious objective of improving transportation efficiency, thus reducing pollution, time and resource wastage, and accidents. In this chapter, after briefly introducing the general architecture of the ICT infrastructure for the new generation of Intelligent Transportation Systems (ITSs), the authors provide a survey of the wireless technologies available for implementing the data network required to transfer information between the peripheral devices, installed roadside and in the vehicles, and the data center where the actual storage and logic resides. Specifically, they consider the following alternatives: IEEE 802.11 in a Wireless Mesh Network (WMN) configuration, IEEE 802.16/WiMAX, Long Term Evolution (LTE), and HiperLAN/2. The latter is investigated in further details by providing results from preliminary laboratory trials carried out in the Italian project IPERMOB.

INTRODUCTION

In the last years, we have witnessed a widespread diffusion of embedded systems in everyday's life, which is now combining together with the advances of communication technologies to cre-

ate a new ecosystem of applications and services that are highly pervasive and have a strong social connotation. The case of Intelligent Transportation Systems (ITSs) is definitely among the domains in which a leapfrogging step forward is envisaged. In general, ITS refers to the automated control of traffic, based on both data collected on real-time and prediction models derived from

DOI: 10.4018/978-1-4666-2223-4.ch003

historical information, so as to achieve a new level of transportation efficiency. This will improve the quality of life of drivers, passengers, and citizens at large, through a significant reduction of accidents and CO2 emissions. Among the others, emergency services are especially important due to their direct impact on society (Martinez, Toh, Cano, Calafate, & Manzoni, 2010). For this reason, at a European level, the application of the ITS Directive for road and urban transport is one of the actions of the Digital Agenda[1] in the pillar ICT for Social Challenges, while similar interest is shown by all developed countries.

One of the first comprehensive reports on ITS is Weissenberg (1998), commissioned by a consortium of public authorities in California, whose findings are still surprisingly valid after 12 years, at least in their essence. In fact, some of the report highlights are that ITS projects need to match local requirements and markets, they are very complex and consisting of "assembled technology" and, hence, require incremental growth and innovation. Finally, it is pointed out that measured data from operational ITS projects is extremely valuable for operations management as well as for regional planning. Especially this last finding is dramatically true nowadays, and applies in particular to urban scenarios, which is the focus of this work, because of the additional challenges it brings with respect to inter-city connection roads and highways. In fact, in densely populated areas, data collection is more difficult, due to the high deployment costs, and traffic behavior is most unpredictable, due to the highly dynamic traffic patterns.

In a modern ITS, gathering of measured data, which is central to the system operation, is carried out by means of devices, which we call sensors. Sensors are generally deployed in the area of interest, possibly in an incremental manner and they are usually fixed entities located roadside for easiest data collection. Data must be conveyed from the sensors to a centralized data center, with storage and analysis functions, which is typically operated by a local authority, e.g., the City Council, or an authorized third party. The deployment of such an information transportation infrastructure with traditional cabled technology, e.g., fiber optic or copper, is overly difficult and tremendously expensive due to high installation costs and physical constraints. Therefore, we argue that the use of wireless technologies is a de facto necessity to reduce the installation time and costs. Our statement is supported by the flourishing of working groups in different standardization bodies for the regulation of ITS wireless communications, including the IEEE, whose reference architecture is described in IEEE P1609.0 Draft Standard for Wireless Access in Vehicular Environments (WAVE) - Architecture, and ETSI 302 665 Intelligent Transport Systems (ITS); Communications Architecture.

The main contribution of this work is a critical survey of standard technologies for creating the wireless infrastructure of a urban-scale ITS, which are attractive for their limited equipment and operation costs. Furthermore, we analyze in details the wireless infrastructure that we have realized in a regional Italian project using the HiperLAN/2 radio technology, also reporting the results obtained in a laboratory prototype of the system.

BACKGROUND

In this section we introduce the key components of an ITS for accurate positioning of our contribution. In the following we broadly reuse the ETSI 302 665 terminology.

An ITS is composed of four main sub-systems. The roadside sub-system is a static device, often called Roadside Unit (RSU), positioned along the road for collecting measurements through sensors, actuating feedbacks via, e.g., Variable Message Signs (VMSs), and acting as a gateway for vehicle communications. The vehicle sub-system, often called On-Board Unit (OBU), resides into the car, which can be equipped with sensors and wireless networking equipment for communication with other cars, in a Vehicle-to-Vehicle (V2V) manner, and roadside units, in a Vehicle-to-Infrastructure (V2I) manner. The personal sub-system is embedded in portable devices used by pedestrians and citizens for collecting travel information and news. The central sub-system, also called data center, which stores and elaborates data from the peripheral sub-systems and possibly provides them with feedbacks/actions. This architecture is designed to flexibly adapt to many possible application scenarios.

For example, suppose a car A records a new traffic flow sample, and it is not in the communication range of any roadside unit. It can send the sample to another car B in the vicinity, which in turn is close to an RSU. The definition of an optimal strategy for routing and forwarding of packets in V2V and V2I communications is a research area on its own (Chen, Guha, Kwon, Lee, & Hsu, 2008), which includes approaches based on clustering (Miller, 2008), geographical dissemination (Bakhouya, Gaber, & Wack, 2009), and cross-layer (Chen, Xiang, Jian, & Jiang, 2009).

Resuming our example, assume car B then relays the sample to the data center, which will store the sample for off-line analysis, e.g., predictive models based on historical datasets, and also elaborate in real-time the data by determining that the road of car A is congested. Then, the data center sends such information to an RSU nearby the position indicated by car A, which can modify the variable speed limit signs or simply indicate congestion alerts to drivers. Even though this example only shows the tip of the ITS iceberg, nonetheless it helps understanding the potential of new ICT techniques compared to traditional approaches, where VMSs are programmed manually by the road administrators, definitely failing to capture the rapid evolution of traffic patterns,

especially in urban environments (Shi, et al., 2009). Techniques for an effective positioning of RSUs are being studied, e.g., Li & Jia (2009), so as to maximize the impact while keeping the costs feasible in scenarios of practical interest.

With regard to the wireless technology for V2V and V2I communication, there is general agreement that a modified version of the very popular IEEE 802.11, called IEEE 802.11p, will be the undisputed enabler. On the other hand, there is no market or industrial consensus on how the data can be transported back and forth between the peripheral sub-systems and the central sub-system, which we call wireless backhauling and is the subject of this chapter.

WIRELESS BACKHAULING SOLUTIONS

In this section we introduce the most relevant technologies for realizing a wireless backhauling to convey data between a data center and the RSUs in a urban ITS. To be feasible in practical applications, there are some requirements that must be obeyed by the wireless technology. First, it should support pervasive connectivity in urban areas. This excludes all those technologies where Line-Of-Sight (LOS) is required, since it would be impractical to mount high towers or poles to surpass the height of buildings. Moreover, it should have a very long-term support, because the expected lifetime of an ITS infrastructure is a few decades, and be cost-effective, to favor capillary diffusion. Therefore, the use of standard technologies is suggested, which reduces the risk of proprietary lock-in and incurs lower costs than proprietary solutions, especially for small installations.

The following technologies are considered: IEEE 802.11, in a Wireless Mesh Network (WMN) configuration, IEEE 802.16/WiMAX, Long Term Evolution (LTE), and HiperLAN/2.

IEEE 802.11/WMNs

Wireless Mesh Networks (WMNs) are a recently available technology providing high-bandwidth networks in industrial and residential settings. A WMN consists of a backbone and several end-user devices, see (Akyildiz, Wang, & Wang, 2005) for a survey. The backbone devices are fixed and form a multi-hop wireless link between end-users and the Internet. End-user devices, on the other hand, are typically mobile or nomadic mesh clients. Each mesh client is connected to a backbone device in order to have its packets forwarded from/to the Internet. In the ITS context, the backbone devices are co-located with the RSUs, and the end-user devices can be vehicle and personal sub-systems. An example of WMN deployment is illustrated Figure 1.

The most common technology for implementing a WMN is the IEEE 802.11, which is very cost effective due to the huge number of chips produced and sold in the last 10 years. Actually, the IEEE 802.11 technology does not provide native support for multi-hop forwarding. For this reason within the IEEE 802.11 working group, a task group 's' has been created in order to amend the standard and add the missing multi-hop functions. While the standardization process has not yet finished, the IEEE 802.11s draft is supported by a wide variety of industry leaders and has been analyzed in many scientific works, e.g., Cicconetti, Lenzini, and Mingozzi (2008) and Hiertz, Denteneer, Max, Taori, Cardona, Berlemann, and Walke (2010). The key advantage of using IEEE 802.11 in a WMN for ITS is that installation is very simple because of its self-configuration and self-healing properties characteristics. For instance, if a link between two RSUs fails because of poor planning or changed wireless conditions, e.g., a new building or seasonal foliage, then the network will automatically discover new paths for creating a virtual connection between the temporarily disconnected RSUs. Therefore, the overall network will remain fully operational provided that there is not a total isolation of one or more RSUs from the rest of them. Such an occurrence can be easily avoided by overprovisioning the number of IEEE 802.11 stations in a dense manner, due to the low cost of equipment and installation.

Unfortunately, there are two main disadvantages with this technology, which does not make it suitable in 100% of the scenarios. In fact, a packet has to be relayed from one RSU to another until it receives the data center; hence, wireless resources are consumed multiple times for each packet. This creates a scalability issue: the more RSUs are added, the more resources are consumed with such "relaying," until eventually the performance degrades for some or all the RSUs in a significant and difficult to anticipate manner. The second problem is that strict Quality of Service (QoS) guarantees, e.g., bounded transfer delays for real-time applications, are impossible to provide because of the multi-hop nature combined with a fully distributed management of resources.

IEEE 802.16/WiMAX

The IEEE 802.16 standard was originally designed for fixed Broadband Wireless Access (BWA), where Subscriber Stations (SSs) are deployed within the coverage range of a Base Station (BS), which coordinates medium access in both down-

Figure 1. Example of WMN deployment

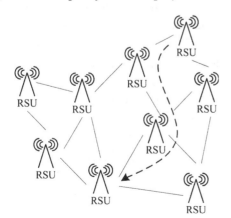

link (from the BS to the SSs) and uplink (from the SSs to the BS). The air interface used was based on either Single Carrier (SC) or Orthogonal Frequency Division Multiplexing (OFDM). More recently the standard was enhanced to support Mobile Stations (MSs) and the air interface was changed to Orthogonal Frequency Division Multiple Access (OFDMA), which is more suitable in mobile environments due to its higher resilience to Doppler and multipath fading effects. Unlike the IEEE 802.11, the IEEE 802.16 specifies QoS support at the Medium Access Control (MAC) layer to enable interactive and multimedia applications along with traditional best-effort services (Cicconetti, Erta, Lenzini, & Mingozzi, 2007). An example of IEEE 802.16 deployment as the wireless backhauling of an ITS is illustrated in Figure 2, where each cell is assumed to have an hexagonal shape and to be divided into three sectors. Each sector is served by a dedicated directional antenna, or group of antennas, operating on either the same (i.e., with reuse factor 1) or different frequencies as the others (i.e., with reuse factor 3).

The WiMAX Forum[2] industrial alliance has released in the last years a number of profiles for use in fixed and mobile environments, in both licensed and license-free spectrum. BSs and SSs are widely available in the market as both chipsets and off-the-shelf products, though their cost is not as low as that of IEEE 802.11 radios due to the mass production of the latter. The high cost

problem applies in particular to the BS, whose installation and configuration requires complex planning activities, which are only marginally simpler than those for cellular technologies, even in license-free frequency bands. Therefore, the addition of a new RSU is seamless only if the existing BS, or set of BSs, already covers the target area; otherwise, the deployment of a new BS is required. Such a cost associated to the expansion of the wireless backhauling beyond the initially planned coverage area is the main disadvantage of IEEE 802.16 for its use as the wireless backhauling technology in an ITS.

Long Term Evolution

The Third Generation Partnership Project (3GPP) is a collaboration among five international groups of telecommunications associations, including ETSI, and it is intended to make globally applicable standards for mobile communications. Established in 1998, it has developed several very successful standards to support the increasing needs of mobile communications, including GSM and UMTS, which were, however, mostly focused on supporting efficiently voice calls. On the other hand, the newer releases, namely HSxPA and LTE, represent a major step towards the service of heterogeneous requests of modern mobile terminals, with optimized support of both voice and data transmission. LTE, in particular,

Figure 2. Example of IEEE 802.16 deployment with sectorized antennas

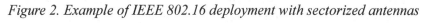

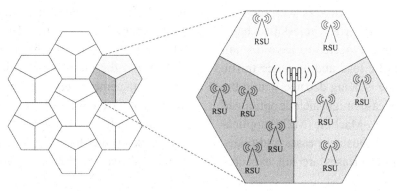

can now be considered the mature leading technology for mobile cellular systems with capabilities beyond 3G (Dahlman, Parkvall, Skold, & Berning, 2008). The configuration of the radio part of an LTE network is similar to that described in Figure 2 for IEEE 802.16. Its main characteristics and relevance to wireless backhauling are described in the following.

LTE supports very high peak rates, up to 300 Mb/s in downlink and 75 Mb/s in uplink, with a combination of the following technical features: flexible spectrum usage, from 1.25 MHz to 20 MHz; support of high-order modulations, up to 64-QAM; use of Multiple-Input-Multiple-Output (MIMO) techniques, which allow two or more antennas to be used at the same time for communications between the BS and the mobile terminal, by exploiting space diversity (Raleigh, & Cioffi, 1998); reduced user and control plane latency, in the order of 5 ms and 100 ms, respectively; QoS support through dynamic resource scheduling. These characteristics make the LTE technology suitable for the interconnection of RSUs in an ITS.

The main drawback is that, unlike the other technologies surveyed in this chapter, the spectrum allocated for LTE is subject to licensing in all developed countries, and can be operated lawfully only by mobile network operators. Therefore, it is necessary for the ITS operator to acquire and maintain service agreements with the local telecom operators. This can be unexpectedly costly, because the predefined services provided by latter are designed with requirements of people in mind, e.g., flat monthly costs for a given number of free call hours, and might not fit very well the type of operations required for a wireless backhauling, where RSUs are expected to have a small but continuous traffic load and no voice traffic at all. Such an issue is being debated within the 3GPP, and future releases might include optimized support to Machine-to-Machine (M2M) applications and appropriate business cases and plans. Unfortunately, these releases are not expected

be available in the market earlier than five years from the time of writing.

ETSI HiperLAN/2

ETSI HiperLAN/2 is a standard technology, defined by European Telecommunications Standards Institute (ETSI) in the Broadband Radio Access Networks (BRAN) project. It can use 5.8 GHz Industrial, Scientific, and Medical (ISM) radio bands, which are unlicensed and much less crowded than the 2.4 GHz one used by most IEEE 802.11 devices. The air interface of HiperLAN/2 is IEEE 802.11a/h compliant, which yields very low costs for chipsets because of their long-lasting popularity. Like IEEE 802.11 and IEEE 802.16, HiperLAN/2 can be operated in both LOS and non-LOS environments, with different transmission rates, and this allows great flexibility in the installation. Another legacy of IEEE 802.11, however, is its limited coverage, in the order of hundreds of meters, in non-LOS environments where the use of omni-directional antennas is envisaged. Such limitation can be substantially overcome when there is a clear path between the transmitter and receiver units, in which case directive antennas with high gains can easily boost the range up to kilometers. Again, this demonstrates that the best choice among the candidate technologies available very much depends on the landscape of installation and its foreseeable future evolution.

Two possible deployments exist, which are illustrated in Figure 3. Which alternative is better depends on the environment where the network has to be installed and on the number of radio link pairs to be placed, as discussed in the following. In a Point-To-Point (PTP) configuration, also called HiperLink, the number of radio links installed in the data center is equal to the number of sites where data are collected and a gateway, with a dedicated radio link, is present. In this case, each radio link installed has a directive antenna oriented to the RSU where the corresponding radio link is placed. To limit the radio interferences, each radio link pair is configured in order to transmit/receive on a different channel. This kind of configuration works very well when the number of radio link pairs is less than or equal to the number of available channels. In this configuration the expansion of the wireless backhauling is cost-effective as long as the newly added RSU can be reached from the data center with a suitable antenna. On the other hand, the Point-To-Multipoint (PMP) configuration is similar to that of cellular systems, and also illustrated in Figure 3. The communication channel is one and data are multiplexed according to the specific HiperLAN MAC following the Dynamic TDMA technique, which is known to provide deterministic QoS guarantees (Lenzini, & Mingozzi, 2001), unlike the IEEE 802.11. Again, like IEEE 802.16, a BS is much more complex and expensive than a subscriber unit; hence, the expansion of the wireless backhauling beyond the original coverage area is costly.

Summary

The prominent characteristics of the wireless technologies analyzed in this section are summarized in Table 1.

As can be seen from the table, there is a clear distinction between the WMN solution using IEEE 802.11 radios and all the others. Specifically, the former is very appealing due to its low cost of installation and operation and also because it allows an incremental expansion of the wireless infrastructure. However, due to the distributed nature of the WMN and because of the use of unlicensed spectrum, it is very difficult to provide strict guarantees on QoS and service continuity. This disadvantage can be critical for all ITS applications including safety, where the data transmitted are important and urgent. On the other hand, the IEEE 802.16e, LTE, and HiperLAN/2 technologies offer good support to such applications, because of how the MAC and management layers have been designed and are implemented by vendors. Furthermore, they can cover a much wider area than typical IEEE 802.11 radios. Both advantages come at the expense of higher installation, maintenance, and operation costs, and their single-hop nature limits the future geographical expansion of the network.

To conclude, as already briefly introduced above, these considerations clearly show that there is not a "killer" technology for the wireless backhauling in ITSs. Rather, for every scenario,

Figure 3. Possible deployments with HiperLAN/2

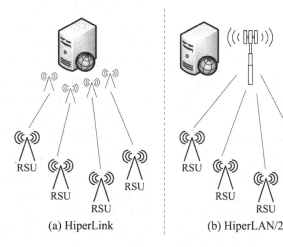

(a) HiperLink

(b) HiperLAN/2

the best candidate, or set of candidates, should be selected based, e.g., on the geographical layout, the number of users, the type of ITS applications envisaged, the estimated growth in the medium and long term.

HIPERLAN/2 TESTBED

In this section we report the results obtained in the IPERMOB project[3] (Infrastruttura Pervasiva Eterogenea Real-time per il controllo della Mobilità – A Pervasive and Heterogeneous Infrastructure to control Urban Mobility in Real-Time), with regard to the wireless backhauling for intelligent transportation. The overall objectives of IPERMOB are: to develop a multi-tier information system for urban mobility; to propose a new generation of integrated systems based on the optimization and interoperability of the chain formed by data collection systems; new aggregation, management, and on-line control systems; new off-line systems aiming at infrastructure planning; new information systems targeted to citizens to handle and rule the vehicle mobility. As testbed, IPERMOB provides real-time information about parking availability and vehicle flows on the landside of the International Airport of Tuscany located in Pisa.

Before reporting the experimental results and describing the conditions under which they have

Table 1. Comparison of the wireless technologies surveyed

	802.11	802.16e	LTE	HiperLAN/2
Deployment	Mesh	PMP	PMP	PMP/PTP
Cost (HW)	Low	BS: High, RSU: Low		
Cost (operation)	Low	Medium	High	Medium
Radio range	Short	Long	Long	(see text)
QoS	No	Yes	Yes	Yes
Expansion	Easy	Easy if in coverage, otherwise difficult		

been collected, we sketch the IPERMOB data management infrastructure.

The IPERMOB Data Management Architecture

In IPERMOB, the data management architecture is centralized: the information gathered from sensors and vehicles are expected to be centrally stored (in a database) and accessible from a control room. The network infrastructure consists of two tiers: a collection tier where the data coming from sensors are fused by the so-called coordinators, and the backhauling tier.

The overall requirements of the network infrastructure include: scalability: the throughput and latency performance should not degrade significantly when new sensors are added, up to the size of a medium city; QoS: low jitter and bounded delays are needed for some time-critical applications; security: only the intended recipients must be able to decode the data transmitted over the air.

In IPERMOB the Gateway (GW) is responsible for collecting and forwarding the data coming from several sources, i.e., sensors and RSUs, assuring a suitable Quality of Service (QoS), by means of traffic shaping, packet scheduling, traffic policing, and packet dropping. The data are coming from the vehicular, wireless sensor networks and, optionally, surveillance cameras.

The GW allocates more or less bandwidth to the data coming from the different traffic sources and gives a priority to the messages, managing several traffic queues and forwarding the data according to the chosen policy. The data are forwarded from each gateway via HiperLAN/2 to a software application called Message Manager (MM) that interfaces with the Database Management System (DBMS) and the so-called Control Room, all residing in the data center. The MM is in charge of collecting all the data coming from different gateways and conveying: to the DBMS: the raw data about traffic flow intensity and parking lot status from sensors; the position of vehicles and

Figure 4. Packet loss per traffic class

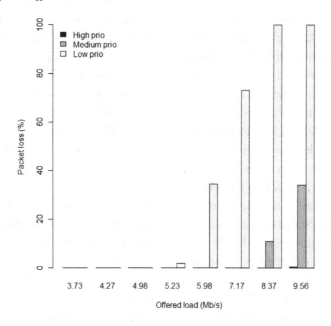

estimated travel times, periodically, from vehicles; to the control room: all the messages concerning network configuration; messages concerning the authentication of vehicles, which also pass through the DBMS. The DBMS then notifies the control room when a parking slot has changed its status, from available to busy or vice versa. In the opposite direction, feedback to vehicles about the

parking lot occupation and estimate travel time is issued by the DBMS on demand.

Testbed Results

A laboratory testbed has been used for carrying out experiments under repeatable and fully controllable conditions. The testbed consists of

Figure 5. 95th percentile of end-to-end delay per traffic class

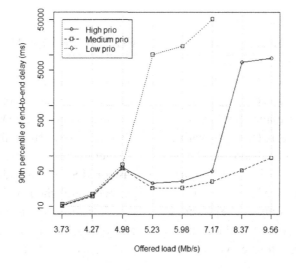

the full transmission chain from the GW to the MM. The wireless sensor networks and the concentrators have been emulated by means of the element called Message simulator in the figure, which is a workstation connected to the GW with enough computational capabilities to create traffic corresponding to thousands of sensors. Each simulated sensor sends UDP packets to the GW, which aggregates all the data and conveys it to the MM via a single TCP connection. The size of packets was set to 255 bytes, which is deemed to be large enough to contain a sample for most practical ITS applications. Statistics are collected on the MM, without the inclusion of the DMBS and the Control Room in the testbed, because we were only interested in the performance of the wireless backhauling. The HiperLAN/2 system has been configured to use the minimum bitrate, which is 6 Mb/s, to simulate a worst-case propagation scenario, while including all the wireless protocol overhead and latencies.

We now report the results from experiments when varying the total traffic load from 3.73 Mb/s to 9.56 Mb/s. Specifically, this behavior has been obtained by changing the period at which the emulated sensors generate data, from 1 s to 1.6 s, and the number of emulated sensors, from 3,000 to about 5,000. We have considered three classes of sensors each associated to a different priority level from High to Low. The emulated sensors are evenly distributed among the three traffic classes.

In Figure 4, we show the percentage of packets lost for each traffic class as the load increases. As can be seen the loss is negligible for all traffic classes until the offered load reaches 5.23 Mb/s, which means that the performance bottleneck is the air link, which has been set to the conservative raw rate of 6 Mb/s. On the other hand, the GW is able to handle the amount of traffic, even though it consists of a low-power embedded device with low computational capabilities, suitable to be powered by solar panels. When the offered load increases further, only the low-priority traffic experiences

packet losses until the load reaches 7.17 Mb/s, at which point the medium priority traffic also begins suffering from packet losses. This shows that the GW is able to achieve an isolation of the traffic classes, which is a necessary requirement to enable safety or real-time applications in the ITS.

Another important metric for these applications is the delay: even without packet losses, real-time applications might now work properly if packets are delayed too much. For instance, if an RSU detects an emergency situation in a road (e.g., a jam), visual indications (e.g., on a VMS) must be triggered with sufficient timeliness to allow both the drivers and their vehicles to react accordingly (e.g., braking until a full stop). Therefore, in Figure 5, we report the 95th percentile of end-to-end delay per traffic class. As can be seen, all the curves are almost overlapping until the offered load is fully sustainable, i.e. until 4.98 Mb/s. Beyond that, the low priority traffic begins dropping packets, which immediately releases some resources for the higher priority classes, whose delay decrease slightly. We can note that, for the delay too, there is a clear isolation of the traffic classes. Moreover, the delay of high-priority traffic is bounded by 100 ms, which includes all the real computational and transmission overheads of communication and provides a safe ground basis for the provisioning of emergency ITS services.

FUTURE RESEARCH DIRECTIONS

The research on this topic has only recently begun; therefore, there are several directions of extension. For instance, while the WMNs and IEEE 802.16e alternatives have been thoroughly investigated in the literature, a comparison analysis in the specific case of ITS, also including HiperLAN/2, has not yet been published, at the best of our knowledge. Another direction is to perform a cost-benefit analysis, where a mix of the wireless technologies is used for creating the wireless backhauling, taking into account the complexity of deploying and managing a heterogeneous network infrastructure. It is worth noting that such a use of varied technologies will be favored in the future with the diffusion of the recent IEEE 802.21 standard, which allows a seamless handover between technologies that are not inter-operable (e.g., LTE towards IEEE 802.16) or for which no explicit handover procedures have been defined (e.g., IEEE 802.11). The interested reader can find a survey of the standard, also including comments on potential applications, in Taniuchi et al. (2009).

CONCLUSION

In this chapter we have discussed the issue of the interconnection of the peripheral entities of an ITS, including vehicles and RSUs, to a data center, where the actual data collection and analysis are performed. Due to the nature of the system and business considerations, standard wireless solutions operating in license-free bands only have been surveyed: WMNs, IEEE 802.16e, LTE, and ETSI HiperLAN/2. The latter has been also further analyzed, based on the results of a regional Italian project on ITS, where a prototype testbed has been realized, whose results have been reported and discussed to show the effectiveness of the HiperLAN/2 solution for practical purposes.

REFERENCES

Akyildiz, I. F., Wang, X., & Wang, W. (2005). Wireless mesh networks: A survey. *Computer Networks*, *47*(3), 445–487. doi:10.1016/j.comnet.2004.12.001

Bakhouya, M., Gaber, J., & Wack, M. (2009). Performance evaluation of dream protocol for inter-vehicle communication. In *Proceedings of the International Conference on Wireless Communication, Vehicular Technology, Information Theory and Aerospace Electronic Systems Technology*, (pp. 289 –293). IEEE.

Chen, W., Guha, R., Kwon, T. J., Lee, J., & Hsu, I. (2008). A survey and challenges in routing and data dissemination in vehicular ad-hoc networks. In *Proceedings of the IEEE International Conference on Vehicular Electronics and Safety*, (pp. 328 –333). IEEE Press.

Chen, Y., Xiang, Z., Jian, W., & Jiang, W. (2009). A cross-layer AOMDV routing protocol for v2v communication in urban vanet. In *Proceedings of the IEEE International Conference on Mobile Ad-Hoc and Sensor Networks*, (pp. 353 –359). IEEE Press.

Cicconetti, C., Erta, A., Lenzini, L., & Mingozzi, E. (2007). Performance evaluation of the IEEE 802.16 MAC for QoS support. *IEEE Transactions on Mobile Computing*, *6*(1), 26–38. doi:10.1109/TMC.2007.250669

Cicconetti, C., Lenzini, L., & Mingozzi, E. (2008). Scheduling and dynamic relocation for IEEE 802.11s mesh deterministic access. In *Proceedings of the Annual IEEE Communications Society Conference on Sensor, Mesh and Ad Hoc Communications and Networks*, (pp. 19–27). IEEE Press.

Dahlman, E., Parkvall, S., Skold, J., & Berning, P. (2008). *3G evolution: HSPA and LTE for mobile broadband*. Boston, MA: Academic Press. doi:10.1587/transcom.E92.B.1432

Hiertz, G., Denteneer, D., Max, S., Taori, R., Cardona, J., Berlemann, L., & Walke, W. (2010). IEEE 802.11s: The WLAN mesh standard. *IEEE Wireless Communications*, *17*(1), 104–111. doi:10.1109/MWC.2010.5416357

Lenzini, L., & Mingozzi, E. (2001). Performance evaluation of capacity request and allocation mechanisms for HiperLAN/2 wireless LANs. *Computer Networks*, *37*(1), 5–15. doi:10.1016/S1389-1286(01)00194-3

Li, R., & Jia, L. (2009). On the layout of fixed urban traffic detectors: An application study. *IEEE Intelligent Transportation Systems Magazine*, *1*(2), 6–12. doi:10.1109/MITS.2009.933858

Martinez, F., Toh, C.-K., Cano, J.-C., Calafate, C., & Manzoni, P. (2010). Emergency services in future intelligent transportation systems based on vehicular communication networks. *IEEE Intelligent Transportation Systems Magazine*, *2*(2), 6–20. doi:10.1109/MITS.2010.938166

Miller, J. (2012). Vehicle-to-vehicle-to-infrastructure (V2V2I) intelligent transportation system architecture. In *Proceedings of the IEEE Intelligent Vehicles Symposium*, (pp. 715–720). IEEE Press.

Raleigh, G. G., & Cioffi, J. M. (1998). Spatio-temporal coding for wireless communication. *IEEE Transactions on Communications*, *46*(3), 357–366. doi:10.1109/26.662641

Shi, W., Wu, J., Zhou, S., Zhang, L., Tang, Z., & Yin, Y. (2009). Variable message sign and dynamic regional traffic guidance. *IEEE Intelligent Transportation Systems Magazine*, *1*(3), 15–21. doi:10.1109/MITS.2009.934642

Taniuchi, K., Ohba, Y., Fajardo, V., Das, S., Tauil, M., & Cheng, Y.-H. (2009). IEEE 802.21: Media independent handover: Features, applicability, and realization. *IEEE Communications Magazine*, *47*(1), 112–120. doi:10.1109/MCOM.2009.4752687

Weissenberger, S. (1998). *Why its projects should be small, local and private*. Research Report UCB-ITS-PRR-98-23. Berkeley, CA: University of California.

ADDITIONAL READING

Anastasi, G., Borgia, E., Conti, M., & Gregori, E. (2005). IEEE 802.11b ad hoc networks: Performance measurements. *Cluster Computing*, *8*(2-3), 135–145. doi:10.1007/s10586-005-6179-3

Astély, D., Dahlman, E., Furuskär, A., Jading, Y., Lindström, M., & Parkvall, S. (2009). LTE: The evolution of mobile broadband. *IEEE Communications Magazine*, *47*(4), 44–51. doi:10.1109/MCOM.2009.4907406

Bézivin, J. (2005). On the unification power of models. *Software & Systems Modeling*, *4*(7), 171–188. doi:10.1007/s10270-005-0079-0

Bruno, R., Conti, M., & Gregori, E. (2005). Mesh networks: Commodity multihop ad hoc networks. *IEEE Communications Magazine*, *43*(3), 123–131. doi:10.1109/MCOM.2005.1404606

Cicconetti, C., Galeassi, F., & Mambrini, R. (2011). A software architecture for network-assisted handover in IEEE 802.21. *The Journal of Communication*, *6*(1).

Commission of the European Communities. (2008). *Action plan for the deployment of intelligent transport systems in Europe*. Technical Report. European Communities.

Ergen, M. (2009). *Mobile broadband–Including WiMAX and LTE*. Berlin, Germany: Springer.

ETSI EN 302 665. (2012). *Intelligent transport systems (ITS): Communications architecture*. Retrieved from http://www.etsi.org

Gambiroza, V., Sadeghi, B., & Knightly, E. W. (2004). End-to-end performance and fairness in multihop wireless backhaul networks. In *Proceedings of the ACM International Conference on Mobile Computing and Networking*, (pp. 287-301). ACM Press.

3GPP TS36. 300. (2012). *Evolved universal terrestrial radio access (E-UTRA) and evolved universal terrestrial radio access network (E-UTRAN): Overall description.* Retrieved from http://www.3gpp.org

3GPP TS 36.201. (2012). Evolved universal terrestrial radio access (E-UTRA): Long term evolution (LTE) physical layer: General description. Retrieved from http://www.3gpp.org

3GPP TS 36.211. (2012). Evolved universal terrestrial radio access (E-UTRA): Physical channels and modulation. Retrieved from http://www.3gpp.org

3GPP TS 36.321. (2012). Evolved universal terrestrial radio access (E-UTRA) medium access control (MAC) protocol specification. Retrieved from http://www.3gpp.org

3GPP TS 36.806. (2012). Evolved universal terrestrial radio access (E-UTRA): Relay architectures for E-UTRA (LTE-advanced). Retrieved from http://www.3gpp.org

Gupta, P., & Kumar, P. R. (2000). The capacity of wireless networks. *IEEE Transactions on Information Theory, 46*(2), 388–404. doi:10.1109/18.825799

IEEE P1609.0. (2012). *Draft standard for wireless access in vehicular environments (WAVE) - Architecture.* Retrieved from http://www.ieee.org

IEEE P802.11p. (2012). *Local and metropolitan area networks - Part 11: Wireless LAN medium access control (MAC) and physical layer (PHY) specifications amendment 7: Wireless access in vehicular environments.* Retrieved from http://www.ieee.org

Kim, K.-H., & Shin, K. G. (2006). On accurate measurement of link quality in multi-hop wireless mesh networks. In *Proceedings of the ACM International Conference on Mobile Computing and Networking,* (pp. 38-49). ACM Press.

Koenig, J. G. (1980). Indicators of urban accessibility: Theory & application. *Transportation, 9*(2), 145–172. doi:10.1007/BF00167128

Koutsonikolas, D., Salonidis, T., Lundgren, H., LeGuyadec, P., Hu, Y. C., & Sheriff, I. (2008). TDM MAC protocol design and implementation for wireless mesh networks. In *Proceedings of the International Conference on Emerging Networking Experiments and Technologies,* (pp. 1-12). ACM Press.

Kurtev, I., Bézivin, J., Jouault, F., & Valduriez, P. (2006). Model-based DSL frameworks. In *Proceedings of the ACM SIGPLAN Symposium on Object-Oriented Programming Systems, Languages, and Applications,* (pp. 602–616). ACM Press.

Liu, X., Sridharan, A., Machiraju, S., Seshadri, M., & Zang, H. (2008). Experiences in a 3G network: Interplay between the wireless channel and applications. In *Proceedings of the ACM International Conference on Mobile Computing and Networking,* (pp. 211-222). ACM Press.

Magrini, M., Moroni, D., Nastasi, C., Pagano, P., Petracca, M., & Pieri, G. ... Salvetti, O. (2010). Image mining for infomobility. In *Proceedings of the International Workshop on Image Mining Theory and Applications,* (pp. 35-44). Angers, France: INSTICC Press.

Osman, A., & Mohammed, A. (2008). Performance evaluation of a low-complexity OFDM UMTS-LTE system. In *Proceedings of the IEEE Vehicular Technology Conference,* (pp. 2142-2146). IEEE Press.

Pagano, P., Piga, F., & Liang, Y. (2009). Real-time multi-view vision systems using WSNs. In *Proceedings of the ACM Symposium on Applied Computing,* (pp. 2191-2196). ACM Press.

Remagnino, P., Shihab, A. I., & Jones, G. A. (2004). Distributed intelligence for multi-camera visual surveillance. *Pattern Recognition, 37*(4), 675–689. doi:10.1016/j.patcog.2003.09.017

Rong, B., Qian, Y., & Lu, K. (2007). Integrated downlink resource management for multiservice WiMAX networks. *IEEE Transactions on Mobile Computing*, 6(6), 621–632. doi:10.1109/TMC.2007.1028

Std, I. E. E. E. 802.16e-2005. (2005). *Amendment to IEEE standard for local and metropolitan area networks - Part 16: Air interface for fixed broadband wireless access systems*. Retrieved from http://www.ieee.org

Std, I. E. E. E. 802.11-2009. (2009). *Wireless LAN medium access control (MAC) and physical layer (PHY) specifications*. Retrieved from http://www.ieee.org

WiMAX Forum. (2007). *Mobile system profile – Release 1.0 approved specification*. WiMAX.

Xiao, Y. (2007). *WiMAX/MobileFi: Advanced research and technology*. Boca Raton, FL: Auerbach Publications. doi:10.1201/9781420043525

KEY TERMS AND DEFINITIONS

Central Sub-System: Functional entity that stores and elaborates data from the peripheral sub-systems and possibly provides them with feedbacks/actions.

Intelligent Transportation Systems: Complex systems deployed over a geographical area to collect data from multiple type of sensors, take appropriate decisions on how to improve road safety and optimize transportation, and provide actions to drivers on how to implement them with a combination of methods.

Personal Sub-System: Device embedded in portable devices used by pedestrians and citizens for collecting travel information and news.

Point-To-Multipoint: Network topology where a single device, called base station, communicate to multiple wireless subscriber units in a broadcast manner and coordinates transmissions from the latter.

Point-To-Point: Network topology where two wireless devices that are in the transmission range of one another communicate through direct messages.

Roadside Sub-System: Static device positioned along the road for collecting measurements through sensors, actuating feedbacks via, e.g., Variable Message Signs (VMSs), and acting as a gateway for vehicle communications.

Vehicle Sub-System: Device that resides into the car, equipped with sensors and wireless networking equipment for communication with other cars.

Wireless Backhauling: Data communication network that enables communication between the peripheral devices and the central sub-system of an ITS.

Wireless Mesh Network: Network topology where point-to-point is used between nodes that can communicate directly, and data is relayed in a multi-hop manner for communication between out-of-range nodes.

ENDNOTES

[1] http://ec.europa.eu/information_society/digital-agenda/
[2] http://www.wimaxforum.org/
[3] http://www.ipermob.org/

Section 2
Applications and RSU Deployment

Chapter 4
Real Time Acquisition of Traffic Information through V2V, V2R, and V2I Communications

Alessandro Bazzi
National Research Council (CNR-IEIIT), Italy

Barbara M. Masini
National Research Council (CNR-IEIIT), Italy

Gianni Pasolini
University of Bologna, Italy

ABSTRACT

Many vehicles are currently equipped with On-Board Units (OBUs) that are in charge of collecting and processing data for some specific purposes (such as for travel monitoring, as requested by many insurance companies). These devices are connected to the cellular network by means of their Vehicle-to-Infrastructure (V2I) communication interface, and are thus able to transmit and receive information also related to real time traffic, pollution, local events, etc. Of course, as the number of OBU-equipped vehicles increases, the cost of this service increases as well, both in terms of network load and billing. In this chapter, the authors discuss the possibility of taking advantage of vehicle-to-vehicle (V2V) and Vehicle-to-Roadside (V2R) communications to save V2I resources, thus reducing the cellular network burden and, consequently, the service cost.

INTRODUCTION

Making road traffic safer and smarter is a challenge that researchers, industries, and standardization bodies are facing worldwide. A fundamental contribution to the achievement of this objective is provided by wireless communications networks, which are enabling advanced services targeted to Intelligent Transportation Systems (ITS).

As a matter of fact, an increasing number of vehicles travelling worldwide is currently equipped with monitoring devices that make them act as

DOI: 10.4018/978-1-4666-2223-4.ch004

sensors collecting and transmitting information about themselves and their surroundings. These equipments embed a Global Positioning System (GPS) receiver, a cellular device providing a Vehicle-to-Infrastructure (V2I) interface, and, in case, other sensors.

Several applications that target transport efficiency could make use of the vast information collected by vehicles: safety, traffic management, smart navigation, pollution monitoring, tourist information, etc. (Conti, 2009). In Italy, for instance, huge amount of data concerning vehicles' position and speed (and ultimately, the traffic on the road network) are acquired by over one million vehicles equipped with On-Board Units (OBUs) (Bazzi, 2010). OBUs continuously collect and store information about the vehicle status (position, speed, acceleration, etc.); these data are periodically sent to a traffic-monitoring control center, which can therefore derive, in real time, the average vehicular speed in any given road travelled by OBU-equipped cars.

Providing this information back to vehicles (including those without the OBU) allows on-board navigators to always choose the optimal route to the destination on the basis of the actual traffic conditions.

Apart from third party OBUs, some navigators' manufacturers directly embed this traffic monitoring capability in their top-level products, which are therefore equipped with a cellular communication device.

Of course, in both cases the service cost is highly affected by the frequent transmissions carried out over the cellular network. These costs are usually hidden in the service subscription fee and represent an obstacle to the widespread diffusion of this kind of devices, which is a fundamental condition to have an accurate monitoring of the road network.

Even not considering economical aspects, the frequent transmissions performed by on-board devices could overload the mobile network, thus reducing the quality of service experienced by users. Moreover, transmissions performed by uncoordinated devices would refer, in many cases, to the same road segment, thus causing an useless resource occupation; if OBUs were able to communicate to each other through a Vehicle-to-Vehicle (V2V) interface, measurements performed almost simultaneously by different vehicles over the same road could be merged before being transmitted to the control center over the cellular network, thus avoiding duplicates and reducing the overall cost of the service as well as increasing the network efficiency and the quality of service (Campolo, 2010).

Of course, the presence of a dedicated roadside communication infrastructure, able to collect data coming from vehicles and to forward in the opposite direction (toward vehicles) information coming from the control center, would further reduce the load offered to the cellular network, with obvious advantages in terms of cost and resource saving.

In this chapter we investigate the advantages achievable by sharing, aggregating and transmitting the collected traffic information through short range ad hoc V2V and Vehicle-to-Roadside (V2R) communications aimed at reducing cellular V2I connections from vehicles to the control center. The benefits will be assessed adopting a simulation platform that takes into account a realistic vehicular traffic in an urban area, simulated through the microscopic Vissim commercial tool (Vissim, 2010), and network aspects through the simulation platform for heterogeneous interworking networks (SHINE) developed in our laboratories (Bazzi, 2006).

Answers will be given in particular to the following questions:

- Which are the advantages provided by V2V communications?
- Which are the further benefits that can be achieved providing vehicles also with V2R communication capabilities?

BACKGROUND

Several standardization processes and research works are currently carried out in the field of vehicular networks (VANETs) with particular reference to the Wireless Access in Vehicular Environments (WAVE) based on the IEEE 802.11p technology (IEEE 802.11p, 2010; WAVE, 2006), for both safety and non-safety applications (Eichler, 2007; Jiang, 2008; Uzcategui, 2009; Wang, 2008). In Stibor (2007), the maximum coverage range that can be achieved given a constraint on the transmitted power was derived (for instance, about 90% of successful communications happened at distances smaller than 750m). In Gukhool (2008), the impact of speed (from 90 km/hr to 140 km/hr) on successful transmissions was assessed finding out that packet error rates should be less than 10% for packets of 1000 bytes for speeds up to 140 km/hr.

As far as propagation models are concerned, in Martinez (2009), three different radio propagation models that capture the effects of signal attenuation with distance and the presence of buildings on VANETs are proposed.

Due to the highly dynamic topology of VANETs, many studies refer to routing protocols in various traffic conditions (Li, 2007). Among the most adopted we cite the greedy routing (Jerbi, 2009) and the Greedy Perimeters Stateless Routing (GPSR), a geographic routing scheme that uses position of nodes to make packet forwarding decisions (Karp, 2000).

In spite of the large literature on this issue, still few works address specific questions directly related to particular applications, such as real time traffic monitoring. In Campolo (2010), the performance of WAVE/IEEE 802.11p VANETs are evaluated in terms of delay and packet delivery ratio assuming no cellular network and roadside access points to be installed in given positions, but the advantages of the roadside infrastructure for real time services was not investigated.

In Bazzi (2010) and Aktiv (2009), the authors investigated the impact on the network capacity and users' satisfaction of real time acquisition of traffic information through V2I cellular communications when no V2V interface is adopted.

To the authors' best knowledge, still no work considers the possibility of exploiting additional communication networks to share and aggregate traffic information with the aim to reduce the cellular network load.

ENABLING TECHNOLOGIES

Research activities on communication systems supporting vehicular mobility are currently mainly focused on two technologies, targeted to long-range and short-range coverage: cellular systems and WAVE IEEE 802.11p.

As far as cellular systems are concerned, they can be used to collect information from vehicles and, in the opposite direction, to transmit information to vehicles. Their main advantage is the large-scale coverage they provide and the fact that cellular devices are, in many cases, already embedded into on-board equipments (e.g., satellite navigators).

On the other side, the WAVE standard based on IEEE 802.11p represents the new WLAN technology enabling short range V2V and V2R communications.

The main characteristics of both technologies, as well as their usability and interoperability in vehicular contexts are summarized in the following.

Cellular Systems

The pervasive coverage of cellular networks allows communications almost everywhere, also in high mobility scenarios. This is the fundamental reason for their success and their widespread diffusion, that fostered the evolution from second generation (2G) circuit-switched networks toward 3G packet switched networks, up to all-IP 4G networks.

Until year 2010 most of the traffic volume on cellular networks was generated by voice communications. Since voice calls do not require huge bandwidth, the 2G GSM system is still the most popular and widespread cellular technology, allowing data rate up to 9.6 Kb/s in 200 KHz bands. GSM is based on the GMSK single carrier modulation and manages the multiple access to radio resources through an hybrid F-TDMA technique, dividing a 25 MHz uplink or downlink band in 200 KHz channels made up of eight time slots each, and dedicating a channel to each single user for the whole call duration (Holma, 2007).

With the increase in data traffic demand, this rigid resource allocation strategy was not satisfactory anymore. Hence, GSM evolved toward the packet switched solution of GPRS (also known as 2.5G), which allows data rate up to 140.8 Kbit/s, achieved thanks to a flexible resource sharing between data services and voice services. This also simplifies the wireless access, allowing multiple users to share the same physical channel.

GPRS is still characterized, however, by unsatisfactory data rates and not negligible access times, especially considering users' demand for high QoS and high data rates multimedia-services, also in high mobility environments (Masini, 2004; Masini, 2006).

These limits were the driving forces that brought to the development of 3G UMTS, which allows personalized voice, data, and video services with data rates up to 2 Mb/s (UMTS allows variable bit rates to offer bandwidth on demand), and guarantees different QoS requirements on a single connection (from delay-sensitive real-time traffic to flexible best-effort packet data) (Holma, 2007). To make this possible, UMTS adopts the 4-QAM modulation in a larger bandwidth with respect to GSM and GPRS (both FDD and TDD duplexing modes are available: in FDD-mode two separate bands of 5 MHz are adopted for the uplink and downlink respectively, whereas in TDD-mode a

5 MHz band is time shared between the uplink and the downlink), and a CDMA technique is adopted for the multiple access. This way, all users share the same bandwidth at the same time, being identified by spreading codes. Data bits are, in fact, multiplied by pseudo-random spreading codes with a fixed chip rate of 3.84 Mchip/s. To support variable data rates services, the use of variable spreading factors and multi-code connections is foreseen.

This technique allows a unitary frequency reuse between different cells, giving higher spectral efficiency with respect to 2G and 2.5G systems. At the same time, the use of tight power control strategies and soft handover is required to reduce the amount of mutual interference among users.

The need for additional wireless capacity as well as the need for lower cost data delivery and the competition of other wireless technologies (such as WiMAX) forced UMTS to evolve toward HSPA (3.5G) with data rates up to 28 Mb/s in the downlink and 7 Mb/s in the uplink, and toward LTE (4G) that will provide data rates up to 1 Gb/s in downlink and 500 Mb/s in uplink.

While HSPA is still CDMA based, LTE will be based on OFDMA in the downlink and SC-FDMA in the uplink, and through the adoption of adaptive modulation and coding schemes as well as MIMO techniques, it will drastically improve the spectral efficiency, reduce the latency, and increase the system flexibility.

Among these cellular technologies, GSM and GPRS are still the most widespread; for this reason current top-level satellite navigators usually embed GSM/GPRS devices in order to transmit and receive updated road traffic information. Thanks to the already existent communication infrastructure the immediate provision of advanced ITS services is thus possible. On the other hand the cellular network is loaded with a new kind of data traffic (short and frequent transmissions of measured data performed by OBUs in the uplink and traffic updates or other information transmitted toward OBUs in the downlink, to and from a high number of vehicles) that reduces the amount of resources available for other cellular services.

It is likely, therefore, that in the next future new short range technologies will be taken into account to provide real time services supporting vehicular mobility, even though new on board and roadside equipments will be needed: communication links will be dynamically established to support V2V and V2R communications and will be probably based on the WAVE IEEE 802.11p technology hereafter discussed.

WAVE IEEE 802.11p

Vehicular ad hoc networks allow V2V and V2R communications without depending on cellular networks in order to address real time services concerning, for instance, road safety, road-charge, gateway access, awareness of parking lots, etc.

On this regard, IEEE created the 802.11p working group, whose task was the definition of a new standard for V2V and V2R communications. An amendment to the IEEE 802.11 standard was finally released in 2010, aimed at improving wireless access in vehicular environments and at supporting ITS applications in the licensed 5.9 GHz band.

The IEEE 802.11p amendment is part of the so-called WAVE standard, which defines an architecture and a complementary set of services and interfaces (WAVE, 2006; IEEE 802.11p, 2010).

The IEEE 802.11p physical layer is based on the OFDM multi-carrier modulation; each subcarrier is adaptively modulated and coded to provide communication capabilities of 3, 4.5, 6, 9, 12, 18, 24, and 27 Mb/s. Low rates will most likely be chosen for safety applications, owing to the high reliability requirement of this kind of services, whereas higher rates will be adopted for multimedia and commercial purposes (Bai, 2011; Kiokes, 2009; Karedal, 2011; Sen, 2008).

The multiple access is based on the Enhanced Distributed Channel Access (EDCA) technique. EDCA uses the CSMA/CA strategy, meaning that network nodes listen to the wireless channel before transmitting, in order to avoid collisions (Sikdar, 2008; Menouar, 2006).

The key purpose of the IEEE 802.11p amendment at the MAC level is to enable very efficient communication group setup without much of the overhead typically needed in the nomadic IEEE 802.11 MAC, simplifying the Basic Service Set (BSS) operations in a truly ad hoc manner for vehicular usage. For instance, the transmission of alert messages cannot subdue the conventional channel-scanning procedure of the IEEE802.11 standard and to the subsequent multiple handshakes phase. A key amendment introduced by WAVE/IEEE 802.11p is thus the "WAVE mode": a station in WAVE mode is allowed to transmit and receive data frames with the wildcard BSS identity (ID) value and without the need to belong to a particular BSS. Hence, two vehicles can immediately communicate in a very short time without any additional overhead as long as they operate in the same channel using the wildcard BSSID (Jiang, 2008).

TAKING ADVANTAGE OF V2V AND V2R FOR ROADS SENSING

The main issue concerning intelligent transportation services is the burden that weighs on the cellular network, which, at the present time, is the only technology in charge of conveying all data collected by on-board devices to the control center by means of the V2I interface.

In a scenario where a relevant fraction of vehicles will be equipped with on-board traffic-monitoring devices, this could be a significant drawback, which affects the service cost, the experienced quality of service, and the network efficiency.

In order to overcome this obstacle, the V2I communication interface could be assisted by V2V and V2R communications interfaces. The former would help reducing the amount of data to be transmitted to the control center, allowing the deletion of packets that, although collected by different vehicles, carry information on the same road, while the latter would be adopted (when available) instead of the V2I interface to convey collected data to the control center.

In the following paragraphs, the benefits provided by V2V and V2R communications are assessed considering realistic conditions. In particular, we assume as reference scenario a portion of the Italian city of Bologna and we investigate three different cases:

- Vehicles are equipped with the V2I cellular interface only (GPRS, for instance) (see Figure 1),
- Vehicles are also equipped with an additional V2V communication interface (IEEE 802.11p) (see Figure 2),
- Vehicles have also V2R communication capabilities (IEEE 802.11p, for instance) (see Figure 3).

When the V2V technology is available, each vehicle communicates with those that are within its coverage distance: following some strategies (that will be detailed in the following), nearby vehicles elect a master and transmit to it all their

data. The master is then in charge of transmitting all collected data to the control center; to this aim, V2R connections will be exploited whenever available, otherwise the cellular V2I interface will be used.

Scenario and Performance Metrics

In order to assess the benefits of V2V and V2R communications in the scenario here considered, we performed simulations under realistic traffic conditions.

The road-network layout of a portion (1.6 x 1.8 squared kilometers) of the city of Bologna (see Figure 4) has been provided as input to the microscopic traffic simulation tool Vissim (2010), that reproduces the movements of vehicles on roads, allowing to consider realistic sources and destinations, as well as movements constrained by the 3-D structure of vehicles and by road rules (Vissim, 2010; Toppan, 2010).

The digital-map of the road network has been provided by Tele Atlas (Tele Atlas, 2009).

We assume that vehicles are equipped with a cellular communication interface for V2I connections and (when present) with the IEEE 802.11p communication interface for short-range V2V and V2R connections.

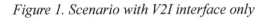

Figure 1. Scenario with V2I interface only

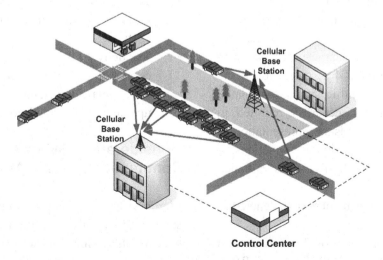

Figure 2. Scenario with V2I and V2V interfaces

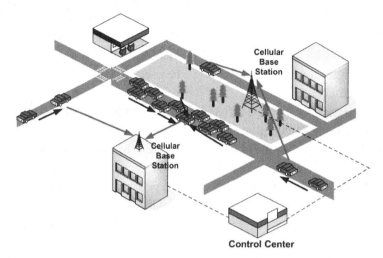

A parametric percentage of vehicles moving in the scenario is assumed equipped with an OBU, that periodically acquires several vehicle related parameters, such as speed and position (which are referred in the following as "measured data").

The following conditions will be considered for numerical results:

- Both normal traffic conditions, characterized by a smooth vehicular flow (hereafter denoted as normal traffic), and congested traffic conditions, with car-queues arising in the proximity of many crossroads (hereafter denoted as heavy traffic). The former scenario is characterized by 150 vehicles per squared kilometer, in average, whereas an average density of 230 vehicles per squared kilometer characterizes the latter scenario. In Figure 4 a screenshot of the Vissim dynamic traffic simulation related to the heavy traffic scenario is reported, in order to provide a visual representation of traffic conditions nearby busy junctions.
- Either 10% or 100% of vehicles equipped with the OBU;
- A variable measurement period, denoted as SamplingInterval;
- A radio coverage range of 30 m for V2V and V2R; this distance results from an EIRP of

0 dBm, a receiver sensitivity of -88 dBm, an antenna gain plus power losses at the receiver of 0 dB, and the following path-loss expressed in dB: $PL(d)=PL_f(1)+27.5 \log_{10}(d)$, where $PL_f(d)$ is the free space path loss and d is expressed in meters (Cheng, 2007).

Measured data are stored in the OBUs transmission queues and then transmitted according to strategies that will be discussed in the following. The use of V2V and V2R is envisioned in order to reduce:

- The cellular network load, which represents the main component of the service cost;
- The delivery delay, that impacts on the accuracy of the traffic conditions estimation; lower delay, in fact, means a more frequent update of traffic conditions.

Considerations When Only V2I Communications are Available

Moreover, an overly short SamplingInterval would surely lead to highly correlated measurements and thus to highly redundant data. In order to highlight this effect, the percentage of measurements that in

Figure 3. Scenario with V2I, V2V, and V2R interfaces

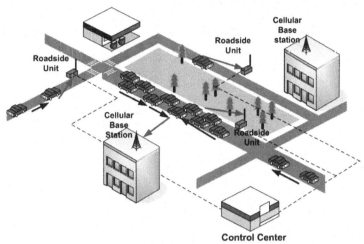

average refer to a new road segment is shown in Figure 5 as a function of SamplingInterval for both the normal and the heavy traffic scenarios; it can be noticed that assuming SamplingInterval lower than 20 seconds in the more crowded scenario leads to about the 10% of measurements referring to a road segment already monitored (road segments refer to the Tele Atlas cartography).

Of course, these results refer to the particular road layouts of our scenario. Nonetheless, they provide an insight on the order of magnitude of reasonable values for SamplingInterval.

As far as the transmission of measured data to the control centre is concerned, a dedicated cellular (tipically GPRS) physical channel is usually assigned; in order to make the unavoidable signalling overhead negligible with respect to the amount of data to be transmitted, a certain number of measurements must be collected before starting the transmission through the V2I interface. Of course,

Figure 4. Realistic scenario considered for numerical results

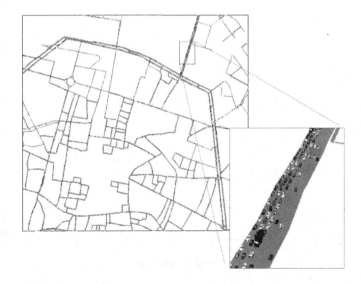

Figure 5. Average ratio of packets generated by the generic OBU that refer to a new road, considering both the normal traffic and the heavy traffic scenarios

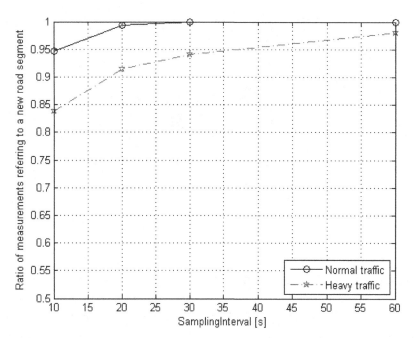

Figure 6. Average ratio of V2I resources that can be saved thanks to the adoption of V2V communication, if measurements referred to the same road segment are merged together before transmission to the control centre

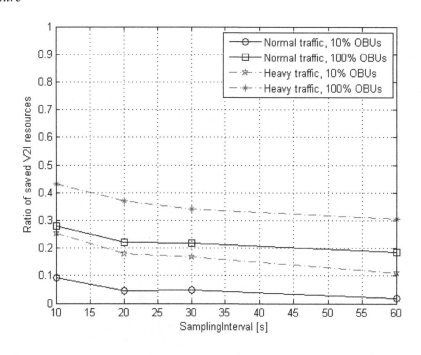

Figure 7. Average delivery delay exploiting V2V communication

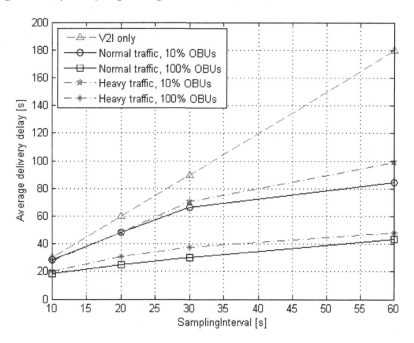

increasing the number of measurements collected for a single transmission session increases the average delivery delay as well. This entails that a trade-off between the signalling overhead and the delivery delay must be sought. Hereafter we assume that the V2I communication is performed when one of the following conditions occurs:

- A given NMaxPackets threshold of packets waiting in the transmission queue is reached;
- The waiting time of the first packet in the queue exceeds a given TimeOut threshold.

Please note that when only the V2I interface is available, one of the two limits is always more stringent than the other; in particular, the NMaxPackets threshold is always reached before the TimeOut threshold if NMaxPackets · SamplingInterval < TimeOut.

When, on the contrary, also V2V communications are envisioned (as done in the following paragraph), either one or the other condition may occur.

Taking Advantage of V2V Communication

Let us discuss, now, the benefits achievable when a V2V communication interface is also available, in addition to the V2I interface. Although the V2I interface must still be used to finally reach the remote control center, packets collected in the transmission queue can be passed from one vehicle to another by means of V2V communications, thus providing two potential benefits: on the one hand, measurements referring to the same road segments (carried out by different vehicles) could be merged together, thus avoiding duplicated information and reducing the overall V2I load; on the other hand, a higher number of packets could be "concentrated" in the same vehicle (the master), whose transmission queue will reach the NMaxPackets threshold more quickly, thus reducing the average delivery delay.

With the aim to minimize delivery delay, the following strategy is assumed: vehicles under radio visibility transmit all their queued packets to the one with the highest number of queued packets,

Figure 8. CDF of delivery delay exploiting V2V communication: SamplingInterval=30 s

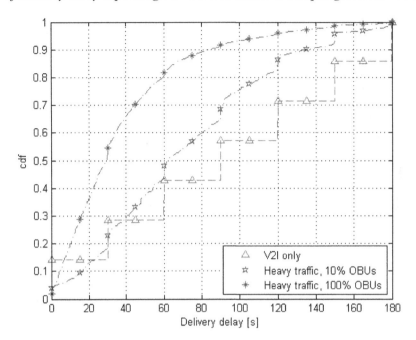

that becomes the master; in case of same queue length the master is randomly selected. In the master's queue, measurements are then compared, and those referred to the same road segment (and the same direction) are merged together in order to reduce the overall V2I load without lowering the information given to the control centre. As previously introduced, packets are finally trans-

Figure 9. Reference scenario with RSU sites

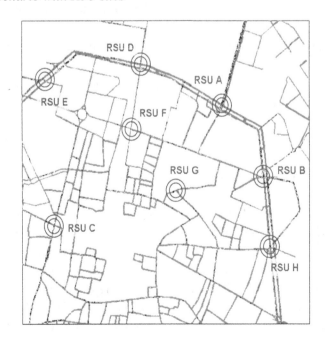

Figure 10. Average ratio of V2I resources that can be saved thanks to the adoption of V2V and V2R communication

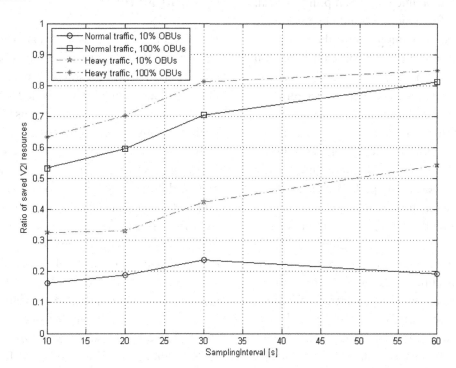

mitted through V2I when either NMaxPackets or TimeOut are reached.

Numerical results are hereafter shown in the reference scenario, assuming NMaxPackets =10 and TimeOut = M · SamplingInterval, with M=6.

On this regard, Figure 6 shows the V2I resource saving, provided by the additional V2V interface, in terms of the ratio between packets that are not transmitted through the cellular network and all packets reaching the remote control centre; resource saving is given as a function of Sampling Interval, varying the traffic conditions and the percentage of vehicles equipped with the OBU.

It can be noticed that all the considered parameters have a significant impact on resource saving: both a higher traffic density and a higher penetration of OBUs make V2V more effective. In particular, the use of V2V communications allows even 40% of resource saving in heavy traffic conditions if all the vehicles are equipped

with the OBU. It must be observed, however, that in normal traffic conditions with a limited penetration of the service (e.g., 10% of vehicles equipped with OBUs), only a small percentage of V2I resources can be saved: as expected, the introduction of the V2V interface does not provide a significant benefit when only few vehicles can rely on it.

Let us discuss now the impact of V2V communications in terms of delivery time. With our settings, in the presence of the sole V2I interface M packets are always collected before transmission, since NMaxPackets is never reached. This means that the average delivery delay is deterministic and equal to TimeOut/2. When, on the contrary, also the V2V interface is available, some vehicles (the masters) act as packets concentrators, thus their NMaxPackets threshold is easily exceeded before TimeOut expiration. Results, in terms of delivery delay, are shown in Figures 7 and 8.

Figure 7 shows, in particular, the average delivery delay as a function of SamplingInterval, varying the traffic conditions and the percentage of vehicles that are equipped with the OBU.

As can be observed, a significant reduction of the delivery delay can be obtained exploiting V2V communications. This benefit is negligible only with a too short SamplingInterval and a very limited penetration of OBUs. A reduction of 75% of the average delay is achieved, on the contrary, in the case of heavy traffic, SamplingInterval=60 s, and 100% vehicles equipped with OBUs. It can be also noticed that traffic conditions have a very minor impact on the average delay reduction.

In order to deepen our investigation on the delivery delay, in Figure 8 we reported the cumulative distribution function (cdf) of delivery delay. Here we assumed heavy traffic conditions and SamplingInterval=30 s; results for both 10% and 100% equipped vehicles are compared to the case where V2I only is assumed. The relevant impact of the percentage of OBU penetration is clearly evident.

Taking Advantage of V2R Communication

Besides the advantages that can be achieved exploiting V2V communication, a significant reduction in transmission costs and delivery delay can be obtained if Roadside Units (RSUs) are deployed in strategic positions. Delivering packets through V2R interfaces allows, in fact, a significant reduction of V2I transmissions.

In this section both the V2I resource saving and the delivery delay reduction are shown when both V2V and V2R interfaces are available and used according to the following strategy: vehicles under RSUs coverage immediately transmit their queued packets by means of the V2R interface, while all other vehicles use the V2V interface to move all measured data to the vehicle nearest (in the sense of Euclidian distance) to the RSUs (the distance is assessed by each OBU exploiting GPS information). The position of RSUs is assumed known by OBUs (for instance, either due to on-board roadmaps with OBUs' coordinates or because the remote control center periodically

Figure 11. CDF of delivery delay exploiting V2V and V2R communication: SamplingInterval=30 s

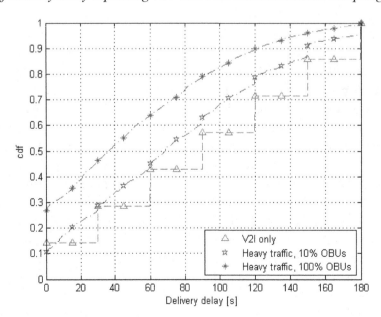

Figure 12. Impact of RSU sites on the average ratio of V2I resources that can be saved thanks to the adoption of V2V and V2R communication. Heavy traffic, 100% vehicles equipped with OBUs.

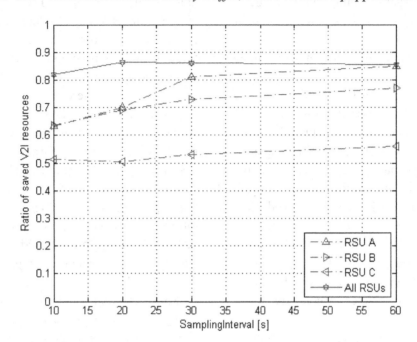

sends the coordinates of OBUs in the surrounding). When neither a RSU nor other useful vehicles are within the coverage distance before TimeOut is exceeded or before NMaxPackets is reached, packets are transmitted through the V2I interface.

The simple greedy forwarding routing algorithm above described, also known as most forward within the transmission radii (MRF) (Takagi, 1984), was chosen in order to minimize costs and complexity. This protocol, in fact, only requires that each vehicle knows its own position and the position of the 1-hop neighbors, allowing low processing burden and memory occupation.

Of course the positions of RSUs have a significant impact on the achievable performance. The sites we considered for RSUs deployment in our reference scenario are shown in Figure 9, corresponding to the mostly crowded junctions. Major junctions are suitable sites also owing to the likely presence of lighting/traffic lights and therefore of power supply.

Let us start, however, our investigation considering a simpler scenario, with only RSU A:

RSU A is positioned, in particular, in the busiest crossroad of the whole scenario.

The average ratio of saved V2I resources that can be achieved in this case, taking advantage of both V2V and V2R communications, is shown in Figure 10 as a function of SamplingInterval, the traffic conditions, and the percentage of vehicles equipped with the OBU. To increase the probability to reach the RSU before the deadline for transmission over the cellular link, without excessively increase the average delay, NMaxPackets is here set to a very high value (i.e., 1000) in order that the TimeOut (with M=6) is always reached first.

Results show that even when a single, but properly positioned, RSU is deployed in large area a significant amount of data can be transmitted to the V2R interface thanks to the joint adoption of V2V communications. Let us observe, in fact, that even with a small SamplingInterval (lower than 30 s) and only the 10% of vehicles equipped with OBUs, the resource saving is still significant (about 20% in the case of normal traffic conditions).

Note that the amount of saved resources increases with larger sampling intervals due to a higher probability to meet a RSU in a longer lasting time interval.

Clearly, the primary objective of the assumed strategy is to foster V2R communications: packets are, in fact, concentrated in those vehicles moving towards the RSU (whereas in the absence of V2R interfaces information was concentrated in those vehicles having the highest number of queued packets). The drawback of this choice is that the average delivery delay is increased with respect to the one achieved with the strategy adopted when V2R was not available. The impact on delay is shown in Figure 11, where the cdf of delivery delay is shown assuming heavy traffic conditions, and SamplingInterval=30 s; results for both 10% and 100% equipped vehicles are compared to the case with V2I only.

The comparison of Figure 11 with Figure 8 confirms that the assumed strategy has worse performance in terms of delay with respect to the one adopted when only V2I and V2V are available; as shown in Figure 11; however, when a large amount of equipped vehicles moves on roads (giving a high probability to reach the RSUs through multi-hop communications among vehicles), delay is still significantly lower with respect to the case where only V2I is assumed.

So far, only a single RSU has been considered which is located in the most crowded junction of the investigated scenario. Of course, the impact of RSUs position on the achievable benefit they can provide is very relevant: in order to investigate this aspect we report in Figure 12 the average ratio of saved V2I resources considering different positions of a single RSU (RSU A, RSU B, and RSU C) and, as element of comparison, all RSUs depicted in Figure 9.

For the sake of conciseness, only the case of heavy traffic and 100% equipped vehicles is considered. Curves are shown as a function of the SamplingInterval.

Figure 13. Comparison of the average ratio of V2I resources that can be saved thanks to the adoption of either V2V and V2R or V2R only communication. Heavy traffic, 100% vehicles equipped with OBUs.

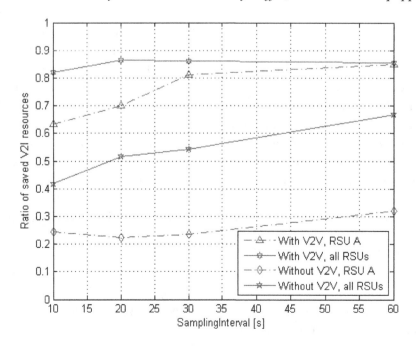

Observing Figure 12, we can infer that RSU B and RSU C, being located in less busy junctions, are less effective than RSU A, owing to lower number of vehicles passing in their proximity. Furthermore, comparing the benefit provided by RSU A to the one achievable with all RSUs simultaneously active we can infer that the advantage obtained deploying all RSUs is not very high with respect to the one achievable deploying only RSU A and would probably not justify the investments required.

The great effectiveness of RSU A suggests that a relevant role is played also by V2V communications. It is likely, in fact, that also vehicles not passing in the proximity of RSU A manage transmitting their information to vehicles moving toward RSU A (which is in a very strategic position), thus increasing its effectiveness.

In order to highlight the combined effect of V2V and V2R communications we also considered a scenario where no V2V information exchange takes place. The outcomes of our investigation are reported in Figure 13, which refers to both the extreme cases of all active RSUs (see Figure 9) and only RSU A active.

Here we can observe that the effectiveness of the roadside infrastructure is significantly enhanced by the joint adoption of V2V communications, thus confirming the synergy of the two communication strategies.

Of course, when the V2V interface is not available the number of deployed RSUs becomes decisive in order to reduce cellular communications through the V2I interface.

FUTURE RESEARCH DIRECTIONS

Different and adaptive strategies could be considered for V2V and V2R communications. In fact, depending on the environment and on the number of equipped vehicles, the propagation channel can be more or less critical, suggesting from time to time to communicate with the nearest vehicle, rather than with the vehicle moving toward the roadside beacon, and adaptively change the communication strategy on the basis of:

- The radio propagation conditions: in dense urban environments affected by interference, in fact, the hidden node problem could have a not negligible impact on the number of collisions;
- The foreseen application: for instance, when traffic management applications are foreseen, in congested scenarios less updates per vehicle are necessary than in fluent traffic conditions.

Furthermore, the reader may observe that, in spite of the fact that the focus of this chapter is on the acquisition of traffic information in the uplink (i.e., from vehicles to a control center), also the transmission of information in the downlink have a great impact on the communication network load. Hence, roadside units could also be exploited to:

- Broadcast to all vehicles in their proximity information on the traffic in the surroundings;
- Transmit dedicated information upon requests.

In any case, a deep investigation on the performance of vehicular networks comparing broadcast and unicast transmission strategies, and the impact on the road traffic has still to be performed.

CONCLUSION

In this chapter, we investigated the benefits arising from the adoption of V2V and V2R communication interfaces, in addition to the cellular V2I interface, in a scenario where vehicles equipped with on board units periodically acquire and transmit information on vehicle's position and speed.

The benefits provided by V2V and V2R communications have been derived in terms of reduction of cellular resource usage and of packet delivery delay. It was shown, in particular, that even without V2R communications the 30-40% of the cellular network resources can be saved thanks to V2V communications, that allow the aggregation of information related to the same road segment, with up to the 70-75% reduction of the average delivery delay. A further significant reduction of cellular network load (up to 80-90%) was gained through the introduction of RSUs and V2R communications.

Furthermore, it is important to observe that it is the joint adoption of V2V and V2R communications that allows a reduction of more than the 80% of cellular resources and that such result is achieved even with a very limited number of deployed RSUs.

ACKNOWLEDGMENT

Authors would like to thank all colleagues at Wilab (www.wilab.org) and, in particular, Prof. O. Andrisano.

© 2012 IEEE. Reprinted, with permission, from A. Bazzi, B. M. Masini, G. Pasolini, "V2V and V2R for Cellular Resources Saving in Vehicular Apllications," IEEE Wireless Communications and Networking Conference (WCNC), Apr. 2012.

REFERENCES

Aktiv CoCar Project. (2009). *Website.* Retrieved from http://www.aktiv-online.org/english/aktiv-cocar.html

Bai, B., Chen, W., Letaief, K., & Cao, Z. (2011). Low complexity outage optimal distributed channel allocation for vehicle-to-vehicle communications. *IEEE Journal on Selected Areas in Communications, 29*(1), 161–172. doi:10.1109/JSAC.2011.110116

Bazzi, A., Masini, B. M., & Andrisano, O. (2010). On the impact of real time data acquisition from vehicles through UMTS. In *Proceedings of the IEEE International Symposium on Personal, Indoor and Mobile Radio Communications, PIMRC.* Istanbul, Turkey: IEEE Press.

Bazzi, A., Pasolini, G., & Gambetti, C. (2006). SHINE: Simulation platform for heterogeneous interworking networks. In *Proceedings of the IEEE International Conference on Communications,* (Vol. 12, pp. 5534-5539). IEEE Press.

Campolo, C., & Molinaro, A. (2010). Vehicle-to-roadside multihop data delivery in 802.11p/WAVE vehicular ad hoc networks. In *Proceedings of the GLOBECOM, IEEE Global Telecommunications Conference,* (pp. 1 –5). IEEE Press.

Cheng, L., Henty, B. E., Stancil, D. D., Bai, F., & Mudalige, P. (2007). Mobile vehicle-to-vehicle narrow-band channel measurement and characterization of the 5.9 GHz dedicated short range communication (DSRC) frequency band. *IEEE Journal on Selected Areas in Communications, 25*(8), 1501–1516. doi:10.1109/JSAC.2007.071002

Conti, A., Bazzi, A., Masini, B. M., & Andrisano, O. (2009). *Vehicular networks: Techniques, standards, and applications.* Boca Raton, FL: Auerbach Publications.

Eichler, S. (2007). Performance evaluation of the IEEE 802.11p WAVE communication standard. In *Proceedings of the Vehicular Technology Conference,* (pp. 2199 –2203). IEEE Press.

Gukhool, B., & Cherkaoui, S. (2008). IEEE 802.11p modeling in ns-2. In *Proceedings of the 33rd IEEE Conference on Local Computer Networks, LCN,* (pp. 622–626). IEEE Press.

Holma, H., & Toskala, A. (2004). *WCDMA for UMTS - Radio access for third generation mobile communications* (4th ed.). New York, NY: Wiley.

IEEE 802.11p. (2010). *Standard for information technology- Telecommunications and information exchange between systems- Local and metropolitan area networks-Specific requirements part 11 - Amendment 6: Wireless access in vehicular environment.* Washington, DC: IEEE.

Jerbi, M., Senouci, S.-M., Rasheed, T., & Ghamri-Doudane, Y. (2009). Towards efficient geographic routing in urban vehicular networks. *IEEE Transactions on Vehicular Technology, 58*(9), 5048–5059. doi:10.1109/TVT.2009.2024341

Jiang, D., & Delgrossi, L. (2008). IEEE 802.11p: Towards an international standard for wireless access in vehicular environments. In *Proceedings of the Vehicular Technology Conference, VTC Spring*, (pp. 2036–2040). IEEE Press.

Karedal, J., Czink, N., Paier, A., Tufvesson, F., & Molisch, A. F. (2011). Path loss modeling for vehicle-to-vehicle communications. *IEEE Transactions on Vehicular Technology, 60*(1), 323–328. doi:10.1109/TVT.2010.2094632

Karp, B. N. (2000). *Geographic routing for wireless networks.* Boston, MA: Harvard University.

Kiokes, G., Amditis, A., & Uzunoglu, N. K. (2009). Simulation-based performance analysis and improvement of orthogonal frequency division multiplexing – 802.11p system for vehicular communications. In *Proceedings of the IET Intelligent Transport Systems*, (pp. 429–436). IET.

Li, F., & Wang, Y. (2007). Routing in vehicular ad hoc networks: A survey. *IEEE Vehicular Technology Magazine, 2*(2), 12–22. doi:10.1109/MVT.2007.912927

Martinez, F., Toh, C.-K., Cano, J.-C., Calafate, C., & Manzoni, P. (2009). Realistic radio propagation models (rpms) for VANET simulations. In *Proceedings of the Wireless Communications and Networking Conference, WCNC*, (pp. 1–6). IEEE Press.

Masini, B. M., Fontana, C., & Verdone, R. (2004). Provision of an emergency warning service through GPRS: Performance evaluation. In *Proceedings. The 7th International IEEE Conference on Intelligent Transportation Systems*, (pp. 1098-1102). IEEE Press.

Masini, B. M., Zuliani, L., & Andrisano, O. (2006). On the effectiveness of a GPRS based intelligent transportation system in a realistic scenario. In *Proceedings of the IEEE Vehicular Technology Conference, VTC*, (vol. 6, pp. 2997-3001). IEEE Press.

Menouar, H., Filali, F., & Lenardi, M. (2006). A survey and qualitative analysis of MAC protocols for vehicular ad hoc networks. *IEEE Wireless Communication, 13*, 30–35. doi:10.1109/WC-M.2006.250355

Sen, I., & Matolak, D. (2008). Vehicle-vehicle channel models for the 5- Ghz band. *IEEE Transactions on Intelligent Transportation Systems, 9*(2), 235–245. doi:10.1109/TITS.2008.922881

Sikdar, B. (2008). Design and analysis of a MAC protocol for vehicle to roadside networks. In *Proceedings of the Wireless Communications and Networking Conference*, (pp. 1525-3511). IEEE.

Stibor, L., Zang, Y., & Reumerman, H.-J. (2007). Evaluation of communication distance of broadcast messages in a vehicular ad-hoc network using IEEE 802.11p. In *Proceedings of the IEEE Wireless Communications and Networking Conference, WCNC*, (pp. 254–257). IEEE Press.

Takagi, H., & Kleinrock, L. (1984). Optimal transmission ranges for randomly distributed packet radio terminals. *IEEE Transactions on Communications, 32*(3), 246–257. doi:10.1109/TCOM.1984.1096061

TeleAtlas. (2010). *Web site.* Retrieved from http://www.teleatlas.com

Toppan, A., Bazzi, A., Toppan, P., Masini, B. M., & Andrisano, O. (2010). Architecture of a simulation platform for the smart navigation service investigation. In *Proceedings of the 16th International Conference on Wireless and Mobile Computing, Networking and Communications (WiMob),* (pp. 548 –554). IEEE Press.

Uzcategui, R., & Acosta-Marum, G. (2009). WAVE: A tutorial. *IEEE Communications Magazine, 47*(5), 126–133. doi:10.1109/MCOM.2009.4939288

Vissim. (2009). *Website.* Retrieved from http://www.ptvamerica.com/software/ptv-vision/vissim/

Wang, Y., Ahmed, A., Krishnamachari, B., & Psounis, K. (2008). IEEE 802.11p performance evaluation and protocol enhancement. *ICVES IEEE International Conference on Vehicular Electronics and Safety,* (pp. 317-322). IEEE Press.

WAVE. (2006). *IEEE trial-use standard for wireless access in vehicular environments (WAVE) - Multi-channel operation, standard.* Washington, DC: IEEE.

ADDITIONAL READING

Andrisano, O., Verdone, R., & Nakagawa, M. (2000). Intelligent transportation systems: The role of third-generation mobile radio networks. *IEEE Communications Magazine, 38*(9), 144–151. doi:10.1109/35.868154

ASTM. (2003). *Standard specification for telecommunications and information exchange between roadside and vehicle systems — 5 GHz band dedicated short range communications (DSRC) medium access control (MAC) and physical layer (PHY).* ASTM E2213-03. Retrieved from http://www.astm.org/Standards/E2213.htm

Bazzi, A., Masini, B. M., Conti, A., & Andrisano, O. (2008). Infomobility provision through MBMS/UMTS in realistic scenarios. In *Proceedings of the ITSC 11th International IEEE Conference on Intelligent Transportation Systems,* (pp. 25-30). IEEE Press.

Bazzi, A., Masini, B. M., Pasolini, G., & Torreggiani, P. M. (2010). Telecommunication systems enabling real time navigation. In *Proceedings of the 13th International IEEE Conference on Intelligent Transportation Systems (ITSC),* (pp. 1057-1064). IEEE Press.

Blum, J., & Eskandarian, A. (2006). Fast, robust message forwarding for inter-vehicle communication networks. In *Proceedings of the IEEE Intelligent Transportation System Conference,* (pp. 1418–1423). IEEE Press.

Blum, J., Eskandarian, A., & Hoffman, L. (2003). Mobility management in IVC networks. In *Proceedings of the IEEE Intelligent Vehicles Symposium,* (pp. 150–155). IEEE Press.

Blum, J., Eskandarian, A., & Hoffman, L. (2004). Challenges of intervehicle ad hoc networks. *IEEE Transactions on Intelligent Transportation Systems, 5*(4), 347–351. doi:10.1109/TITS.2004.838218

Briesemeister, L., Schäfers, L., & Hommel, G. (2000). Messages among highly mobile hosts based on inter-vehicle communication. In *Proceedings of the IEEE Intelligent Vehicle Symposium,* (pp. 522–527). IEEE Press.

Car2Car Communication Consortium. (2012). *Website.* Retrieved from http://www.car-to-car.org

Cartalk. (2000). *Website.* Retrieved from http://www.cartalk2000.net

COMeSafety. (2012). *Website.* Retrieved from http://www.comesafety.org

Drive-Thru Internet Project. (2012). *Website.* Retrieved from http://www.drive-thru-internet. org/index.html

Fujii, H., Hayashi, O., & Nakagata, N. (1996). Experimental research on inter-vehicle communication using infrared rays. In *Proceedings of the IEEE Intelligent Vehicles Symposium*, (pp. 266–271). IEEE Press.

Hui, F. W., & Mohapatra, P. (2005). Experimental characterization of multi-hop communications in vehicular ad hoc network. In *Proceedings of the 2nd ACM International Workshop on Vehicular Ad Hoc Networks*. ACM Press.

Katragadda, S. (2003). A decentralized location-based channel access protocol for inter-vehicle communication. In *Proceedings of the 57th IEEE Vehicular Technology Conference*, (pp. 1831–1835). IEEE Press.

Kosch, T., Schwingenschlögl, C., & Ai, L. (2002). Information dissemination in multihop inter-vehicle networks. In *Proceedings of the 5th IEEE International Conference on Intelligent Transportation Systems*, (pp. 685–690). IEEE Press.

Liu, Y., Ozgüner, U., & Acarman, T. (2006). Performance evaluation of inter-vehicle communication in highway systems and in urban areas. *IEEE Intelligent Transportation Systems, 153*, 63–75. doi:10.1049/ip-its:20055013

Maeshima, O., Cai, S., Honda, T., Urayama, H., & Taira, A. (2007). Transmission performance evaluation of a roadside-to-vehicle communication system with antenna beam switching. In *Proceedings of the 3rd International Workshop on Vehicle-to-Vehicle Communications*, (pp. 35-41). Istanbul, Turkey: IEEE Press.

Michael, L. B., Kikuchi, S., Adachi, T., & Nakagawa, M. (2000). Combined cellular/direct method of inter-vehicle communication. In *Proceedings of the Intelligent Vehicles Symposium*, (pp. 534-539). IEEE Press.

Ming-Fong, J., & Wanjiun, L. (2008). On cooperative and opportunistic channel access for vehicle to roadside (V2R) communications. In *Proceedings of the IEEE Global Telecommunications Conference*, (pp. 1-5). IEEE Press.

Nagaosa, T., & Hasegawa, T. (2000). A new scheme of nearby vehicles' positions recognition and inter-vehicle communication without signal collision — V-PEACE scheme. In *Proceedings of the 51st IEEE Vehicular Technology Conference*, (pp. 1616–1620). IEEE Press.

Network-on-Wheels. (2012). *Website.* Retrieved from http://www.network-on-wheels.de/vision. html

Niyato, D., & Hossain, E. (2010). A unified framework for optimal wireless access for data streaming over vehicle-to-roadside communications. *IEEE Transactions on Vehicular Technology, 59*(6), 3025–3035. doi:10.1109/TVT.2010.2048769

Niyato, D., Hossain, E., & Wang, P. (2009). Competitive wireless access for data streaming over vehicle-to-roadside communications. In *Proceedings of the IEEE Global Telecommunications Conference*, (pp. 1-6). IEEE Press.

Pasolini, G., & Verdone, R. (2002). Bluetooth for ITS? In *Proceedings of the 5th IEEE International Symposium on Wireless Personal Multimedia Communication*, (pp. 315–319). IEEE Press.

Path. (2012). *Website.* Retrieved from http://www. path.berkeley.edu

Rongyan, X., Chen, Y., & Dongdong, Z. (2010). Vehicle to vehicle and roadside sensor communication for intelligent navigation. In *Proceedings of the 6th International Conference on Wireless Communications Networking and Mobile Computing (WiCOM)*, (pp. 1-4). WiCOM.

SAFESPOT. (2012). *Website.* Retrieved from http://www.safespot-eu.org

Sikdar, B. (2008). Medium access control in vehicle to roadside networks. In *Proceedings of the IEEE International Conference on Communications*, (pp. 2830-2834). IEEE Press.

Sikdar, B. (2010). Characterization and abatement of the reassociation overhead in vehicle to roadside networks. *IEEE Transactions on Communications*, *58*(11), 3296–3304. doi:10.1109/TCOMM.2010.091310.090406

Sourour, E., & Nakagawa, M. (1999). Mutual decentralized synchronization for inter-vehicle communications. *IEEE Transactions on Vehicular Technology*, *48*(6), 2015–2027. doi:10.1109/25.806794

Sugiura, A., & Dermawan, C. (2005). In traffic jam IVC-RVC system for ITS using Bluetooth. *IEEE Transactions on Intelligent Transportation Systems*, *6*(3), 302–313. doi:10.1109/TITS.2005.853704

Tokuda, K. (2001). Applications of wireless communication technologies for intelligent transport systems. *Wireless Personal Communications*, *17*, 343–353. doi:10.1023/A:1011258622298

Wang, S. Y. (2006). Integrating inter-vehicle communication with roadside wireless access points to provide a lower-cost message broadcasting service on highways. In *Proceedings of the IEEE 17th International Symposium on Personal, Indoor and Mobile Radio Communications*, (pp. 1-5). IEEE Press.

Wang, S. Y. (2007). The potential of using inter-vehicle communication to extend the coverage area of roadside wireless access points on highways. *IEEE International Conference on Communications*, (pp. 6123-6128). IEEE Press.

Wischhof, L., Ebner, A., & Rohling, H. (2005). Information dissemination in self-organizing intervehicle networks. *IEEE Transactions on Intelligent Transportation Systems*, *6*(1), 90–101. doi:10.1109/TITS.2004.842407

Yamao, Y., & Minato, K. (2009). Vehicle-roadside-vehicle relay communication network employing multiple frequencies and routing function. In *Proceedings of the 6th International Symposium on Wireless Communication Systems*, (pp. 413-417). IEEE.

Yang, X., Liu, J., Zhao, F., & Vaidya, N. (2004). A vehicle-to-vehicle communication protocol for cooperative collision warning. In *Proceedings of the 1st Annual International Conference Mobile and Ubiquitous System: Networking and Services*, (pp. 1–4). IEEE.

Zhu, J., & Roy, S. (2003). MAC for dedicated short range communications in intelligent transport system. *IEEE Communications Magazine*, *41*(12), 60–67. doi:10.1109/MCOM.2003.1252800

Chapter 5
RSU Deployment for Content Dissemination and Downloading in Intelligent Transportation Systems

Massimo Reineri
Politecnico di Torino, Italy

Claudio Casetti
Politecnico di Torino, Italy

Carla-Fabiana Chiasserini
Politecnico di Torino, Italy

Marco Fiore
INSA Lyon, INRIA, France

Oscar Trullols-Cruces
Universitat Politecnica de Catalunya, Spain

Jose M. Barcelo-Ordinas
Universitat Politecnica de Catalunya, Spain

ABSTRACT

The focus of this chapter is twofold: information dissemination from infrastructure nodes deployed along the roads, the so-called Road-Side Units (RSUs), to passing-by vehicles, and content downloading by vehicular users through nearby RSUs. In particular, in order to ensure good performance for both content dissemination and downloading, the presented study addresses the problem of RSU deployment and reviews previous work that has dealt with such an issue. The RSU deployment problem is then formulated as an optimization problem, where the number of vehicles that come in contact with any RSU is maximized, possibly considering a minimum contact time to be guaranteed. Since such optimization problems turn out to be NP-hard, heuristics are proposed to efficiently approximate the optimal solution. The RSU deployment obtained through such heuristics is then used to investigate the performance of content dissemination and downloading through ns2 simulations. Simulation tests are carried out under various real-world vehicular environments, including a realistic mobility model, and considering that the IEEE 802.11p standard is used at the physical and medium access control layers. The performance obtained in realistic conditions is discussed with respect to the results obtained under the same RSU deployment, but in ideal conditions and protocol message exchange. Based on the obtained results, some useful hints on the network system design are provided.

DOI: 10.4018/978-1-4666-2223-4.ch005

INTRODUCTION

In most countries the time that a person spends in a car ranges between one and two hours per day. Thus, most carmakers are striving to create an in-vehicle environment which is as comfortable and entertaining as possible. Most newly manufactured vehicles boast multimedia capabilities that were once thought to belong to a living room, like LCD screens or gaming consoles. Such technological wealth, however, is not complemented with live features besides radio broadcasts. The presence of multiple LCD screens for passengers begs, as it were, for advanced infotainment services of various nature, ranging from email/social network access to more bandwidth-demanding contents, such as newscasts or local touristic clips. Without affecting drivers' attention, navigational aids may be integrated by short videos showing traffic congestion and recommending alternate routes. Furthermore, in keeping with the explosive growth of social networks, it is envisioned that car passengers may show a high interest in car-oriented social networking and multiplayer games. Finally, professional drivers could access services for efficient vehicle fleet coordination, up-to-the-minute updated goods deliveries or re-routing, and customized cab pick-ups.

Currently, the only connectivity option for vehicles amounts to accessing a 3G network, which could provide high-speed network availability but is hampered by restricted competition among network operators. In addition, the lack of a local infrastructure, which is specifically dedicated to geolocalized services, makes the realization of the above scenarios hard to implement and limits its features. However, the emergence of communication standards for vehicular networks is bringing new visions and opportunities that could come close to the always-connected paradigm. Globally referred to as Intelligent Transportation System (ITS), this new vision aims at improving transportation in terms of safety, mobility, traffic efficiency, impact on the environment, and productivity.

Motivated by such a vision, this Chapter deals with the dissemination of information from RSUs to vehicular users within a geographical region, as well as the downloading from RSUs of delay-tolerant (e.g., map services, touristic information) and bandwidth-demanding (e.g., video streaming) content, by passing-by vehicles. More specifically, the presented study tackles the issue of deploying an ITS infrastructure based on the IEEE 802.11p technology, which efficiently achieves the goal of information dissemination and downloading in spite of the fleeting connectivity, highly dynamic traffic patterns, and constrained node movements. To this end, the following key issues are investigated:

1. Assuming that an area, with an arbitrary road topology, must be equipped with a limited number k of infrastructure nodes, what is the best deployment strategy to maximize the dissemination process or the downloading throughput?
2. Given such an optimal RSU deployment, what is the actual throughput performance that can be achieved by users when realistic traces are used to represent the vehicular mobility?

The answers to the above questions are given in the remainder of the Chapter, which is organized as follows.

- The section entitled "Background" reviews existing approaches to the problem of optimal RSU deployment, and discuss them by highlighting the differences and the performance they can achieve.
- In the section entitled "RSU Deployment for Content Dissemination and Downloading," different formulations of the infrastructure deployment problem

are presented. The most complete one, referred to as Maximum Coverage with Time Threshold Problem (MCTTP), aims at guaranteeing that a large number of vehicles travel under the coverage of one or more RSUs for a sufficient amount of time. Such a formulation attempts to maximize the number of covered vehicles while ensuring a minimum coverage time to the users, and it can be adapted to the dissemination and downloading contexts by tuning a single parameter. The MCTTP is a more general case of the Maximum Coverage Problem (MCP), which is known to be NP-hard. Therefore, heuristic algorithms are presented, which exhibit different levels of complexity and require different knowledge on the system.

- Section "Mobility Scenarios" describes the real-world mobility scenarios we use in order to study the performance of content dissemination and downloading. Different mobility traces, including urban, suburban, and rural road topologies, where the vehicular mobility is reproduced by means of state-of-the-art simulators, are considered.

- The section titled "Performance Analysis of the Heuristics under Ideal Network Settings" uses the aforementioned heuristics to derive an optimal RSU deployment in the realistic mobility scenarios under study. In this case, ideal channel access and propagation conditions are considered and no protocol aspects are accounted for. The obtained results are analyzed in order to identify which regions of the road layout can be more efficiently served by RSUs, so that a large amount of vehicular users can be covered at a minimum deployment cost. Based on the outcome of the presented analysis, useful hints are derived that lead to planning guidelines, in terms of RSU number and position.

- Simulation results obtained through the network simulator ns2 are presented in the section entitled "Performance Analysis of the Heuristics in Realistic Environments." Again, real-world road topologies and vehicular traces are used. The optimal RSU deployment, computed as outlined above, is taken as an input to the simulation, and vehicular users are assumed to either receive the same information (dissemination service) or download a different information item each, from the fixed Internet through 802.11p RSUs. Using such a realistic simulation environment, the performance of content dissemination is evaluated in terms of percentage of informed vehicles and delay in receiving the information, while the performance of content downloading is studied in terms of per-user throughput and delay in starting the content retrieval.

- Finally, in the last section the major lessons learnt through the presented study are summarized and some guidelines for RSU deployment in ITSs are highlighted.

BACKGROUND

Several works in the literature have addressed the problem of the deployment of RSUs for vehicular access, although with a number of significantly different objectives. In this Chapter, the focus is on RSU deployments for (1) the dissemination of information to all vehicles in a geographic region, and (2) the downloading of content from Internet-based servers, by a subset of the vehicles.

The simplest solution possible to the RSU placement problem, i.e., a random deployment, is evaluated by Marfia (2007): such a strategy, representative of unplanned access networks like those identified in the real world by Bychkovsky (2006), is shown to help the routing of data within urban vehicular ad-hoc networks. Similarly, intuitive RSU deployments, that are not justified by means of a theoretical or experimental analysis, are evaluated by Ding (2007), with the goal of improving delay-tolerant routing among vehicles, by letting each AP work as a static cache for contents that have to be transferred between vehicles visiting it at different times. However, although they benefit from the routing process, random or intuitive placements cannot represent, in general, an optimal solution to the RSU deployment problem. Fiore (2009), Trullols-Cruces (2010) and Malandrino (2011) have demonstrated that such simple strategies are easily outperformed by more sound approaches, for both the dissemination and the downloading objectives. As a consequence, in the following the focus will be on deployment strategies that are instead built upon a precise placement rationale.

Firstly, note that standard maximum graph coverage approaches, such as those adopted by Krumke (2002), Whitaker (2005), Kim (2005), Oyman (2004), and Poe (2007) do not fit the RSU deployment problem as considered in this Chapter. Indeed, these placement strategies are designed for sensor or cellular networks, and thus assume that the infrastructure nodes form a connected network or provide a continuous coverage of the road topology. Moreover, many standard infrastructure deployment techniques have an energy efficiency goal that instead is not of interest in a vehicular environment.

Secondly, the mobility of vehicles is rather unique, as it obeys traffic regulations, is constrained by the street layout and alternates very high and very low speeds in relatively short times pans. As a consequence, the scenario differs significantly from those studied by Qiu (2004), which deals with the deployment of Internet access points in a static network, and by Hu (2009), which targets a mobile sensor network.

Zheng (2009) and Zheng (2010) target the maximization of the amount of time each vehicle is within range of at least one RSU, an objective that may be seen as beneficial for both the dis-

semination and downloading objectives. More precisely, these works formulate optimization problems whose solutions provide the RSU positions that maximize the coverage time. In the work by Zheng (2009), a minimum coverage requirement is guaranteed, while that by Zheng (2010) maximizes the minimum contact opportunity. However, both RSU deployment strategies assume that a predefined set of paths over a given road topology is provided, which makes their application limited to the particular case where only a subset of the total traffic is to be covered by RSUs.

Within the context of information dissemination to all vehicles in a geographical region, Ahn (2011) recently formulated an optimization problem that aims at maximizing the spreading of an information within a temporal horizon. However, this work assumes that RSU positions are given, and thus does not address the issue of the identification of the RSUs locations.

Recently, multiple dissemination schemes have been evaluated in the context of vehicular environments by Withbeck (2011), with the aim of leveraging opportunistic vehicle-to-vehicle communication so to offload the cellular infrastructure from the need of forwarding some small information to all vehicles in a geographical region. However, again, this work does not cope with the placement of RSUs, since the access network is represented by a pervasive and ready-to-use cellular network.

Lochert (2008) formulates an optimization problem for the planning of RSU locations, solvable with genetic algorithms. However, the deployment is intended to facilitate the aggregation of data, collected by the vehicles, on the road traffic conditions, rather than the dissemination of information.

Trullols-Cruces (2010) formulate optimization problems for the deployment of RSUs, whose objective is that of the dissemination of information to vehicles in the shortest time possible. In this Chapter, the formulation and results of this work are discussed and employed as the starting point for a simulative performance evaluation campaign.

RSU deployments that aim at maximizing content downloading are instead proposed by Fiore (2009) and Malandrino (2011). However, the associated optimization problems are designed for a cooperative downloading, i.e., a process where direct RSU-to-vehicle data exchanged are augmented through vehicle-to-vehicle communication: the cooperative downloading thus leverages opportunistic contacts among vehicles to increase the downloading speed. Of the two, the formulation by Malandrino (2011) is the most complete, measuring the actual per-user throughput in presence of realistic data transmission rates, channel access and interference. In addition, Abdrabou (2011) adopts a theoretical framework to study the RSU deployment density that minimizes the uploading delay via vehicle-to-vehicle multi-hop communication. However, RSU placement strategies that assume cooperative approaches and vehicle-to-vehicle data transfers will not be further discussed in this Chapter, since the focus here is on the downloading via direct RSU-to-vehicle communication.

Also, related to the transfer of data in vehicular environments are the work by Zhao (2008) and Yoon (2007). The former deals with the collection at the RSUs of small-sized data generated by vehicles, and thus targets content uploading rather than the dissemination and downloading, which are addressed in this Chapter. The latter focuses instead on the scheduling of data packets at RSUs, while it assumes the infrastructure deployment to be given: therefore, it does not concern the RSU placement problem considered here.

RSU DEPLOYMENT FOR CONTENT DISSEMINATION AND DOWNLOADING

In this section, the problem of planning vehicular networks for information dissemination and downloading is studied taking into account the peculiarities of the vehicular environment. In order to capture both the dissemination and downloading applications with a single framework, the problem is cast as that of deploying a limited number of RSUs so as to maximize

1. The number of vehicles served (i.e., covered) by the RSUs, and
2. The connection time between vehicles and RSUs.

Such an approach fits well both the targeted applications, which can be modeled as separate instances of the same problem above, characterized by different durations of the desired connection time. As a matter of fact, on the one hand, a dissemination process typically concerns small pieces of information and large amounts of vehicles, thus it requires that as many vehicles as possible enjoy a small connection time. On the other hand, the downloading application limits the number of mobile users involved in the process, since only a fraction of them is interested in retrieving some content from the Internet at the same time; however, each of such vehicles must be covered for a long time, so as to be able to download the whole amount of the data it demanded.

RSU Deployment as an Optimization Problem

Formally, an urban road topology of area size equal to A is considered, including N intersections. RSUs can be deployed at any of the N intersections, since, as proved by Trullols-Cruces (2010), placing RSUs at road junctions yields significant advantage over positioning them along road segments, in terms of both covered vehicles and connection time. Each RSU is assumed to have a service range equal to R. Such a service range may map into the transmission range of the RSU, or into a multiple of its transmission range if information delivery can be performed through multi-hop communication. Also, denote by V the number of vehicles that transit over the area A during a given time period, hereinafter called observation period.

The goal is then to deploy k RSUs so as to maximize the number of covered vehicles, among the possible V, so that the connection time between vehicles and RSUs is above a given threshold τ. Notice that this problem can be seen as a generalization of the well-known Maximum Coverage Problem (MCP), as also detailed next. However, the fact that vehicles may be covered by more than one RSU during their route to destination, jointly with the connection time constraint embodied by the threshold τ, makes most of the generalizations to the MCP unsuitable to the problem studied in this Chapter. Therefore, in the following several solutions to the problem outlined above are discussed, as presented by Trullols-Cruces (2010).

Contact-Only RSU Deployment

As a baseline strategy to compare with, an RSU deployment is first introduced that only considers the number of vehicle-to-RSU contacts, while it neglects the connection time aspect.

The goal is then to maximize the number of vehicles covered by k RSUs, that can be deployed at the N intersections located in the road topology. To that end, by analyzing the vehicular mobility in the selected area, define an N x V matrix P whose generic element is given by

$$P_{ij} \begin{cases} 1 \_ if \_ vehicle \_ i \_ crosses \_ junction \\ j \_ during \_ the \_ observation \_ period \\ 0 \_ otherwise \end{cases}$$

The problem is modeled as a Maximum Coverage Problem (MCP), which can be formulated as follows. Given a collection of sets $S = \{S_1, S_2,..., S_N\}$, where each set S_i is a subset of a given ground set $X = \{X_1, X_2,..., X_V\}$, the goal is to pick k sets

from S so as to maximize the cardinality of their union. To better understand the correspondence with the problem posed above, consider that the elements in X are the vehicles that transit over the considered road topology during the observation period. Also, for i =1, 2,..., N, we have

$$S_i = \left\{ x_j \in X, j = 1,...,V : P_{ij} = 1 \right\}$$

i.e., S_i includes all vehicles that cross intersection i at least once over the observation period. Thus, by solving the above problem, the set of k intersections where an RSU should be placed can be obtained so as to maximize the number of covered vehicles.

Unfortunately, the MCP problem is NP-hard; however, as reported by Ageev (1999), it is well known that the greedy heuristic achieves an approximation factor of $1-(1-1/m)^m$, where m is the maximum cardinality of the sets in the optimization domain. The greedy heuristic, hereinafter also called MCP-g, picks at each step a set (i.e., an intersection) maximizing the weight of the uncovered elements.

Now, consider an auxiliary collection of sets G, subset of S, and let W_i (with i = 1,..., N) be the number of elements covered by S_i, but not covered by any set in G. The steps of the greedy heuristic are reported in Figure 1.

We stress that, although the MCP-g algorithm provides a very good approximation of the optimal solution, it requires global knowledge of the road topology and network system, as well as the identity of the vehicles that have crossed the N intersections during the observation period.

Coverage Time-Based RSU Deployment

Next, consider the case of actual interest, i.e., k RSUs have to be deployed at the road intersections so as to favor both the number of covered vehicles, as well as the time for which they are covered. To this end, define an N x V matrix T whose generic element, T_{ij}, represents the total time that vehicle j would spend under the coverage of an RSU if the RSU were located at intersection i, i.e., the contact time between a vehicle j and an RSU located at intersection i. Then, the following problem can be formulated, named Maximum Coverage with Time Threshold Problem, or MCTTP: given k RSUs to be deployed, the aim is to serve as many vehicles as possible, for (possibly) at least τ seconds each, i.e.,

$$\max \sum_{j=1}^{V} \min \left\{ \tau, \sum_{i=1}^{N} T_{ij} y_i \right\}$$

$$s.t. \sum_{i=1}^{N} y_i \leq k; y_i \in \{0,1\} \forall i$$

Note that in the first equation above an RSU is placed at an intersection so as to maximize the number of vehicles that are covered, taking into account a vehicle contact time up to a maximum value equal to τ. RSUs that provide coverage for at least τ seconds to a given vehicle do not further contribute to the overall gain of covering such a vehicle. The constraint in the second equation instead limits the number of RSUs to k.

Figure 1. Algorithm for the greedy MCP heuristic

The MCP-g heuristic
Require: k, **P**, $\mathscr{S}$
1:　$G \leftarrow \emptyset,\ C \leftarrow 0,\ U \leftarrow \mathscr{S}$
2:　$W_i = \sum_{j=1}^{V} \mathbf{P}_{ij},\ i = 1,\dots,N$
3:　**repeat**
4:　　Select $S_i \in U$ that maximizes W_i
5:　　$G \leftarrow G \cup S_i$
6:　　$C \leftarrow C + 1$
7:　　$U \leftarrow U \setminus S_i$
8:　　$W_i = \sum_{\substack{j=1 \\ j:x_j \notin G}}^{V} \mathbf{P}_{ij}, i = 1,\dots,N$
9:　**until** $C = k$ or $U = \emptyset$

It can be easily verified that the MCP is a particular case of the above formulation, obtained by setting τ = 1 and $T_{ij} = P_{ij}$. Hence, MCTTP is NP-hard and a greedy heuristic is proposed for its solution, denoted by MCTTP-g. The heuristic picks an intersection at each step so as to maximize the provided coverage time, although only the contribution due to vehicles for which the threshold τ has not been reached is considered.

Let G, subset of S, be a collection of sets and let now W_i (with i = 1,…, N) be the total contact time provided by intersection i, considering for each vehicle a contribution such that the vehicles coverage time due to the union of the G and S_i sets does not exceed the threshold τ. The greedy heuristic is reported in Figure 2.

Again, notice that the time-threshold heuristic requires knowledge of the global road topology and of the vehicles identity. While the first assumption appears realistic, the second may not always be so: therefore, it needs to be relaxed, proposing an RSU deployment strategy that is unaware of the vehicles identities.

Absence of Information of Vehicles Identities

When the vehicles identities are not available, the only information that can be exploited is the total time that all vehicles would spend under the coverage of an RSU if it were located at intersection i, i.e.,

$$T_i = \sum_{j=1}^{V} T_{ij} \qquad i = 1,\dots,N$$

Thus, in this case the objective is to maximize the total contact (service) time offered to vehicles when k RSUs are deployed. In this case, the problem can be formulated as a 0–1 Knapsack Problem (KP), which is defined by Pisinger (2004) as follows. A set of N intersections (items) $I = \{I_1, I_2,\dots, I_N\}$ is given; each intersection has a value

Figure 2. Algorithm for the greedy MCTTP heuristic

The MCTTP-g heuristic

Require: $k, \mathbf{T}, \tau, \mathscr{S}$

1:    $G \leftarrow \emptyset, C \leftarrow 0, U \leftarrow \mathscr{S}$
2:    $t_j = 0, j = 1, \ldots, V$
3:    **repeat**
4:      $W_i = \sum_{j=1}^{V} \min(\tau - t_j, \mathbf{T}_{ij}), i = 1, \ldots, N$
5:      Select $S_i \in U$ that maximizes W_i
6:      $G \leftarrow G \cup S_i$
7:      $C \leftarrow C + 1$
8:      $U \leftarrow U \setminus S_i$
9:      $t_j = \min(\tau, t_j + \mathbf{T}_{ij}), j = 1, \ldots, V$
10:   **until** $C = k$ or $U = \emptyset$

T_i and unitary weight, and the maximum number of selected intersections (maximum weight) must be equal to k. The goal is to select a subset of k intersections that maximizes the overall service time provided to vehicles, i.e.,

$$\max \sum_{i=1}^{N} T_i y_i$$

$$s.t. \quad \sum_{i=1}^{N} y_i \leq k; \qquad y_i \in \{0,1\} \quad \forall i$$

The 0–1 KP is an NP-hard problem in general; however in the case under study, where each intersection has a constant weight, it can be solved in polynomial time by simply sorting the intersections in decreasing order by their value, and selecting the first k intersections. This algorithm, which requires the knowledge of the T_i coefficients (with i = 1,…, N), is referred to as KP-T.

Computational Complexity

The computational complexity of both MCP and MCTTP is $O(VN^k)$: given N intersections, all possible combinations where the k RSUs can be placed have to be considered and the weight of

each intersection is computed over V vehicles. The cost of both greedy heuristics, MCP-g and MCTTP-g, is O(KVN), since, for k times, the best choice among the candidate intersections (initially set to N) has to be selected, and again the selection is based on the weight computed over V elements. The complexity of the algorithm to solve the 0–1 KP is O(VN+N logN), since it is enough to consider each of the N intersections and sort the values to obtain the best k choices.

MOBILITY SCENARIOS

In order to carry out the performance evaluation of the information dissemination and downloading services, real-world road topologies from the canton of Zurich, in Switzerland, are used. Realistic traces of the vehicular mobility in such a region, generated by the Simulation and Modeling Group at ETH Zurich, are made available by Naumov (2006). These traces describe the individual movement of cars through a queue-based model calibrated on real data: as detailed in Cetin (2003), they provide a realistic representation of vehicular mobility at both microscopic and macroscopic levels.

The four road topologies depicted in Figures 3(a)-3(d) are considered; they represent 100 km^2 portions of the downtown urban areas of the cities of Zurich, Winterthur, and of the suburban areas of Baden and Baar. For each topology, half an hour of vehicular mobility is extracted, in presence of average traffic density conditions.

In order to remove partial trips (i.e., vehicular movements starting or ending close to the border of the square area), the trace is filtered by removing cars that traverse only three intersections or less, as well as those spending less than 1 minute in the considered region. The selected thresholds result in a low percentage of cars being removed from the traces of the scenarios characterized by a higher traffic density (Zurich and Winterthur), while the filtering is heavier on the traces of the suburban scenarios (Baden and Baar), where the conditions set above are harder to meet. However, the resulting numbers still guarantee the statistical validity of the tests conducted over all road topologies. Specifically, we have 83, 43, 38 and 46 intersections and a number of vehicles equal to 21373, 4942, 5914, and 3736, in the Zurich, Winterthur, Baden, and Baar scenarios, respectively.

PERFORMANCE ANALYSIS OF THE HEURISTICS UNDER IDEAL NETWORK SETTINGS

In this section, a first statement on the performance of the algorithms previously introduced is provided. To this end, the different heuristics are solved in presence of real-world road topologies, assuming ideal conditions from a network engineering viewpoint, i.e., no channel losses, ideal disc-like propagation with radius equal to 100 m, perfect medium access, and instantaneous vehicle-to-RSU communication without any need for control messages. The resulting RSU deployments are evaluated in terms of information dissemination capabilities. In the following, the results obtained with the different deployment algorithms maximizing coverage and contact times are compared.

Heuristics Performance

The RSU placement provided by the coverage time-based heuristics presented earlier varies depending on the threshold τ. Indeed, this parameter allows the control of the objective of the deployment, so as to favor:

- A dissemination application, by choosing a low value of τ and thus maximizing the number of short-lived contacts that are needed to spread a small content from the

RSUs to as many passing-by vehicles as possible;

- A downloading application, by imposing a high value of τ and thus maximizing the number of vehicles that are covered for the arbitrarily long time periods needed to retrieve large-sized files from Internet-based servers.

As a result, let us first observe how the performance of the quasi-optimal deployment obtained through the MCTTP-g algorithm varies as a function of the τ parameter. Figure 4(a) focuses on the Zurich road topology and reports the coverage ratio, i.e., the fraction of vehicles that are covered by at least one RSU during their route throughout the scenario, versus the number k of deployed RSUs. The parameter τ ranges between 5 and 120 s, and the plot shows the result of the MCTTP-g scheme along with those obtained under the MCP-g and KP-T solutions. Looking at the results, it can be seen how MCTTP-g falls in between an algorithm that maximizes vehicle-to-RSU contacts, i.e., MCP-g, and one that maximizes the overall coverage time, i.e., KP-T. In particular, for low values of τ, MCTTP-g tends to MCP-g, since the time constraint is easily satisfied (a contact with a single RSU is often sufficient to reach the desired coverage time) and the algorithm can thus focus on maximizing the coverage. Instead, when τ is high enough, MCTTP-g tends to KP-T, since the desired coverage time is seldom reached, and thus the same vehicles end up contributing to the optimization: the focus of the algorithm then shifts onto coverage times.

A confirmation to this analysis comes from the CDFs of the per-vehicle coverage time, in Figure 4(b), where the same behavior of the MCTTP-g algorithm is observed, as τ varies and for k = 6. It can be noted, however, how MCTTP-g with τ = 5 s matches MCP-g in terms of coverage ratio, but outperforms it in terms of coverage time. Similarly, MCTTP-g with τ = 120 s match-

Figure 3. Road topology layout: Zurich (a), Winterthur (b), Baden (c), Baar (d)

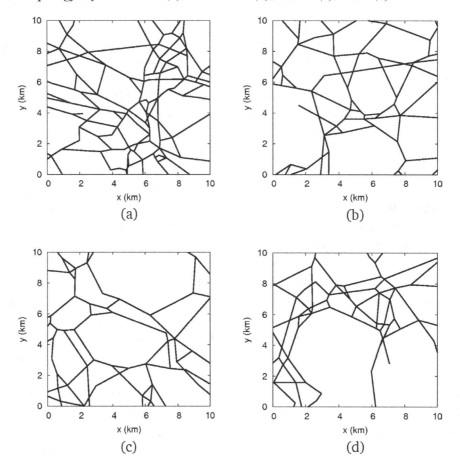

(a)   (b)

(c)   (d)

es KP-T as far as the coverage time is concerned, but provides a better coverage ratio. The combined maximization of contacts and coverage time can thus achieve better performance than contacts-only, or time-only driven solutions, even in borderline conditions.

Thus, it can be concluded that the coverage time threshold τ can be leveraged to calibrate the RSU deployment so as to fit the goals of the different types of services.

Next, it is important to evaluate the role that different mobility scenarios play in the RSU deployment problem. This aspect is evaluated by fixing the threshold τ to 30 s, a contact duration that should be largely sufficient to transfer a few kbytes from RSUs to vehicles. The MCTTP-g

algorithm is compared to the optimal solution to the original MCTTP formulation, which, as mentioned, is NP-hard and thus solvable only for small instances of the problem (in the case under study, up to $k = 6$) via a brute-force approach. The outcome of the KP-T algorithm is reported as well, along with that of a random RSU deployment, so to benchmark the performance of the other schemes.

The coverage ratio achieved by such algorithms, in different road topologies and as the number of deployed RSUs varies, is depicted in the plots of Figures 5(a)-5(d). Observe that, regardless of the road topology considered, the MCTTP-g solution is always extremely close to the optimal one. Moreover, the availability of information on the vehicular mobility plays a

Figure 4. Coverage ratio versus number deployed RSUs (a) and CDF of the coverage time for 6 deployed RSUs (b) in the Zurich scenario

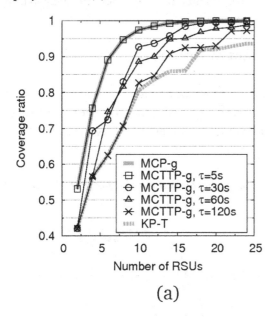

(a)

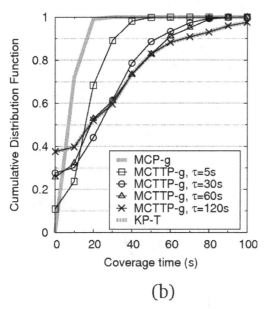

(b)

the vehicular trajectories. Such a result is consistent throughout all scenarios, although the entity of the difference in the coverage ratio provided by the different deployment algorithms varies with the considered road topology. More precisely, a more complex road topology, such as that of the Zurich area, leads to more significant differences between the schemes that are mobility-aware and those that are not.

Figures 6(a)-6(d) report instead the distribution of the coverage time, in the specific case in which k = 6 RSUs are deployed over each road topology. Recall that the goal is to maximize the time spent by vehicles under coverage of RSUs, up to the threshold time τ of 30 s, identified by the vertical line in the plots. The common result in all road topologies is that random deployments lead to small coverage times, whereas the other schemes tend to behave similarly, although KP-T is characterized by a more skewed distribution than those of the MCTTP, in both its optimal solution and greedy approximation. As a matter of fact, the deployments determined by KP-T result, at a time, in more vehicles with very low coverage times, and more vehicles with very high coverage times. Conversely, the MCTTP leads to more balanced distributions, where many vehicles experience a coverage time around the threshold τ. Once more, these observations hold for all the scenarios considered.

When comparing the coverage times in Figures 6(a)-6(d) with the corresponding coverage ratios in Figures 5(a)-5(d), notice that MCTTP and MCTTP-g provide very similar performance, generally superior to those achieved by the other schemes. Indeed, a random deployment of RSUs induces both a lower number of vehicle-to-RSU contacts and a shorter coverage time with respect to the solutions above. The KP-T solution leads to a performance comparable to that of MCTTP and relative heuristics in terms of coverage time, although with the skewness discussed before; however, this result is paid at a high coverage ratio cost.

major role in favoring contacts among vehicles and RSUs: as a matter of fact, the random solution performs poorly, the KP-T algorithm provides an improved coverage of the vehicles, but the best performance is achieved by the MCTTP-g scheme, which leverages the most detailed knowledge of

In conclusion, the MCTTP formulation represents an efficient solution to the RSU deployment problem which enjoys the desirable properties of

1. Being configurable to a specific application by properly setting the value of the τ parameter,
2. Having an inexpensive greedy heuristics that well approximates the optimal solution, and

3. Yielding results that are consistently better than those achieved with unplanned RSU placements or Knapsack Problem-based formulations.

Impact of Routes

The figures in the previous section are averaged over space, aggregating the coverage ratio and time of all vehicles moving in the region under study.

Figure 5. Coverage ratio versus the number deployed RSUs, in the Zurich (a), Winterthur (b), Baden (c), and Baar (d) scenario

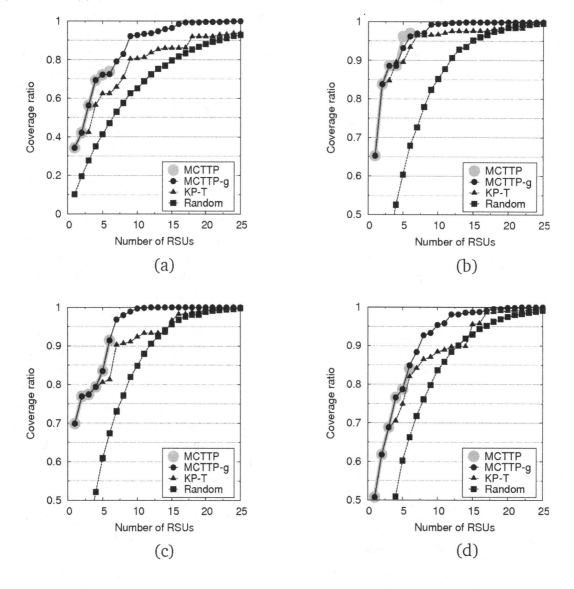

As a further step in the analysis, observe how the route traveled by a car affects the coverage it enjoys during its movement. To that end, the MCTTP heuristics is considered and the coverage time on a per-route basis is computed by aggregating the performance referring to vehicles that followed the same route through the road topology scenario.

Figures 7(a)-7(d) show the coverage time measured on different routes traveled by vehicles, in the different mobility scenarios, when the threshold τ is set to 30 s and the number of deployed RSUs is varied. The x-axis of the plots reports the route identifier, which is assigned according to a decreasing coverage ratio ordering (which implicitly leads to monotonically decreasing curves). Observe that when just one RSU is placed in a region, the coverage time is around 20 s (i.e., approximately the duration of one vehicle-to-RSU contact) along a subset of routes (i.e., those passing by the location of the lone RSU). This result is consistent for all the road scenarios, although the number of routes with non-zero coverage time varies depending on the street layout: clearly, more complex topologies imply that more combinations of consecutive segments are available, and thus that a higher number of possible routes will pass by the deployed RSUs.

When the number of deployed RSUs increases, as one could expect, more routes become covered for a longer time. However, note that disparity among routes grows along with the number of RSUs deployed: when more RSUs become available, the luckiest routes tend to get coverage durations that are 5 to 10 times those experienced by vehicles traveling on the less fortunate routes. This result evidences how some routes are more prone to enjoy better coverage than others are, even in presence of a coverage that is approximating the optimal one.

The impact of the time threshold τ on the per-route performance is instead evaluated in Figures 8(a)-8(d), when the number of RSUs is fixed to 10. It is quite evident that lower values of τ allow a fairer distribution of RSUs over the road topology, as more routes are covered, even if for a shorter amount of time on average. On the contrary, increasing the τ threshold forces an RSU deployment that is significantly more clustered, with the result that a smaller subset of routes enjoys a high coverage time, while the rest is left uncovered or almost so. This behavior can be observed over all road topologies, but it is especially evident in the Zurich scenario, due to the larger choice of routes enabled by the more complex street layout. A visually-intuitive representation of such a disparity is provided in Figures 9(a)-9(d): the plots show maps of the four road scenarios, where darker and thicker lines represent road segments traveled by vehicles that have higher coverage times. The results refer to the case of 10 RSUs and τ equal to 30 s, but similar figures were obtained under any other parameter combination.

According to these results, it can be concluded that RSU deployments can be significantly unfair, and, as a consequence, that a given average coverage time does not necessarily mean that all vehicles will spend such a time interval under coverage of RSUs. Indeed, especially when the number of RSUs or the minimum time constraint grow, a dramatic disparity can emerge in the performance observed by individual vehicles traveling in the same region but along different routes.

PERFORMANCE ANALYSIS OF THE HEURISTICS IN REALISTIC ENVIRONMENTS

In order to provide a realistic assessment of our heuristics, we ran ns2 simulations tracking vehicle movements in the four maps. Each vehicle is assumed to be equipped with an IEEE 802.11p interface with which it communicates with RSUs. All RSUs use the same frequency channel, 20-MHz wide, for beacons (issued every 0.2 s) and any other communication with the vehicles. For

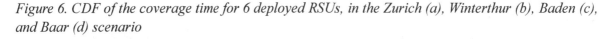

Figure 6. CDF of the coverage time for 6 deployed RSUs, in the Zurich (a), Winterthur (b), Baden (c), and Baar (d) scenario

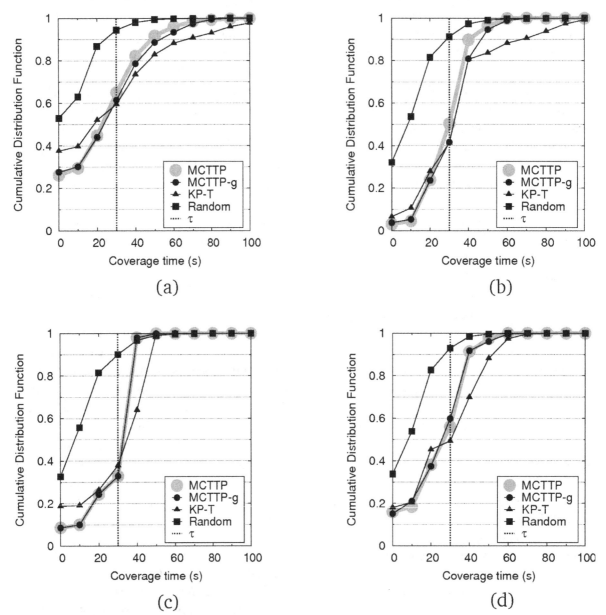

(a)

(b)

(c)

(d)

simplicity, the link between vehicles and RSUs is established on the service channel, operating at a data rate of 54 Mb/s, which, due to the channel switching of IEEE 802.11p, translates to an effective maximum throughput of about 13 Mb/s at the application layer, in absence of contention and of transmission errors. The link is simulated

according to a shadowing model defined by Karendal (2011), with urban parameters for the Zurich and Winterthur maps (resulting in shorter-range coverage), and with suburban parameters for the Baded and Baar maps (resulting in a longer-range coverage). For each scenario, the transmission power of vehicles and RSUs is set in such a way that 95% of the transmitted packets are correctly received at a distance of 100 m.

In the dissemination case, the information is included with the beacon issued by the RSU (the beacon size is increased from 22 to 1000 bytes), while in the downloading case the vehicle sends a request packet upon receiving the first beacon from an RSU. The request packet specifies the size of the file to be downloaded.

Each downloader wishes to retrieve a file whose size follows the experimental distribution derived in Aidouni (2009). Each file is divided into chunks of 1400 bytes each and the RSU starts sending it as soon as the request is received. Chunks carry application-layer sequence numbers, thus vehicles can selectively request the retransmission of missing chunks.

We start by looking at the dissemination case. Based on the discussion presented in the previous section, the parameter τ is set to 30 s, and RSUs are placed on each map according to the MCTTP-g heuristic. Several experiments are carried out for each of the four road layouts, with a number of RSUs ranging from 5 to 25.

Figure 10(a) shows the coverage ratio, computed as the ratio between the number of vehicles that receive at least one beacon and the total number of vehicles in the area. Note that the results match the behavior of the coverage ratio metric obtained in the various scenarios under ideal settings (see Figures 5(a)-5(d)), although lower performance is achieved due to the fact that realistic propagation conditions are now modeled. Interestingly, though being both classified as urban areas (and thus being simulated with the same channel model), Zurich and Winterthur provide both the worst and the best coverage ratio, for any number of RSUs. The reason lies in the lower average vehicle speed and higher number of roads in the Zurich scenario, resulting in a longer travel time (compared to the simulation length) before reaching an RSU. This is confirmed by the delay between entering the map and receiving a beacon, shown in Figure 10(b),

that is much higher for Zurich than for Winterthur. Concerning the suburban scenarios, Baar achieves slightly better performance than Baden because it has a lower number of roads, all crossing the same limited area; thus, a better coverage of the vehicles can be achieved.

Figure 10(c) reports the CDF of the coverage time, when the number of RSUs is fixed to 6. The coverage time is computed, for each vehicle, as the sum of the intervals between back-to-back beacons received from the same RSU. Again, comparing this plot with the ones in Figures 6(a)-6(d), it can be seen that qualitatively similar results are obtained in the different road layouts. Also, note that the coverage times reflect the behavior of the coverage ratio shown in Figure 10(a); in particular, the probability of having zero coverage time is in agreement with the percentage of vehicles that do not receive any beacon, in all scenarios under study.

Next, the performance of content downloading is shown in Figures 11(a)-11(c). For each scenario, 1% of the total number of vehicles in the traces were selected to be downloaders. Their performance was monitored by setting τ equal to 1000 s and placing a varying number of RSUs according to the MCTTP-g heuristic.

Looking at the plots, it can be seen that results are affected by the road layout, the number of downloaders and the node mobility in the different scenarios. In particular, for a fixed number of RSUs that are deployed, a shorter total road length, and a lower average vehicle speed result in a higher coverage time (Figure 11a), hence in a higher throughput (Figure 11b). This effect is especially evident by comparing the results obtained in the Baar area, where the total road length is shorter (hence RSUs are necessarily placed closer to each other) to those derived in the other suburban area, i.e., Baden, which is characterized by a larger total road length coupled with faster vehicles. Similar considerations hold for the comparison between the two urban scenarios, i.e.,

Figure 7. Average coverage time versus route, for a varying number of RSUs, in the Zurich (a), Winterthur (b), Baden (c), and Baar (d) scenario

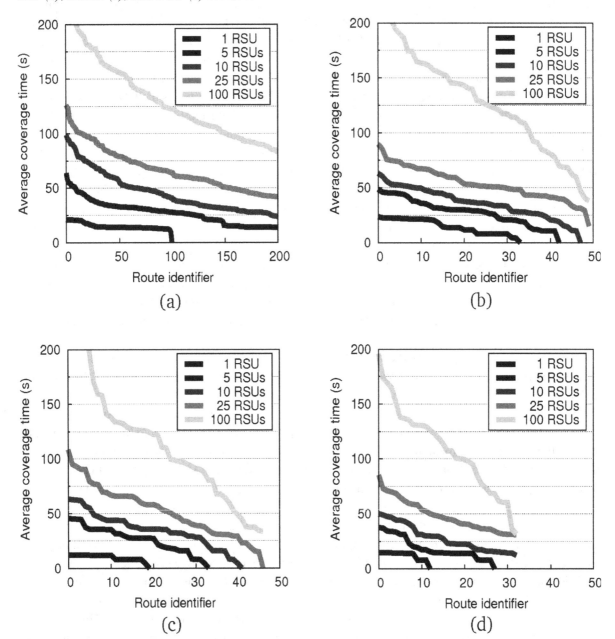

Zurich and Winterthur, where the former exhibits a larger road length than the latter.

Another important factor in determining the performance is the number of vehicles under the same RSU that concurrently download information. The Baden and Zurich scenarios are the ones that exhibit a larger number of downloaders, and,

consistently, feature a lower throughput than the others. It follows that the relationship between throughput and coverage time (the latter shown in Figure 11b) is not as strong as one would expect.

Note also that the average per-downloader throughput is computed at the application layer, over the vehicles that are able to start download-

Figure 8. Average coverage time versus route, for a varying threshold τ, in the Zurich (a), Winterthur (b), Baden (c), and Baar (d) scenario

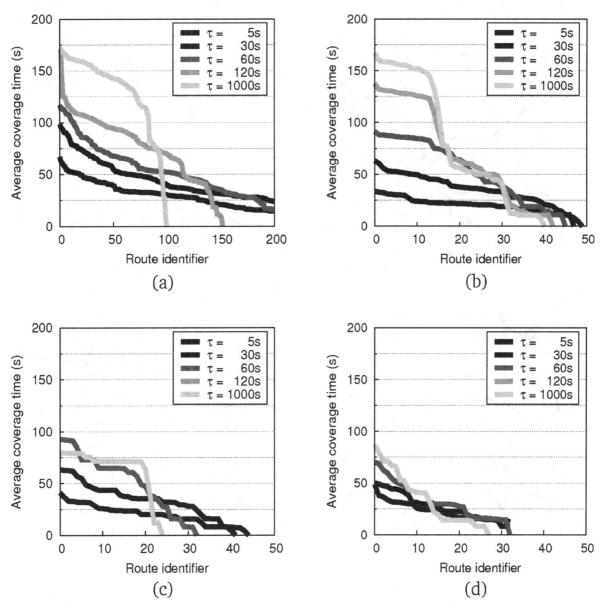

ing the file. An important metric to observe is therefore the percentage of downloaders that can retrieve not even a chunk, as well as the percentage of downloaders that is never under coverage of any RSU. Such results are reported in Table 1, for the various scenarios and as the number of deployed RSUs varies. It can be seen that the Baden and Baar areas, which are both suburban, exhibit better performance than the urban regions

of Zurich and Winterthur. This is mainly due to the fact that in the former scenarios almost all vehicles travel on a few major roads, while in the urban environments downloaders may travel also on narrow roads with little RSU coverage. Furthermore, better performance is achieved in the Baar scenario than in the Baden area; indeed, the smaller number of roads, all within the same

Figure 9. Per-road coverage time, for 10 RSUs and τ=30 s, in the Zurich (a), Winterthur (b), Baden (c), and Baar (d) scenario

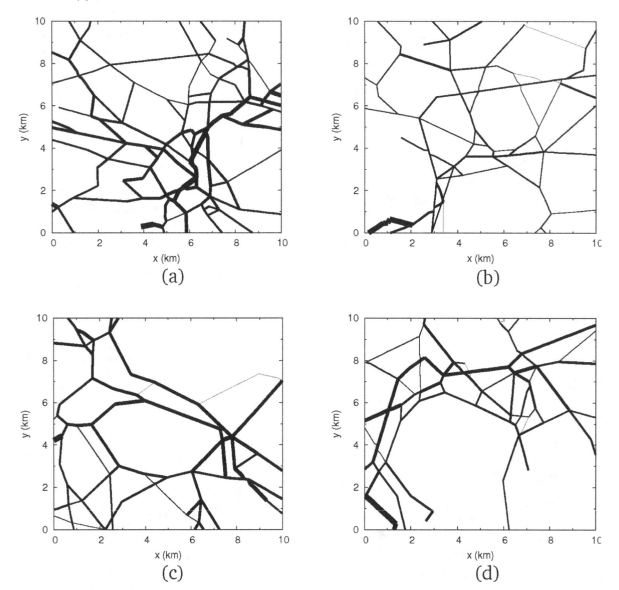

limited area, that characterizes the Baar layout leads to a larger coverage ratio.

Finally, Figure 11(c) depicts the average delay between the time instant when the downloader enters the service area and the time at which it receives the first chunk (note that only downloaders that receive at least one chunk have been considered, in order to compute such a delay). Observe that the mobility scenario has little impact on such a metric, as the number of deployed RSUs is not as small as in the case of dissemination services; thus, it is likely that a downloader finds an RSU after a reasonable amount of time independently of the road layout. In addition, as ex-

Figure 10. Dissemination case in the four scenarios: coverage ratio versus number of RSUs (a), delay between entering the map and receiving a beacon versus number of RSUs (b), CDF of the coverage time per vehicle with 6 deployed RSUs (c)

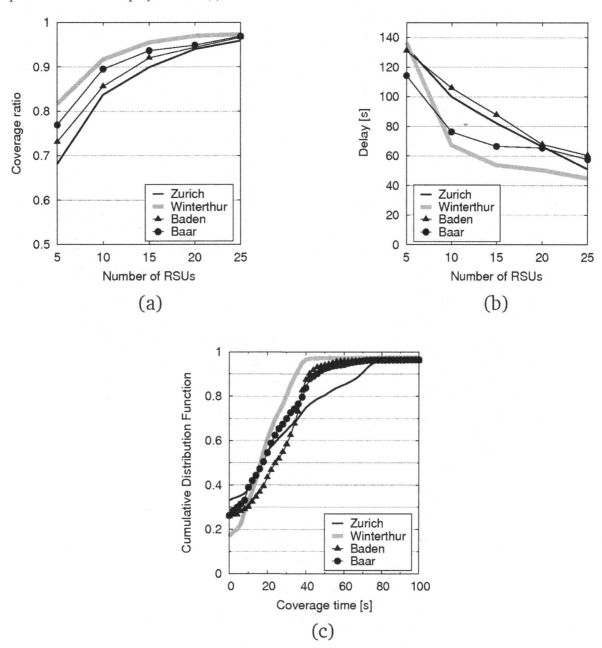

(a)

(b)

(c)

pected, the larger the number of RSUs, the lower the travel time before reaching an RSU, hence the experienced delay.

CONCLUSION AND FUTURE RESEARCH DIRECTIONS

This Chapter addressed two fundamental information delivery services in vehicular networks with

Figure 11. Downloading case in the four scenarios: average coverage time (a), average throughput achieved by downloaders (b), and delay between entering the map and receiving the first chunk (c), versus number of RSUs

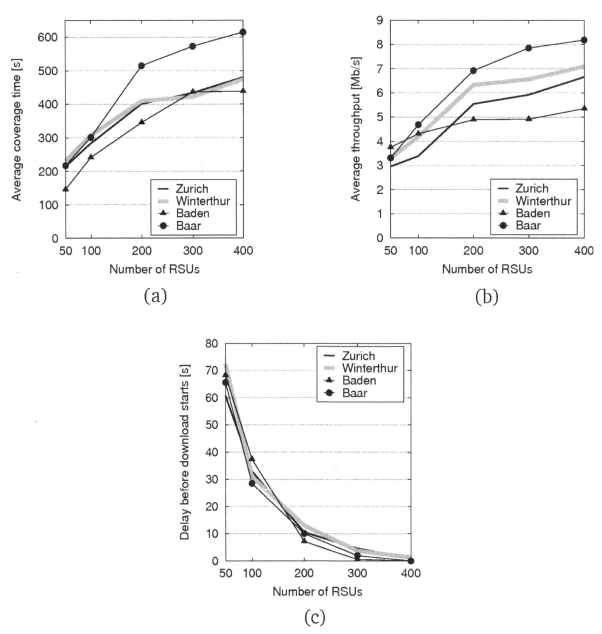

(a)

(b)

(c)

infrastructure support: information dissemination from RSUs to passing-by vehicles and content downloading by vehicular users through nearby RSUs.

In order to ensure good performance for both services, RSU deployment was investigated, by casting it as an optimization problem, and different formulations of the problem were presented.

Among such formulations, the one named Maximum Coverage with Time Threshold Problem (MCTTP) aims at guaranteeing that a large number of vehicles travel under the coverage of

Table 1. Content downloading: percentage of downloaders experiencing zero throughput, percentage of downloaders experiencing zero coverage

Scenario/ No. RSUs	50	100	200	300	400
Zurich	[13.09, 12.99]	[12.4, 12.19]	[4.00, 2.00]	[2.00, 2.00]	[2.00, 2.00]
Winterthur	[12.50, 12.50]	[12.50,12.50]	[4.17, 4.17]	[2.09, 2.09]	[0, 0]
Baden	[15.75, 13.11]	[9.84, 9.84]	[4.84, 3.23]	[0, 0]	[0, 0]
Baar	[14.62, 12.50]	[3.12, 3.12]	[0, 0]	[0, 0]	[0, 0]

one or more RSUs for a sufficient amount of time, denoted by τ. Such a formulation also leverages, with respect to the others, the knowledge of the vehicular trajectories. The (either optimal or approximate) solution of the MCTTP problem emerged as the most suitable to support different information delivery services in vehicular networks, for a number of reasons.

Firstly, it was shown that, by varying the minimum required coverage time, τ, in the MCTTP formulation, the RSU deployment can be calibrated so as to achieve a combined maximization of contacts and coverage time, which yields better performance than contacts-only or time-only driven solutions.

Secondly, the MCTTP formulation leads to a more balanced distribution of the coverage time over the vehicles, with respect to other formulations: when RSUs are deployed according to the MCTTP solution, many vehicles experience a coverage time around the minimum required value threshold τ.

Simulation results, both under ideal and realistic conditions, also highlighted some interesting effects. A factor which is often underestimated, and that was investigated in this Chapter, is the effect of the constraint on the coverage time. Simulation results showed that lower values of τ allow a fairer distribution of RSUs over the road topology, as more routes are covered, even if for a shorter time on average. On the contrary, increasing the τ threshold yields a more clustered RSU deployment, with the result that a smaller subset of routes enjoys a high coverage time, while the rest is left uncovered or almost so. We thus concluded that aiming at a given average coverage time does not necessarily mean that all vehicles will be under coverage of RSUs for so long, and fair coverage cannot be achieved.

Furthermore, simulations allowed us to establish the impact of factors such as vehicle speed, vehicle density, and road density, highlighting the need to collect these types of statistics when designing the coverage, for both information dissemination and content downloading.

In conclusion, RSU deployment cannot be addressed through random or intuitive placements, since neither one represents, in general, an optimal solution to the RSU deployment problem. Such simple strategies are easily outperformed by more sound approaches, for both the dissemination and the downloading objectives. The MCTTP formulation of the RSU deployment problem, which leverages the knowledge of the vehicles trajectories, represents an efficient solution and enjoys the desirable properties of (1) being configurable to a specific application by properly constraining the coverage time, (2) having an inexpensive greedy heuristics that well approximates the optimal solution, and (3) yielding results that are consistently better than those achieved with unplanned RSU placements or Knapsack Problem-based formulations.

An important aspect to the performance of data delivery services that should be addressed by future research, and that is complimentary to the study presented in this Chapter, is the interaction between the deployed RSUs and the vehicle-to-vehicle information transfer. Indeed, this chapter highlighted the unfairness in RSU coverage that may arise in realistic road layouts. A way to mitigate such an (often) unavoidable effect is to let vehicles share data of common interest in areas where connectivity with an RSU in not possible. If the amount of data exchanged through vehicle-to-vehicle communication could be predicted by the RSUs, an effective synergy could be created between roadside infrastructure and vehicles within the ITS.

REFERENCES

Abdrabou, A., & Zhuang, W. (2011). Probabilistic delay control and road side unit placement for vehicular ad hoc networks with disrupted connectivity. *IEEE Journal on Selected Areas in Communications, 29*(1), 129–139. doi:10.1109/JSAC.2011.110113

Ageev, A. A., & Sviridenko, M. I. (1999). Approximation algorithms for maximum coverage and max cut with given sizes of parts. *Lecture Notes in Computer Science, 1610*, 17–30. doi:10.1007/3-540-48777-8_2

Ahn, J., Krishnamachari, B., Bai, F., & Zhang, L. (2011). *Optimizing content dissemination in heterogeneous vehicular networks*. Technical Report. Retrieved from http://ceng.usc.edu/assets/002/69415.pdf

Aidouni, F., Latapy, M., & Magnien, C. (2009). Ten weeks in the life of an eDonkey server. In *Proceedings of the Sixth International Workshop on Hot Topics in Peer-to-Peer Systems (Hot-P2P 2009)*. Rome, Italy: Hot-P2P.

Bychkovsky, V., Hull, B., Miu, A. K., Balakrishnan, H., & Madden, S. (2006). A measurement study of vehicular internet access using in situ wi-fi networks. In *Proceedings of the ACM/IEEE International Conference on Mobile Computing and Networking (MobiCom)*. Los Angeles, CA: ACM/IEEE.

Cetin, N., Burri, A., & Nagel, K. (2003). A large-scale multi-agent traffic microsimulation based on queue model. In *Proceedings of the Swiss Conference on Transport Research (STRC)*. Ascona, Switzerland: STRC.

Ding, Y., Wang, C., & Xiao, L. (2007). A static-node assisted adaptive routing protocol in vehicular networks. In *Proceedings of the ACM International Workshop on Vehicular Ad Hoc Networks (VANET)*. Montreal, Canada: ACM Press.

Fiore, M., & Barcelo-Ordinas, J. M. (2009). Cooperative download in urban vehicular networks. In *Proceedings of the IEEE International Conference on Mobile Adhoc and Sensor Systems (MASS)*. Macau, China: IEEE Press.

Hu, Y., Xue, Y., Li, Q., Liu, F., Keung, G. Y., & Li, B. (2009). The sink node placement and performance implication in mobile sensor networks. [MONET]. *Journal on Mobile Networks and Applications, 14*, 230–240. doi:10.1007/s11036-009-0158-5

Karedal, J., Czink, N., Paier, A., Tufvesson, F., & Molisch, A. F. (2011). Path loss modeling for vehicle-to-vehicle communications. *IEEE Transactions on Vehicular Technology, 60*, 323–328. doi:10.1109/TVT.2010.2094632

Kim, H., Seok, Y., Choi, N., Choi, Y., & Kwon, T. (2005). Optimal multi-sink positioning and energy-efficient routing in wireless sensor networks. In *Proceedings of the International Conference on Information Networking (ICOIN)*. Jeju Island, Korea: ICOIN.

Krumke, S. O., Marathe, M. V., Poensgen, D., Ravi, S. S., & Wirth, H.-C. (2002). Budgeted maximum graph coverage. *Lecture Notes in Computer Science, 2573,* 321–332. doi:10.1007/3-540-36379-3_28

Lochert, C., Scheuermann, B., Wewetzer, C., Luebke, A., & Mauve, M. (2008). Data aggregation and roadside unit placement for a VANET traffic information system. In *Proceedings of the ACM International Workshop on Vehicular Ad Hoc Networks (VANET).* San Francisco, CA: ACM Press.

Malandrino, F., Casetti, C., Chiasserini, C. F., & Fiore, M. (2011). Content downloading in vehicular networks: What really matters. In *Proceedings of the IEEE International Conference on Computer Communications (INFOCOM).* Shanghai, China: IEEE Press.

Marfia, G., Pau, G., Giordano, E., De Sena, E., & Gerla, M. (2007). Evaluating vehicle network strategies for downtown Portland: Opportunistic infrastructure and importance of realistic mobility models. In *Proceedings of the ACM International Workshop on Mobile Opportunistic Networking (MobiOpp).* San Juan, Puerto Rico: ACM Press.

Naumov, V. (2011). *Realistic vehicular traces.* Retrieved April 6, 2011, from http://lst.inf.ethz.ch/ad-hoc/car-traces

Oyman, E. I., & Ersoy, C. (2004). Multiple sink network design problem in large scale wireless networks. In *Proceedings of the IEEE International Conference on Communications (ICC).* Paris, France: IEEE Press.

Pisinger, D. (2004). Where are the hard knapsack problems? *Computers & Operations Research, 32,* 2271–2284. doi:10.1016/j.cor.2004.03.002

Poe, W. Y., & Schmitt, J. B. (2007). *Minimizing the maximum delay in wireless sensor networks by intelligent sink placement.* Technical Report 362/07. Kaiserlautern, Germany: University of Kaiserslautern.

Qiu, L., Chandra, R., Jain, K., & Mahdian, M. (2004). Optimizing the placement of integration points in multi-hop wireless networks. In *Proceedings of the IEEE International Conference on Network Protocols (ICNP).* Berlin, Germany: IEEE Press.

Trullols-Cruces, O., Fiore, M., Casetti, C., Chiasserini, C. F., & Barcelo-Ordinas, J. M. (2010). Planning roadside infrastructure for information dissemination in intelligent transportation systems. *Elsevier Computer Communications, 33*(4), 432–442.

Whitaker, R. M., Raisanen, L., & Hurley, S. (2005). The infrastructure efficiency of cellular wireless networks. *Elsevier Computer Networks, 48*(6), 941–959. doi:10.1016/j.comnet.2004.11.014

Whitbeck, J., Lopez, Y., Leguay, J., Conan, V., & Dias de Amorim, M. (2011). Relieving the wireless infrastructure: When opportunistic networks meet guaranteed delays. In *Proceedings of the IEEE International Symposium on a World of Wireless, Mobile and Multimedia Networks (WoWMoM).* Lucca, Italy: IEEE Press.

Yoon, S., Ngo, H. Q., & Qiao, C. (2007). On "shooting" a moving vehicle with data flows. In *Proceedings of the IEEE Workshop on Mobile Networks for Vehicular Environments (MOVE).* Anchorage, AK: IEEE Press.

Zhao, J., & Cao, G. (2008). VADD: Vehicle-assisted data delivery in vehicular ad hoc networks. *IEEE Transactions on Vehicular Technology, 57*(3), 1910–1922. doi:10.1109/TVT.2007.901869

Zheng, Z., Lu, Z., Sinha, P., & Kumar, S. (2010). Maximizing the contact opportunity for vehicular internet access. In *Proceedings of the IEEE International Conference on Computer Communications (INFOCOM).* San Diego, CA: IEEE Press.

Zheng, Z., Sinha, P., & Kumar, S. (2009). Alpha coverage: Bounding the interconnection gap for vehicular internet access. In *Proceedings of the IEEE International Conference on Computer Communications (INFOCOM)*. Rio de Janeiro, Brasil: IEEE Press.

ADDITIONAL READING

Ahmed, A., & Kanhere, S. S. (2006). VANET-CODE: Network coding to enhance cooperative downloading in vehicular ad hoc networks. In *Proceedings of the ACM (IWCMC)*. Vancouver, Canada: ACM Press.

Amaldi, E., Capone, A., Cesana, M., & Malucelli, F. (2004). Optimizing WLAN radio coverage. In *Proceedings of the IEEE International Conference on Communications (ICC)*. Paris, France: IEEE Press.

Burgess, J., Gallagher, B., Jensen, D., & Levine, B. (2006). MaxProp: Routing for vehicle-based disruption-tolerant networks. In *Proceedings of the IEEE International Conference on Computer Communications (INFOCOM)*. Barcelona, Spain: IEEE Press.

Chaintreau, A., Le Boudec, J. Y., & Ristanovic, N. (2009). The age of gossip: Spatial mean-field regime. In *Proceedings of the ACM International Conference on Measurement and Modeling of Computer Systems (SIGMETRICS)*. Seattle, WA: ACM Press.

Chen, B. B., & Chan, M. C. (2009). MobTorrent: A framework for mobile internet access from vehicles. In *Proceedings of the IEEE International Conference on Computer Communications (INFOCOM)*. Rio de Janeiro, Brasil: IEEE Press.

Cohen, R., Raz, D., & Aezladen, M. (2009). Locally vs. globally optimized flow-based content distribution to mobile nodes. In *Proceedings of the IEEE International Conference on Computer Communications (INFOCOM)*. Rio de Janeiro, Brazil: IEEE Press.

Fiore, M., & Harri, J. (2008). The networking shape of vehicular mobility. In *Proceedings of the ACM (MobiHoc)*. Hong Kong, China: ACM Press.

Frenkiel, R. H., Badrinath, B. R., Borras, J., & Yates, R. (2000). The infostations challenge: Balancing cost and ubiquity in delivering wireless data. *IEEE Personal Communications Magazine*, *7*(2), 66–71. doi:10.1109/98.839333

Gass, R., Scott, J., & Diot, C. (2006). Measurements of in-motion 802.11 networking. In *Proceedings of the IEEE WMCSA/HotMobile*. Seattle, WA: IEEE Press.

Huang, H. Y., Luo, P. E., Li, M., Li, D., Li, X., Shu, W., & Wu, M. Y. (2007). Performance evaluation of SUVnet with real-time traffic data. *IEEE Transactions on Vehicular Technology*, *56*(6), 3381–3396. doi:10.1109/TVT.2007.907273

Hui, F., & Mohapatra, P. (2006). Experimental characterization of multi-hop communications in vehicular ad hoc networks. In *Proceedings of the ACM International Workshop on Vehicular Ad Hoc Networks (VANET)*. Koln, Germany: ACM Press.

Nandan, A., Das, S., Pau, G., Gerla, M., & Sanadidi, M. Y. (2005). Cooperative downloading in vehicular ad-hoc wireless networks. In *Proceedings of the Conference on Wireless on Demand Network Systems and Service (WONS)*. St. Moritz, Switzerland: WONS.

Ott, J., & Kutscher, D. (2004). Drive-thru internet: IEEE 802.11b for automobile users. In *Proceedings of the IEEE International Conference on Computer Communications (INFOCOM)*. Hong Kong, China: IEEE Press.

Sardari, S., Hendessi, F., & Fekri, F. (2009). Infocast: A new paradigm for collaborative content distribution from roadside units to vehicular networks. In *Proceedings of IEEE (SECON)*. Rome, Italy: IEEE Press. doi:10.1109/SAHCN.2009.5168939

Sollazo, G., Musolesi, M., & Mascolo, C. (2007). TACO-DTN: A time-aware content-based dissemination system for delay tolerant networks. In *ACM International Workshop on Mobile Opportunistic Networking (MobiOpp)*. San Juan, Puerto Rico: ACM Press.

Trullols-Cruces, O., Morillo, J., Barcelo-Ordinas, J., & Garcia-Vidal, J. (2009). A cooperative vehicular network framework. In *Proceedings of the IEEE International Conference on Communications (ICC)*. Dresden, Germany: IEEE Press.

Tutschku, K. (1998). Demand-based radio network planning of cellular mobile communication systems. In *Proceedings of the IEEE International Conference on Computer Communications (INFOCOM)*. San Francisco, CA: IEEE Press.

Wright, M. H. (1998). Optimization methods for base station placement in wireless applications. In *Proceedings of the IEEE Vehicular Technology Conference (VTC)*. Ottawa, Canada: IEEE Press.

Wu, H., Fujimoto, R., Guensler, R., & Hunter, M. (2004). MDDV: A mobility-centric data dissemination algorithm for vehicular networks. In *Proceedings of the ACM International Workshop on Vehicular Ad Hoc Networks (VANET)*. Philadelphia, PA: ACM Press.

Zhang, J., Zhang, Q., & Jia, W. (2007). A novel MAC protocol for cooperative downloading in vehicular network. In *Proceedings of the IEEE (GLOBECOM)*. Seattle, WA: IEEE Press.

Zhao, J., & Cao, G. (2006). VADD: Vehicle-assisted data delivery in vehicular ad hoc networks. In *Proceedings of the IEEE International Conference on Computer Communications (INFOCOM)*. Barcelona, Spain: IEEE Press.

KEY TERMS AND DEFINITIONS

802.11p: Approved amendment to the IEEE 802.11 standard to add wireless access in vehicular environments.

Content Dissemination: Push-based delivery of small pieces of information to large sets of users.

Content Downloading: Pull-based delivery of possibly large-sized data to one specific interested user.

Heuristic Algorithm: Algorithm producing an approximate solution to a complex problem, within a time and employing a set of resources that make it practical with respect to the perfect solution.

Mobile Networks: Communication networks whose nodes are mobile and communicate via wireless.

Optimization Problem: Mathematical problem whose solution allows to choose the best element from some set of available alternatives.

RSU Deployment: Placement of the access infrastructure over a road topology.

Vehicular Networks: Communication networks where nodes are vehicles.

Chapter 6
Employing Traffic Lights as Road Side Units for Road Safety Information Broadcasts

Navin Kumar
University of Aveiro, Portugal

Luis Nero Alves
University of Aveiro, Portugal

Rui L. Aguiar
University of Aveiro, Portugal

ABSTRACT

There is great concern over growing road accidents and associated fatalities. In order to reduce accidents, improve congestion and offer smooth flow of traffic, several measures, such as providing intelligence to transport, providing communication infrastructure along the road, and vehicular communication, are being undertaken. Traffic safety information broadcast from traffic lights using Visible Light Communication (VLC) is a new cost effective technology which assists drivers in taking necessary safety measures. This chapter presents the VLC broadcast system considering LED-based traffic lights. It discusses the integration of traffic light Roadside Units (RSUs) with upcoming Intelligent Transportation Systems (ITS) architecture. Some of the offered services using this technology in vehicular environment together with future directions and challenges are discussed. A prototype demonstrator of the designed VLC systems is also presented.

INTRODUCTION

Fatality rates on road are becoming severe even with the introduction of many intelligent communication devices on board vehicles and alongside the road. Road crashes are the second leading cause of death globally among young people aged five to 29 and the third leading cause of death among people aged 30 to 44 years. Over 1.2 million people are killed annually because of road accidents (World Health Organization, 2008). The study predicted that road accidents would become the sixth largest cause of death in

DOI: 10.4018/978-1-4666-2223-4.ch006

the world in 2020 whereas it was the ninth largest cause of death in 1990.

To minimize road accidents and fatalities, various modes of vehicular communications, such as Vehicle-to-Infrastructure (V2I), Vehicle-to-Vehicle (V2V), and Infrastructure-to-Vehicle (I2V), are being investigated. The emergence of the IEEE 802.11p standard (IEEE 802.11p, 2010) for short to medium range inter-vehicle communication and the allocation of a dedicated frequency band for ITS communication in Europe have paved the way for future implementations of communication-based ITS safety applications. ITS (2010), which interrelates humans, roads, and vehicles through state-of-art Information Technology (IT) are new transport systems for the purpose of the solution of the road transportation problems, aiming for efficient traffic flow and reduction of the environmental load. Recently, ITS have drawn a lot of attention to solve various traffic problems.

There are many projects being investigated and realized related to ITS worldwide, such as PREVent (Prevent IP, 2010) and CALM (ISOTC-204WG16, 2010) to reduce road fatalities. VIDAS (VIsible light communication for advanced Driver Assistant Systems) is another challenging project which promises to be used over existing infrastructures, resulting in low cost communication systems by exploring traffic lights as road side units based on VLC. VLC is normally based on Light Emitting Diodes (LED) which has many advantages such as highly energy efficient, long life, harmless to human and friendly to environment (green technology).

LED-based VLC (Akanegawa, Tanaka, & Nakagawa, 2001) systems can be deployed in vehicular environment on existing infrastructure such as LEDs traffic signal lights. The VLC systems can broadcast road traffic safety information minimizing the possible accidents and increasing smooth flow of traffic on road. Furthermore, LED-based road light can offer Ubiquitous Road to Vehicle Communication (URVC) (Kitano, Haruyama, & Nakagawa, 2003) throughout travel.

This chapter presents LED-based traffic lights as RSU for traffic information broadcast (I2V mode) using VLC systems. A VLC system's architecture suitable for information broadcast is discussed. Some of the related works in this area are also presented. The concept of VLC system integration with RSUs and ITS architecture is briefly introduced. Few important road safety services offered by VLC systems are also discussed. Finally, chapter highlights some of challenges in the technology and implementation issues.

ITS AND VEHICULAR COMMUNICATION

With the growth of population in major urban areas and accelerated increase in number of cars, traffic is becoming generically chaotic. The problem of congestion, differently from what many might think, not only affects the day-to-day life of citizens but also has a great impact on business and economic activities. These issues therefore generate less income, affecting the sustainable growth of cities throughout the world.

Considering current problems of traffic management, control, and planning, especially fearing the consequences of their medium and long-term effects, both practitioners and the scientific communities have strived to tackle congestion in large urban networks. Research has been carried out basically towards the design and specification of future transport solutions featuring autonomy, putting the user in the center of all concerns and largely oriented to services. Such efforts were eventually to culminate in the emergence of the concept of ITS. Now the user is a central aspect of transportation systems, forcing architectures to become adaptable and accessible by different means so as to meet different requirements and a wide range of purposes.

Two of the main features of today's intelligent transportation are as follows:

Automated computation is an important requirement of ITS. Future transport systems must make decisions automatically, analyzing input information and acting accordingly, triggering coordinated actions to improve system performance. Demand for flexibility and freedom of choice is another important aspect on the user's side. The current lack of flexibility in transportation systems limits their potential to users, especially in that concerning personalized services, which is a major target for criticism by many users. ITS then should be open to flexibility, different options, and driver choices, as well as personalized services. As transportation systems are greatly dependent on the network topology and other characteristics, intelligent infrastructures become fundamental. New communication technologies, including mobile, wireless and ad-hoc networks are improving infrastructures a great deal, enabling it to become an active and interactive part of the system.

A distributed architecture, accounting for asynchronous, control algorithms, coordination and management autonomous elements is undoubtedly one of the major currently researched areas of ITS. There are several requirements that must be satisfied, from user-centered to service-based functionalities, turning intelligent transportation into a complex, heterogeneous and intricate artificial society. Current research already considers that ITS architecture must explore distributed algorithms using exogenous information from various sources, making greater use of parallelism and asynchronous capacities of pro-active entities.

ITS encompass a broad range of wireless and wired communications-based information, control and electronics technologies. When integrated into the transportation systems infrastructure, and in vehicles themselves, these technologies help monitor and manage traffic flow, reduce congestion, provide alternate routes to travelers, enhance productivity, and save lives, time, and money. Based on wireless short-range technology, vehicles are able to exchange information with RSUs spontaneously. However, with advancement of long-range wireless systems, vehicles are able to communicate among themselves. Thus vehicular communication combined with ITS is becoming extremely important. They offer numerous services in vehicular environment.

IMPORTANT SERVICES IN VEHICULAR ENVIRONMENT

One of the important factors of success of a technology is its different kinds of applications and offered quality of services by it. With the expansion of applications scenarios from safe navigation and collision avoidance to content distribution, emergency operations recovery (natural disasters, terrorist attacks, etc.) and urban pervasive sensing, a brand new set of services will emerge in the Vehicular Network, such as priority oriented broadcast of vehicle alarms, vehicle to vehicle routing, and so on. The new vehicular applications will also place new service requests to the Internet infrastructure, such as geo addressing as opposed to (or in addition of) traditional IP addressing, directory service support, service discovery, mobile resource monitoring, and mobility management (GeoNET, 2010).

There are many high priority road safety applications and services of VLC systems in vehicular environment. All of them assist drivers with making safe decisions in traffic and complying with traffic regulations. The traffic signal violation warning and curve speed warning applications allow infrastructure to transmit to vehicles with traffic light states and curvature of road, respectively.

Vehicular applications span different network scenarios as discussed before and require a range of network services. Furthermore, the information dissemination in these scenarios can occur over multiple hops or be limited to single hop. These network services, either stand-alone or combined, provide all the services required for vehicular applications. Main network services for the support of various applications are given in Table 1 (IEEE 802.11p, 2010; ITS, 2010; Prevent IP, 2010).

I2V or Roadside-to-Vehicle Communication (RVC) Systems assume that all communications take place between roadside infrastructure (including RSUs) and vehicles. Depending on the application, two different types of infrastructure can be distinguished, Sparse RVC (SRVC) and Ubiquitous RVC (URVC) systems. SRVC systems are capable of providing communication services at hot spots. A busy intersection scheduling traffic light, a gas station advertising its existence (and prices), and parking availability at an airport, are examples of applications requiring an SRVC system. An SRVC system can be deployed gradually, thus not requiring substantial investments before any available benefits.

An URVC system is the holy grail of vehicular communication: providing all roads with high-speed communication, which would enable applications unavailable with any of the other systems. Unfortunately, an URVC system may require considerable investments for providing full (even significant) coverage of existing roadways (especially in large and developing countries like the India, China, etc.).

Table 1. Vehicular network services

Network Services	Description and important applications/services
I2V One-Hop Broadcasting	Required by traffic signal violation warning and curve speed warning applications. Combined with the V2I one-hop anycasting, it can provide service for the left turn assistant, and stop sign movement assistant applications where bi-directional information exchange between the vehicles and the infrastructure nodes is required.
V2I One-Hop Anycasting	On receipt of information, infrastructure node processes through backbone network. This network service, along with I2V one-hop broadcasting service, can be combined with the multihop inter-vehicle forwarding. The combination maximizes the utilization of the backbone infrastructure network and vehicles as relays and the chance to reach every node.
Multihop Inter-Vehicle Forwarding	In this case each vehicle acts as a relay and forwards data packets following a set of rules to prevent unnecessary broadcast flooding, e.g., there is a time-to-live limit on each packet, and a packet is forwarded only once by each vehicle. This network service maximizes the possibility that information is disseminated quickly and reliably among a large number of vehicles. Therefore, it is suitable for providing service to event-triggered, urgent message delivering applications, such as cooperative forward collision warning, pre-crash sensing, and emergency electronic brake lights.
Limited Neighbor Broadcasting	This service also operates in the V2V scenario, but over single hop. Each vehicle broadcasts information from all of its transmitters to its neighboring vehicles. But, the information dissemination is limited to one hop, and the neighboring vehicles do not forward information that they receive. Thus, this network service only provides vehicles with information in close vicinity; by limiting the extent of broadcasting. It prevents network performance degradation due to high volume flooding. Thus, it provides service to the applications that need periodic, local information. For example, the lane change warning application requires this network service because vehicles constantly need to know about the positions of the nearby vehicles when making lane changes, but information from other distant vehicles is irrelevant.
Vehicle-To/From-Infrastructure Unicasting	The vehicle-to/from-infrastructure unicasting network service takes place in the V2I and I2V network scenarios, with each scenario providing uplink and downlink for vehicular Internet access applications respectively. This service works over single hops and multiple hops to/from a gateway infrastructure node. By using routing protocols, vehicles first find routes to a gateway infrastructure node and then start transmission to that gateway, which may use other vehicles as relays. This service requires routing protocols to discover routes, and other services and paths to vehicles and infrastructure nodes via single hop transmissions and multihop broadcasting.

However, for these services and applications; vehicular networks require interaction in virtually all levels. And ITS in fact; rely on distributed and advanced communication infrastructure. Interoperability and integration become crucial in this scenario. This novel scenario has been motivating and challenging practitioners and scientific community. In the following section, we highlight ongoing development of ITS architectural scenario to accomplish this.

INTEGRATION OF COMMUNICATION SYSTEMS WITH ITS ARCHITECTURE

Existing in-vehicle safety systems enhanced with new cooperative approaches using wireless communications between vehicles can potentially decrease the number of accidents on the roads and smooth traffic flow. ITS use a number of technologies and many more are likely to be used as we progress. In this situation, it becomes very important for an ITS architecture to be flexible enough to accommodate integration of new systems.

Ongoing development towards ISO TC 204 ITS architecture (ISOTC204WG16, 2009) by the European Telecommunications Standards Institute (ETSI) is considered to be a major breakthrough in the area of ITS. ITS development is strongly driven by large-scale research and development projects on cooperative systems (CVIS, SAFESPOT, COOPERS) complemented by more focused projects (GEONET, SEVECOM) (GeoNET, 2010; SeVeCom, 2010). To consolidate these efforts towards a European solution, the COMeSafety project (COMeSafety, 2010) defines a common European ITS communication architecture as a basis for future development and standardization. This architecture framework is currently being refined and complemented by the European research and development project PRE-DRIVE C2X (2010) working towards future field operational tests for cooperative systems.

In summary, the COMeSafety architecture framework specifies a reference protocol architecture of ITS. ITS represents a generic model for the integration of services, vehicles and roadside communication infrastructures. The reference protocol architecture basically obeys the ISO/OSI reference model, vertically extended by a management and a security layer (Figure 1).

ITS standards (ISOTC204WG16, 2009; Evensen, 2010) promise to offer various access technologies. This family of standards specifies a common architecture, network protocols and communication interface definitions for wired and wireless communications using various access technologies including cellular 2G, 3G, satellite, infrared, 5GHz micro-wave, 60GHz millimeter-wave, and mobile wireless broadband. These and other access technologies that can be incorporated are designed to provide broadcast, unicast, and multicast communications between mobile stations, between mobile and fixed stations and between fixed stations in the ITS sector. Networking and Transport layer offers Internet connectivity and routing and consists of many basic transport protocols and Internet protocol specifically IPv6. For communication support, application support, service announcement and so on, facility layer is included into the model while safety related, efficient traffic relay and value added dedicated applications are handled using application layer. A security layer monitors and offer authentication for extended services and applications. A management and control layer becomes necessary for the reference model for proper control and operation of various components.

The National ITS Architecture (ISOTC-204WG16, 2009) can be viewed as a framework that ties together the transportation and telecommunication world. This framework enables the creation and effective delivery of the broad spectrum of ITS services. There are also many challenges in interconnecting the disparate components of any end-to-end ITS solution, encompassing various transportation and communication issues. It has

Figure 1. Reference model for ITS

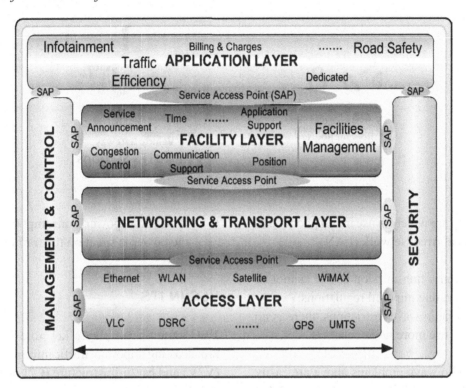

been critical, therefore, to promote an architectural concept that mitigates the complexity of interconnecting many transportation systems with multiple types of communication links.

An ITS communication architecture as shown in Figure 2 is a communication system made of four physically separated subsystem components: 1) the vehicle subsystem component (Vehicle Station); 2) the mobile subsystem component (Personal Station); 3) the roadside subsystem component (Roadside Station); and 4) the central subsystem component (Central Station). ITS communication architecture contains the ITS subsystem components and usually a vehicle gateway connecting the ITS Station to legacy systems. The vehicle requires a vehicle gateway connected to the vehicle station and to the vehicle manufacturer's proprietary vehicle network. These components are inter-linked by a communication network. The communication between the vehicle subsystem component and the mobile subsystem component are performed over a short-range wireless or wired communication media. Similarly, vehicle communication systems interact with RSUs, which consist of many communication infrastructures and access networks.

Access point routers, variable message sign and gateways are responsible for offering information data connectivity between mobile units (vehicles) and Internet. However, these radio systems are not cost effective. It is very difficult to use wireless based access point all along the road at small intervals. Furthermore, it is noted that it may provide the biological damages to humans by the electromagnetic wave. In addition, the Radio Law does restrict the free usage of the radio wave wireless communication. On the other hand, the VLC does not require any license at present. Also, due to the limited licensed bandwidth, the radio spectrum is becoming increasingly congested. In summary, the radio wireless communications have the following problems

Figure 2. Communication architecture

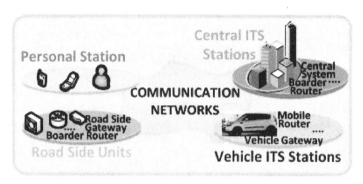

although they are widely in use in cell phones and wireless Local Area Network (LAN):

- The electric transmission power cannot be increased due imposed regulations;
- Due to radio wave restrictions, there is no room to use more radio channels.

These radio wave problems above are easily solved by the use of VLC. A LED-based VLC system would consume less energy than the radio system, allowing the expansion of communication networks without added energy requirements and potentially reducing carbon emissions over the long term. This technology leads a Green growth as it uses eco-friendly IT green technology which is an added benefit to ITS. In comparison to the radio wireless communication, VLC systems have the following main advantages:

- There are no licensing requirements or tariffs for its utilization;
- There are no RF radiation hazards, visible light is safe for human;
- It has a large bandwidth, which enables very high data rates;
- It is small, light, and compact;
- Traffic lights are set everywhere. Then, wireless transmission can be easily established through the VLC device attached to the lightings;

- It has low power consumption—most of the power is spent on the traffic signaling.

VLC IN ITS

VLC systems can play a key role in ITS from broadcasting important traffic information to C2C (V2V) and car2infrastructure (C2I or V2I) communication facilities. Akanegawa, Tanaka, and Nakagawa (2001) carried out basic study on traffic information system using LED traffic lights. They analyzed basic performance and defined a service area for requisite data rate using basic intensity modulation. Road-to-Vehicle communication system using LED traffic light was discussed in Wada, Yendo, Fujii, and Tanimoto (2005) and Iwasaki, Wada, Endo, Fujii, and Tanimoto (2007). Authors in these studies proposed a parallel OWC system based on LED traffic light as transmitter and high-speed camera as receiver. They discussed modulating LED individually and receiving by its corresponding camera. A communication protocol for the inter-vehicle communication system was proposed in Takayuki and Ryuji (2000). The proposed system configures a dynamic Code Division Multiple Access (CDMA) network by changing the spreading code using the code hopping technique every packet. A new fast responding VLC receiving system suitable for ITS applications was proposed by Toshiki, Shinya, Tomohiro, Toshiaki and Masayuki (2007). In this proposal, the authors discuss the imaging optics, based on photo-diodes and the tracking mechanism.

VLC is not only suitable for a broadcast system, as road-to-vehicle or I2V communication systems, but it can be equally effective in V2V and V2I communication systems. In case of V2V scenario, a vehicle in the front of traffic light receives the traffic safety information and passes it using brake light to the vehicle running behind. They can even form vehicle adhoc network and share information among themselves. An example of a scenario is illustrated in Figure 3. Similarly, the running car can request information from RSUs using LED-based front head light thereby forming full duplex communication systems.

RSUs such as, LED-based traffic lights are well suited for broadcast communication in I2V mode of vehicular communication systems. Traffic safety related information can be continuously broadcasted without extra power usage enhancing smooth traffic flow as well as reducing accident fatality. The light emitted from a traffic light (consisting of an array of LEDs) is modulated at a frequency undetectable to human eyes.

The modulated light is then detected by a Photo Diode (PD) based receiver on the vehicle, providing useful safety information to the driver in advance. More advanced perspectives may employ inter-vehicle communication means, as a way to convey information between vehicles stopped near a traffic control post.

Hence, LED-based traffic light offers very suitable option to be included as RSU and integrated with ITS architecture. One of the suitable scenarios of interaction and communication from RSU to vehicle communication is presented in Figure 4 Along with many access technologies, LED-based VLC can be used. An additional traffic control and monitor unit is included which can provide additional support information in conjunction with other RSUs. In this systems therefore, integrating LED-based traffic light unit for broadcasting safety related information offer a cost effective method of implementation. Since, replacement of conventional traffic light with LED-based traffic light getting momentum. It is highly desirable to use the dual function of LED; in this case, signaling and traffic broadcast unit.

Figure 3. Application scenario-outdoor

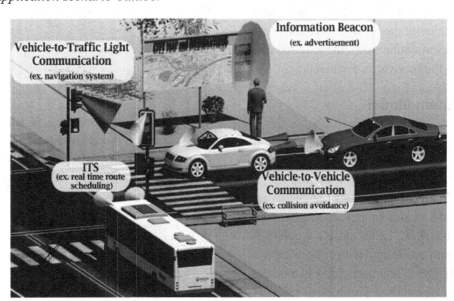

Moreover, traffic lights are already being replaced by LEDs all over the world. Even vehicles are now equipped with LEDs brake and head light. Therefore, VLC can be considered as supplementary communication systems not only for broadcast but also uplink communication connectivity and V2V communication facility. However, we have focused mainly in a broadcast system using LED-based VLC system for road safety application. A brief description follows in following section.

EXPLORING A LED-BASED TRAFFIC LIGHT AS ROAD SIDE UNIT

LED-based traffic light can be used as medium-range beacon in broadcast mode, distributing traffic safety information for drivers on their approach. Examples of such information include traffic flow, road conditions, on-going construction sites and many more. This traffic light can be called as a RSU and can be a part of an access networks such as WiFi, WiMax, and so on, for ITS architecture.

We present LED-based traffic light system set-up as shown in Figure 5. A suitable model for safety information broadcast is designed and developed. A service area for uniform and high illumination coverage to enhance data communication is defined through simulation study, the required gain for designing the receiver is discussed.

Traffic System Model

This section presents the traffic system set-up and develops a model for the emitter and channel. A generic multilane traffic light system is shown in Figure 5. Table 1 summarizes the design parameters for the system model. The traffic light consists of an array of LEDs closely wired to fit into the standard traffic light with either a 200mm or 300mm diameter, and each LED is modeled considering a generalized Lambertian radiation

pattern. The irradiance distribution or illuminance are both, cosine functions of the viewing angle. A practical approximation of the irradiance distribution is given by (Barry, 1994):

$$E(d,\theta) = E_0(d)\cos^m(\theta) \tag{1}$$

where θ is the viewing angle and $E_0(d)$ is the irradiance (W/m^2), also given in luminous flux (lm) on the axis at a distance d from the LED. Parameter m characterizes the directivity index of the LED, given as:

$$m = -\frac{ln(2)}{ln\left[cos\left(\varnothing_{\frac{1}{2}}\right)\right]} \tag{2}$$

is the mode number that specify the directivity of the transmitter. At far-field the distribution from an array of LEDs placed in a circular concentric ring pattern is also found to be approximately Lambertian. Supported by the geometry of Figure 4 and the parameters presented in Table 2, the LoS channel gain is given as (Kumar, Terra, Lourenco, Alves, & Aguiar, 2011):

$$H_{multiring(x,y,z)} = E(0)p(t)\frac{m+1}{2\pi}\Sigma_{k=1}^{N_{ring}}\Sigma_{i=1}^{N_k}$$
$$\frac{\cos^m(\varphi_i)\cos(\sigma_i)}{d_{i^2}}rect\left(\frac{\sigma_i}{FOV}\right) \tag{3}$$

where, N_{ring} is the no. of rings, N_k is the LEDs on ring k, d is the direct distance from each LED (emitter) to receiver, $E(0)$ is the axial irradiance of LED, *FOV* is the field of view of receiver which is a *rect* function, and

$$\cos(\varphi_i) = \frac{z}{\sqrt{[(x-x_i)^2 + (y-y_i-h)^2 + z^2]}} \tag{4}$$

Figure 4. A scenario of traffic light integration with ITS architecture

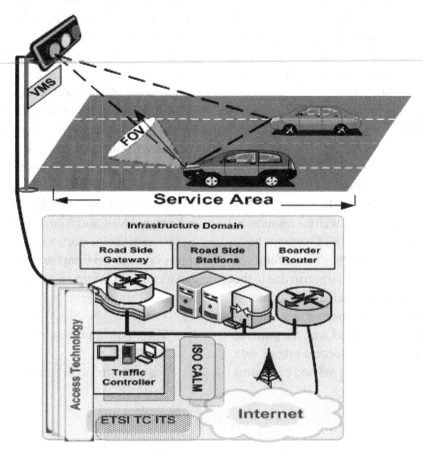

and

$$\cos(\beta_i) = \frac{(y - y_i - h)\cos(\theta) + z\sin\theta}{\sqrt{[(x - x_i)^2 + (y - y_i - h)^2 + z^2]}}$$

$$(5)$$

where h is the height of the traffic light and θ is the angle of orientation of the receiver. This model provides a significant advantage when designing a VLC system for traffic lights as it enables a preview of the expected output radiation pattern in function of several implementation parameters. Channel loss over distance is plotted and shown in Figure 6.

VLC SYSTEM ARCHITECTURE FOR INFORMATION BROADCAST

System Architecture

A VLC system consists of VLC transmitter and receiver, which are physically different and functionally separated. The transmitter modulates information at lighting sources, such as LEDs. This modulation takes place at high frequencies that humans' bare eyes cannot perceive any difference in lighting compared to that when there is no modulation. A VLC receiver consists of photodiodes either as stand-alone elements or in the form of an image sensor. The block diagram representation of the system architecture is shown in Figure 7. Devices such as laptop, mobile phones can be used for transmitting and receiving information signal. The transmitter part consists of a light source, modulator, and a pulse shaper to switch the LEDs at the rate of data transmission. The light source emits data using light wave as the medium while illuminating.

VLC Transmitter

A VLC Transmitter (also called emitter) is an optic-electronic transducer device that transmits information using visible light waves as the transmission medium, usually with the resource to high brightness (HB)-LED's. VLC systems have become a more viable technology for the future of wireless data transmission, in large part due to the developments in the area of solid-state lighting.

The digital data signal is passed to a data encoder that modulates the signal with the purpose to switch the LEDs at the expected rate of data transmission. The modulation method used must offer high robustness to background light and at the same time, it should be as bright as possible. The Pulse Position Modulation (PPM) of Intensity Modulation (IM) as in the case of IR can be used (Khan & Barry, 1997). Other option is to use a simple Non-Return-to-Zero (NRZ) encoding with an On-Off-Keying (OOK) amplitude modulation. Spread Spectrum is another technique that can be considered. It increases resistance to interference and jamming, and also allows the establishment of secure communications. Various modulation schemes have been investigated and discussed in Kumar, Alves, and Aguiar (2011).

In a practical aspect, the modulator also receives information from the traffic control unit so that it can hold information while the light color changes. This ensures:

1. There is no transmission in the brief period; and

2. Transmission synchronization.

Figure 5. Traffic system set up information broadcast

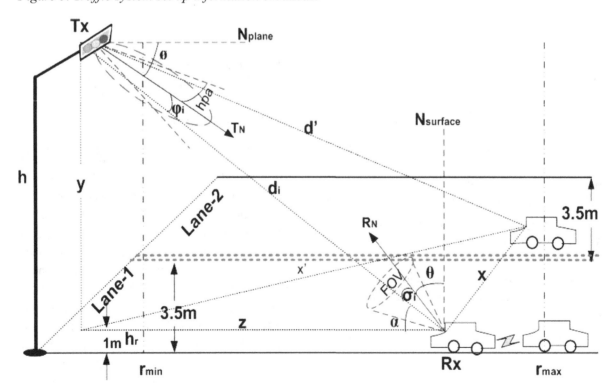

Table 2. Traffic system design parameters

Parameters	Definition and Values
h	Height of traffic light.
$(h-l)$	Height of traffic light from the receiver.
z	Distance from traffic light base to the vehicle in lane 1.
x	Distance from traffic light base to the vehicle in lane 2.
d_i	Direct distance from emitter to the detector on lane
hpa	Half power angle.
φ_i	Angle of irradiation.
θ	Orientation of receiver.
σ_i	Angle of incidence.
Lane width	3,5 meters
Width of the vehicle	1,8 meters

Heights and distances are defined in meters. Angles and orientations are defined in degrees.

The resulting signal is then used to control the switching of the LED through the output driver. The output driver combined with the control signal should ensure sufficient optical power, in order to achieve the expected range of communication. Sometimes the electrical characteristics of the different color LED's, like the maximum forward current or the forward voltage, might imply the usage of an output driver with distinct channels and a slightly different switching.

The encoder can be integrated, or the range of input signals specified. To build this block, a microprocessor is a relatively cost effective solution but upgrading it is not an easy process. Using a Field Programmable Gate Array (FPGA) would be more expensive, but has better data processing capabilities, and it also makes upgrading easier.

Figure 6. Channel attenuation over distance

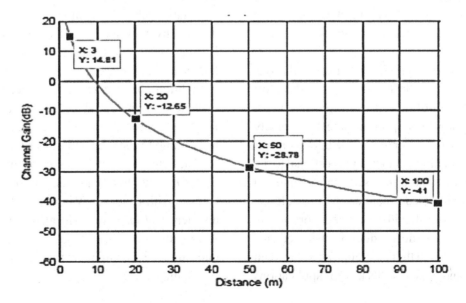

Figure 7. VLC transmitter and receiver block representation

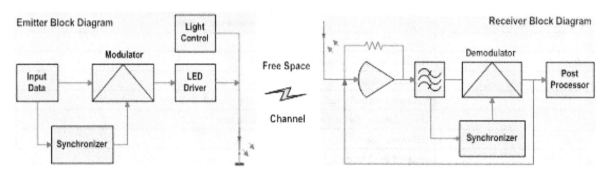

In the front-end electronics, integrating the LED matrix is essential to specify power consumption, optical range, and maximum operating frequency, etc.

VLC data rate is limited by the switching speed of the emitter LEDs. On the other hand, long distance communication is limited by the transmitted power and background light sources.

VLC Receiver

The VLC receiver is an optic-electronic transducer that receives information, previously modulated in the visible light spectrum, and converts it into electrical signal capable of being processed by a demodulator-decoder. The correct design of this device is crucial to ensure good performance of the overall VLC system. Among other concerning factors are the presence of low-level signals and high noise interference.

The visible light pulses, originated at the system's emitter, are collected in the photo-detector; an optical IR cut-off filter is a viable solution for eliminating unwanted spectral content. Reversely biased photodiode operates in the photoconductive mode generating a current proportional to the collected light. This current is of a small value and a preamplifier is used to convert it into a voltage. This preamplifier should have low distortion and a large gain-bandwidth product. Transimpedance amplifiers represent the best compromise between bandwidth and noise for this kind of applications

(Aguiar, Tavares, Cura, de Vasconcelos, Alves, Valadas, & Santos, 1999). The resulting voltage is then applied to a low-pass filter to remove any high-frequency noise. The signal is then further amplified in the final voltage amplifier stage. Also, DC signal filtering is applied at the input of the amplifying and filtering stages, which helps reduce the DC noise component of the captured signal as well as low-frequency components. The final voltage signal should correspond to the received light pulses, which are then decoded in the final decoder block, thus extracting the digital data. This final block performs the inverse function of the emitter's encoder block, but it can also be implemented with a microprocessor or, even better, an FPGA (Ghassemlooy & Boucouvalas, 2005). The demodulate scheme will depend on the modulation scheme used in emitter side. A practical down-conversion technique that can be considered is direct detection. Clock recovery is necessary to synchronize the receiver with the transmitter. In addition, the system will also need the clock management unit and data/clock recovery block for the synchronization of received packets corresponding to the received power level.

The detector is characterized by the parameter Field Of View (FOV). For a larger service area, a receiver with a wider FOV is preferable. However, a wider FOV leads to performance degradation. Among the received signals, there are also many undesired noise components, which are processed simultaneously.

Figure 8. LoS link and diffused link scenario

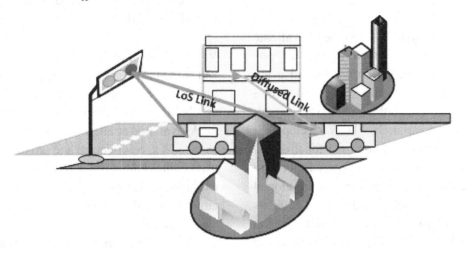

The Channel

One of the stringent requirements of the VLC is direct Line-of-Sight (LoS). However, in some instances of indoor applications diffused channel are also used. Figure 8 illustrates some link examples. The emitted light from LED carries data information in wireless medium. Thus, the intensity of light of the emitter becomes an important parameter on which range of transmission depends. There are many external light sources such as Sun light, road/street lights. These are the major issues to be considered in link design. They deteriorate the intensity of emitter light and may cause false triggering of photo diode. Optical filters, color filters should be used to minimize the effect.

Figure 9. VLC prototype for traffic information broadcast in ITS

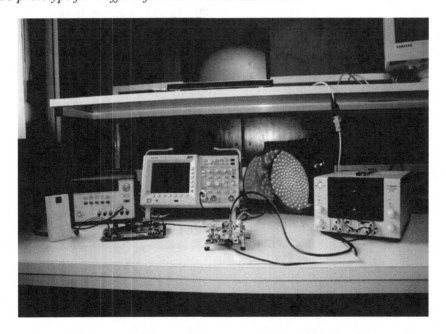

Prototype VLC Systems

A prototype VLC system is designed to validate the theoretical analysis. Opto-electronic parts of transmitter and receiver are designed using discrete components while signal processing parts of both the transmitter and the receiver are implemented in Spartan-3E FPGA development kits. The modulation scheme used for this system is based on direct sequence spread spectrum techniques. The transmitter parts are developed to ensure data transmission at the rate of 200kbps (however, configurable) and efficiently drive an arrays of LEDs. The receiver samples the signal 5-times higher at a maximum of 1Mega samples per second (Msps) (limited by the ADC speed in our kit) using Analog-to-Digital Converter (ADC).

A snapshot of experiment in laboratory is shown in Figure 9. This figure illustrates FPGA board for transmitter and receiver, optoelectronic VLC transmitter (traffic light and associated driver units) and receiver, a laptop showing sent and received messages, signal waveform on oscilloscope and necessary power supply. Packet error rate performance of the system is also presented as shown on Figure 10. However, outdoor experiment is still under progress.

RECENT DIRECTIONS AND CHALLENGES

VLC systems leveraging benefits from LED advancements have been recognized as one of the important technologies. This can be considered as ubiquitous for the reason that light can be made available at all places. Many devices such as PC, TVs, cell phones, and advertising boards use visible light. LED components are recently exploited to these devices. IrDA and small LED lamps attached to home appliance have been often utilized everywhere. VLC can be seamlessly employed in conjunction with these devices and terminals. Thus, it will be possible to have a human interface communication system which is secure, high-speed response, high data rate, low power consumption and cleaner harmless to humans. VLC is very suitable to the ubiquitous environment in terms of human interface to assure comfortable human life. Towards this end, IEEE personal area network working group is discussing on standardization of the VLC technology.

Standardization

Important steps have already been taken by IEEE 802.15 VLC working group towards standardiza-

Figure 10. PER for different SNR

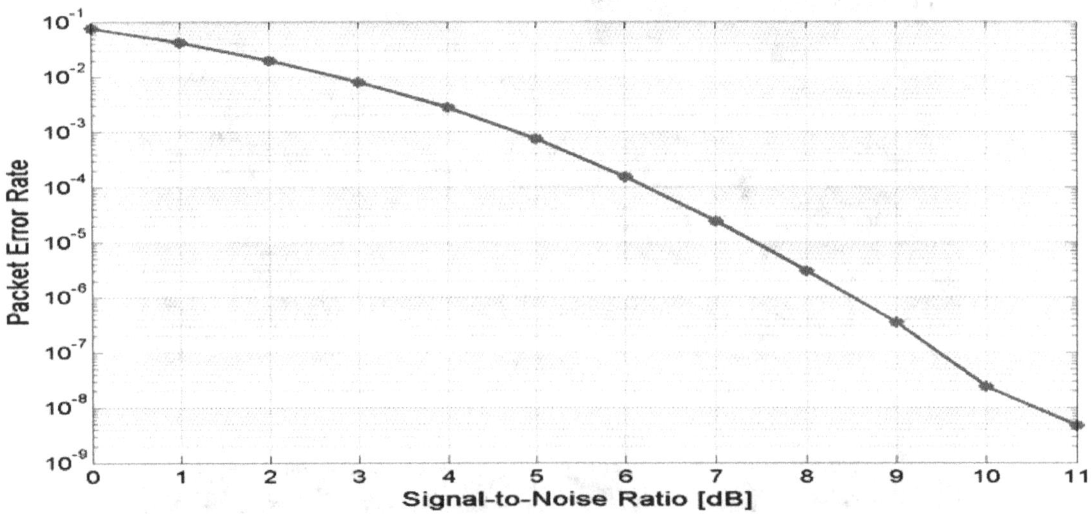

132

tion (IEEE 80.15.7, 2010). The standard would be recognized as IEEE 802.15.7. The working group standardizes PHY and MAC for VLC personal area networks. They have been discussing for last two years and by the end of this year, they are expected to bring forward the draft version. Therefore, the technology is expected to be more popular in coming years.

However, VLC systems have multiple benefits but a number of complex challenging issues need to be addressed. We briefly outline the major challenges as given:

- **Long Range Limitation:** Because of LoS path requirement, the technology is suitable for short-range communication.
- **Ambient and other sources of heavy noise:** In outdoor applications, overcoming and minimizing the effect of natural and artificial lights is a major challenging task.
- **Increasing data rate:** The limited bandwidth of the LEDs is another major challenge for high-speed communication.
- **Provision of Uplink:** Using illumination sources is naturally suited to broadcast applications. Providing uplink communication will be problematic.
- **Complex modulation:** The most simple and useful modulation technique based on direct detection intensity modulation finds too weak to overcome many challenges. A complex modulation technique would be needed to support effective and desirable data communication.
- **Parallel communication (Optical Multiple-Input-Multiple-Output [MIMO]):** It is an interesting scenario of VLC. However, theoretically, it can be realizable but implementation would be a real challenge.
- **Complex receiver based on equalizer:** As an extension of IR, some studies proposed the use of equalizers at the receiver at the cost of increased complexity.
- **Regulatory challenges:** VLC is subject to regulation (in most cases) by non-communication standard such as eye-safety standard, automotive standard. Therefore, coordination across regulatory bodies and frameworks become challenging.

CONCLUSION

Visible Light Communication is becoming an alternative choice for next generation wireless technology by offering unprecedented bandwidth and ubiquitous infrastructure support. Their applications in outdoor vehicular environment such as ITS is very important for road safety however, very challenging. Providing uplink from V2I mode using VLC systems is not easy. This chapter discusses LED-based traffic light as a road side unit for I2V mode of communication using VLC. It describes how VLC can be used and integrated with ongoing ITS architecture. The chapter also highlights important characteristics and challenges.

REFERENCES

Aguiar, R. L., Tavares, A., Cura, J. L., de Vasconcelos, E., Alves, L. N., Valadas, R., & Santos, D. M. (1999). Considerations on the design of transceivers for wireless optical LANs. In Proceedings of the IEE Electronics & Communications, Colloquium on Optical Wireless Communications. London, UK: IEE.

Akanegawa, M., Tanaka, Y., & Nakagawa, M. (2001). Basic study on traffic information system using LED traffic lights. *IEEE Transactions on Intelligent Transportation Systems, 2*(4), 197–203. doi:10.1109/6979.969365

Akanegawa, M., Tanaka, Y., & Nakagawa, M. (2001). Basic study on traffic information systems using LED traffic lights. *IEEE Transactions on Intelligent Transportation Systems, 2,* 197–203. doi:10.1109/6979.969365

Barry, J. R. (1994). *Infrared communications.* Dordrecht, The Netherlands: Kluwer Academic Publishers. doi:10.1007/978-1-4615-2700-8

COMeSafety. (2010). *Communication for esafety.* Retrieved Jul. 2010 from http://www.comesafety.org/

Evensen, K. (2010). Intelligent transport systems, European standardization for ITS: WG2 architecture. In *Proceedings of the ETSI TC ITS Workshop.* ETSI.

GeoNET. (2010). *Geographic addressing and routing for vehicular communications.* Retreived Nov. 2010 from http://www.geonet-project.eu/

Ghassemlooy, Z., & Boucouvalas, A. C. (2005). Indoor optical wireless communications systems and networks. *International Journal of Communication Systems, 18,* 191–193. doi:10.1002/dac.698

IEEE 802.11p. (2010). *Website.* Retrieved July 2010, from http://www.ieee802.org/11/Reports/tgp update.htm

IEEE 802.15.7. (2010). *Website.* Retrieved March 2010 from http://www.ieee802.org/15/pub/TG7.html

ISOTC204WG16. (2009). *Communication access for land mobile.* Retreived Aug. 2009 from http://www.isotc204wg16.org/concept

ISOTC204WG16. (2010). *Communication access for land mobile.* Retrieved from http://www.isotc204wg16.org/concept

ITS. (2010). *Website.* Retrieved from http://www.its.dot.gov/research.htm

Iwasaki, S., Wada, M., Endo, T., Fujii, T., & Tanimoto, M. (2007). Basic experiments on parallel wireless optical communication for ITS. In *Proceedings of the IEEE Intelligent Vehicles Symposium,* (pp. 321-326). IEEE Press.

Khan, J. M., & Barry, J. R. (1997). Wireless infrared communications. *Proceedings of the IEEE, 85,* 265–298. doi:10.1109/5.554222

Kitano, S., Haruyama, S., & Nakagawa, M. (2003). LED road illumination communication system. In *Proceedings of the IEEE Vehicular Technology Conference,* (vol. 5, pp. 3346-3350). IEEE Press.

Kumar, N., Alves, L. N., & Aguiar, R. L. (2011). *Performance study of direct sequence spread spectrum based visible light communication systems for traffic information transmission.* Unpublished.

Kumar, N., Terra, D., Lourenço, N., Alves, L. N., & Aguiar, R. L. (2011). *Visible light communication for intelligent transportation in road safety application.* Paper presented at 7th International Wireless Communications and Mobile Computing Conference. Istanbul, Turkey.

PreDRIVE C2X. (2010). *Preparation for driving implementation and evaluation of car 2 X communication technology.* Retrieved Jul. 2010 from http://www.pre-drive-c2x.eu/index.dhtml/444d919dde59571535mo/-/deDE/-/CS/-/

Prevent, I. P. (2010). *Website.* Retrieved from http://www.prevent-ip.org/

SeVeCom. (2010). *Secure vehicle communication.* Retreived Nov. 2010 from http://www.sevecom.org/

Takayuki, T., & Ryuji, K. (2000). Inter-vehicle communication protocol using common spreading code. In *Proceedings of the IEEE Intelligent Vehicles Symposium.* IEEE Press.

Toshiki, H., Shinya, I., Tomohiro, Y., Toshiaki, F., & Masayuki, T. (2007). A new receiving system of visible light communication for ITS. In *Proceedings of the 2007 IEEE Intelligent Vehicles Symposium.* Istanbul, Turkey: IEEE Press.

Wada, M., Yendo, T., Fujii, T., & Tanimoto, M. (2005). Road-to-vehicle communication using LED traffic light. In *Proceedings of the 2005 IEEE Intelligent Vehicles Symposium,* (pp. 601-606). IEEE Press.

World Health Organization. (2008). *The top ten causes of death. Fact sheet No. 310.* Geneva, Switzerland: WHO.

ADDITIONAL READING

Car to Car Communication Consortium. (2012). *Website.* Retrieved from http://www.car-to-car. org/

Ernst, T., & De La Fortelle, A. (2006). *Car-to-car and car-to-infrastructure communication system based on NEMO and MANET in IPv6.* Retrieved from http://hal.inria.fr/docs/00/10/24/43/PDF/ITSWC-2006-IPv6.pdf

Gans, J. S., King, S. P., & Wright, J. (2004). Wireless communications. *Handbook of Telecommunication Economics, 2.*

Kumar, N., Lourenço, N., Spiez, M., & Aguiar, R. L. (2008). Visible light communication conception and VIDAS. *IETE Technical Review, 25*(6). doi:10.4103/0256-4602.45428

Chapter 7
WiMAX for Traffic Control in Urban Environments

Mohamed Ahmed El-Dakroury
Ain Shams University, Egypt

Hassanein H. Amer
American University, Egypt

Abdel Halim Zekry
Ain Shams University, Egypt

Ramez M. Daoud
American University, Egypt

ABSTRACT

This chapter addresses the wireless communication aspect of traffic control in an urban vehicular environment. The IEEE 802.16e-2005 standard is used for Infrastructure to Vehicle communication. An architecture is developed with the target of minimizing overall data loss. Access Service Network Gateway (ASN-GW) is used to manage vehicle communication while roaming. OPNET simulations show that using ASN-GW gives good performance in mobility management. Simulations also show that introducing an interference source drastically degrades system performance. Using Dual Trigger HO (DTH) in a congested scenario improves system performance and reduces the impact of interference on the system.

INTRODUCTION

Traffic congestion has a number of negative effects on world economy as well as people's lives (Mohandas, 2009). Significant activities are underway worldwide to accelerate the development of Intelligent Transportation Systems for safe, efficient, and convenient driving. For example, the department of transportation in the USA funds projects like IntelliDrive (Weil, 2009). In Europe, the European Union funds projects like CityMobil (Wahl, 2008), COOPERS (Toulminet, 2008), and

DOI: 10.4018/978-1-4666-2223-4.ch007

GeoNet (Mariyasagayam, 2008). On the other side of the world, the Ministry of Land, Infrastructure, Transport, and Tourism in Japan funds the SmartWay project for driving safety support systems based on vehicle-highway cooperation (Oyama, 2008).

ITS is about integrating wireless communications, computing, and advanced sensor technologies into vehicular and transportation systems. One of the main challenges in providing a complete ITS is the design of protocols for Vehicle-to-Vehicle (V2V) and/or Infrastructure-to-Vehicle (I2V) networking that adapt to changes of roadway conditions in order to provide fast, reliable communications technologies while achieving security and privacy standards (Chen, 2009).

Research was conducted in the context of V2V communication in highway environments and produced good results (Schwartz, 2010). On the other hand, in city centers, V2V was not an optimal choice as the area is smaller and the flow of vehicles is more complex. Introducing central node (Correspondent Node, CN) was a very attractive solution to control the traffic flow and measure the load on every segment of the roads; vehicles sent status to the CN (V2I) and the CN sent information to the vehicles (I2V) (Daoud, 2006).

There are a lot of protocols that can provide wireless communication for the vehicles like WiFi, GPRS, 3G, WiMAX, and others (Rebeiro, 2005). GPRS and 3G appear to be an attractive solution as the networks are already in place and can easily be integrated with the CN. However, from a practical point of view, commercial networks have limited bandwidth which is costly for the operators; furthermore, they are already congested and hence, cannot guarantee the QoS for the ITS traffic. The other option is to build a dedicated network for the vehicles communication. WiFi is a big step in the world of wireless internetworking and communication. WiFi offers better data rates than the GPRS and 3G of the personal mobile communication systems. It is operating in the unlicensed Industrial Scientific and Medical (ISM) band. The ISM band is a free band under power regulations by the federation of each country.

The Hand-off HO (or Handover) mechanism is an issue for wireless networks. WiFi (IEEE 802.11 protocols) does not define a built-in handover mechanism in its layer (layer 2) of the stack. Providing mobility in WiFi requires a higher layer (layer 3 or the IP layer) to control the mobility. Each wireless node is identified by a unique Internet Protocol (IP) address. It is then difficult to maintain connectivity when the Mobile Node (MN) changes its point of attachment to the network, because it changes its IP address.

The large growth in network use generally demands a new address protocol to accommodate this large number. After Internet Protocol version 4 (IPv4), Internet Protocol version 6 (IPv6) is introduced and is currently being deployed. A big share of the network cards manufacturers are now making these cards IPv6 compatible (wired as well as wireless).

With the presence of both IPv4 and IPv6, hand-off task forces worked first on MIPv4 (Mobile IPv4) and then migrated to MIPv6 (Mobile IPv6) to support mobility in IPv4 and IPv6, respectively (RFC3775, 2004; RFC4260, 2005). Many efforts are put in this context to provide a solution for wireless communication using WiFi in light urban areas and make use of the free band the WiFi is utilizing. The solution includes a lot of techniques to overcome the impact of the long handover delays generated from the layer 3 handover of the MIP protocols (Daoud, 2007). The same techniques could not provide an acceptable solution in urban or more congested environment due to the limitation of the coverage area of WiFi in urban areas and the long handover delay in the layer 3 handover protocols.

The rapid development and deployment of Worldwide Interoperability for Microwave Access (WiMAX) and the introduction of the mobility concept made it possible to use this system in traffic control. The IEEE 802.16e commercially known as mobile WiMAX is an attractive wireless solution to cover large areas and provide wireless access with carrier grade performance, as well as real-time experience for users by efficiently handling handovers during user movement.

In El-Dakroury (2010), an infrastructure was proposed to manage downtown vehicle traffic. The infrastructure was based on the mobile WiMAX IEEE 802.16e standard to maintain the communication between the Infrastructure (Correspondent Node) and the vehicle (MN). A Correspondent Node was star-connected to all serving Base Stations (BSs). Mobile IP version 6 (MIPv6) was used as a handover protocol. Dual Trigger Handover

(DTH) was introduced to optimize the handover initialization in the system. DTH is an improved type of fixed hysteresis handover mechanisms that does not depend on network measurements. DTH is a technique to reduce the unwanted HO's that occur due to wrong handover decisions. Different speeds and Inter-Packet Transmission rates (IPT's) were tested using DTH. Results based on a 95% confidence analysis showed that DTH improved performance by decreasing the unwanted HO from 8-10% to less than 2%.

In this chapter, a similar problem to the one studied in El-Dakroury (2010) is investigated using Access Service Network Gateway (ASN-GW) to manage the communication of the MN while roaming instead of using MIPv6. MN initiated handover is used for better efficiency of network resources and better expandability. IEEE 802.16e is still used and the MN moves under the ITU vehicular environment and in a congested situation. A network architecture is designed based on the IEEE 802.16e-2005 standard using ASN-GW to manage the mobility of the vehicles.

The issue of Infrastructure to Vehicle (I2V) communication is studied using OPNET. A comparison is made between the performances of network when using ASN-GW to manage the mobility and when using MIPv6 for the same task. The interference impact on the network performance is studied by modeling a congested scenario. Results show that the network performance drastically degrades. For improvement, DTH is used. DTH improves performance by decreasing the unwanted handovers. The comparison is based on the performance improvement in terms of the amount of packets dropped.

BACKGROUND

Mobile Worldwide Interoperability for Microwave Access (WiMAX) or IEEE802.16 is one of the IEEE standards dealing with the last mile connections in Metropolitan Area Networks (MAN)

(IEEE 802.16e-2005, 2006). The IEEE 802.16 standard defines the air interface physical layer as well as the MAC layer to provide a reliable end-to-end link. The air interface is defined as a single-carrier modulated air interface with 5, 10, 20 MHz bandwidth with 512, 1024, 2048 Orthogonal-Frequency Division Multiplexed (OFDM) sub-carriers consecutively. The OFDM-based air interfaces are suitable for NLOS operation due to the simplicity of the equalization process for multi-carrier signals. The MAC Layer of IEEE 802.16 was designed for Point to Multi Point (PMP) broadband wireless access applications. There are 2 main standards defined under the IEEE 802.16 group, the IEEE 802.16-2004 which defines the fixed WiMAX protocol and IEEE 802.11e-2005 which defines the mobile WiMAX (Andrews, 2007).

Mobile WiMAX or IEEE 802.16e-2005 defines several mechanisms to handle handovers: hard handover, Fast Base Station Switching (FBSS), and Macro Diversity Handover (MDHO). The hard handover mechanism is based on received signal strength measurements done on the OFDMA frame preamble. When the MN notices that the Carrier to Interference Noise Ratio (CINR) is below a preset threshold, it starts the scanning procedure. During the scanning period, the MN measures the CINR for the neighbor BSs of the serving BS. The hard handover is triggered, if the CINR of the serving BS becomes low enough and there is a BS with a better CINR value available. The CINR of the target BS has to exceed a certain hysteresis margin to avoid a ping-pong situation. On the other hand, FBSS as well as MDHO are soft handover mechanisms. FBSS is based on CINR measurements done on pilot subcarriers in both DownLink (DL) and UpLink (UL) sub-frames. Both MN and BS maintain a Diversity Set of BSs that is involved in FBSS. MN only communicates with an Anchor BS, which is defined among the Set. The MN may add or drop a BS from the list. It is clear that the hard handover mechanism is a break before make mechanism where the MN breaks with the serving BS before connecting to a new BS. On the other hand, hard handover can be implemented in both MN initiated HO and BS initiated HO while soft HO can only be implemented when using BS initiated HO systems (Majanen, 2009).

Handover is still one of the hot topics under research as it is one of the main contributors in the overall performance of wireless systems. There has been a lot of research to determine the perfect time for HO initiation to minimize the number of undesired HO as well as latency. One approach is to use a pre-coordination mechanism (Jenhui, 2007). Another approach is to optimize the HO trigger parameters, mainly the hysteresis value and minimum CINR. The use of a single fixed value for the hysteresis will make it very hard to maintain precise HO decisions, especially in harsh environments. Dynamic hysteresis was introduced to make use of the BS measurements and change the hysteresis value depending on the dynamics of the system to maintain optimized HO decisions (Lal, 2007). Although dynamic hysteresis can improve the precision of HO decisions, it is not applicable for MN initiated HO as it depends on the BS measurements (these measurements are not transmitted to the MN). MN initialed HO is used in broadcast type of networks to avoid centralized calculation and tracking of all MN's in the network. It is also more beneficial in case of network expandability as it does not require linear expansion of the network. Dual fixed Trigger HO (DTH) was introduced to provide optimized HO decisions in case of MN initiated HO (El-Dakroury, 2010).

DTH is an improved type of fixed hysteresis handover mechanisms that does not depend on network measurements. It is a technique to reduce the unwanted HO's that occur due to wrong handover decisions. WiMAX HO depends on 2 parameters: minimum CINR and minimum hysteresis. The minimum CINR and hysteresis values should achieve a compromise between the quality of the serving BS, decreasing the MN disconnected time, power saving for the MN and decreasing the number of HO's (ping-pong situation). It is not realistic to achieve a good compromise by using a single fixed value for CINR and hysteresis. Usually, it either leads to ping-pong cases or sections without signal. Using 2 values for CINR and 2 values for hysteresis (DTH) gives more precise HO decisions and eventually better performance. DTH introduces 2 values for hysteresis's and correspondent minimum CINRs, low hysteresis, low minimum CINR and high hysteresis, high minimum CINR. The second value of the CINR is calculated within the MN depending on the CINR set from the network. This way, DTH does not require any change in the protocol. When the Down Link CINR reaches the high Minimum CINR value set, the MN node will trigger the HO initiation process. The MN will not perform the HO unless there is a targeted BS with CINR better that the serving BS with high hysteresis. If these is no BS has the required signal quality, the MN will wait until the second trigger is initiated (El-Dakroury, 2010). Figure 1 shows flow chart for the DTH.

Proposed Architecture

In this research, an infrastructure is proposed to manage downtown vehicle traffic. The infrastructure is based on the IEEE 802.16e-2005 standard on the 2.5 GHz band and 10 MHz bandwidth to maintain the communication between the Infrastructure (Correspondent Node) and the vehicle (Mobile Node) (Andrews, 2007). A Correspondent Node is star-connected to all serving Base Stations (BSs). All BSs are distributed over a city with Manhattan map topography. The Stigmergic approach is used by the CN to calculate the fastest route for vehicles to move from one location to another (Sallez, 2005). Access Service Network Gateway node (ASN-GW) is used to maintain the MN connectivity during handover between cells

Figure 1. DTH flow chart

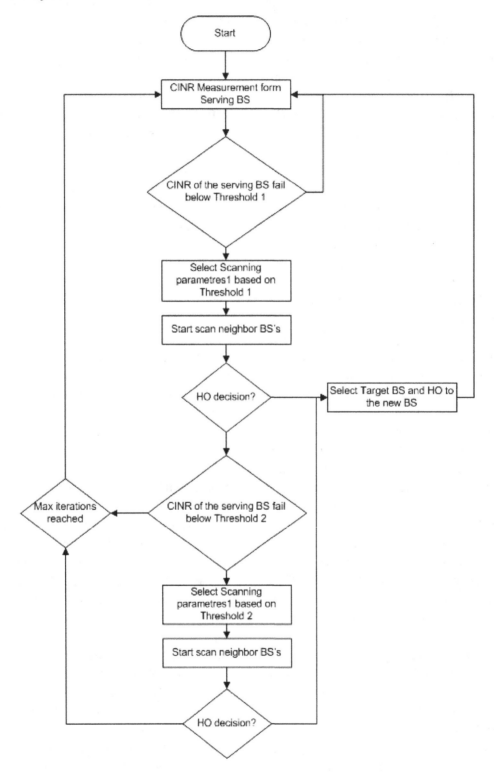

Figure 2. Network architecture

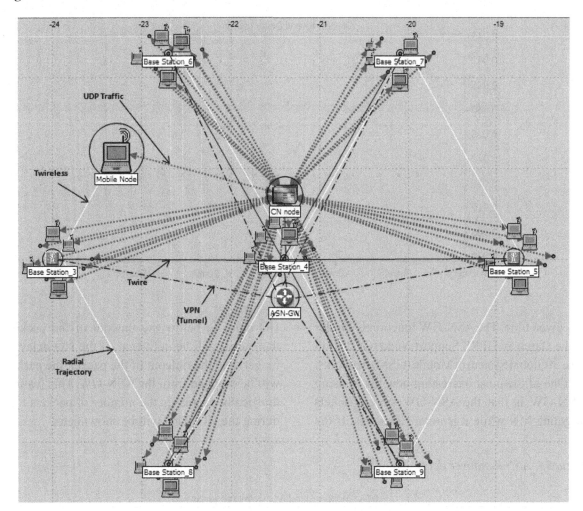

without the need to change the IP address of the MN. MN initiated HO is used to maintain simple expandability of the system.

ASN Gateway aggregates subscribers and control traffic from base stations. It manages the roles of Subscriber management and forwarding of all subscriber traffic. During the network setup, a two-way tunnel (Virtual Private Network VPN) connection is established between the ASN-GW and every BS in the network served by this ASN-GW (Sim, 2009). The number of ASN-GW's in the network depends on the network load and ASN-GW capacity. ASN-GW capacity depends on the number of BSs attached or the number of MNs

served or the data rate passing through the ASN or a mix between all these parameters (Motorola Wi4, 2008). In the scenario under study, only one ASN-GW is used and all BS's are connected to it. All traffic from any MN in the network is forwarded by the serving BS to the ASN-GW through the established tunnel and the ASN-GW delivers it to the right destination. On the other hand, all traffic targeting any of the MN's is routed to the ASN-GW and the ASN-GW tunnels it to the right BS. Using this technique, the MN will not change its IP address while moving from the serving BS to another BS and the ASN-GW will manage the delivery the traffic to the serving BS at

Figure 3. Network latency

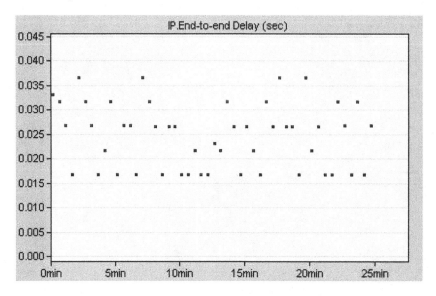

any given time. The ASN-GW function is similar to the Gateway GPRS Support Node (GGSN) in case of Global System of Mobile (GSM) networks.

One of the most interesting benefits of using ASN-GW is that the ASN-GW stores packets targeting MN while it is in an HO status. If the HO delay is below the timeout of the packet, the packet will be delivered. If the HO delay is longer than the timeout of the packet, the packet will be dropped from the ASN-GW. This feature drastically decreases the number of packets lost during the HO. This will be shown later.

Figure 4. ASN handover delay

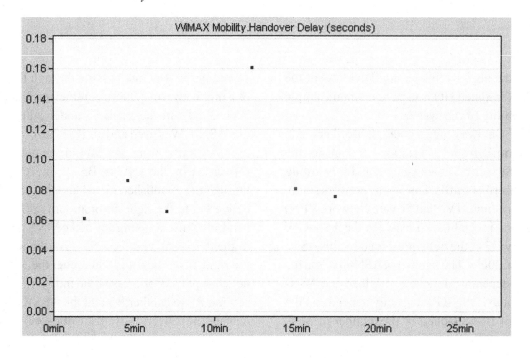

Figure 5. Comparison between ASN and MIPv6

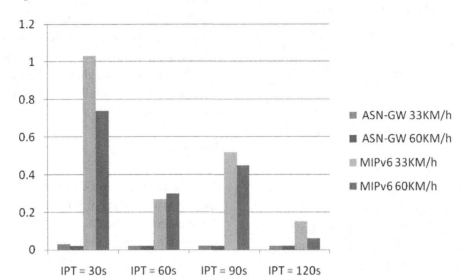

The scenario includes a honey-cell layout and one moving MN traversing all 7 BS's coverage areas in a radial path as shown in Figure 2. "ITU Vehicular Environment" path loss model (shown in equation 1) is modeled (ITU 5D/469-E, 2009).

$$L = 40 \ (1 - 4 * 10^{-3} \ \Delta h_b) \ \log_{10} R - 18 \ \log_{10} \Delta h_b - 21 \ \log_{10} f + 80 \ \text{dB} \tag{1}$$

where R is the base station—mobile station separation (km), f is the carrier frequency in MHz, and Δh_b is the base station antenna height in meters, measured from the average rooftop level. The "Vehicular B" model for multipath is used in the study (ITU 5D/469-E, 2009).

Table 1. Confidence analysis for the number of packets lost for MN moving at 33km/hr

Inter-Packet Transmission Time	μ	σ	Range
30s	1.30	1.02	(0.96, 1.65)
60s	1.15	0.80	(0.88, 1.42)
90s	0.58	0.50	(0.40, 0.75)
120s	0.55	0.50	(0.37, 0.72)

The WiMAX model parameters are set as per the recommendation of the WiMAX forum as well as Intel products datasheets (Mobile WiMAX-P1, 2007). Shadow fading of σ = 4dB is modeled (ITU-R M.1225, 1997). Partial Usage of Sub-Carriers (PUSC) with reuse factor of 3 is used to avoid interference between cells. Different MN speeds are tested: 6Km/hr, 33Km/hr and 60Km/hr. These speeds are a mix between walking speed (6 km/hr) and the maximum speed for a moving vehicle in an urban area (60 km/hr). OPNET simulations are performed to find the optimum inter-center distance between adjacent cells: 2.6Km. The search criterion was to find the minimum packet loss during handover.

Based on the Stigmergic approach used by the CN and the Manhattan map, the CN needs to broadcast 100B of information about the road status every 30, 60, 90 or 120 seconds (Daoud, 2006). These times represent the Inter-Packet Transmission (IPT) times in the proposed network architecture. This traffic represents the I2V traffic in the scenario under study. The I2V data traffic is sent as generic UDP application in the OPNET modeler (OPNET). Next, two speeds are simulated: 33Km/hr and 60 Km/hr. 60 Km/

Table 2. Confidence analysis for the number of packets lost for MN moving at 60km/hr

Inter-Packet Transmission Time	μ	σ	Range
30s	1.39	0.83	(1.11, 1.68)
60s	0.79	0.65	(0.67, 1.01)
90s	0.60	0.50	(0.44, 0.78)
120s	0.21	0.42	(0.37, 0.35)

hr represents the maximum speed in urban areas under consideration. At the speed of 6 Km/hr, it is assumed that the MN is stuck in a traffic jam and the information sent from the CN is superfluous. An average speed of 33 Km/hr is simulated beside the 60 Km/hr.

For every speed of the MN, the four IPT's are simulated. A 95% confidence analysis is performed for 33 simulation runs using 33 different seeds. The key performance indicators affecting the packet lost are the propagation latency and handover delay.

Propagation Latency

Propagation latency (Tp) is the time the data packets consume propagating from the CN and reaching the MN.

$$Tp = Twireless + Twire + Tprocessing \qquad (2)$$

where Twireless is the latency of the wireless channel, Twire is the delay through the wire connection and Tprocessing is the processing delays in the Base stations (BS), CN and ASN-GW. Practically, Twireless varies depending on the location of the MN while Tprocessing varies with time depending on the status of the node.

Based on this scenario presented in Figure 2, simulation results show that Tp varies from 15 ms to 40 ms as shown in Figure 3.

Comparing Tp while using ASN-GW vs. using MIPv6 as a HO technique, it is noticed that Twire-

less and Twire are equal in case of using MIPv6 or ASN-GW as they depend on the topology of the network. Tprocessing is less in case of using ASN-GW as there is no layer 3 routing and everything is done through VPN connection; however, this value is small as all traffic is passing though the ASN-GW.

Handover Delay

The handover delay (Th) is the time the MN spends changing its Air interface from a serving BS to a new serving BS. The HO process results in the interruption of the data flow. The handover delay always consists of 2 layers handover, layer 2 (L2) and layer 3 (L3). Since there is only one ASN-GW as an access network node, the MN will not go through a layer 3 HO (T_{L3}) and the IP will not change. This can be expressed as follows.

$$Th = T_{L2} \qquad (3)$$

T_{L2} is the time between the HO initiation and the MN connection restoration. T_{L2} directly depends on the round-trip time of layer 2 binding packets.

$$T_{L2} = (\text{\# Binding packets}) \times (Twireless) \qquad (4)$$

In some cases, the target BS may skip some of the re-entry steps to speed up the process (Majanen, 2009). Simulation results show that Th can reach 160ms (see Figure 4).

Table 3. Confidence analysis for the number of packets lost for MN moving at 33km/hr using DTH

Inter-Packet Transmission Time	μ	σ	Range
30s	0.82	0.85	(0.53, 1.11)
60s	0.91	0.77	(0.65, 1.17)
90s	0.55	0.51	(0.37, 0.72)
120s	0.27	0.45	(0.12, 0.43)

Table 4. Confidence analysis for the number of packets lost for MN moving at 60km/hr using DTH

Inter-Packet Transmission Time	μ	σ	Range
30s	0.61	0.61	(0.40, 0.81)
60s	0.55	0.56	(0.35, 0.74)
90s	0.58	0.50	(0.40, 0.75)
120s	0.06	0.24	(0.00, 0.14)

Since the system has a maximum HO delay of 160ms, a very low rate of packet loss is expected to occur during the HO. The highest mean of packets lost is 0.03 packets per complete trajectory. This small mean number of packet lost is due to the fact that the HO delay is very low and the fact that the ASN stores the packets for the MN not connected to the network while performing HO.

Figure 5 shows complete results and a comparison between the number of packets lost when using ASN-GW (STH or DTH as they are the same) and MIPv6 for MN passing through the same trajectory over the same environment.

Although the above results are optimum with almost no packets lost in most of the scenarios, they ignore any kind of congestion in the network. In this section, a congested scenario is studied. The scenario has the same setup as the previous scenario except for adding a source of congestion. The source of congestion is represented by 8 wireless nodes around each BS (56 stationary nodes). This represents a load of 9 served MNs at any given time. A 95% confidence analysis is performed using 33 seeds testing the 2 speeds for the MN (33Km/h and 60 Km/h) using the 4 IPT's (30sec, 60sec, 90sec, and 120sec).

The results show that increasing the load of the system increases the number of handovers and the number of wrong handovers which increases the number of packets lost in the network. The average number of packets lost increases from 0.03 packets in the whole trajectory to 1.4 packets.

Complete results of the simulations are shown in Tables 1 and Table 2.

Solutions and Recommendations

Since the increase in number of packets lost is mainly due to the wrong handover decisions, therefore using DTH will decrease the number of packets lost. DTH is more suitable for the scenario under study as it supports MN initiated HO and does not require much processing in the network side. Running the same sets of simulations using DTH and applying the same confidence analysis using the same 33 seeds gives better performance. The results show that the maximum number of packets lost decrease from 1.39 packets to 0.91 packets. Complete results of simulations are shown in Table 3 and Table 4. These tables show better results than the single value trigger handover shown in Tables 1 and 2. The number of wrong handover decisions that lead to ping-pong situation, decreases drastically.

This leads to a bigger improvement in the overall number of packets lost. Figure 6 shows how the DTH decreases the number of wrong HO decisions, which improves network performance.

FUTURE RESEARCH DIRECTIONS

The capacity of the ASN-GW is relatively limited. HO between 2 different ASN-GW's requires change of IP. The inter-ASN-GW handover with MIPv6 operation is a good point of future research. Adding on-board entertainment traffic is another interesting approach. The prioritization of the different streams is critical for overall system performance.

CONCLUSION

This chapter addresses the issue of traffic control in a vehicular environment. The analysis is

Figure 6. STH vs DTH number of HO's

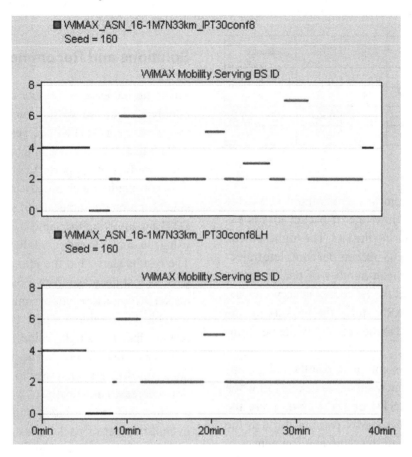

based on the Stigmergic approach. The problem addressed is the wireless communication aspect between the Infrastructure and the vehicles. A network architecture is designed based on the IEEE 802.16e-2005 standard using ASN-GW to manage the mobility of the vehicles. The architecture consists of several 7 Base Stations (BSs) distributed in a honey-cell layout that provides complete coverage of the environment under study.

The issue of Infrastructure to Vehicle (I2V) communication is studied using OPNET. A quantitative comparison is made between the performances of network when using ASN-GW to manage the mobility and when using MIPv6 for the same task. The comparison is based on the performance improvement in terms of the amount of packets dropped. A performance enhancement

is observed as expected when using ASN-GW and the mean number of packets lost drops to below 0.03 for MN moving at 33 Km/h and Inter-packet transmission time of 30 second. In the case of 60 Km/hr, the mean number of packets lost drops to below 0.025. These results are based on a 95% confidence analysis.

The interference impact on network performance is studied by modeling a congested scenario. Results show that network performance drastically degrades. The mean number of packets lost rises to 1.39. For improvement, DTH is used. DTH improves performance by decreasing the unwanted HOs. For example, using DTH, the mean number of packets lost for an MN moving at a speed of 60Km/h and using an IPT of 30 drops from 1.39 to 0.61.

REFERENCES

Andrews, J., Ghosh, A., & Muhamed, R. (2007). *Fundamentals of WiMAX: Understanding broadband wireless networking.* Upper Saddle River, NJ: Prentice Hall.

Chen, W., Delgrossi, L., Kosch, T., & Saito, T. (2009). Topics in automotive networking. *IEEE Communications Magazine, 47*(11), 82–83. doi:10.1109/MCOM.2009.5307470

Daoud, R. M., El-Dakroury, M. A., Amer, H. H., Elsayed, H. M., & El-Soudani, M. (2007). *WiFi architecture for traffic control using MIPv6.* Paper presented at the IEEE Mediterranean Conference on Control & Automation MED. Athens, Greece.

Daoud, R. M., El-Dakroury, M. A., Amer, H. H., Elsayed, H. M., El-Soudani, M., & Sallez, Y. (2006). *Wireless vehicle communication for traffic control in urban areas.* Paper presented at the 32nd Annual Conference of the IEEE Industrial Electronics Society IECON. Paris, France.

Document, I. T. U. 5D/469-E. (2009). *Guidelines for using IMT-Advanced channel models.* Retrieved August 6, 2009, from http://projects.celtic-initiative.org/winner+/WINNER+%20and%20ITU-R%20EG%20documents/R07-WP5D-C-0469!!MSW-E%20%28Guidelines%20Finland%29.pdf

El-Dakroury, M. A., Zekry, A. H., Amer, H. H., & Daoud, R. M. (2010). *Traffic control using WiMAX with dual trigger handover.* Paper presented at the 6th International Engineering conference on Computer Engineering ICENCO. Cairo, Egypt.

IEEE Standard 802.16e-2005. (2006). *Amendment to IEEE standard for local and metropolitan area networks – Part 16: Air interface for fixed broadband wireless access systems – Physical and medium access control layers for combined fixed and mobile operation in licensed bands.* Retrieved February 15, 2009, from http://ieee802.org/16/pubs/80216e.html

ITU-R M.1225 Recommendation for IMT-2000 Radio Interfaces. (1997). *Guidelines for evaluation of radio transmission technologies for IMT-2000.* Retrieved June 6, 2009, from http://www.itu.int/dms_pubrec/itu-r/rec/m/R-REC-M.1225-0-199702-I!!PDF-E.pdf

Jenhui, C., Chih-Chieh, W., & Jiann-Der, L. (2007). *Pre-coordination mechanism for fast handover in WiMAX networks.* Paper presented at the 2nd International Conference on Wireless Broadband and Ultra Wideband Communications (AusWireless). Sydney, Australia.

Lal, S., & Panwar, D. K. (2007). *Coverage analysis of handoff algorithm with adaptive hysteresis margin.* Paper presented at the 10th International Conference on Information Technology ICIT. Rourkela, India.

Majanen, M., Perala, P. H. J., Casey, T., Nurmi, J., & Veselinovic, N. (2009). *Mobile WiMAX handover performance evaluation.* Paper presented at the IEEE Fifth International Conference on Networking and Services ICNS. Valencia, Spain.

Mariyasagayam, M. N., Menouar, H., & Lenardi, M. (2008). *GeoNet: A project enabling active safety and IPv6 vehicular applications.* Paper presented at IEEE International Conference on Vehicular Electronics and Safety (ICVES). Columbus, OH.

Mobile WiMAX – Part 1. (2007). *A technical overview and performance evaluation*. Retrieved August 27, 2008, from http://www.wimaxforum. org/technology/downloads/Mobile_WiMAX_ Part1_Overview_and_Performance.pdf

Modeler Key Features, O. P. N. E. T. (2009). *OPNET modeler official website*. Retrieved January 15, 2010, from http://www.opnet.com/ solutions/network_rd/modeler.html

Mohandas, B. K., Liscano, R., & Yang, O. (2009). *Vehicle traffic congestion management in vehicular ad-hoc networks*. Paper presented at the IEEE 34th Conference on Local Computer Networks LCN. Zürich, Switzerland.

Motorola Wi4 WiMAX Access Service Network ASN Gateway Data Sheet. (2008). *Website*. Retrieved April 6, 2010, from http://www. motorola.com/web/Business/Products/Wire-lessBroadbanNetworks/WiMAX/WiMAXAc-cessPoints/WAP600/_Documents/Static_files/ wi4_WiMAX_Access_Service_Network_ASN_ Gateway_Data_Sheet_Copy.pdf

Oyama, S. (2008). *Vehicle safety communications: Progresses in Japan*. Paper presented at the IEEE International Conference on Vehicular Electronics and Safety ICVES. Columbus, OH.

Papadimitratos, P., La Fortelle, A., Evenssen, K., Brignolo, R., & Cosenza, S. (2009). Vehicular communication systems: Enabling technologies, applications, and future outlook on intelligent transportation. *IEEE Communications Magazine, 47*(11), 84–95. doi:10.1109/ MCOM.2009.5307471

RFC3775. (2004). *Website*. Retrieved from http:// www.ietf.org/rfc/rfc3775.txt

RFC4260. (2005). *Website*. Retrieved from http:// ietfreport.isoc.org/idref/rfc4260/

Ribeiro, C. (2005). *Bringing wireless access to the automobile: A comparison of Wi-Fi, WiMAX, MBWA, and 3G*. Paper presented at the 21st Computer Science Seminar. Troy, NY.

Sallez, Y., Berger, T., & Tahon, C. (2005). *Stigmergic approach and potential field based method for intelligent routing in FMS*. Paper presented at the International Conference on Industrial Engineering and Systems Management IESM. Marrakech, Morocco.

Schwartz, R. S., van Eenennaam, M., Karagiannis, G., Heijenk, G., Wolterink, W. K., & Scholten, H. (2010). *Using V2V communication to create over-the-horizon awareness in multiple-lane highway scenarios*. Paper presented at the 4th IEEE Intelligent Vehicles Symposium (IV). San Diego, CA.

Sim, S., Han, S., Park, J., & Lee, S. (2009). Seamless IP mobility support for flat architecture mobile WiMAX networks. *IEEE Communications Magazine, 47*(6), 142–148. doi:10.1109/ MCOM.2009.5116811

Toulminet, G., Boussuge, J., & Laurgeau, C. (2008). *Comparative synthesis of the 3 main European projects dealing with cooperative systems (CVIS, SAFESPOT, and COOPERS) and description of COOPERS demonstration site 4*. Paper presented at the 11th International IEEE Conference on Intelligent Transportation Systems ITSC. Maastricht, The Netherlands.

Wahl, R., Tørset, T., & Vaa, T. (2008). *Large scale introduction of automated transport which legal and administrative barriers are present?* ITS World 2008. Retrieved March 13, 2010, from http://www.citymobil-project.eu

Weil, T. (2009). *Service management for ITS using WAVE (1609.3) networking*. Paper presented at the IEEE GLOBECOM Workshops. Hawaii, HI.

Section 3
Quality of Service Provisioning

Chapter 8
A Novel Distributed QoS Control Scheme for Multi-Homed Vehicular Networks

Hamada Alshaer
Khalifa University, UAE

Thierry Ernst
l'Ecole des Mines Paristech, France

Arnaud de La Fortelle
l'Ecole des Mines Paristech, France

ABSTRACT

Resource availability in vehicular mobile networks fluctuates due to wireless channel fading and network mobility. Multi-homed mobile networks require a Quality-of-Service (QoS) control scheme that can select a routing path to guarantee high quality of communications with Correspondent Nodes (CNs) while using the maximum available bandwidth of wireless and radio communication technologies. In this chapter, the authors develop an intelligent distributed QoS control scheme which inter-operates between mobile routers, managing vehicular networks mobility, and Road Communication Gateways (RCGs). This proposed scheme manages Vehicle-to-Infrastructure (V2I) communications through enabling multi-homed vehicular networks to optimally distribute traffic among egress links of their mobile routers based on vehicular communication policies and available bandwidth and performance metrics of selected routing paths. This scheme considers the data control plane as a collaborative entity and specifies detailed operations to be performed in the mobile routers and RCGs. Simulation experiments show that the proposed scheme can improve the Congestion Window (CWND) of TCP and the e2e packet loss of video traffic, despite network mobility. It also guarantees the service parameter settings of uplink and downlink connections while achieving reasonable utilization efficiency of network resources and fairly sharing them.

DOI: 10.4018/978-1-4666-2223-4.ch008

INTRODUCTION

Highway communication system gains momentum efforts to set up a transport communication network to let vehicles communicate with each other and with roadside communication stations. Some highway tests have already been completed for the Vehicle Infrastructure Integration (VII) systems (Costlow, 2008), which aim to reduce accidents and congestion. Because of wireless channel fading and network mobility, QoS provisioning in wireless and mobile networks is more challenging than in fixed networks (Xie & Narayanan, 2010; Gu, Jung, & Kim, 2010). Multi-homing in Intelligent Transportation Systems (ITSs) often refers to the connection of a vehicular mobile network (NEMO) to multiple Internet Service Providers (ISPs) through different wireless and radio communication technologies (Alshaer, Ernst, & Fortelle, 2012). Multi-homing is also used by large enterprises or stub ISPs to connect to the Internet in order to get more service benefits in terms of cost, reliability or performance (Bates & Rekhter, 1998). Multi-homing enables vehicular NEMOs to be reached anywhere anytime under varying network topologies and communication circumstances.

Different wireless interfaces are available on the market, which can enable NEMOs to access Internet. This includes WLAN IEEE , WiMax , wireless access vehicular environment (WAVE) IEEE , Dedicated Short-Range Communication (DSRC), satellite, GPRS (Generalized Packet Radio Switching) and UMTS (Universal Mobile Telecommunication System) (Johnson, Perkins, & Arkko, 2004; Chen & Guizani, 2006). Ng, Ernst, Paik, and Bagnulo (2007) investigated different multi-homing configurations for vehicular NEMOs. However, throughout this Chapter, we will focus on the multi-homing configuration depicted in Figure 1, where the root Mobile Router (MR) of NEMO is equipped with wireless, radio and satellite cards to reach Internet through multiple routing paths. NEtwork MObility Basic Support Protocol (NEMO-BSP) (Devarapalli, Wakikawa, Petrescu, & Thubert, 2005) is employed to manage communications between NEMOs through egress interfaces of their mobile routers and Home Agents (HAs), as shown in Figure 1. NEMOs can send and receive traffic through multiple routing paths established with HAs. The upstream traffic can be managed by MR of NEMO, meanwhile the downstream traffic can be managed by and Road Communication Gate-

Figure 1. A multi-homed nested NEMO connected to a number of ISPs

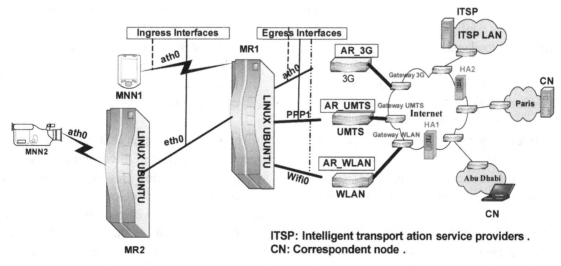

ITSP: Intelligent transport ation service providers .
CN: Correspondent node .

ways (RCGs). Therefore, an intelligent distributed QoS control scheme is required to inter-operate between MR and RCGs to fully manage traffic on wireless and wired segments of selected routing paths with HAs and CNs.

Multi-homing Intelligent Route Control (IRC) systems often use Cisco Optimized Edge Routing (OER) (Cisco, 2006) which automatically detects service degradation, enabling them to reroute traffic through a different routing path. This dynamic change of routing path is done in a reactive manner to avoid transit congestion periods. In this Chapter, however, our challenging problem is that: NEMO does not have a priori knowledge about the network topology and capacity of the upstream routing paths that reach HAs, Correspondent Nodes (CNs) or Intelligent Transportation Service Providers (ITSPs). Thus, at the conceptual level, a multi-homing optimal load distribution system like MR_1 should be enabled to determine the available bandwidth on routing paths with HA, CN, or ITSP, and detect failed access links and divert Internet traffic around them. From a Mobile Network Node (MNN) standpoint, an ideal multi-homing optimal load distribution system should be plug-and-play and requires no other modifications to the existing network infrastructure than adding more access links.

This Chapter introduces a distributed QoS control scheme which inter-operates between mobile routers configured on vehicular mobile networks and road communication gateways to:

1. Establish reliable connections based on defined vehicular communication policies, users' preferences, ITSP Service Level Agreements (SLAs) with on-board users,
2. Select and switch autonomously to the best available routing path with CNs,
3. Manage the mobility of vehicular networks, and
4. Optimally distribute traffic among the wireless and wired segments of selected routing paths with the HAs and CNs.

PROBLEM DESCRIPTION

Figure 1 depicts our multi-homed vehicular NEMO model. It is a nested NEMO connected to the Internet through a number of Internet Service Providers (ISPs), where each ISP provides the Internet services through a different wireless or radio communication technology. Thus, each egress interface of MR_1 routes upstream traffic flows through a different routing path to CNs (destinations), though the different selected routing paths may overlap in upstream domains toward the different destinations. This Chapter aims to provision an optimal multi-homing configuration for a multi-homed vehicular NEMO. Wang, Xie, Qi, Siberschatz, and Yang (2005) and Tao, Xu, and Xu (2004) studied a similar problem, but for large wired stub and content distribution networks or multi-homed users. We, however, consider network mobility which dynamically changes the egress interfaces status of MR_1, shortening egress interfaces (ISPs) selection timescales, and routing path switching between these egress interfaces. To this end, more tasks are required to provision the optimal multi-homing configuration, such as:

- Defining policies for Vehicle-to-Infrastructure (V2I) communications in MR_1 to select the most optimal egress interface (routing path) with correspondent nodes (destinations). The selected routing path should guarantee the e2e QoS required for real-time traffic connections while guaranteeing the minimum e2e QoS requirements for other classes of traffic connection.

The transit congestion periods can be solved in a reactive manner using OER in multi-homing IRC systems (Cisco, 2006). However, dynamic path switching can result in sub-optimal multi-homing configuration due to vehicular network mobility and dynamic change of the egress interfaces of MR_1. Thus, the selection process of egress routing path should run periodically to guarantee optimal multi-homing configuration for vehicular NEMOs. We envision that the selection process of routing path would be repeated according to a predetermined policy while dynamic path switching would take place in the time scale of seconds to guarantee the e2e QoS required for the different classes of traffic connection, as well as network resources optimally utilized (Alshaer, Ernst, & Fortelle, 2012). The objectives of provisioning optimal multi-homing are determined by the following requirements:

1. **Guarantee of e2e QoS:** MR1, RCGs, and HA should be enabled to guarantee the e2e QoS required for upstream and downstream traffic connections. This requires carefully selecting the egress interface of MR, measuring and monitoring the utilization of network resources. Traffic connections should not be routed through a limited-capacity ISP to avoid congested routing paths and congested points in network. MR1, RCGs, and HA should be enabled to provide routing paths diversity to destinations so that traffic connections can be rerouted on alternative (backup) routing paths, when the primary (selected) routing path to destinations fails or becomes unavailable due to traffic congestion.

2. **Vehicle-to-infrastructure communication policies:** Under normal conditions where all egress interfaces of MR1 are active, MR1 should select an egress interface according to predetermined communication policies. This might be based on the cost of traffic transmission through the different egress interfaces, NEMO's geographical position: If it is in urban or rural area; if it is connected to its home network or a visited network. The policy can also determine through which egress interface network resources reservation should be made for real-time traffic connections. Under abnormal conditions where the status of MR1 egress interfaces changes

dynamically, the policy might be based on NEMO's speed to determine handover frequency and order, whether it is from WLAN to 3G or to satellite and vice-versa. It can also relate to security issues associated to each egress interface.

RELATED WORK

Reliable and real-time vehicle-to-road communication (V2R) is the key for supporting numerous intelligent transportation services and applications. Hossain and Mahmud (2007) proposed a system architecture based on V2R communications to provide secure software download and update for road safety, traffic management, and driver-support applications. A virtual market place, i.e., FleaNet, based on V2R communications was proposed in Lee, Park, Amir, and Gerla (2006). This system can be used by users on-board vehicles to buy and sell concert tickets when the vehicle approaches the concert hall. Jungum, Doomun, and Ghurbhurrun (2008) proposed a collaborative driving support system which uses wireless technology to provide time-sensitive information about traffic conditions and roadside facilities to a driver.

The performance of a V2R communication system based on the IEEE technology was reported in Cai and Lin (2005). To provide efficient data transmission between road communication gateways and MRs of NEMOs, the Maximum Freedom Last (MFL) scheduling algorithm was proposed in Chang, Cheng, and Shih (2007) for dedicated short-range communication networks. A cross-layer protocol, i.e., the Coordinated External Peer Communication (CEPEC) protocol, for V2R communications using the IEEE Worldwide Inter-operability for Microwave Access (WiMAX) technology was proposed in Yang, Ou, Chen, and He (2007). Lin, Lai, and Chen (2003) showed that caching can improve the application performance in wireless networks by reducing the data outage probability. Persone and Grassi (2003) evaluated the performance of using caching in a palm top-based navigational tool in the vehicular environment. With caching and pre-fetching, the latency of retrieving road maps and locations can be significantly reduced. However, this can complicate proxy buffer management and may cause traffic loss. Therefore, the impact of selecting the best routing path for video transmission on proxy buffer management and QoS required for transmitted streaming traffic was not considered.

Many applications, e.g., emergency video transmission, roadside video advertisement, and inter-vehicle video conversation, require seamless and ubiquitous video streaming over wireless, radio and satellite communication links in a vehicular network. The problem of wireless video streaming over Vehicle-to-Vehicle (V2V) links was studied in Guo, Ammar, and Zegura (2005) and Xie, Hu, Wan, and Ho (2007). Soldo, Cigno, and Gerla (2008) proposed a protocol for supporting audio/video streaming over V2R links. A tree network is formed by using the positioning and timing information (e.g., through a satellite) of each vehicle to relay streaming data from a roadside unit to the destination vehicle. The protocol supports synchronization among vehicles to avoid transmission collision. A proxy buffer-management scheme was proposed in Mancuso and Bianchi (2004) for data streaming to multiple users over V2R communications links. Chung and Cho (2003) analyzed the performance of real-time data transmission over Code-Division Multiple Access (CDMA)-based V2R communications. However, the selection of best routing path to reach the Internet was not considered in this work.

Our contributions in this Chapter can be described in three folds: First, in addition to dispatching traffic connections or packets onto egress links of MR, a probing mechanism is integrated in MR_1 to evaluate the available bandwidth on these links. Second, policies for vehicle-to-infrastructure communications and mobile weighted round robin scheduling service

discipline are integrated in MR_1 to select egress links that can guarantee optimal distribution of traffic load among these egress links and thus achieve optimal multi-homing configuration for NEMOs. Third, a probing mechanism based on burst traffic transmission is integrated in road communication gateways to allocate routing paths with HA and MR for upstream and downstream connections, respectively. These contributions have been integrated in a distributed QoS control scheme, which inter-operates between mobile routers of NEMOs and Road Communication Gateways (RCGs) to allocate network resources for upstream and downstream real-time traffic connections and hence guarantee their QoS requirements.

In the following section, we introduce a general architecture framework for supporting reliable vehicle-to-infrastructure communications.

VEHICLE-TO-INFRASTRUCTURE COMMUNICATIONS ARCHITECTURE

Traffic generated from vehicular communications can be uploaded and downloaded at different data rates according to the availability of wireless, radio, and satellite link connectivity. This can be affected due to network mobility and channel fading of the vehicle-to-infrastructure communication link. For example, under favourable conditions, traffic can be uploaded and downloaded to the buffer of RCG and MR, respectively, at a rate higher than the playout rate. The excess downloaded traffic can be stored for future playout when link connectivity to the RCG is not available. A vehicular NEMO should be enabled to efficiently access Internet through available communication networks to support QoS-sensitive applications in a cost-effective manner.

Figure 2 shows our architectural overview of typical intelligent transportation services oriented in vehicular networks, which mainly include on mobile routers (NEMOs), road communication gateways, home agents and application servers (ITSPs). This architecture operates on both wireless and wired networks in a unified framework conceived to enable Network Service Providers (NSPs) and intelligent transportation service providers to guarantee high quality in provisioned services and applications for mobile networks and user on-board vehicular networks. The role and functionality of each entity in this architecture proposed for reliable V2I communications is described as follows:

- **Road Communication Gateway (RCG):** The road communication gateways belong to a Network Service Provider (NSP). A RCG selects a downlink wireless, radio or satellite channel and allocates bandwidth for downstream traffic destined to vehicular networks. It offers both reservation-based and on-demand Internet access service. The RCG also computes and allocates routing paths with HA.

- **Network Service Provider (NSP):** The NSP that owns the RCGs optimally sets the price of bandwidth for Internet access so that the revenue is maximized. The price of bandwidth for reservation-based Internet access is set by the NSP on a longer time scale and is assumed to be fixed here.

- **Mobile Router (MR):** The MR performs wireless, radio and satellite access as well as routing path selection through the RCG in a service area with either reservation or on-demand mode. The decision on selected routing path and wireless, radio or satellite access is made in the MR to support QoS-sensitive applications while minimizing the cost of wireless, radio or satellite access.

Figure 2. An architecture for vehicle-to-infrastructure communications

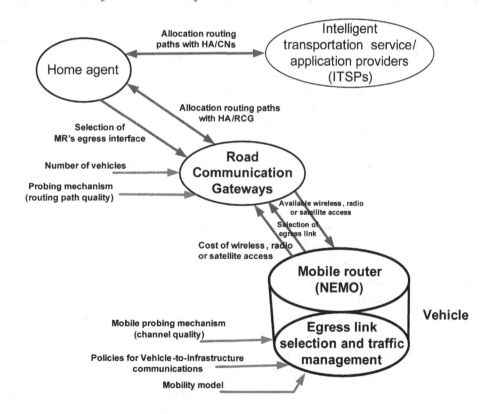

- **Intelligent Transportation Service Provider (ITSP):** The ITSP that owns the MRs decides to buy bandwidth from the NSP for reservation-based wireless, radio or satellite access at different service areas so that the long-term cost of Internet access is minimized. They are also registered with a HA to reach vehicular networks anywhere anytime. Recall that the HA through NEMO-BSP can trace and localize vehicular mobile networks by binding their home-of-address (HoS) with care-of-address (CoS) (Devarapalli, Wakikawa, Petrescu, & Thubert, 2005).

This framework is used to obtain the following decisions, which can support QoS-sensitive traffic over V2I communication links.

- In the first level of the framework, the decision of the ITSP is optimized to reserve bandwidth for wireless, radio or satellite access through RCGs in specific locations so that the cost for Internet access is minimized over the long term. This decision is made based on the cost of wireless, radio or satellite access using reservation and on-demand modes (i.e., based on reservation price and on-demand price). This decision takes into account the randomness of the number of vehicles in a service area.
- In the second level of the framework, the optimal short-term decision on routing path selection and Internet access by the MR is obtained. Given the availability of communication channels through the RCGs in different locations using either on-demand or reservation mode, the MR makes a decision to download or upload traffic so that the cost of wireless, radio or satellite connectivity is minimized, while satisfying the QoS required for traffic. This decision takes into consideration vehicle

mobility and quality (availability) of communication links.

In the following section, we introduce our proposed QoS scheme architecture to guarantee QoS in provisioned services for vehicular networks and users-on board vehicular networks.

PROPOSED E2E QOS SCHEME ARCHITECTURE

The in a vehicle has a finite buffer of length packets to buffer the upstream and downstream traffic. Figure 1, shows NEMO, via , can reach Internet through multiple operators by using different communication networks. The operation of Medium Access Control (MAC) services supported through these communication technologies is connection-oriented. A connection is defined as a unidirectional mapping between MR and Road Communication Gateways (RCGs) MAC peers for the purpose of transporting a service flow's traffic. A service is a unidirectional flow of MAC service data units with predefined QoS parameters. A connection is defined by its unique Connection Identifier (CID) based on which it is implicitly provided. To accommodate upper layer applications with different service requirements, our proposed scheme defines two types of MAC scheduling service: non-elastic and elastic services. Each connection is categorized into one of these two service categories according to the property application carried by this connection.

A road communication gateway can request for each downstream connection its desired bandwidth by sending a stand-alone MAC header. Though the bandwidth is requested for a connection, the grant is, however, issued to the corresponding road communication gateway, which decides about the consumption of a particular bandwidth allocation. As a result, the road communication gateway can perform some connection level functionalities performed by the Access Routers

(ARs [BSs]), which limit the signaling overhead, while keeping the QoS required for connection low. In what follows we introduce the first entity in our proposed e2e QoS architecture, which is responsible for selecting egress links of MRs with road communication gateways. This entity consists of several components for ensuring optimal multi-homing configuration for vehicular mobile networks.

Available Bandwidth Measurement Unit

This unit is integrated in our proposed scheme to measure the available bandwidth on egress links. It obtains the instant bandwidth request of each connection according to the buffer length of connection and MAC headers required to transmit the backlogged traffic. This bandwidth request is upper-bounded by the eligible bandwidth request of connection, which is calculated as:

$$r_i^e = \max \left\{ \frac{R_i^{\max}}{8} \times [t - S_i(t)], 0 \right\} \qquad (1)$$

where is the eligible bandwidth request of connection , is the maximum sustained traffic rate in (bits/second) of this connection and is the system (i.e, MR or RCG in upstream or downstream connections, respectively) time. represents the value of the connection service timer at time. The MR allocates traffic connections whatever available bandwidth on the selected routing paths to guarantee their QoS requirements.

QoS Enforcement Unit

This unit maintains a QoS timer (priority value) for each non-elastic upstream and downstream connections running in the MR and road communication gateway, respectively. The QoS timer enforces the service rate of connection to meet a guaranteed value. The QoS timer is synchronized

with the system clock and ticks with the following value upon the service of each packet in the corresponding connection:

$$A_i = \frac{8 \times B_i}{\rho_i} \qquad (2)$$

where is the increment of connection service timer, upon the service of a packet of size bytes. ρ_i is the service timer, where this value should be. For the QoS timer, the value of ρ_i should be , i.e., the minimum reserved traffic rate (in bps) of connection. The reason behind designing two virtual times for a connection requiring minimum service rate is to have the received service rate guaranteed but not limited at its minimum reserved traffic rate. The operations performed by the QoS enforcement module include two steps: (i) For each non-elastic (bandwidth guaranteed) or elastic (non-bandwidth guaranteed) connection, divide its bandwidth request into Bandwidth Guaranteed (BG) part and Non-Bandwidth Guaranteed (NBG) part, i.e., and , according to the corresponding value of QoS timer, denoted as , i.e:

$$r_i^{BG} = 0, Q_i(t) \geq t \qquad (3)$$

$$r_i^{BG} = \min \left\{ r_i, \frac{R_i^{\min}}{8} \times [t - Q_i(t)] \right\}, Q_i < t$$

where , which can be offered to BE connections.

Vehicle-to-Infrastructure Communication Policies Unit

Traffic packets or flows are scheduled onto an ingress link of MR, if there is enough available bandwidth to accommodate them such that their QoS requirements are guaranteed (Alshaer & Elmirghani, 2009).The connection admission and resource allocation functions are proactive, which can be based on anticipatory utilization on egress links. However, the selection process of an egress link is based on specific policies integrated in MR for vehicle-to-infrastructure communications or services provisioned through communication operators. For example, an egress link is selected because it offers the required service with reasonable cost, or it has enough bandwidth and guarantees high quality of traffic transmission.

Mobile Weighted Round Robin Scheduling Service Discipline

A Mobile Weighted Fair Queuing (MWFQ) Scheduling Service Discipline (SSD) has been integrated into our proposed scheme to serve traffic connections based on their class and capacity sharing of egress links. It allocates an amount of available bandwidth to traffic connections based on their priority class, but does not adapt incoming traffic data rate to the available bandwidth on the egress links of MR. Figure 3 depicts the flowchart of our proposed Mobile Weighted Round Robin Scheduling Service Discipline (MWRR SSD). To manage traffic on egress links of MR, the maintains a number of tables: Capacity of egress links, , available bandwidth table, , flow table, , link table, , weight table, , number of flows table, , packet table, , number of packets table, ,. records the capacity of egress links. records the available bandwidth on egress links. records the flows assigned to egress links. records the packets assigned to egress links. records the utilized bandwidth on egress links after admitting packets/flows. records the weights assigned to egress links based on the available bandwidth. records the number of flows assigned to egress links. records the number of packets assigned to egress links.

The uses probing to measure the available bandwidth on egress links. Each interface is assigned a weight, ω_i, based on the available bandwidth measured on this interface, γ_i, as follows:

$$\omega_i = \frac{\gamma_i}{C_i} \tag{4}$$

Equation (1) calculates the bandwidth required for a traffic connection. The Number of Flows () scheduled onto an egress link can be calculated as follows:

$$NF_i = \frac{\gamma_i}{r^e} \tag{5}$$

$$NFT[i][0] = NFT[i][0] + [\omega_i * NF_i] * r^e \tag{6}$$

The number of packets () scheduled onto egress links can be calculated as follows:

$$NP_i = \frac{\gamma_i}{L_p} \tag{7}$$

$$NPT[i][0] = NPT[i][0] + [\omega_i * NP_i] * L_p \tag{8}$$

where represents the size of each packet scheduled onto the egress link. The capacity of egress links in and is incremented by the bandwidth allocated for admitted flows or packets based on the flow or packet dispatching scheme, respectively. By calculating the number of flows or packets, which can be dispatched onto egress links, traffic can be better balanced among egress links. This increases the utilization of egress links, while controlling the resource allocated for traffic connections with different QoS requirements. In what follows, we introduce the second entity in our proposed e2e QoS scheme architecture, which is responsible for computing and selecting routing paths with HAs and CNs. This entity consists of local and global traffic load balancing.

LOCAL TRAFFIC LOAD BALANCING

Recall that MR as well as other network nodes should ensure optimal or even distribution of traffic among output links so that traffic can be optimally or evenly distributed across the network (Hsiao, Hwang, Kung, & Vlah, 2001; Thaler & Ravishankar, 1998). MNNs generate traffic connections at different data rates, where egress interfaces (output links) of MR as well as other network nodes serve traffic at different service rates. Based on the traffic arrival rates at each of the input links and service rates at the output links of any network node, optimal weights can be dynamically calculated for each output (outbound) link to upper bound the amount of transmitted traffic.

Usually, ISPs can only provide static routing for router access to better manage and control traffic in their network domains. To avoid managing BGP routing table, many networking systems perform link sharing based on the NAT mechanism or stripping traffic connections, packet or users into the different output links (Thaler & Ravishankar, 1998; Yuen & Chung, 2007). This would increase the multiplexing gain by enabling traffic connections to efficiently use the capacity of output links. Note that the weights of outbound links should not be simply set proportional to their link rate or the number of next hops (Thaler & Hopps, 2000), instead it is better to be calculated based on the input traffic rate and available capacity measured or estimated at the output links.

When the weights are calculated at each output link of any network node between NEMO and correspondent nodes, then, traffic load balancing can be achieved by using a simple Class-Based Queuing (CBQ) SSD or WRR scheduling service discipline. In case of NEMOs, the service rates of output links change as function of time and geographical positions of NEMOs; therefore, our proposed mobile WRR SSD adjusts dynamically the weights based on the available capacity measured at the output links. Furthermore, the output links have different characteristics, depending on the employed communication technology,

thus the weights of the output links should be assigned dynamically to serve traffic based on network status. However, since routing protocols have not self-knowledge of current traffic load of each link, they cannot achieve real traffic load balancing through the multiple links to the Internet for the inbound/outbound traffic. Thus, local traffic load balancing should be integrated with a global traffic load balancing to avoid any eventual congestion and guarantee traffic load balancing across the network.

GLOBAL TRAFFIC LOAD BALANCING

Traffic connections contend to the available resources on the different routing paths, which connect a NEMO through its MR and road communication gateways to home agents and correspondent nodes. There are numerous techniques to avoid contention by balancing the traffic load across the network. Most routing-based techniques involve two stages: routing path calculation and selection. The routing path calculation can be divided into two categories, namely static and dynamic. In static-route calculation, one or more routes are calculated ahead of time, based on some metrics, such as number of hops. For example, in fixed alternate routing paths, one or more routes can be computed using Dijekstra's shortest-path algorithm, which calculates a routing path based on single or multiple performance metrics.

Static route calculation techniques can work effectively when the traffic is fairly steady; however, this is not the case of NEMO since traffic over the different routes may fluctuate over a short time scale, particularly on the route segments connecting NEMO to access routers (or RCGs). Therefore, dynamic routing should be used to dynamically calculate routes based on certain transient dynamic traffic information such as link congestion, number of connections contending on the link, Signal to Noise Ratio (SNR) and bandwidth availability. The information regarding

Figure 3. Mobile weight round robin SSD algorithm

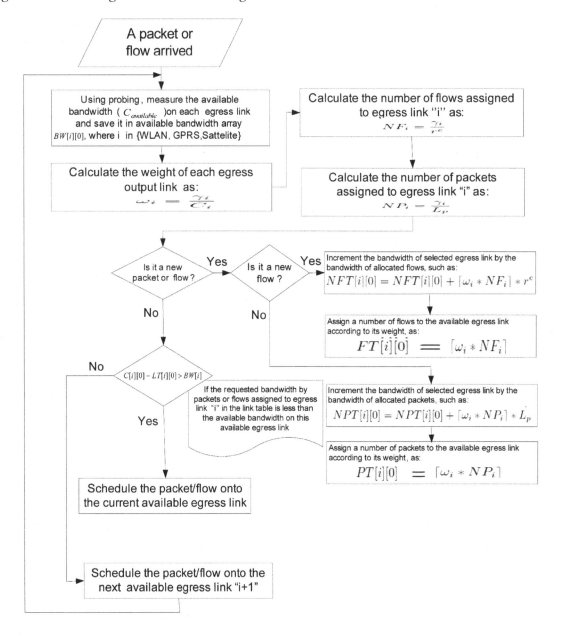

these links can be obtained in two ways, namely probe-based or broadcast approaches. In this chapter, we employ the probe-based approach and an optimal broadcast approach to collect information regarding the status of the different routing paths connecting a vehicular network to CNs.

In the probe-based approach, before MR routes (or initiates) traffic connections generated by MNNs, a road communication gateway sends a probe packet to the HA serving NEMO. The probe packet collects the necessary information from the links and network nodes along the routes connecting NEMO and RCG to HA and returns to the RCG with the necessary information to select a routing path. In the broadcast approach, network nodes and RCGs perform an active role by transmitting

Figure 4. Multi-homed NEMO simulation environment in OMNeT++

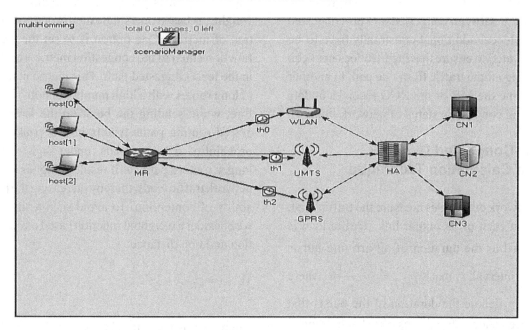

relevant congestion information periodically to all edge nodes including RCGs and MRs (vehicles), respectively. The RCG can send the probe packet either once for every handover performed by the MR (NEMO) or periodically based on an interval ô (Alshaer & Elmirghani, 2009).

The RCG sends traffic data using burst mode, where data can be buffered and sent when a route path has been calculated and allocated for traffic connections. Since the duration of the transmitted data is short, the probe can be sent periodically based on some intervalô. In order to reduce the control packet traffic (overhead) in the broadcast approach, the feedback information about a link can be sent to all edge nodes if the traffic load on the link exceeds a maximum congestion load threshold, ρ^{max}. Note that NEMOs through probing each duration will be notified if there is a change on the congestion status from the previous value of the links connecting them to RCGs. By doing so, the core nodes and RCGs can eliminate sending status packets in certain intervals altogether, thereby ensuring that there is minimal feedback to all the edge nodes (RCGs) and

NEMOs, respectively. It is noteworthy that additional memory overhead is needed at the core nodes to maintain the load status of each of their output links.

When the routing paths are selected statically or dynamically, one of these paths is selected for transmitting arrived traffic. If the calculation technique for routing paths computes only a single path, the selection process of routing path is omitted; thus, the selection of routing path primarily applies to static routing path computation techniques that calculate multiple routes. In static routing path selection techniques, a fixed fraction of traffic is sent on each of the alternate routes. The amount of traffic sent on each alternate path is decided based on feedback information. Dynamic route-selection policies are based on feedback information and operate similar to the dynamic route-calculation techniques. Using the information and the dynamic route selection policy, the data is transmitted on the selected route.

Stabilization is a significant point in dynamic routing path calculation and selection techniques. It is possible that different NEMOs react to congestion simultaneously, which will result in oscillation between congested and un-congested states. Hence, additional constraints have to be incorporated to ensure that the MR does not keep switching all the traffic from one path to another every time the MR or the RCG receives update regarding congestion status of network links.

Least-Congested Dynamic Route Calculation Technique

The network core nodes measure the traffic load, $\rho_{(i,j)}$, on each of its output link. Traffic load is expressed as the duration of all arriving bursts over the interval, τ, that is $\rho_{(i,j)} = \dfrac{\tau_s + \tau_d}{\tau}$, where τ_s and τ_d denote the duration of the bursts that have been successfully transmitted and dropped during the interval τ, respectively. The traffic load of each link is calculated every τ units of time,

where the routes are computed again. Let the weight, , is based on a single metric or a combination of metrics. One option is to set the weight function equal to the congestion metric, resulting in the least congested path. This metric may lead to long routes with a high number of hops. Therefore, while sending the burst on the least congested routing paths results in low packet loss probability at lower loads, under higher loads, longer routing paths will result in higher overall network traffic loads, thereby increasing the probability of contention. To avoid such a situation, we consider a weighted function based on congestion and hop distance:

$$W_{(i,j)} = \rho_{(i,j)} + 1 \tag{9}$$

where $\rho_{(i,j)}$ is the offered traffic load on the link. This weighted function results in better performance in term of loss, since the minimal number

Figure 5. The impact of network mobility on TCP congestion window

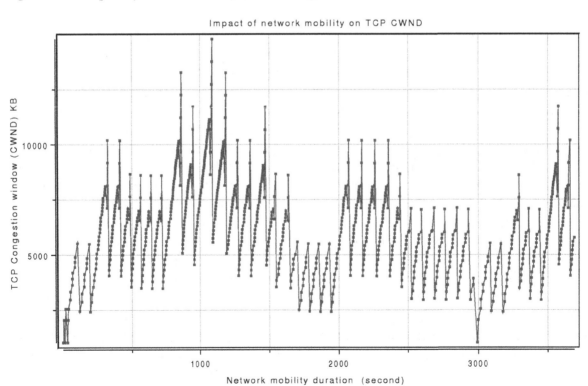

Figure 6. Performance of TCP packet and flow splitting schemes under CBQ scheduling

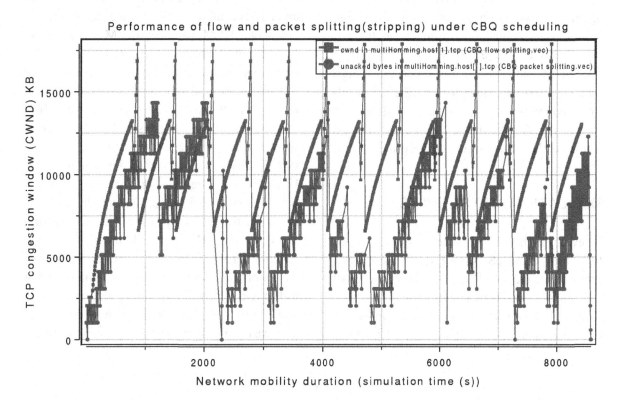

of nodes are selected in a routing path, thereby reducing the probability of contention. Another option is to define the weighted function based on congestion and propagation delay.

$$W_{(i,j)} = \rho_{(i,j)} + \frac{d_{(i,j)}}{d^{\max}} \qquad (10)$$

where $d_{(i,j)}$ is the delay propagation of the link and $d^{\max}$ is the maximum delay propagation of any link in the network. This weighted function may result in better performance in terms of propagation delay and congestion, since minimum congestion and propagation delay on links are selected in a routing path, thereby reducing the congestion and e2e delay.

Parameter Selection

The duration over which the offered traffic load on a link is computed, ô, significantly affects the performance of the load balancing algorithm. There are three factors which should be considered in selecting the value of : the amount of control overhead, the accuracy of algorithm and the effect of outdated information. The average traffic load obtained in larger value of ô is more accurate. A short value of ô will increase the control overhead in the network and load status computed during this interval may be not accurate.

The selection of $\rho^{\max}$ is also critical, since the value determines whether the link is congested or not. Hence, the value of $\rho^{\max}$ should be chosen based on the desired operating load range of the network. Setting a low value to $\rho^{\max}$ will lead to better route selection decisions when the load is low. However, when the operating loads are much higher, $\rho^{\max}$ will be ineffective, since $\rho^{\max}$ will signal congestion on all the alternate paths, thereby not providing any useful information for the edge node. On the other hand, setting a high value of $\rho^{\max}$ will result in good decisions at high loads. However, at lower load all the paths will not be congested between a source and destination. Hence, all the traffic will be sent on the primary path, leading to a congested primary path.

SIMULATION AND RESULTS

To evaluate the performance of our proposed distributed e2e QoS control scheme, we have integrated it, under OMNeT++, with NEMO-BSP (Devarapalli, Wakikawa, Petrescu, & Thubert, 2005) in the network topology shown in Figure 4. In this, a multi-homed vehicular NEMO is connected to Internet through WLAN, UMTS, and GPRS communication technologies. A single HA serves NEMO and enables MNNs and CNs to communicate based on NEMO-BSP. Along the simulation time, 3MB to 6MB files were constantly transferred from MNNs (host0, host1, and host2) to CNs. NEMO was moving at a random speed (10 m/s, 20 m/s, 30 m/s) to measure the effect of network mobility on the communication performance metrics. Most of the Internet applications use TCP/IP as an underlying transport protocol; therefore, we have conducted simulation experiments with the aims to: (1) analyze the TCP Congestion Window (CWND) size while the CBQ SSD is functioning in the MR, (2) evaluate the performance of traffic splitting schemes, namely packet traffic and flow traffic splitting schemes (PTSS and FTSS), and (3) evaluate the performance of the least congestion and minimum hop-based

Figure 7. The impact of network mobility and route selection on video packets

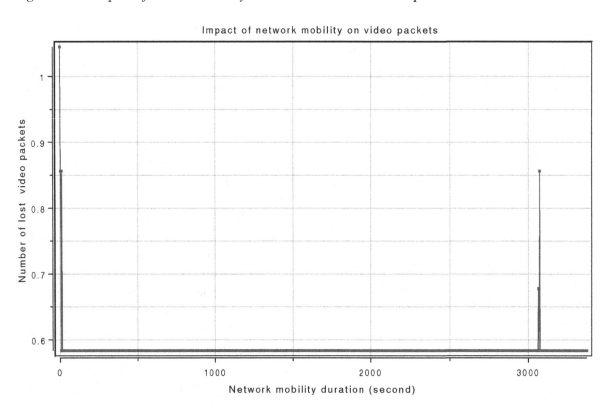

dynamic route calculation technique in reducing the impact of network mobility on video traffic. The TCP CWND bounds the amount of data which can be sent per round-trip time (RRT) of any connection. The slow start threshold (ssthresh) sets the value of the TCP CWND, which corresponds to the estimated available bandwidth along the selected routing path and accordingly regulates the transmission rate based on:

$$Bandwidth = \frac{1.22 * MTU}{RTT * \sqrt{}} \qquad (11)$$

$$ssthresh = bandwidth * RTT_{\min} \qquad (12)$$

where MTU denotes the maximum transmission unit, L denotes the loss probability along the routing path and RTTmin denotes the minimum propagation RTT between a MNN and its CN.

As a result, Figure 5 shows that the TCP CWND varies according to the network mobility and selected routing path, where MNNs could send at a higher data rate when the MR selected the WLAN egress interface or NEMO was moving at a low speed such as 10 m/s. Thus, NEMO should carefully select the egress interface according to network mobility and NEMO speed. Figure 6 shows a result where NEMO speed was sat to 30 m/s. It demonstrates that the FTSS performs better than the PTSS in term of TCP CWND, enabling MNNs to send at a higher data rate. Furthermore, the TCP CWND appears to be more stable in case of FTTS than that resulting from the PTSS. This can be attributed to the fact that traffic packets which are forwarded to different egress interfaces incase of PTSS, their TCP connections converged to different ssthresh values based on the Equations (12) and (11) and therefore the CWND size varies on a short time scale, decreasing the e2e throughput. This explains the problem of the TCP CWND size, where competing connections might not be allocated equal network resources,

because the TCP CWND size might converge to different CWND values.

Figure 7 shows that the proposed distributed e2e QoS control scheme performs better when the routes selection is based on the weighted function described in Equation (9). This is represented by the low video traffic loss during network mobility (0 - 3000 s) where the probing duration was long and routing paths were selected based on the congestion and hop distance. Thereafter, however, the proposed scheme selects routing paths based only on congestion where longer routes were selected for video traffic and hence a spike appeared, representing the increase in video traffic loss.

RESEARCH DIRECTIONS

- Traffic caching can improve the application performance in wireless networks by reducing the data outage probability. The performance of using caching in a palm top-based navigational tool was evaluated in the vehicular environment. With caching and pre-fetching, the latency of retrieving road maps and locations can be significantly reduced. However, more research is still required to consider the impact of network pricing on proxy buffer management and data access (Lin, Lai, & Chen, 2003; Persone & Grassi, 2003).

- The performance of real-time data transmission over Code-Division Multiple Access (CDMA)-based Vehicle-to-Road (V2R) communications was analyzed. However, more research work is still required to study the cost of wireless streaming over V2R links and optimization of wireless access (Mancuso & Bianchi, 2004; Chung & Cho, 2003).

- More research work is still needed to further develop our proposed distributed e2e

QoS control scheme to consider the application requirements, the cost of communication access channel and its utility.

SUMMARY

Network mobility has a significant impact on MNNs throughput due to the variations of the TCP CWND on a short time scale. This can be improved by enabling NEMOs to dynamically select routes based on the measured (probed) available bandwidth along the different routes connecting it to CNs. This Chapter has introduced an e2e QoS control scheme, which integrates three main entities: Scheduling service discipline, traffic splitting, dynamic routing path computation and selection, which ensure optimal multi-homing configuration for vehicular NEMOs by enabling mobile routers and road communication gateways to optimally distribute traffic among egress interfaces with RCGs and routing paths with HAs and CNs, respectively. By integrating local and global traffic load balancing, each network node can contribute in optimally distributing traffic load across the whole network. Simulation results have shown the promising performance of our proposed distributed e2e QoS control scheme. This will be further developed to integrate other network entities, which can contribute in ensuring optimal multi-homing configuration for vehicular NEMOs.

REFERENCES

Alshaer, H., & Elmirghani, J. M. H. (2009). Road safety based on efficient vehicular communications. In *Proceedings of the IEEE Intelligent Vehicle Symposium*. XI' an, China: IEEE Press.

Alshaer, H., & Elmirghani, J. M. H. (2009). Fourth-generation (4G) wireless networks: Applications and innovations. In *An end-to-end QoS framework for vehicular mobile networks*. Hershey, PA: IGI Global.

Alshaer, H., Ernst, T., & Fortelle, A. D. L. (2012a). An integrated architecture for multi-homed vehicle-to-infrastructure communications. In *Proceedings of the 13th IEEE/IFIP Network Operations and Management Symposium (NOMS)*, (pp. 1042—1047). IEEE Press.

Alshaer, H., Ernst, T., & Fortelle, A. D. L. (2012). A QoS architecture for provisioning high quality in intelligent transportation services. In *Proceedings of the 13th IEEE/IFIP Network Operations and Management Symposium (NOMS)*, (pp. 595—598). IEEE Press.

Bates, T., & Rekhter, Y. (1998). *Scalable support for multihomed multi-provider connectivity*. RFC 2260. Retrieved from http://tools.ietf.org/html/rfc2260

Cai, H., & Lin, Y. (2005). Design of a roadside seamless wireless communication system for intelligent highway. In *Proceedings of the IEEE Network Sensors Control*, (pp. 342–347). IEEE Press.

Chang, C.-J., Cheng, R.-G., Shih, H.-T., & Chen, Y.-S. (2007). Maximum freedom last scheduling algorithm for downlinks of DSRC networks. *IEEE Transactions on Intelligent Transportation Systems*, 8(2), 223–232. doi:10.1109/TITS.2006.889440

Chen, H.-H., & Guizani, M. (2006). *Next generation wireless systems and networks*. New York, NY: John Wiley and Sons Ltd. doi:10.1002/0470024569

Chung, Y., & Cho, D.-H. (2003). Performance evaluation of soft handoff for multimedia services in intelligent transportation systems based on CDMA. *IEEE Transactions on Intelligent Transportation Systems, 4*, 189–197. doi:10.1109/TITS.2003.821343

Cisco Systems. (2006). *Optimized edge routing.* Retrieved from http://www.cisco.com/en/US/products/ps6628/products_ios_protocol_option_home.html

Costlow, T. (2008). VII (vehicle infrastructure integration) highway communication system gains momentum. *Automotive Engineering International, 116*, 44–45.

Devarapalli, V., Wakikawa, R., Petrescu, A., & Thubert, P. (2005). *Network mobility (NEMO) basic support protocol.* IETF RFC3963. Retrieved from http://www.ietf.org/rfc/rfc3963.txt

Gu, B., Jung, J., Kim, K., Heo, J., Park, N., Jeon, G., & Cho, Y. (2010). SWICOM: An SDR-based wireless communication gateway for vehicles. *IEEE Transactions on Vehicular Technology, 59*, 1593–1605. doi:10.1109/TVT.2009.2040004

Guo, M., Ammar, M.-H., & Zegura, E. W. (2005). V3: A vehicle-to-vehicle live video streaming architecture. In *Proceedings of IEEE International Conference on PerCom*, (pp. 171–180). IEEE Press.

Hossain, I., & Mahmud, S. M. (2007). Analysis of a secure software upload technique in advanced vehicles using wireless links. *Proceedings of IEEE ITS, C*, 1010–1015. IEEE Press.

Hsiao, P., Hwang, A., Kung, H. T., & Vlah, D. (2001). Load balancing routing for wireless access network. Cambridge, MA: INFOCOM. *Proceedings of INFOCOM, 2*, 986–995.

Johnson, D., Perkins, C., & Arkko, J. (2004). *Mobility support in IPv6.* RFC 3775. Retrieved from http://www.ietf.org/rfc/rfc3775.txt

Jungum, N. V., Doomun, R. M., Ghurbhurrun, S. D., & Pudaruth, S. (2008). Collaborative driving support system in mobile pervasive environments. In *Proceedings of ICWMC*, (pp. 358–363). ICWMC.

Lee, U., Park, J.-S., Amir, E., & Gerla, M. (2006). Fleanet: A virtual market place on vehicular networks. In *Proceedings of the International Conference on Mobile Ubiquitous Systems Workshops*, (pp. 1–8). IEEE.

Lin, Y.-B., Lai, W.-R., & Chen, J.-J. (2003). Effects of cache mechanism on wireless data access. *IEEE Transactions on Wireless Communications, 2*, 1247–1258. doi:10.1109/TWC.2003.819019

Mancuso, V., & Bianchi, G. (2004). Streaming for vehicular users via elastic proxy buffer management. *IEEE Communications Magazine, 42*, 144–152. doi:10.1109/MCOM.2004.1362558

Ng, C., Ernst, T., Paik, E., & Bagnulo, M. (2007). *Analysis of multihomming in network mobility support.* RFC 4980. Retrieved from http://ietfreport.isoc.org/idref/rfc4980/

Persone, V. N., & Grassi, V. (2003). Performance analysis of caching and prefetching strategies for palmtop-based navigational tools. *IEEE Transactions on Intelligent Transportation Systems, 4*(1), 23–34. doi:10.1109/TITS.2002.808416

Soldo, F., Cigno, R. L., & Gerla, M. (2008). Cooperative synchronous broadcasting in infrastructure-to-vehicles networks. In *Proceedings of Conference WONS*, (pp. 125–132). WONS.

Tao, S., Xu, K., Xu, Y., Fei, T., Gao, L., & Guerin, R. ... Towsley, D. (2004). Exploring the performance benefits of end-to-end path switching. In *Proceedings of the ICNP*. ICNP.

Thaler, D., & Hopps, C. (2000). *Multipath issues in unicast and multicast next-hop selection.* RFC. Retrieved from http://www.ietf.org

Thaler, D., & Ravishankar, C. V. (1998). Using name-based mappings to increase hit rates. *IEEE/ACM Transactions on Networking, 6,* 1–14. doi:10.1109/90.663936

Wang, H., Xie, H., Qi, L., Siberschatz, A., & Yang, Y. R. (2005). Optimal ISP subscription for internet multihoming: Algorithm design and implication analysis. In *Proceedings of the IEEE Infocom.* IEEE Press.

Xie, F., Hua, K. A., Wang, W., & Ho, Y. (2007). Performance study of live video streaming over highway vehicular ad hoc networks. In *Proceedings of IEEE VTC Spring,* (pp. 2121–2125). IEEE Press.

Xie, J., & Narayanan, U. (2010). Performance analysis of mobility support in IPv4/IPv6 mixed wireless networks. *IEEE Transactions on Vehicular Technology, 59,* 962–973. doi:10.1109/TVT.2009.2034668

Yang, K., Ou, S., Chen, H.-H., & He, J. (2007). A multihop peer-communication protocol with fairness guarantee for IEEE 802.16-based vehicular networks. *IEEE Transactions on Vehicular Technology, 56,* 3358–3370. doi:10.1109/TVT.2007.906875

Yuen, A., & Chung, T. (2007). *Traffic engineering for multi-homed mobile networks.* (PhD Thesis). The University of New South Wales. Sydney, Australia.

Chapter 9

QoS–Aware Chain–Based Data Aggregation in Cooperating Vehicular Communication Networks and Wireless Sensor Networks

Zahra Taghikhaki
University of Twente, The Netherlands

Yang Zhang
University of Twente, The Netherlands

Nirvana Meratnia
University of Twente, The Netherlands

Paul J.M. Havinga
University of Twente, The Netherlands

ABSTRACT

Vehicular Communication Networks (VCNs) and Wireless Sensor Networks (WSNs) are emerging types of networks, which have individually been extensively explored. However, their cooperation and exploring advantages offered by their integration are poorly explored. Such integration helps better investigate impacts of human mobility and transportation behaviors on safety and well-being of cities, their residents, their surrounding environments, and ecology. In this chapter, the authors propose a QoS-Aware Chain-based data Aggregation (QoS-ACA) technique for wireless sensor networks cooperating with vehicular communication networks, which fast, reliably, and energy efficiently aggregates sensor data and sends the aggregated value to the road side units. Ensuring quality of service parameters has been put forward as an essential consideration for wireless sensor networks, which are often deployed in unattended and open environments and are characterized by their limited resources. To this end, in-network data aggregation is an efficient solution to save energy and bandwidth and to provide meaningful information to end-users.

DOI: 10.4018/978-1-4666-2223-4.ch009

INTRODUCTION

Vehicular Communication Networks (VCNs) are an emerging type of networks, in which vehicles and Road Side Units (RSUs) communicate with each other to provide real-time information to drivers and policy makers. Popularity and importance of VCNs have increased in recent years as they can support a wide range of applications. Although VCNs have some similarities with VSNs (Vehicular Sensor Networks), they have important differences. VCNs exploit sensing and communication infrastructure deployed along-side the roads to monitor vehicles (e.g. presence, type, speed) and the environment (e.g. pollution). This information is gathered by the RSUs in order to manage traffic congestion and safety, among others. VSNs, on the other hand, are sensing and communication infrastructures formed by equipping vehicles with onboard sensing and communication devices to enable vehicles to collect sensory information about themselves (e.g. speed, location) or the environment (pollution) and to communicate with each other or RSUs in order to transmit information about vehicular traffic control and accidents, among others. Figure 1 (b) illustrates the difference between VCNs and VSNs.

Similarly to VCNs, Wireless Sensor Networks (WSNs) have also received much attention in recent years. A WSN consists of a large number of spatially distributed autonomous wireless sensor nodes which are usually deployed in an unattended environment to monitor physical or environmental conditions, such as temperature, sound, vibration, pressure, motion, or pollution (Akyildiz et al., 2002; Romer & Mattern, 2004; Haenselmann, 2006). VSNs can be considered as a special type of Wireless Sensor Networks (WSNs). Unlike WSNs, however, VSNs are highly mobile and do not have the sever resource constraints (in terms of battery, processing, and memory) of the WSNs.

In this paper, we focus on VCNs and WSNs and their cooperation. This is because while VCNs and WSNs have individually been extensively ex-

plored, their cooperation and exploring advantages offered by their integration are poorly explored. Such integration helps better investigate impacts of human mobility and transportation behaviours on safety and well-being of cities, their residents, their surrounding environments, and ecology. Wild animals living on the border of cities are hit very often by cars passing by. Areas in which people frequently commute are subject to more pollution, which in turn threat asthma, COPD, and heart patients more. Road traffic noise and congestion are to be blamed for increase stress and frustration of citizens of big and crowded cities. Fine grained monitoring and (near) real-time reasoning capability of wireless sensor networks alongside the already available communication infrastructure of vehicular communication networks can facilitate more efficient study and more reliable and accurate investigation of human beings mobility parameters and their effects.

To this end, we consider a scenario in which a WSN with CO_2 and sound sensors are deployed along-side the VCNs as illustrated in Figure 1(a). We aim to detect the highly polluted areas in terms of both sound and CO_2 and provide reliable information to be able to redirect the traffic to the unpolluted and clean areas. By doing so, we aim not only to detect busy areas potentially facing traffic jams but also to inform heart and lung patients about areas to avoid.

The Need for Data Aggregation

To detect highly polluted areas, either every sensor node should send all its row data to a RSU or it should be able to detect pollution and its density locally. In case of the former, it is very expensive (in terms of communication) for the sensor nodes to send their raw data to the RSU very frequently. The raw data transmission from every sensor node to the RSU will deplete wireless sensor nodes' limited energy, which consequently influences the quality and quantity of sensor nodes' measurements. Ensuring high quality of sensor data

Figure 1. a) An example of coexistence and cooperation of VCNs and WSNs; b) An example of a VSN

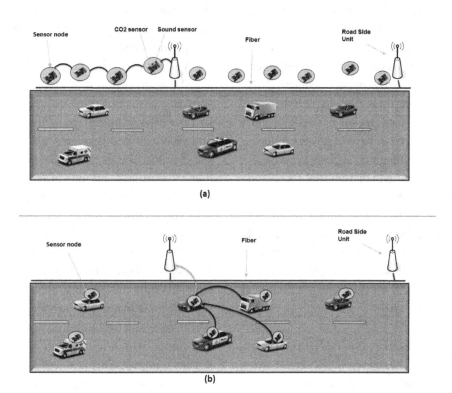

(a)

(b)

and preserving energy resources of the sensor nodes go hand in hand. Therefore, a decentralized method, in which sensor data can be aggregated and processed within the network, out of which patterns can be detected locally, is highly preferred. Use of data aggregation techniques not only helps save energy by communicating less data but also provides meaningful information to the end-users and prevents them from being flooded with huge amount of data.

Since sensor nodes are usually inexpensive hardware components, they are highly vulnerable to malicious attacks and often malfunction or fail. Malfunctioning of radios or sensors can result in generation of missing or wrong sensor values which in turn has detrimental effects on the overall performance of the network and decision making process. On the other hand, due to the fact that sensor nodes are often deployed in unattended and open environments, occurrence

of unexpected situations such as being hacked or replaced by untrustworthy nodes is very likely. These events influence data quality and reliability. Decisions made based on incorrect and unreliable sensor data cannot be trusted and may lead to serious inefficiencies throughout the whole network. Aggregation of inaccurate data contributes to data inaccuracy and error even further. Therefore, data aggregation needs to take both energy efficiency and reliability into account.

Data aggregation is considered as a significant primitive in the large and real-time networks, which helps save energy and bandwidth by reducing data transmission. There are two types of data aggregation in a network:

- Concatenating the payloads of the packets: In this case, as illustrated in Figure 2, only the headers of packets are merged and the payload parts are concatenated. This type of aggregation results in a bigger packet size compared with the several original small packets. Indeed, combining multiple packets into one eliminates number of communications and the cost associated with transmitting the packet headers. This type of aggregation is useful when the size of aggregated data packet is small. It can also be employed in case of having heterogeneous measurements, such as the case of our application, which requires CO_2 and sound measurements.

- Combining the payloads of packets: In this case, both headers and payload are merged separately so the size of the resultant packet remains the same as the original packets. This approach is useful in case of having homogenous data.

As stated in (Palazzo et al., 2009), use of data aggregation approaches in wireless sensor networks offers: i) reducing energy consumption, ii) eliminating overheads of the redundant packets, iii) decreasing total load of the network, and iv) making a meaningful data for the end user exploiting smart filtering of data. The same reference states that the main shortcomings of the data aggregation techniques may include: i) imposing extra data latency, ii) decreasing accuracy and data integrity in case of inappropriate aggregation. iii) the need to handle duplicated data in case of having a complex aggregation function, and iv)

the need for proper coding (Palazzo et al., 2009). Being aware of these advantages and disadvantages helps find a proper trade-off while utilizing aggregation techniques.

While routing the data from sensor nodes to a RSU, aggregation task can be done either on specific sensor nodes or on every sensor node. In case of not opting for aggregation on every node, having fixed aggregators should be avoided. This is due to the fact that these fixed aggregators may become single points of failures. Therefore, instead of having fixed aggregators, it is better to select nodes that satisfy best the necessary criteria of being an aggregator. By doing so, the role of aggregator can be rotated among all sensor nodes. Data aggregation techniques are very often tightly coupled with the routing approaches. If some links fail and do not relay sensor nodes' data for a while, the result of the aggregation may be highly inaccurate, which in turn can have a significant negative impact on the overall network performance. Most of existing routing approaches are designed for tree-base or cluster-based topologies and cannot be applied to the linear topology of cooperating WSN and VCN

Contribution

In this chapter, we propose QoS-ACA, a novel QoS-aware data aggregation approach for a wireless sensor network deployed along-side a vehicular communication network. The linear

Figure 2. Concatenation type of aggregation

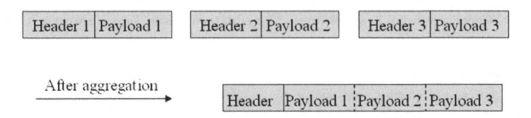

topology of these two cooperative networks implies that we consider a chain structure, in which aggregation is performed within clusters and aggregated data is routed to a RSU through cluster headers of adjacent clusters. To route aggregated data from the sensor nodes to road side units, we present a latency-, energy-, and reliability-aware cluster head election algorithm, which is applied both within clusters and outside clusters and aim to find nodes that best satisfy the criteria to be an aggregator on the basis of the networks provided transmission reliability, residual and required energy. We consider nodes physical position in a chain and also their distance to the RSU to have the best economical selection in terms of latency. In order to reach reliability, we utilize an error correction technique in the form of retransmission and send a packet n times (the exact value of n is calculated for each link) to provide the required reliability of the links.

The rest of this chapter is organized as follows. In what follows we briefly discuss state of the art, the model of our system and the problem statement, the proposed method and its performance evaluation. Finally we conclude this chapter by concluding remarks and future work.

STATE OF THE ART

The design of efficient and effective data aggregation techniques for WSNs is a challenging task, on which extensive research has been performed in recent years. Since topology of the network plays a vital role in performance of data aggregation techniques, we categorize existing data aggregation techniques based on their supported topology and present an architecture-based taxonomy. We first present the basic concept of these data aggregation methods and address their main advantages and limitations. Furthermore, we describe a number of chain-based data aggregation techniques, as these are the most relevant to the topic of this chapter. In addition, we present the

relevant work concerned with data aggregation in vehicular sensing networks (VSNs).

Taxonomy of Data Aggregation Techniques for WSNs

As illustrated in Figure 3, and based on their supported topology, existing data aggregation techniques for WSNs can be categorized into cluster-based, chain-based, tree-based, multi-path based, and hybrid methods.

Cluster-Based Data Aggregation Techniques

Cluster-based data aggregation techniques (Heinzelman et al., 2002; Jung et al., 2009; Busse et al., 2006; Chen & Son, 2005) organize nodes into a number of clusters and a local aggregator or cluster head aggregates data from sensor nodes of its cluster and transmits the aggregated data to a base station. The cluster heads can communication with the base station directly via long range communication or via multi-hops through other cluster heads.

Chain-Based Data Aggregation Techniques

Chain-based data aggregation techniques (Lindsey & Raghavendra, 2002; Tabassum et al., 2006; Shin & Suh, 2008; Du et al., 2003) build a linear chain connecting all nodes of a (sub) network and enable each node to transmit the data only to its closest neighboring node along the chain for data aggregation. Eventually the leader node which is similar to the cluster head transmits the aggregated data to a base station. Effectiveness of chain-based data aggregation techniques depends heavily on the construction of an effective chain. Compared to cluster-based techniques, chain-based techniques reduce excessive energy consumption for communicating with the base station, when it is located far from the cluster heads.

Figure 3. Taxonomy of data aggregation techniques for WSNs

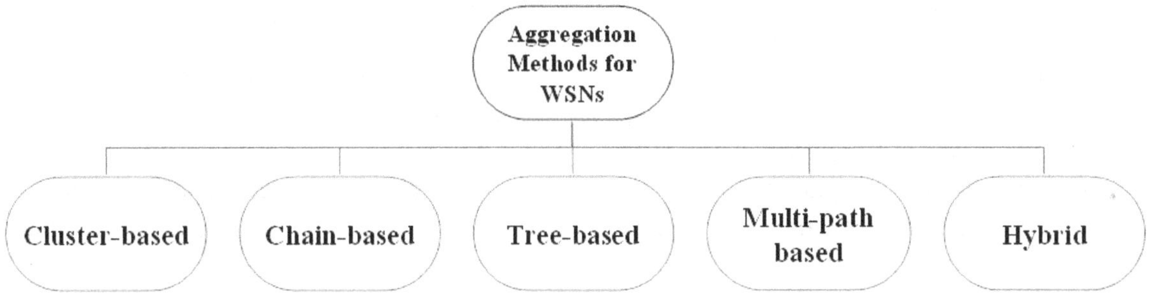

Tree-Based Data Aggregation Techniques

Tree-based data aggregation techniques (Tan & Korpeoglu, 2003; Kim & Han, 2005) organize nodes into a tree structure, where data aggregation is performed on intermediate nodes along the tree. Eventually the root node which is similar to the cluster head transmits the aggregated data to a base station. Compared to chain-based techniques, tree-based techniques allow parallel aggregation and shorten the routing delay. However, the maintenance of the tree needs many control messages which lead to a high volume traffic.

Multi-Path-Based Data Aggregation Techniques

Multi-path-based data aggregation techniques (Vidhyapriya & Vanathi, 2007; Ramadan, 2009) build multiple paths among sensor nodes for data transmission and data aggregation. In these techniques, one node sends its data to multiple neighbors instead of one neighbor. Multi-path-based techniques improve the robustness and gain maximum data accuracy and reliability in presence of link/node failure or packet loss. However, they have higher energy consumption and generate more data traffic to maintain the multi-paths.

Hybrid-Based Data Aggregation Techniques

Hybrid data aggregation techniques (Fan & Zhou, 2007; Lai & Jimmy, 1997; Stephanie et al., 2002; Taghikhaki et al., 2011) utilize a combination of different aggregation techniques and architectures.

Chain-Based Data Aggregation Techniques

There is not much work on data aggregation in the chain-based network architecture. A very first chain-based data aggregation technique is PEGASIS (Lindsey & Raghavendra, 2002). In PEGASIS, nodes are organized into a linear chain by using a greedy algorithm. The greedy chain formation assumes that all nodes have global knowledge about the network. The furthest node from the base station initiates chain formation and at each step, the closest neighbor of a node is selected as its successor in the chain. In each data gathering round, a node receives data from one of its neighbors, fuses the data with its own, and transmits the fused data to its other direct neighbors along the chain. Eventually the leader node transmits the aggregated data to the base station. PEGASIS effectively reduces the energy consumption in communication since the distances, from which most of the nodes transmit their data, are much less compared to cluster-based techniques, especially when cluster heads are far away from sensor nodes. However, the main disadvantage of PEGASIS is its strong assumption that all nodes have global knowledge about the entire network to pick suitable neighbors and minimize the neighbor distance. Additionally, due to the fact that only one leader exists in the entire network, PEGASIS causes an excessive delay for the nodes at the end of the chain, which are far away from the base station.

To alleviate the excessive delay in PEGASIS, two chain construction techniques, namely COSEN and MSC, were presented in (Tabassum et al., 2006; Shin & Suh, 2008). COSEN (Tabassum et al., 2006) is a hierarchical chain-based technique, in which sensor nodes are organized into one higher level chain and several lower level chains. In every lower level chain, nodes transmit the data to a chain leader, which is elected based on the residual energy. Then all lower level leaders send the aggregated data to a higher level leader, which has the highest energy among all lower level leaders. Eventually, the higher level leader performs final data aggregation and forwards the result to the base station. Compared to PEGASIS, COSEN has much lower latency because of using multiple chains and hierarchical structure to aggregate and route data. Shin & Suh (2008) propose an algorithm to build up a chain by leveraging Minimal Spanning Chain (MSC). This technique aims to enhance PEGASIS by reducing the chain length in order to decrease delay. This algorithm has two main steps, i.e., (i) configuring an initial chain, and (ii) link exchange. The first step uses Kruskal Minimal Spanning Tree (Kruskal, 1956) algorithm with maximum degree of two in order to make an initial chain. They verified that the Kruskal algorithm performs better than Prime algorithm, which PEGASIS employs. The rationale

behind this claim is that the Kruskal algorithm selects the minimum link among more links. The second step involves reducing the total chain length considering links' cost and by avoiding link crossing, which makes a chain longer and affects the delay, energy consumption and lifetime. The proposed technique does not exhibit any crossing links, while PEGASIS has many links.

The above two chain construction techniques (Tabassum et al., 2006; Shin & Suh, 2008) effectively alleviate the excessive delay in PEGASIS, however, they keep the same energy consumption of chain construction. To develop an energy efficient chain construction algorithm, Du et al. (2003) propose a multiple-chain technique that uses a sequence of insertions to add the least amount of energy consumption to the whole chain. The multiple chain technique divides the whole network into four regions centered at the node that is the closest to the center of the sensing region. For each region, a linear chain is constructed which ends at the center node. The multiple chain technique aims to decrease the total transmission distance for all-to-all broadcasting. In the greedy chain construction algorithm proposed in PEGASIS, the process starts with the furthest node from the sink. This node is the head of the chain. At each step, a non-chain node which is the closest to the chain head is selected and appended to the chain as the new head. The procedure is repeated until all nodes are in the chain.

Although most of chain-based data aggregation techniques for WSNs consider network lifetime and latency (time delay), they do not consider transmission reliability. Due to the fact that an aggregator may become a single point of failure, a robust data aggregation technique should not have just one special aggregator all the time. Thus, a suitable data aggregation for WSNs should ensure the transmission reliability as well as reduce energy consumption and time delay. This is the very contribution of our technique.

Data Aggregation Techniques for VSNs

To the best of our knowledge, there is no relevant work about coexistence of VCNs and WSNs in relation with data aggregation. Also, little work has been addressed for data aggregation in VSNs. Here we describe two techniques used in VSNs incorporating data aggregation.

Lim and Ko (2009) propose a multi-hop data harvesting method for VSNs, in which the vehicles are able to receive the data from multiple sensor nodes. A cluster-based data aggregation technique for this method is also introduced to alleviate the problem of packet collisions and transmission delays when replicas of sensing data in a similar region are created. A vehicle first transmits a geo-cast request message, which is then forwarded by the intermediate nodes until the first targeted sensor node inside the geo-cast region receives it. The first sensor node in the geo-cast region announces itself as a cluster head and forwards the request message to all the sensor nodes in the geo-cast region. The other sensor nodes become the cluster child nodes and transmit their data packets to the cluster head instead of transmitting them to the intermediate nodes. Finally, the cluster head aggregates the packets and transmits the aggregated data back to the vehicle.

Han et al. (2010) proposes a secure probabilistic data aggregation method for VSNs, in which the security issues especially on how to ensure authenticity and integrity of aggregation results in dynamic vehicular environment receive much attention. The data aggregation used in this method focuses on the specific aggregation operation for received data instead of routing in a dynamic network topology. It aggregates data based on Flajolet-Martin sketch (Flajolet & Martin, 1985) and a series of sketch proof techniques.

SYSTEM MODEL AND PROBLEM STATEMENT

Network Model

We make the following assumptions regarding the wireless sensor network deployed along-side the vehicular communication network:

- As illustrated in Figure 4a, the wireless sensor network consists of N sensor nodes deployed in a linear topology.
- The network is divided into sub-networks such that every sub-network is located between two road side units.
- The wireless sensor network uses VCN's road side units as its base stations. Road side units have a high speed communication link, e.g. fiber. Cluster/chain leaders are able to reach one of the road side units.
- In case of not being a cluster/chain leader, sensor nodes can only communicate with their direct neighbors.
- The location of sensor nodes and the base stations are fixed and are known a priori.

Radio Model

We utilize the first order radio model discussed in (Heinzelman et al., 2000). As stated in (Heinzelman et al., 2000), the energy dissipation of the radio in order to run the transmitter or receiver circuitry is $E_{elec} = 50nJ / bit$ and to run transmitter amplifier is $E_{amp} = 100pJ / bit / m^2$.

In order to transmit a k-bit packet over a distance d, the radio expends:

$$E_{Tx}(k, d) = E_{elec} \times k + E_{amp} \times k \times d^2.$$

The energy consumption in the receiver is expressed as $E_{Rx}(k, d) = E_{elec} \times k$.

For the energy consumption of the processing task, we only consider the energy cost for data aggregation, which is expressed as $E_{agg} = 5nJ \: / \: bit \: / \: message$.

Two-Tier Architecture Model

It should be mentioned that because our proposed algorithm can be applied to each sub-chain independently, we only focus on one sub-chain and hereafter we refer to a sub-chain as our given network. We assume the number of nodes for all sub-chains is the same. Therefore, if the number of sub-chain is denoted by N_{cl}, each sub-chain has $N_{sn/cl} = \dfrac{N}{N_{cl}}$ sensor nodes. We consider a static cluster-based wireless sensor network and a two-tiers architecture model, as illustrated in Figure 4b. Every sensor node in a cluster must send its data to its upstream neighbor, which has been selected in the chain construction phase. Within each cluster, intermediate nodes along the path to the local aggregator aggregate the data received from the downstream nodes with their own data and forward the local aggregated value towards to the cluster head. The cluster head that we call the aggregator must perform final aggregation on the data received from its neighboring clusters and then forward the result to the RSU through the cluster head of other clusters.

Network Operation Modes

We consider the wireless sensor network to be used for both periodic data collection as well as event detection.

Problem Statement

The problem we deal with is to find a reliable and well-balanced scheme to deliver data packets gathered by the sensor nodes to a RSU by taking the residual and needed energy of the nodes into account in order to keep all sensor nodes alive simultaneously. This is because data of all sensor nodes is important and if some nodes die sooner than the rest, network operation will be hindered by created 'holes'. We also consider the latency parameter in order to shorten the delay of receiving data by the RSU. This is especially important for event detection operation mode of the network.

Since within a network, sensor nodes that are not chain leader can only communicate with their two direct neighbors, routing algorithm is not very complicated. Therefore, we mostly concentrate on the cluster head and aggregator election algorithm instead of routing.

QUALITY OF SERVICE PARAMETERS

Before explaining our technique, we first discuss a number of Quality of Service (QoS) parameters, which are of importance to our scenario and explain our approach to ensure them.

Transmission Reliability

Ensuring transmission reliability is important for applications of wireless sensor networks, however, different applications require different degree of reliability. Decision making applications such as event detection need high degree of transmission reliability, as events detected locally in the network or critical data should certainly be received by the RSUs. Periodic monitoring applications can better tolerate missing data and therefore need lower degree of reliability. Depending on network density, different measurements can be utilized to ensure the required reliability.

We consider reliability metric to be the ratio between the numbers of packets received by the RSU and the total number of packets transmitted.

Figure 4. a) The network model b) Two-tiers architecture model

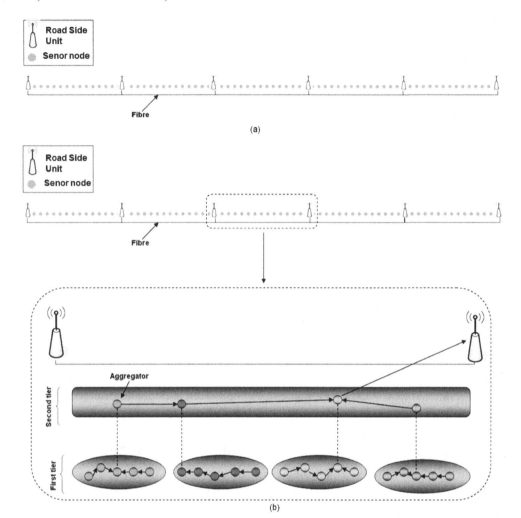

Ensuring Reliablity for Event Detection Applications

One of the usual approaches to achieve reliable transmission in a failure prone environment is sending several copies of one packet from each source node towards the destination node. This operation can be accomplished in two different ways:

- Using acknowledgement in order to identify whether the packet has been received by the destination. In this way, the source node sends the copy of one given packet till it receives an acknowledgement. If the acknowledgement packet is lost due to link/network failure, source node continues sending copies of the received data in spite of receiving data by the destination. This approach suffers from possibly high communication overhead, which can lead to high energy dissipation.

- Sending multiple copies without sending any acknowledgement. Although this approach reduces the acknowledgement overhead, it must find a solution to ensure that the data will be received by the destination after sending n copies of a packet. A good option to calculate n is using $n = \log_{p_{pktloss}}^{1-R_{Req}}$. R_{Req} represents the reliability requested by the application for each link and $p_{pktloss}$ is the packet loss probability of the network. In our technique, as will be explained later, we apply this equation for each link in the chain. Hence, $p_{pktloss}$ is the packet loss probability of a given link. The number of copies (n) must be calculated for each link individually since probability of packet loss may vary between different links.

To ensure reliability, we send multiple copies of the same data from every sensor nodes to its neighbor. In doing so, the position of cluster head is not important. The rationale behind this is that every node just tries to have a reliable transmission with its upstream neighbor who also aims to achieve this reliability and is responsible to forward data (or aggregated data which includes its own data and the data of its downstream node) of its downstream node to its upstream node.

Ensuring Reliability for Periodic Monitoring Applications in Dense Networks

Retransmission approaches are highly preferable for applications requiring high degree of reliability. For applications requiring less degree of reliability, such as periodic monitoring application we do not employ data retransmission and each data packet is sent just once.

Figure 5. Hop-by-hop reliability in a given chain

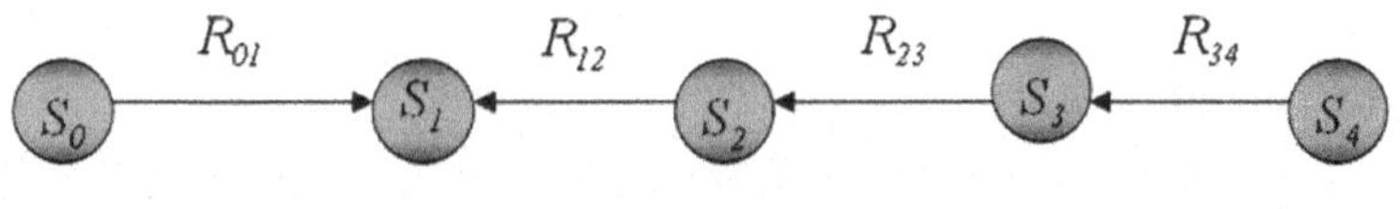

In a dense network, we aim to maximize transmission reliability by finding the best place for the leader while we calculate sum of the end-to-end reliabilities between each sensor node and the designated leader, i.e., $\sum_{i=0}^{N_{SN/cl}} EE - \mathrm{Re}\,liability$.

The end-to-end reliability is obtained by the product of the hop-by-hop reliability of the sensor nodes along the path to the given leader.

In the example shown in Figure 5, the hop-by-hop reliabilities are denoted by $R_{i,i+1}$ for every link. For example the end-to-end reliability for S_4 when S_1 is a leader is

$$EE\_\mathrm{Re}\,liability(S_4, S_1) = R_{34} \times R_{23} \times R_{12}.$$

The higher the value of $\sum_{i=0}^{N_{SN/cl}} EE - \mathrm{Re}\,liability$, the more data will be received by the designated leader. Consequently more data will reach the RSU.

Finding the best leader is done by the RSU every T_l time period. T_l is an application dependent parameters. A small T_l value leads to more adaptability to the environment changes, higher reliability, and higher energy consumption, which leads to shorter network life time.

In order to properly select the leader for each sub-chain, the RSU must be aware of the last changes of the environment as much as possible. Also, some applications require knowing the state of all sensor nodes at each time period. To this end, we exploit the flag part of the data packets.

The RSU uses the flags of data packet in order to identify whether the result which is in aggregated data field includes the data of all sensor nodes in a chain. RSU maintains one table, called *nmbrRcvd* which includes the number of received data from each sensor node in the sub-network and updates this table every time period by looking at the flag fields of the received packets. Each row of this table belongs to one sensor node in the given sub-network. Base station increases the value of corresponding row of a sensor node in the *nmbrRcvd* table if the flag of that sensor node is 1.

$$nmbrRcvd_{S_i} = \begin{cases} nmbrRcvd_{S_i} + 1 & if \ flag_{S_i} = 1 \\ nmbrRcvd_{S_i} & if \ flag_{S_i} = 0 \end{cases}$$

Each leader in every T_l time period must find the loss probability of each link using *nmbrRcvd* table. The loss probability of the link between S_i and S_{i+1} is calculated using:

$$p_{pktloss}(S_i, S_{i+1}) = 1 - \frac{nmbrRcvd_{S_i}}{total \ packet \ must \ be \ received \ from \ S_i}$$

These loss probabilities are sent to the RSU every T_l time period through nodes of the second-tier (see Figure 4b.). It should be mentioned that we assume the reliability or packet loss probability for one link is symmetric, therefore $p_{pktloss}(S_i, S_{i+1}) = p_{pktloss}(S_{i+1}, S_i)$.

Having these loss probabilities, the hop-by-hop reliability between two sensor nodes will be obtained using

$$HH - \mathrm{Re}\,liability(S_i, S_{i+1}) = 1 - p_{pktloss}(S_i, S_{i+1})$$

By having the hop-by-hop reliabilities, the RSU must evaluate the appropriateness of each sensor node to be an aggregator. To this end, the RSU first calculates the end-to-end reliability from each sensor node to the designated leader by employing the equation in Box 1.

At the second step, the RSU finds the provided reliability of each designated leader by summing up the end-to-end reliability of each sensor node by considering the designated leader ID as the LeaderID in:

$$\mathrm{Pr}\,ovided - \mathrm{Re}\,liability(S_k) = \frac{1}{N_{SN/cl} - 1} \times \sum_{i=0}^{N_{SN/cl}} EE - \mathrm{Re}\,liability(S_i, S_k).$$

After finding all the provided reliability values in a chain, the RSU selects the sensor node which offers the maximum provided reliability as the leader for a given chain. This selection ensures the maximum reliability that this chain can provide.

Our approach to ensure reliability for period monitoring application in dense network tends to select the sensor nodes close to the high reliable links as a leader. Therefore, it is a good option to guarantee reliability for applications which only need to receive data from a sub-chain or area and it does not matter which sensor node sends this data. Most of the time, number of different sensor nodes which participate to make the final aggregation value at the leader is small and probably just a few sensor nodes near the leader make the final aggregation value.

Box 1.

$$EE - \mathrm{Re}\,liability(S_i, LeaderID) = \begin{cases} \prod_{k=i}^{LeaderID-1} HH - \mathrm{Re}\,liability(S_k, S_{k+1}) & LeaderID > i \\ \prod_{k=LeaderID}^{i-1} HH - \mathrm{Re}\,liability(S_k, S_{k+1}) & LeaderID < i \end{cases}$$

Ensuring Reliability for Periodic Monitoring Applications in Sparse Networks

Unlike the previous case, periodic monitoring using sparse networks require data from all sensor nodes and having data from one of sensor nodes in an area of sub-chain does not suffice. In this case to ensure a reliable transmission, we propose another solution that makes only a few changes to the RSU functionality described in the previous subsection.

The RSU first finds the minimum value of *EE—Reliability* for each candidate leader and then selects the leader candidate whose minimum value is greater than others as the leader. This minimum value somehow represents the contribution of the least reliable sensor node in a chain to the value of the aggregated result received by the RSU from this chain. Therefore, the higher this value, the higher the contribution of least reliable node. Indeed, the sensor nodes with higher end-to-end reliability have higher contribution to the final aggregation. In other word, the RSU selects the sensor node which satisfies the equation in Box 2 as the leader.

This approach ensures that the aggregated value received by the RSU from a sub-chain contains data of all sensor nodes in that given sub-chain. This approach tends to provide fairness in terms of contribution of sensor nodes to the aggregated value.

Lifetime

Efficient energy consumption has the highest priority in wireless sensor networks in order to allow network operating for long time. There are different definitions for lifetime of a wireless sensor network. In fact, lifetime is an application-dependent concept. There are some applications, which consider lifetime to be the time at which the first node dies, while others consider lifetime to be the time at which last node dies. Some applications need to have all sensor nodes alive simultaneously in order to fulfill their missions properly. In other words, deaths of the first node may have drastic effects on their mission and may lead to their inability to satisfy their application requirements. In this case, we must opt for load-balancing and evenly assign tasks to the sensor nodes by considering their residual energy ($\mathrm{Re}\,sidualEg_i$). Moreover, the needed energy ($neededEg_i$) to accomplish the assigned task and the initial energy of the given sensor node ($InitialEg_i$) should be taken into account. To ensure this quality of service, we select sensor nodes which maximize

$$\frac{\mathrm{Re}\,sidualEg_i}{InitialEg_i \times neededEg_i} \quad i \in \{1, ..., N_{sn/cl}\}$$

equation as the leader for a given chain.

Latency

In case of having no retransmission, providing latency guarantee depends heavily on the leader position in a chain. In order to shorten the latency in a chain, the leader must be located as close as possible to the middle of the chain. In other words, latency will be in direct proportion to the length of the biggest sub-chain, which is located at one side of the leader's position.

Box 2.

$$Maximum\{Minimum\{EE - \mathrm{Re}\,liability(S_i, S_j)\ i \in \{1, ..., N_{sn/cl}\}\} \quad j \in \{1, ..., N_{sn/cl}\} \wedge j \neq i\}$$

In case of having retransmission in the network, the position of the leader is not very important to find the total latency in a chain. In this situation, latency depends on the number of retransmissions that sensor nodes must perform to reach the desired reliability.

A RELIABILITY-, ENERGY-, AND LATENCY-AWARE AGGREGATION IN LINEAR TOPOLOGY

In this section, we present our QoS-aware data aggregation. One should note that we use the approaches mentioned in the previous section to ensure the quality of service parameters in our aggregation. As we employ a two-tiers architecture model, illustrated in Figure 4b, we make a separation between these two tiers in order to have clarity. The first-tier is the intra-cluster chain, which is created among sensor nodes inside a chain and aims to aggregate data within the chain.

The second-tier is the inter-cluster chain, which is created among the chains leaders and aims to aggregate the data of the chain leaders and route the aggregated data to the RSU. In what follows, we discuss these two tiers.

First-Tier: Intra-Cluster Chain

As previously mentioned, we consider a wireless sensor network, which consists of N sensor nodes deployed in a linear topology. Each sensor node must first be informed about its upstream neighbors. To do so, we employ the chain construction algorithm applied in PEGASIS (Lindsey & Raghavendra, 2002). In the next step, the sensor nodes in this single long chain are divided into several sub-chains or clusters in order to increase the degree of parallelism and to shorten the delay imposed by having a single long chain. Since these tasks are done once at the initial phase, we ignore their overhead. Each formed chain has one chain leader, which we call the aggregator. We assume the number of nodes for all sub-chains is the same.

In each sub-chain, one node must be selected as a leader in order to do the final aggregation and send the final aggregated data of the sub-chain either to the leader of another sub-chain or to the RSU. Before expanding on the criteria that we consider to select the leader in intra-cluster chain, we first take a look at the packet structure that needs to be sent. Figure 6a shows structure of the aggregated data packet. Flag fields are initially set to zero. Each bit flag represents one sensor node in a chain. Upon receipt of data from its downstream node, every upstream nodes aggregates its own data with the data received from its direct neighbors and sends the result to its upstream node. Before sending this packet, the upstream node performs the following tasks:

Setting the flag: If the upstream node receives data from its downstream node, it sets the flag of its downstream node in its own packet to 1. This means that the data stored at the aggregated data field includes the data of this downstream node. If the upstream node does not receive data from its downstream node, it does not change the flag of its packet and keeps zero for the corresponded flag of that node as well as all its neighbors.

Copying the flag of the packet of its downstream node to the corresponding place in its own packet: This means that the aggregated data includes data from the sensor nodes whose flags in the packet are set to 1.

The three QoS parameters which were discussed in details in the previous section will be combined in order to make different criteria for electing a leader. To this end, we introduce the following formula in Box 3.

Where $Delay_i$ denotes the latency introduced by sensor node S_i. Using this formula, the benefit value of each sensor node $(Total - benefit(S_i))$ can be calculated. The higher this benefit value, the higher the probability of being selected as a leader.

Figure 6. a) Structure of the aggregated data packet for the first-tier b) Structure of the aggregated data packet for the second- tier

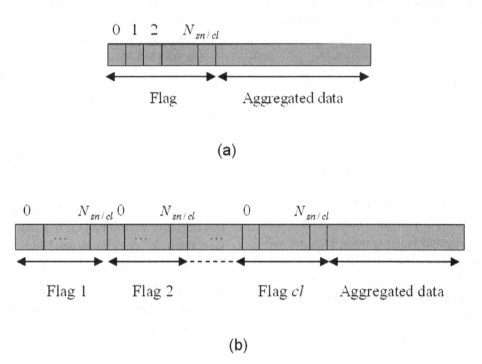

(a)

(b)

As different applications have different requirements, we can change the assigned weights to each part of the above equation in order to satisfy the application requirements. For instance, in traffic jam detection application in which reliability and latency are the main concerns, the weight of the energy parameter can be set lower than reliability and latency (i.e. $w_R=1$, $w_e=0$, $w_D=1$). Although application-dependent, we can assume that these weights vary between (0, 2). If a given parameter is not important, we set its weight to 0. If a given parameter is vital, we set its weight to 2. If a given parameter is important but not much, we set its weight to 1.

Second-Tier: Inter-Cluster Chain

In electing a leader for the inter-cluster chain, lifetime and latency are the most important quality of service parameters. This is due to the fact that, the flag part of the packet structure that we introduced earlier is used to find packet loss probability for each link in a sub-chain and the packet loss probability of links in the second-tier cannot be deduced. This is due to the frequent changes of the elements of the inter-cluster chain, which makes the loss probability found in the current interval useless for the next interval. Therefore, packet loss or reliability cannot be considered

Box 3.

$$Total - benefit(S_i) = (\Pr ovided - \operatorname{Re} liability_i)^{w_R} \times (\frac{\operatorname{Re} sidualEnergy_i}{InitialEg_i \times neededEg_i})^{w_E} \times (\frac{1}{Delay_i})^{w_D}$$

as a criterion to select an inter-cluster leader. To this end, the formula we employ to find out the benefit of being leader of each sensor node in the inter-cluster is as follows:

$$Total-benefit(S_i') = (\frac{\mathrm{Re}\,sidualEg_i}{InitialEg_i \times neededEg_i})^{w_E} \times (\frac{1}{Delay_i})^{w_D}$$

where S' represents a set of sensor nodes in the second-tier which are able to directly communicate with the RSU. Upon receiving data from its downstream node, a sensor node in the second-tier concatenates the flag parts and puts the aggregated value of the downstream node together with its own aggregated value coming from its sub-chain in the first-tier and sends the new packet to its upstream node. This results in a bigger packet (Figure 6b) compared with the packet generated in the first-tier (Figure 6a).

PERFORMANCE EVALUATION

We use Visualsense (Ptolemy team, 2008) as our simulation platform. Each simulation runs 10 times and the simulation time is 5000 rounds.

Scenarios Description

Our sub-network has 100 sensor nodes evenly clustered in 10 sub-chains, i.e., each sub-chain has 10 sensor nodes. The average distance between two sensor nodes is 20m and two RSUs are located at the most right and the most left side of the sub-network. Every $T_1=10$ time period, the leader election procedure will be executed. We assume that one hop transmission takes 1s.

The required transmission reliability for each link $(R_{\mathrm{Re}q})$ at the RSU varies from 0.9 to 0.99 and the packet loss probability $(p_{pktloss})$ on the links changes from 0.1 to 0.4. The initial energy for each sensor node is 0.5J.

We consider three types of applications.

- Event detection (ED)
- Periodic monitoring using a dense network (MDA)
- Periodic monitoring using a sparse network (MSA)

Each of the above applications poses different requirements on quality of service parameters, therefore we assign different weights (*Wr, We, Wd*) to them for the purpose of leader selection.

We consider $R_{\mathrm{Re}q}$ only for event detection application. Therefore, just in this application we utilize retransmission in order to provide high transmission reliability. Due to using retransmission, the $p_{pktloss}$ does not depend on position of the leader because we send a packet until it is received by the next node with the $R_{\mathrm{Re}q}$ probability. Therefore, *Wr* does not have much effect on the leader election procedure especially when $R_{\mathrm{Re}q}$ is selected close to 1.

Results Discussion

We express the lifetime of the network in terms of number of dead nodes over the time.

The network life time for event detection application is plotted in Figure 7a. As expected, when aggregators are chosen based on both latency and energy, the energy consumption is more uniform and balanced among sensor nodes. Therefore, all sensor nodes work together and die approximately at the same time. When aggregators are chosen only based on latency, energy consumption is unbalanced, which leads to creating holes in the network especially when application requires to have all nodes to be alive simultaneously.

Figure 7b and Figure 7c show network lifetime in periodic monitoring applications using sparse and dense networks, respectively. As it can be seen, selecting aggregators based on energy (in addition to the other two parameters) lead to well-balanced energy consumption.

Figure 7. a) Network lifetime in case of event detection; b) Network lifetime in case of periodic monitoring using a sparse network; c) Network lifetime in case of periodic monitoring using a dense network

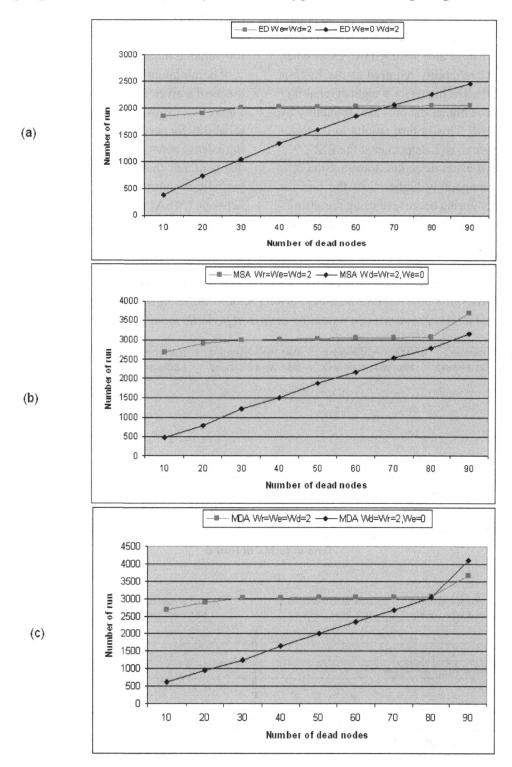

Performance evaluation of QOS-ACA in terms of ensuring transmission reliability is depicted in Figure 8a, from which one can see the impact of choosing different values for weights (*Wr, We, Wd*). We have also included two cases when transmission reliability required at the RSU is 99% and 90%. The higher the weight of reliability parameter, the higher the provided reliability by that candidate. This in turn results in a greater number of received data packet at the RSU.

In case of event detection, transmission reliability is comparably higher than the one for periodic monitoring because of using retransmission mechanism. The transmission reliability for

ceived by the RSU. One can see that in case of Wr=2, We=Wd=0, the first round has the highest reliability. However, because of excessive use of nodes with high reliable link they die soon and low reliable links need to be used instead.

The minimum end-to-end reliability for the elements of a given chain is plotted in Figure 8a and Figure 9b. However, even though the transmission reliability for periodic monitoring application using a dense network (MDA) (illustrated in Figure 8b) is higher than the corresponding graphs of periodic monitoring application using a sparse network (MSA) (illustrated in Figure 8c), the minimum end-to-end reliability for the elements

Figure 8. a) Impact of assigning different weights on transmission reliability; b) Performance evaluation in terms of transmission reliability in case of periodic monitoring using a dense network; c) Performance evaluation in terms of transmission reliability in case of periodic monitoring using a sparse network

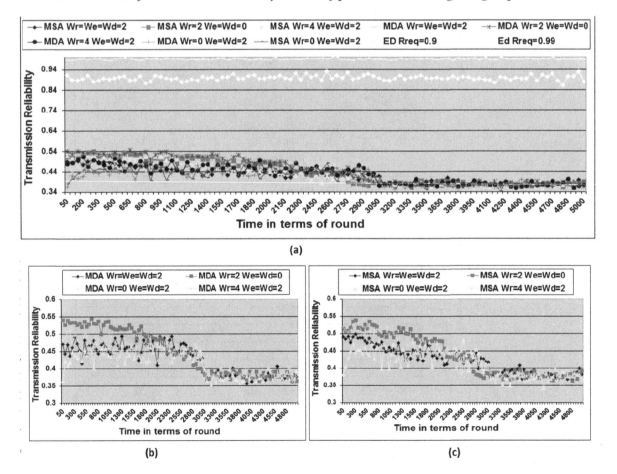

introduces an extra delay that we must consider per hop. This metric represents the temporal accuracy of the monitoring/detecting process. One can see that the latency of event detection application is higher than periodic monitoring using sparse and dense networks. This is due to the fact that in event detection application we employ retransmission mechanism to ensure high reliability. The produced latency is in direct proportion with the number of retransmissions. Number of retransmissions also depends on packet loss probability and the required reliability by the application for each link. High packet loss leads to high latency which is a direct impact of high number of retransmission. One notes that when reliability is not important and is set to zero, latency decreases significantly.

CONCLUSION AND OPEN ISSUES

In this chapter, we propose QoS-ACA, a QoS-aware chain-based data aggregation approach for the wireless sensor network deployed alongside the

Figure 9. a). Minimum end-to-end reliability in a given chain when only reliability is important; b) Minimum end-to-end reliability in a given chain when all weights are equal

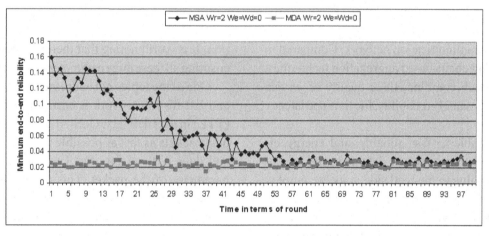

(a)

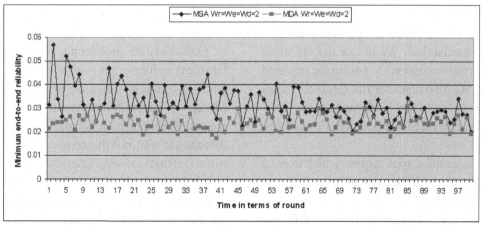

(b)

Figure 10. Latency

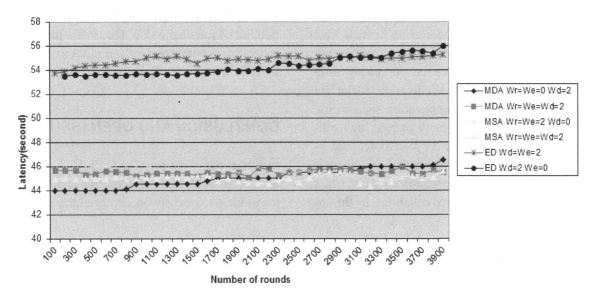

vehicular communication network. Compared to the existing chain-based aggregation techniques, our approach combines three quality of service parameters namely reliability, life time and latency together.

To be able to fast, reliably, and energy efficiently aggregate sensor data and send the aggregated value to the road side units, we employ a chain-based aggregator selection technique which takes individual link transmission reliability and latency as well as residual energy of nodes into account. To ensure reliability, we leverage the benefits of retransmission without using any acknowledgement and use it as a means of error correction mechanism. We utilize the optimum number of retransmissions to ensure the required reliability. We also consider the residual energy of each sensor node and its distance to the RSU as two main criteria to select a sensor node as an aggregator.

We consider three applications, which impose different priority on the three mentioned quality of service parameters. The flexibility of our technique allows application developers to assign different weights to these quality of services parameters depending on the requirements of their applica-

tion. It is worth noting that there is a trade-off in ensuring all these three parameters simultaneously.

One of the topics not addressed in this chapter and left for future work is ensuring time-to-live (TTL) in data delivery. QoS-ACA aims to deliver data packets as fast as possible to the destination and does not consider the Time-to-Live (TTL) parameter of the packet. This means that QoS-ACA does not guarantee delivery of a packet to the RSU within its deadline. This is an important parameter to consider as time-critical applications highly depend on availability of real-time data as in these applications data is neither useful nor valuable if it is received after its TTL.

Outdated data cannot only be useless but also harmless as it may have negative impacts on the decisions made by providing invalid information. Moreover, transmitting expired data depletes the energy of relaying nodes inappropriately. Another direction to continue this research towards relates to the fact that QoS-ACA assumes fixed-size clusters, but it is also likely to have dynamic clusters. In this case, selecting the best candidate as an aggregator within clusters, which do not only overlap in terms of communication but also in terms of sensor measurements pose new challenges.

ACKNOWLEDGMENT

This work is supported by IST FP7 STREP GENESI: Green sEnsor NEtworks for Structural monItoring project.

REFERENCES

Akyildiz, F., Su, W., Sankarasubramaniam, Y., & Cayirci, E. (2002). Wireless sensor networks: A survey. *Computer Networks Elsevier Journal*, *38*(4), 393–422. doi:10.1016/S1389-1286(01)00302-4

Busse, M., Haenselmann, T., & Effelsberg, W. (2006). TECA: A topology and energy control algorithm for wireless sensor networks. In *Proceedings of ACM Modeling Analysis and Simulation of Wireless and Mobile Systems,* (pp. 317-321).

Chen, Y., & Son, S. H. (2005). A fault tolerant topology control in wireless sensor networks. In *Proceedings of ACM/IEEE International Conference on Computer Systems and Applications,* (pp. 57-64).

Du, K., Wu, J., & Zhou, D. (2003). Chain-based protocols for data broadcasting and gathering in sensor networks. *International Parallel and Distributed Processing Symposium,* (pp. 260-267).

Fan, Z., & Zhou, H. (2007). A scalable power-efficient data gathering protocol with delay guaranty for wireless sensor networks. *Lecture Notes in Computer Science*, *4864*, 221–232. doi:10.1007/978-3-540-77024-4_22

Flajolet, P., & Martin, G. N. (1985). Probabilistic counting algorithms for data base applications. *Computer and System Sciences Journal*, *31*(2), 182–209. doi:10.1016/0022-0000(85)90041-8

Haenselmann, T. (2006). *GFDL wireless sensor network textbook*. GFDL.

Han, Q., Du, S., Ren, S., & Zhu, H. (2010). SAS: A secure data aggregation scheme in vehicular sensing networks. *Proceedings of IEE, ICC*, 1–5.

Heinzelman, W., Chandrakasan, A., & Balakrishnan, H. (2000). Energy efficient communication protocol for wireless micro sensor networks. In *Proceedings of the 33rd Annual Hawaii International Conference on System Sciences*, 3005-3014.

Heinzelman, W., Chandrakasan, A., & Balakrishnan, H. (2002). An application-specific protocol architecture for wireless microsensor networks. *IEEE Transactions on Wireless Communications*, *1*, 660–670. doi:10.1109/TWC.2002.804190

Jung, W. S., Lim, K. W., Ko, Y. B., & Park, S. J. (2009). A hybrid approach for clustering-based data aggregation in wireless sensor networks. In *Proceedings of the Third International Conference on Digital Society,* (pp. 112-117).

Kim, H. S., & Han, K. J. (2005). A power efficient routing protocol based on balanced tree in the WSN. In *Proceedings of the 1st International Conference on Distributed Framework for Multimedia Applications,* (pp. 138-143).

Kruskal, J. B. (1956). On the shortest spanning subtree of a graph and the traveling salesman problem. *Proceedings of the American Mathematical Society*, *7*(1), 48–50. doi:10.1090/S0002-9939-1956-0078686-7

Lai, K. K., & Jimmy, W. M. C. (1997). Developing a simulated annealing algorithm for the cutting stock problem. *Computers & Industrial Engineering*, *32*, 115–127. doi:10.1016/S0360-8352(96)00205-7

Lim, K. W., & Ko, Y. B. (2009). Multi-hop data harvesting in vehicular sensor networks. *IET Communications in Special Issue on Vehicular Ad Hoc and Sensor Networks, 4*(7), 768–755.

Lindsey, S., & Raghavendra, C. S. (2002). PEGASIS: Power-efficient gathering in sensor information systems. In *Proceedings of IEEE Aerospace Conference,* Vol. 3, (pp. 1125-1130).

Palazzo, S., Cuomo, F., & Galluccio, L. (2009). Data aggregation in wireless sensor networks: A multifaceted perspective . In Ferrari, G. (Ed.), *Sensor networks: Where technology meets practice* (pp. 103–143). Berlin, Germany: Springer. doi:10.1007/978-3-642-01341-6_6

Ptolemy team. (2008). *Visualsense.* Retrieved from http://ptolemy.berkeley.edu/visualsense/

Ramadan, R. (2009). Agent based multipath routing in wireless sensor networks. In *Proceedings of IEEE Symposium Series on Computational Intelligence,* (pp. 1548-1551).

Romer, K., & Mattern, F. (2004). The design space of wireless sensor networks. *IEEE Wireless Communications, 11*(6), 54–61. doi:10.1109/MWC.2004.1368897

Shin, J., & Suh, C. (2008). Energy efficient chain topology in ubiquitous sensor network. In *Proceeding of the 10th International Conference on Advanced Communication Technology,* (pp. 1688-1693).

Stephanie, L., Cauligi, R., & Krishna, M. S. (2002). Data gathering algorithms in sensor networks using energy metrics. *IEEE Transactions on Parallel and Distributed Systems, 13*(9), 924–935. doi:10.1109/TPDS.2002.1036066

Tabassum, N., Ehsanul, Q., Mamun, K., & Urano, Y. (2006). COSEN: A chain oriented sensor network for efficient data collection. In *Proceedings of the Third International Conference on Information Technology,* (pp. 260-267).

Taghikhaki, Z., Meratnia, N., & Havinga, P. J. M. (2011). Energy-efficient trust-based aggregation in wireless sensor networks. In *Proceedings of the 3rd International Workshop on Wireless Sensor, Actuator and Robot Networks (WiSARN), in conjunction with IEEE InfoCom,* (pp. 10-15).

Tan, H. O., & Korpeoglu, I. (2003). Power efficient data gathering and aggregation in wireless sensor networks. *ACM SIGMOD Bulletin, 32*(4), 66–71. doi:10.1145/959060.959072

Vidhyapriya, R., & Vanathi, P. (2007). Energy efficient adaptive multipath routing for wireless sensor networks. *International Journal of Computer Science, 34*(1).

KEY TERMS AND DEFINITIONS

Cooperating WSN and VCN: Refers to a WSN deployed alongside a VCN and roadside units are used as the base station of the WSN.

Data Aggregation: Combining a number of data packets into one in such a way that it is a representative of original data.

Linear Topology: A topology in which sensor nodes are organized in a linear structure.

Quality of Service: Refers to the quality requirements of one application that must be best satisfied until the application mission is successfully fulfilled.

Chapter 10
User–Centric Vehicular Ad–Hoc Networks and Roadside Units for Public Transports Systems

Fábio Pereira
Technical University Lisbon, Portugal

João Barreto
Technical University Lisbon, Portugal

ABSTRACT

Public transportation is becoming more and more importance in big urban centers, as it is a key ingredient to sustainable cities. Still, richer and more diverse public transport services imply increased complexity to the users of such services. In this chapter, the authors address the problem of journey planning for public transport users. This problem can be described as finding the best route between two given points in a city taking into account the available public transport services. The authors describe and compare traditional approaches that are already deployed in most cities. They then focus their attention on new and promising alternatives that become possible with the emergence of user-centric vehicular ad-hoc networks, complemented with roadside infrastructure. The authors discuss the benefits and challenges behind this new approach for journey planning in public transportation, and propose directions for possible solutions.

INTRODUCTION

With the growing population densities in big urban centers, sustainable mobility is assuming more importance. Gradually, more public transport alternatives are made available to citizens. While this change substantially improves one's mobility, it also makes it more complex to take advantage of public transports efficiently.

The central question that public transport users repeat routinely is "what is the best way to get from A to B by a combination of public transports?" Finding an adequate answer to the question in a reasonable amount of time is crucial to the perceived quality of the public transport

DOI: 10.4018/978-1-4666-2223-4.ch010

service. Let us denote the problem of journey planning in public transport systems.

Given two points in a city, there are typically several ways to travel from one point to the other. Alternatives can vary in many ways, like means of transportation (e.g., subway, train, tram, bus, ferry), operators, estimated durations, prices, number of tickets needed to completion, etc. All those aspects are important for public transport users and they can have a massive impact on the success (or failure) of the journey planning choices that one makes every day.

Any suitable solution to help users with journey planning should fulfill two main requirements. First, it should provide the user with the best route in terms of duration, price, and number of changes, or a possible conjugation of these factors, according to specific user requirements. Second, it is fundamental that the solution is available when the user needs it. Ideally, a journey planning system should be ubiquitous relatively from the user's point of view: whenever the user needs to determine the best route to a target destination, no matter where the user is, the journey planning system should be available to provide a prompt and correct answer.

To fulfill these requirements, journey-planning systems need to overcome some fundamental challenges. The information that drives journey planning is typically complex. It ranges from static information sources, such as maps, timetables and fare information; to dynamic information, such as real-time information about accidents and other events that disturb the transport services.

Furthermore, as public transport networks grow, the larger becomes the above information. Hence, delegating the responsibility of finding the best option to the user is not a good choice.

For example, if a user is standing in Piccadilly Circus and she wants to go visit the Big Ben, we want to provide her with the quickest, the cheapest, and/or shortest alternative, between those two points of the city of London. Furthermore, we pretend this information to be of easy access to her in the starting point, and if possible, that it can move with the user for pervasive and ubiquitous use. It is far from trivial how to achieve these goals. The complexity and amount of information needed are challenges, because in this example the user has a minimum of eight alternatives, using public transports, to travel between those two points (Journey Planner, 2011).

Information dynamism is also an issue due to unpredictable events (e.g., accidents, service interruptions) or abnormal traffic affluences (higher or lower than normal). For example, even if the user chooses the best route option, it can become an invalid "best option" due to these unpredictable events, which can have negative consequences to that option and may invalidate the characteristics that influenced the user's choice.

Sometimes information is not available where it is most needed (i.e., the place where the user currently stands) due to few available information sources. Other times the corresponding information sources are located in far points, from which information needs to be transmitted. In our example, an accident in the best option between Piccadilly Circus and Big Ben is often perceived only when something starts to go wrong (e.g., the user stands in an abnormal traffic jam), and this can be a problem. If the user had received information about the interruption earlier better options could have been made by the user.

To ensure that relevant information is available where public transport users need it, solutions such as electronic panels or on-line Internet-based services are very popular nowadays. Still, these typically incur substantial costs to the operator and, possibly, the user.

Finally, information is often from different operators, which typically do not cooperate between them to provide the user the best information, but the one that best fits their interests. For example, when standing in Piccadilly Circus, the user should know the different alternatives from different operators to travel to the Big Ben. This is a great challenge because existing and already deployed solutions are often property of an operator and they provide only information regarding that operator's services. Therefore, typically they fail in providing the best possible information to the user.

The objective of this chapter is to analyze distinct approaches to the problem of journey planning in public transportation. We describe and compare traditional approaches that are already deployed in most cities. We then focus our attention in new and promising alternatives that become possible with the emergence of user-centric vehicular ad-hoc networks, complemented with roadside infrastructure. We discuss benefits and challenges behind this new approach for journey planning in public transportation, and propose directions for possible solutions.

The remainder of the chapter is organized as follows. In Section 2, we introduce a generic solution to support journey planning in public transports, which will constitute the baseline framework from which the remaining sections will depart. Section 3 describes traditional approaches that are nowadays popular. Finally, in Section 4, we introduce Infrastructure-Informed Ad-Hoc Journey Planning, a hybrid approach involving ad-hoc communication as well as roadside units in some strategic places, explaining the issues, challenges, and advantages of such approach.

A GENERIC SOLUTION

All the solutions we present in the remainder of the chapter can be seen as particular instances of the generic approach that Figure 1 depicts.

The main entities in a system that solves the problem are now described.

The Client is the access platform with which the user interacts.

The Optimizer is the subsystem responsible for the determination of the best route option. The optimizer component accesses static information from static data sources, like databases. Dynamic

information access is performed through information gathered during contacts with other nodes.

Static Source represents a source of static information. Consequently, Dynamic Source represents a source of dynamic information.

The Data Aggregator is an entity or an agglomeration of entities responsible for the organization of information. Sensors are entities that gather dynamic information about public transportation environment.

Finally, the Localizer provides the Client or Optimizer with their current location. This can be important for algorithmic purposes or user assistance. As we previously referred, there are several solutions using this approach, or simpler variants, to solve the routing problem.

TRADITIONAL APPROACHES

In this section, we describe the traditional approaches to solve support journey planning public transportation. Some of these approaches have been in use for years, others are more recent ones. They are all particular instances of the generic approach previously detailed. We also provide some examples of systems employing each of these approaches. Furthermore, we explain that these traditional approaches suffer from some well-known issues, which make this problem open to research on new alternative approaches.

Human-Based Journey Planning

In the most primitive solution to the problem, the public transport user performs most of the main tasks shown in Figure 1. We call this approach Human-based journey planning. Using static sources of information, the user can behave as an optimizer, according to her objectives, using her cognitive capabilities to find the best route option.

Figure 2 illustrates the human-based journey planning approach.

Figure 1. Generic approach

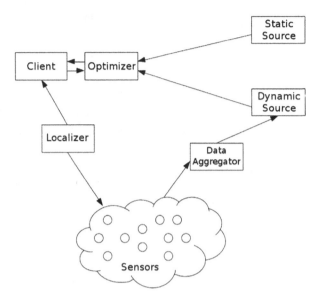

Limited dynamic information can be inferred by human perceptions about the environment. Typically, they are gathered though human senses (e.g., sight, hearing). For example, sometimes gossips travel over transport users reporting that some unpredictable event has occurred, like rumors of a service interruption on the subway or visible events like traffic jams.

Human-based journey planning is far from being the best solution to support journey planning in public transportation. The main issue is that, typically, humans do not perform well in finding the best route option between two given points (Liu, 1996). This issue becomes more problematic when the complexity of available options increases.

In addition, in this approach human user (the optimizer) needs to consider a lot of information. It should be noted, as well, that many times the user has few or none available dynamic information sources, so, many decisions are taken with partial and/or incomplete knowledge about the transportation network.

Concluding, Human-based journey planning has to manage complex, numerous, dynamic, hard to obtain information and it fails to perform well in such conditions.

Infrastructure-Informed Human-Based Journey Planning

Gradually, most transport operators start to shift to more interesting solutions then the human-based journey planning. This second approach consists in an improvement of human-based journey planning. The main focus of lately implemented operators' solutions is to provide more dynamic, complete information to users. This is typically achieved by having some infrastructure gathering dynamic information and delivering it to the user. The main objective of this kind of solutions is to capture real-time information about the transportation network and to make it available through information sources. In this approach, the client and optimizer roles are still performed by the user.

Fixed and/or mobile infrastructure sensors are disseminated through the network. They are responsible for gathering information about the transportation environment and for sending the collected information to an entity that organizes, manages, and publishes it (e.g., servers, traffic control center—any kind of data aggregator/manager).

Localizers are needed because they make it possible for mobile sensors to compute their location, playing an important role in information's capture. They can be implemented according to the requirements and characteristics of the system.

Static sources are the same as in the previous approach. Dynamic sources are much more sophisticated. They can assume many forms, like electronic panels, interactive kiosks, SMS/email query services, etc. Sensors can have communication capabilities between them or be limited to communicate only with the data aggregator/manager, depending on the solution.

Figure 3 shows the Infrastructure-Informed human-based journey-planning scheme.

However, complexity and costs often limit this approach to solve the problem of routing. Infrastructure sensors are usually complex equipment with great reliability, availability properties. These properties make them expensive. The optimization is still performed by a human, which makes infrastructure-informed human-based journey planning approach an improved version of the human-based journey planning, by providing more quality information. Nevertheless, the error probability is still high which can lead to bad routing decisions.

Other limitation is related to the fact that these solutions are typically property of an operator. Therefore, they provide only information about the system's owner services. This is potentially problematic because users typically get information only regarding that operator instead of the best information available for them to make the best choice.

Consider the following scenario:

- A user X standing in a bus stop from operator W at point A;
- X wants to travel to point B;
- Best route option from A to B involves taking a subway from operator Y.

Typically, W will not provide the information that X needs to make the best possible choice. Instead, W will provide the best option involving their services. This usually happens because operators, normally do not cooperate.

Still regarding the cost of these solutions, they often do not cover the entire transportation network. Therefore, this can make them fail on the "Maximize the availability of information" requirement.

Examples

Many operators have applied some solutions based on this approach. We give a brief description of some solutions applied worldwide.

The Régie Autonome des Transports Parisiens (or RATP) has a geolocation system, to detect the position of their fleet vehicles (RATP, 2010). By these means, they can gather and infer important real-time information about their environment (dynamic information). RATP is developing a project which consists on the installation of 3000 electronic panels on the transportation network. These panels will show estimated time of arrivals.

Bus Tracker (Chicago Transit Authority, 2010) is Chicago Transportation Authority's system. Their fleet is equipped with GPS devices, which

Figure 2. Human-based journey planning

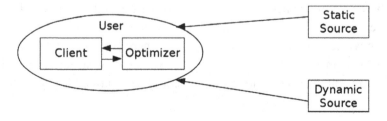

Figure 3. Infrastructure-informed human-based journey planning

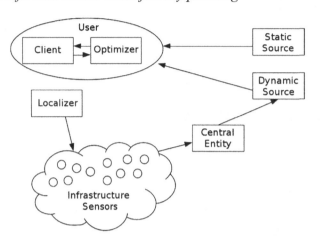

report current vehicle's location. The main difference to the previously described solution is the fact that in BusTracker panels can be installed on convenience stores, coffee shops, etc. BusTracker also provides SMS access to the information.

Carris (2010) has a similar geolocation system. They have 350 bus stops equipped with electronic panels showing the estimated time of arrivals for the buses passing there.

They also provide access to such information through email and SMS services.

London Underground (or the Tube [TFL, 2011]) shows estimated time of arrivals in platform panels.

These brief examples show that operators are concerned with the usability of their infrastructures. Therefore, they try to provide more dynamic information to their users for them to take more informed decisions.

Internet-Based Journey Planners

With the growth of Internet popularity, the emergence of Internet-based journey planners for public transportation happened naturally. Internet-based journey planners are typically transport journey planning services, which can be accessed through an Internet connection. Internet-based journey planners usually prompt the user basic input as the source and destination points, then, they normally provide the best route option between those points. It is important to make a distinction between two different kinds of Internet-based journey planners: static and dynamic Internet-based journey planners. Static Internet journey planners rely only on static information sources, like databases of schedules, prices, routes, etc. On the other hand, dynamic Internet journey planners use both static and dynamic sources.

In the Internet-based journey planning approach, access to the optimizer is made through a client, often an application. The optimizer module is typically a public service that performs the routing, taking into account user input.

The existence of a location system is optional in this kind of systems. Yet, when present, it acts as an improvement to the usability of the system, because it computes the user position instead of asking the user to manually introduce her location.

The automatic computation of the best route is the main advantage of this approach. In this way, error probability is reduced, by reducing the users' contribution to the optimization.

There are several deployed solutions following this approach. Some gather information about many operators, which is an advantage when comparing to the previous approach. However, these systems have some limitations.

Static Internet-based journey planners provide unreliable options, because they do not use real-time information when optimizing the user's route.

Dynamic Internet-based journey planners are hybrid solutions, being backed up by dynamic information provided by some network of sensors running on the operator's infrastructure. Therefore, dynamic Internet-based journey planners inherit some issues from the previous approach.

Another limitation of Internet-based journey planning is the need of an Internet connection between the application and the optimizer. As route optimizers are more useful when users are traveling or about to travel, mobile access is often used to access them, typically, using mobile devices. Therefore, the use of such systems comes often with the cost of mobile Internet fees. This can make these solutions expensive to the user.

Finally, some of these solutions are not optimized and adapted to mobile devices, which makes it hard to access the services using such devices.

Examples

Google Maps (Google, 2011) is a popular Internet-based journey planner. The user can get directions between two given points using public transports.

CTA, MBTA and WMATA (2011) provide trip planning applications, real-time service updates and next train/bus arrivals.

However, the greatest evolution in this area is that operators are opening their systems to developers. BusTracker provides an API, which allows the usage of real-time gathered infrastructure information. WMATA and MBTA also provide an API or open information about their services, like schedules, real-time bus positions, etc. This strategy of opening the systems allows developers to give use to such precious information and increases the number and variety of applications available to public transport users.

São Paulo Metro (Metro, 2011) has an online service that provides real-time status information about their lines. They provide detailed information when something goes wrong.

INFRASTRUCTURE-INFORMED AD-HOC JOURNEY PLANNING

In this section, we describe infrastructure-informed ad-hoc journey planning. This approach tries to overcome the issues identified on traditional approaches by incorporating the voluntary contribution of the users into the journey planning system.

More precisely, it relies on both the operator's network infrastructure (e.g. nodes deployed on stations, vehicles, and stops) and mobile devices carried by the public transport users themselves (e.g. smartphones, personal digital assistants, or palmtops). Overall, by resorting to short-range wireless networking technologies such as like Bluetooth, 802.11b/n/g, the combined set of mobile and stationary nodes will dynamically form spontaneous mobile networks. The journey planning system will rely on such ad-hoc connectivity to acquire, disseminate, and aggregate relevant information.

Nodes are both producers and consumers of information. Each mobile node might be aware of its location to be capable of capturing information about the transportation network.

Hereafter, we shall designate this kind of ad-hoc networks as User-Centric Vehicular Ad-Hoc Networks (or UC-VANETs). Like VANETs, UC-VANETs are formed by mobile devices interconnected by some wireless network. Consequently, UC-VANETs are very sparse and dynamic, due to the brief contacts between nodes, like VANETs.

The crucial distinction is that in UC-VANETs most nodes are portable devices carried by moving users that can migrate between different vehicles; whereas VANETs are classically defined as wireless networks whose nodes are vehicles (not users migrating from one vehicle to another).

Hence, it is important to point out the differences between classical VANET notion and UC-VANET:

- Users may migrate between vehicles during their route, rather than relying on the same vehicle for the whole journey;
- The mobile devices that users carry (e.g. mobile phones) have significantly higher energy constraints than the devices deployed in vehicles;
- Users have less predictable routes, because their movement patterns aren't limited to road infrastructures;
- Most means of public transport obey to schedules, instead of purely continuous traffic as in automobile traffic.

There are a number of scenarios where infrastructure-informed ad-hoc journey planning promises to be advantageous. We illustrate some as follows:

- **First Scenario:** Peter is at Piccadilly Circus and he wants to go to his work at the Big Ben. He does this journey everyday taking the Bus 35 between 9am and 9:30am. He has an average time for completion of 20 minutes. He meets another user whose average time is 10 minutes using another route option. So, Peter receives a notification on his mobile phone that a new best route option is available and he accepts the suggestion.
- **Second Scenario:** Charles is standing at Stamford Bridge Stadium, after a game of his favorite football club, and he wants to go home. Charles has information about three route options. Normally, he chooses to take the subway, because it is the best route option he knows in terms of temporal requirements, taking about 15 minutes. When Charles is heading to the subway, he

meets a user who met another user 10 minutes ago, who claims that he took about 7 minutes to do that journey using Tram Line 5. Therefore, Charles accepts the suggestion and takes the tram.
- **Third Scenario:** John is arriving to the train station on the Train 17. Normally, he drops from the train at this station and goes to the subway. However, today he receives an alert message in his mobile phone claiming that the circulation on the subway is interrupted. Therefore, John takes a bus to avoid arriving late at his work.

Some important challenges arise from the adaptation of UC-VANETs to support journey planning in public transportation.

A first challenge is how to disseminate information efficiently in this sparse scenario. In infrastructure-informed ad-hoc journey planning some events will be captured by some nodes that will want to publish that information to the interested nodes. Therefore, we need efficient mechanisms for one-to-many/many-to-many message dissemination across the UC-VANET. Traditional solutions to this problem assume that networks are fully connected and that it is possible to establish routes between all nodes. In contrast, UC-VANETs are particularly challenged networks with very sparse and disconnection properties.

However, some operations, like information lookups, require one-to-one communication mechanisms. Hence, the system will also need unicast routing protocols that are suitable to UC-VANETs. Once again, as we discuss later on, traditional approaches are not a perfect fit for the specific restrictions of UC-VANETs.

As a third challenge, the expectedly high disconnection periods will force nodes to temporarily store messages in memory-constrained buffers. Hence, appropriate buffer management mechanisms need to be devised.

Furthermore, much of the events occurring in public transports are observed by several users, due to the agglomeration of people in such transport means. Hence, it is important to limit the information reporting such events, because that information will be very similar. The detection and aggregation of such data is important to provide some quality-of-service to an UC-VANET.

The following subsections address each challenge above and describe solution directions.

Information Dissemination in UC-VANETs

Contacts between public transport users are often sporadic and brief. Moreover, if one randomly chooses two public transport users in the all universe of public transport users of a large/medium city, the probability of direct encounters between them is often very small.

Altogether, the sparseness, high mobility, and briefness of contacts in UC-VANETs make classical communication algorithms an unsuitable option for such networks.

In contrast, Delay-Tolerant Networking (or DTN [DTNRG, 2010]) network model seems to fit very well in the problem we are trying to solve. DTNs are characterized by particularly brief contacts between nodes and for frequent absence of end-to-end paths between nodes. Hence, this kind of networks is often sparse and highly disconnected.

DTNs typically rely on Store-Carry-Forward mechanisms. These mechanisms are characterized by forwarding/dissemination algorithms adapted to such characteristics. These mechanisms allow a message generated in a point A to eventually reach a point B even if no end-to-end path exists to such location. Like the name suggests, Store-Carry-Forward mechanisms can be implemented in three parts. A source of important information will rely on other nodes' capabilities to transport that information to whom or where it is needed. This demands the creation of a transport buffer for nodes to keep and manage such information until they forward it. Finally, an efficient forwarding algorithm has to be specified.

We now address the main challenges of information dissemination in UC-VANETs in the public transportation scenario. We dedicate some discussion to communication issues where ad-hoc approaches are particularly challenging. Then, we explain how data aggregation mechanisms may be important in UC-VANETs. Furthermore, we enumerate some security requirements whose consideration we believe it is fundamental on an ad-hoc routing approach.

Message Diffusion/ Information Dissemination

Message diffusion/dissemination protocols are employed to spread information through some network. Event notification, network maintenance, and alert dissemination are some possible applications of message diffusion protocols.

Two fundamental aspects are decisive to the effectiveness of a message dissemination protocol:

- The relay selection strategy, i.e. the task of choosing nodes to carry information;
- Forwarding policy, i.e. the task of specifying the behavior of nodes in case of direct encounter.

A relay is a node responsible for transporting and forwarding information entrusted to it. The simplest solution to this problem is to adopt a flooding-based scheme, where every node relays messages that it receives to all the other nodes available in its vicinity.

However, better alternatives can be designed and implemented if we consider specific scenarios' information, like particular characteristics of the nodes. Such considerations allow the creation of more controlled and sophisticated relay selection strategies and forwarding policies. Several characteristics can be considered: interests, popularity measures, future paths.

Potentially interesting solutions to our public transportation scenario try to verify which nodes are interested in that information. Flooding-based solutions generate much unnecessary network traffic, because several distributed copies are useless to some nodes and so, they eventually get discarded. This situation needlessly increases the network resource usage, which can have a negative impact to the network. Furthermore, overloaded networks can drop really important packets.

Hence, some solutions attempt to analyze past encounters to establish popularity heuristics to drive more intelligent relay selection strategies. If a node has a popularity value greater than some threshold, that node is considered as a good relay for information and a copy of the information is transmitted to it.

Other solutions are based on publish-subscribe models (Yoneki, Hui, Chan, & Crowcroft, 2007), while others try to base their choices in network nodes' movement knowledge or prediction. Therefore, potentially interesting information on a given geographic area is entrusted to nodes heading there (or at least with a high probability of heading there).

By exploiting such metrics, it is possible to control dissemination schemes, providing more acceptable resources usage levels. Therefore, we now describe some different approaches, which try to perform better than flooding-based solutions.

- **Gossip-based dissemination protocols:** There are some proposed schemes that adapt the gossip logic to ad-hoc networking. In Friedman, Gavidia, Rodrigues, Viana, and Voulgaris (2007), the authors analyze the application of gossip protocols to different kinds of ad-hoc networks: dense gossip, sparse gossip, and delay tolerant gossip. The last two scenarios are particularly interesting to this chapter.

  Two kinds of gossip approaches are Broadcast Gossip and Opportunistic Gossip. In Broadcast Gossip the source of information broadcasts to all the nodes on the contact range. Nodes that receive a message decide if they should forward the message using some algorithm. Some examples of metrics that can be used to perform such a decision are:

  ◦ Probabilities (e.g., random probabilities, encounter probabilities);
  ◦ Closeness to the source (e.g., physical distance, network distance);
  ◦ Message Hop Count.

  Some combination of several metrics may be used.

  Opportunistic Gossip uses the knowledge about nodes' movement patterns to select information relays. When relays meet other nodes, some metric-based algorithm (for example, a probabilistic one) is used to decide if a message should be forward to them.

- **Popularity-based dissemination protocols (Yoneki, Hui, Chan, & Crowcroft, 2007; Gao & Cao, 2011):** Some dissemination protocols are based in metrics like node popularity or centrality. The most popular nodes are selected to perform the transport of information through the network. These nodes are expected to perform more contacts with other nodes, so they are considered the best candidates to carry information.

- **Location-based dissemination protocols:** This approach has some similarities with Opportunistic Gossip. In Ye, Chen, Xia, and Zhao (2010), two particularly interesting metrics are introduced, Destination Matching and Arrival Time of Destination, to aid the relay selection strategy. Destination Matching is a metric related to the probable destination for nodes and messages.

  For example, if a node X generates a message it wants to publish at a location A, X will delegate the message transport to a node with probable destination on A.

  Arrival Time of Destination is a metric related to the node's expected time of arrival at a location.

For example, if X founds several nodes heading A, it will delegate the transport to the nodes with lower Arrival Time of Destination values.

With regards to the relays, their operation works as follows: it is established a circular region around the Destination Matching point, when a relay detects that it is inside that region it starts to forward the message using flooding.

However, this solution assumes that it is possible to know or predict node's mobility patterns.

Routing Protocols

All previously presented solutions have one common property. All of them make the assumption that messages are potentially interesting to several nodes. Sometimes, applications need packets to be delivered to only a specific user, instead of several ones. Due to some characteristics of UC-VANETs such as mobility, brief contacts, unreliability/nonexistence of links and low bandwidth, some classical approaches to establish routes fail in providing communication means. The main reason for that is because they spend so much time establishing routes proactively or reactively.

In Spyropoulos, Psounis, and Raghavendra (2005), the authors define routing as a sequence of independent, local forwarding decisions, based on current connectivity information and predictions of future connectivity. This routing notion is very interesting to our challenged scenario.

Proactive protocols (e.g., DSDV [Perkins & Bhagwat, 1994], OLSR [RFC 3626]) try to establish routes and maintain them through network life. This fact invalidates their usage in UC-VANETs.

Reactive protocols (e.g., AODV [Perkins & Royer, 1999], DSR [Johnson & Maltz, 1996]) try to establish routes immediately before the packet exchange. So, due to the brief characteristic of node contacts in UC-VANETs precious time is spent establishing routes, instead of being spent

on packet exchange. Furthermore, there is a high probability that established routes quickly become invalid. These facts make them inappropriate solutions to our problem.

Due to the unsuitability of such protocol types to UC-VANETs many investigation effort has been applied to find solutions to this challenge.

One of the simplest routing algorithms is Epidemic Routing (Vahdat & Becker, 2000). When two nodes meet, they exchange the messages they do not share. This flooding-based routing scheme tries to guarantee eventual delivery of packets. The main goals of this protocol are to minimize both delivery latency of messages and resource usage (e.g., bandwidth, memory usage) and to maximize the message delivery rate. However, this solution fails in achieving some of these goals. The resource usage of a flooding-based routing scheme is high, because many copies of the same message are created and spread through the network. This fact has implications in bandwidth consumption and memory usage which consequently may have negative consequences to message delivery delays and rates.

PROPHET (Lindgren, Doria, & Schelen, 2003) is a probability-based routing scheme. PROPHET assumes that nodes do not move randomly. Node movement is repetitive, routine-oriented and often obeys cyclic patterns. As such, this scheme analyzes past encounters between nodes to decide if a message should be forwarded to a specific node. The metric used in PROPHET is called delivery predictability, $P(a,b)$, which tells the probability of a node to deliver a message to another node. This metric is based on past encounters, aging actualizations and a transitive property.

When nodes meet, the logic is pretty much the same as in Epidemic Routing. Both nodes analyze the messages they have as well as the correspondent delivery predictability values assigned to message destinations. Therefore, it is necessary to adopt a forwarding strategy to decide which messages to exchange. For example, this strategy can be as simple as the establishment of threshold values to delivery predictability.

The performance of the PROPHET protocol depends on the chosen forwarding strategy. Concluding, there is always a trade-off between resource usage and message delivery rates/delays.

Spray and Wait (Spyropoulos, Psounis, & Raghavendra, 2005) is a routing protocol designed to perform better than Epidemic Routing by transmitting a lower number of messages, performing more efficiently in different scenarios in terms of network size and node density.

Spray and Wait can be defined in two distinct phases:

- **Spray:** For each message from a source node, L copies are spread through the network;
- **Wait:** If message's destination is not found in spray phase, each node carrying a copy forwards it to its destination.

However, this definition does not specify how the spray phase is performed. Two distinct types of Spray and Wait models are: Source Spray and Wait, Binary Spray and Wait.

In Source version, the source node forwards the L copies to the first L distinct nodes it meets, then the scheme advances to the Wait phase.

Binary version works as follows:

- Source node creates L copies;

- When a node, A, that possesses more than one copy, meets a node, B, that doesn't possess any copy, A forwards Floor[n/2] copies to B and keeps the remaining ones;
- When a node only possesses one copy, it keeps that copy until it finds the destination node.

MaxProp (Burgess, Gallagher, Jensen, & Levine, 2006) is a routing scheme, which performs scheduling of packets to be transmitted to other nodes and chooses which packets to be dropped when the transport capacity of a node approaches its maximum. This protocol has some differences compared with previous ones. The main assumption is that contacts are brief. So, most of the effort performed by this routing scheme is spent managing packets according to prioritization metrics. Nodes' transport buffers are divided in two zones. These zones are managed in different ways. Figure 4 shows the buffer's organization of a node performing MaxProp.

The first part contains highest priority packets. Highest priority packets are the first ones to be transmitted. The second part contains lowest priority packets. Lowest priority packets are the first ones to be dropped when transport buffers reach maximum capacity. This priority notion is related to the number of hops a packet traveled. If a packet has a number of hops larger than or equal to a given threshold, it is placed in the second part of the transport buffer. Otherwise, the

Figure 4. MaxProp buffer

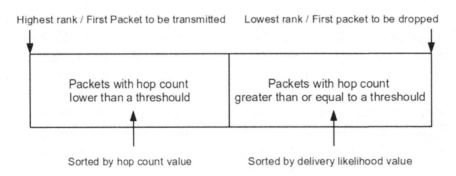

packet is considered as of high priority and it is placed in the first part of the transport buffer. First part is ordered taking into account the number of hops traveled by the packet. This sorting is ascendant. Therefore, packets with less hop count are placed in the head of the first part. The second part of the buffer is ordered by a metric called Delivery Likelihood in a descending order. Delivery Likelihood is a probabilistic value based in past encounters analysis. Each node j has an estimative vector of encounter probability with all the other nodes on the network. In addition, MaxProp uses acknowledgments to inform the nodes when packets are delivered. The main objective of this mechanism is to inform all the nodes, which carry a copy of such message, that they should drop it from their transport buffer.

RAPID (Balasubramanian, Levine, & Venkataramani, 2007), BUBBLE Rap (Hui, Crowcroft, & Yoneki, 2008), and GOSSIP (Haas, Halpern, & Li, 2006) are other examples of routing schemes.

MANETs routing protocols are not necessarily suitable for use in VANETs or UC-VANETs. As Nzouonta et al. discuss, real-time vehicular traffic information can be exploited for more efficient routing in such scenarios (Nzouonta, Rajgure, Wang, & Borcea, 2003). A class of VANET-specific routing protocols has thus been proposed recently. However, the distinct nature of UC-VANETs calls for novel protocols that take the specificities such environments into account.

Buffer Management

As discussed previously, the development of a Store-Carry-Forward mechanism is crucial to solve the problem of journey planning in public transportation. The previously described challenges presented some parts of the problem of developing such mechanism. However, there is still missing one challenge to complete the description of communication challenges. Buffer management is the last but not least important

challenge to overcome if we want to create a good performing Store-Carry-Forward mechanism.

To provide capabilities as "Store" and "Carry," nodes need to have some transport buffers for them to keep messages whose transport was delegated to them. Furthermore, nodes often have limited storage resources. Hence, when transport buffers reach their maximum capacity, it's important to keep providing the service. This task can be ensured by managing the limited storage space, replacing messages when buffers get full. Some buffer management policies are (Chou & DeWitt, 1985; Lindgren & Phanse, 2006):

- **Least Recently Used (LRU):** The least recently used item gets discarded;
- **Most Recently Used (MRU):** The most recently used item gets discarded;
- **First In First Out (FIFO):** Items leave the buffer in the same order they arrive;
- **Most Forwarded (MOFO):** The most forwarded item gets discarded;
- **Shortest Life (SHLI):** The item with the lowest time-to-live value gets discarded;
- **Less Probability (LEPR):** This policy discards the item that has the lowest probability of being delivered by the node.

More than one policy can be used together.

Data Aggregation

To save network important resources as network bandwidth and decrease buffer occupancy rates, it is important to apply some data aggregation mechanisms to reduce the amount of duplicated information that gets disseminated. These mechanisms often consist in summarizing information using algorithms. Some authors (Ahmed & Kanhere, 2009) apply mechanisms of message data aggregation based on Network Coding to solve these issues. Some others (Lochert, Scheuermann, & Mauve, 2007) try to establish probabilistic or mathematical approaches to aggregate data. Other solutions (Rajagopalan & Varshney, 2006) take into account several characteristics about topological structures of the networks and network nodes before choosing data sinks or leaders that will perform data aggregation.

As previously stated, in the context of our problem, plenty of the generated information is identical, due to the characteristic of public transportation. Several nodes will observe the same events. These nodes will generate duplicated messages. So, it's important to detect those duplicates and to limit them. As information often is very similar, differing only in irrelevant details, aggregation mechanisms can be simplified in our scope. One possible solution is: a node chooses one copy to keep from the similar ones (based on creation time, for example) and discards all the rest.

Security

In UC-VANETs nodes are devices carried by people. These people have privacy concerns and requirements that must be fulfilled. In particular, if we regard journey-planning systems, it is clear that privacy is an obvious issue. Badly intended users can exploit a badly designed system. For example, they can take advantage of the system to learn users' routines with malicious intents. Furthermore, they can inject false information on the network, like false alert messages reporting accidents or service interruptions/perturbations. These injections of false information can be harmful to systems credibility.

We can sum up system threats to the following main categories:

- Message sniffing;
- Message injection/modification/removal;
- Message repetition.

Consequently, the following security requirements should be fulfilled to guarantee a properly designed system:

- Integrity;
- Confidentiality;
- Availability.

The use of cryptography can be a solution for many security problems like authentication, integrity and confidentiality. For instance, we can authenticate alert and location messages for the users to know that the message came from the infrastructure.

However, resource usage evaluation must be performed to analyze how systems behave with this additional burden. It is important to remember that security solutions are often complex in terms of the effort necessary to compute some tasks and that mobile devices usually have very restrict computational and power resources.

Ad-Hoc Journey Planning Issues

We now address how an ad-hoc journey planner can be implemented using an UC-VANET approach.

Figure 5 shows an ad-hoc scheme based on our generic approach described in the previous section. In an ad-hoc journey planning system, users have an application installed and running on her mobile phone or other mobile device. Each device represents a network node. In this approach, each node is simultaneously a consumer and a producer of information, as we explain next.

The application is composed of two modules, an interface, and the optimizer. Access to dynamic information is performed through contacts with other network nodes. Wireless communication is often used in UC-VANETs (e.g., 802.11x, Bluetooth). Static information can be integrated at the domain level (like maps, schedules, stops locations, estimated durations) through databases that can be dynamically updated.

Data Aggregators are nodes that have the responsibility, permanent or sporadic, of performing data aggregation. The Localizer is, as already explained, a subsystem responsible for providing the current location to the optimizer as well as to the user. This component is fundamental in an ad-hoc journey planner due to the mobility of the nodes and the special importance of location-awareness to algorithmic purposes.

However, this approach fails in some aspects. These networks are density-dependent in terms of active nodes generating and carrying information. If there is not enough nodes generating and carrying important information, the logic of this approach will fail.

In addition, due to the infrastructure-less characteristics, some information about the network is hard to infer (e.g., service interruptions, accidents). Evidently, these drawbacks represent important problems on ad-hoc networking research.

Our main interest is on systems, which perform content sharing or some kind of information spreading. Ad-hoc lookup systems are also very interesting. Remember that an ad-hoc journey planner must provide as basic communication operations data dissemination and lookup mechanisms. In addition, a location system must be designed and implemented for nodes to know where they are standing. Some authors (Hightower & Borriello, 2001) have dedicated a great effort researching location systems on ubiquitous computing environments. The properties of location systems are driven by the context on which they will be used and by the developers' requirements.

A basic location system can be formalized by the use of GPS-equipped devices. However, this solution invalidates the usage of such system in many devices. For example, a great number of mobile phones do not have a GPS antenna and some of the ones that got it only provide Assisted-GPS, which is a paid service in many countries nowadays. Therefore, this fact can strongly hinder the acceptability of ad-hoc journey planners among public transport users.

At the same time, the ad-hoc approach also has a great advantage if we compare it with other approaches: it provides means for users to share information about different operators overcoming the fact that public transport operators typically do not collaborate. Therefore, a node that observes an event on the subway can deliver information about that event to other nodes arriving on a bus from other operator and that are heading to the subway station.

Infrastructure-Informed Ad-Hoc Journey Planners

Some vehicular ad-hoc network solutions are particularly interesting to the problem of journey

Figure 5. Ad-hoc journey planner architecture

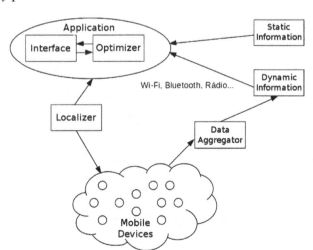

planning in public transportation, because they complement the ad-hoc communication with fixed infrastructure units (roadside units).

All the previous approaches have similarities with this kind of systems. Users, typically drivers, interact with the Optimizer through an application. The Optimizer is often a device installed on the vehicle with a wireless interface. In this way, the vehicle can communicate with other network nodes. Therefore, in these solutions, equipped vehicles which travel in roads are the Sensors. A Localizer is also needed for them to participate in the network in both production and consumption of information. In addition, there are some solutions where some vehicles act as Data Aggregators (Lochert, Scheuermann, Wewetzer, Luebke, & Mauve, 2008; Nadeem, Dashtinezhad, Liao, & Iftode, 2004) (see Figure 6).

It is intuitive to envision the possibility of creating an infrastructure-informed ad-hoc journey planner to the context of public transportation. Imagine that some strategic points in a public transport network are equipped with roadside units. These strategic points can be bus stops, stations, among others. This scheme is very

similar to the ad-hoc journey planner. The only difference lies on the addition of such infrastructure devices that are considered fixed sensors in this approach.

However, it is important to remember that such infrastructure introduction cannot become an expensive burden. Hence, it is fundamental to keep a minimal architecture and to provide only basic functionality to our roadside units. For example, Lochert, Scheuermann, Wewetzer, Luebke, and Mauve (2008) introduced roadside units in their system to increase dissemination performance in sparse scenarios.

Another feature that the presence of roadside units introduces is the fact that stationary nodes are introduced on the network. These stationary nodes can work as geographic references to mobile nodes. Therefore, a simplified location system can be formulated to non-GPS-equipped devices. In our domain, this system does not need rigid accuracy and precision levels. Hence, a system providing: 1) symbolic location (Hightower & Borriello, 2001), an abstract indication about where an object is standing (e.g., near to Big Ben); and 2) computation of location performed

Figure 6. Infrastructure-informed ad-hoc journey planner

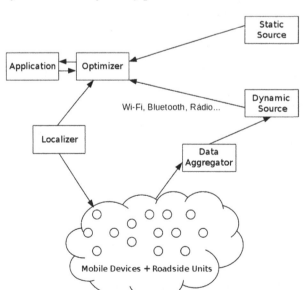

by the mobile phone can fulfill the needs of an infrastructure-informed ad-hoc journey planner.

The location-sensing technique applied by the location system can be based on proximity to the roadside units. By these means, one can build a more applicable system discarding the dependence on GPS capabilities.

Another disadvantage of strict ad-hoc solutions can be overcome in the hybrid approach. Infrastructure warnings can be easily introduced by operators through those units. For example, if a service interruption occurs, operators can use their roadside units to inform theirs users that something is going wrong by creating alert messages.

Furthermore, roadside units can act as information banks, where users can get information about their routes.

Easy-City

The easy-city project (Pereira & Barreto, 2011) aims at developing and deploying a collaborative decentralized route planner for public transport users, based on an infrastructure-informed ad-hoc approach.

In easy-city, the very commodity wireless devices carried by users work together with inexpensive wireless devices installed in public transport vehicles, stations, and stops.

Users gather information about real-time journey times. Stop nodes produce infrastructure warnings about the public transportation network, such as accidents, traffic jams and service information. Opportunistically, vehicles exchange messages with users to inform them when they enter or exit them.

Using the gathered information and a transport network map, easy-City allows users to ask for routes between two given points. Maps have information provided by operators about the public transport offer on a city, like travel times, waiting times and pedestrian times. The knowledge on the map is complemented by the gathered information through time estimative calculations.

Easy-City relies on a message dissemination protocol that uses estimates of each node's future locations to make forwarding, buffer management, and message aggregation decisions.

Based on simulations, it has been shown that users aided by easy-City frequently (20 to 49% times) finish their journeys substantially earlier than they would if they relied on using traditional static journey planners (Pereira & Barreto, 2011).

CONCLUSION AND OPEN RESEARCH ISSUES

In this chapter, we describe possible solutions to support journey planning for public transportation in large urban centers. While this problem is not new, it is receiving increasing importance as effective public transportation services become a crucial requirement for urban sustainability. However, as public transport services become richer and more diverse, they also become more complex to use efficiently by their users.

Lately, public transport operators have increased their offer in terms of traditional solutions. We introduced the concept of UC-VANET, which is the base concept of Infrastructure-informed ad-hoc journey planning. We firmly believe that the future of journey planning for public transports will rely on the mobile devices carried by users themselves and the opportunistic ad-hoc interactions among such devices. However, we consider that presence of roadside units is important to complement the ad-hoc component of networks.

To the best of our knowledge, the easy-city project (Pereira & Barreto, 2011) is the only solution so far that has proposed a complete infrastructure-informed ad-hoc journey planner for public transportation. Using a partially implemented prototype and relying to simulations, the preliminary results of easy-city suggest that this novel approach can achieve considerable advantages to users of complex public transport networks, with low infrastructural costs.

Still, there is still a long road before a real and complete system can be implemented and deployed. All the design issues discussed in the chapter remain open in the context of UC-VANETs in the scenario of public transports.

REFERENCES

Ahmed, S., & Kanhere, S. (2009). HUBCODE: Message forwarding using hub-based network coding in delay tolerant networks. In *Proceedings of the 12th ACM International Conference on Modeling, Analysis and Simulation of Wireless and Mobile Systems (MSWiM 2009)*, (pp. 288-296). New York, NY: ACM Press.

Balasubramanian, A., Levine, B., & Venkataramani, A. (2007). DTN routing as a resource allocation problem. *SIGCOMM Computer Communication Review*, *37*(4), 373–384. doi:10.1145/1282427.1282422

Burgess, J., Gallagher, B., Jensen, D., & Levine, B. (2006). MaxProp: Routing for vehicle-based disruption-tolerant networks. In *Proceedings IEEE INFOCOM 2006, 25TH IEEE International Conference on Computer Communications*, (pp. 1-11). IEEE Press.

Carris. (2010). *Transportes públicos Lisboa*. Retrieved from from http://www.carris.pt/

Chicago Transit Authority. (2010). *Website*. Retrieved from http://www.transitchicago.com/

Chou, H., & DeWitt, D. (1985). An evaluation of buffer management strategies for relational database systems. In *Proceedings of the 11th International Conference on Very Large Data Bases (VLDB 1985)*, (vol 11, pp. 27-141). VLDB Endowment.

DTNRG. (2010). *Delay tolerant networking research group*. Retrieved from http://www.dtnrg.org/

Friedman, R., Gavidia, D., Rodrigues, L., Viana, A., & Voulgaris, S. (2007). Gossiping on MANETs: The beauty and the beast. *SIGOPS Operating Systems Review*, *41*(5), 237–288.

Gao, W., & Cao, G. (2011). User-centric data dissemination in disruption tolerant networks. In *Proceedings of INFOCOM*. IEEE.

Google. (2011). *Map data & Europa technologies, INEGI*. Retrieved from http://maps.google.com/

Haas, Z., Halpern, J., & Li, L. (2006). Gossip-based ad hoc routing. *IEEE/ACM Transactions on Networking*, *14*(3), 479–491. doi:10.1109/TNET.2006.876186

Hightower, J., & Borriello, G. (2001). Location systems for ubiquitous computing. *Computer*, *34*(8), 57–66. doi:10.1109/2.940014

Hui, P., Crowcroft, J., & Yoneki, E. (2008). Bubble rap: Social-based forwarding in delay tolerant networks. In *Proceedings of the 9th ACM International Symposium on Mobile Ad Hoc Networking and Computing (MobiHoc 2008)*, (pp. 241-250). New York, NY: ACM.

Johnson, D., & Maltz, D. (1996). Dynamic source routing in ad hoc wireless networks. In Imielinski, T., & Korth, H. F. (Eds.), *Mobile Computing* (pp. 153–181). Dordrecht, The Netherlands: Kluwer International. doi:10.1007/978-0-585-29603-6_5

Journey Planner. (2011). *Transport for London*. Retrieved from http://journeyplanner.tfl.gov.uk/

Lindgren, A., Doria, A., & Schelén, O. (2003). Probabilistic routing in intermittently connected networks. *SIGMOBILE Mobile Computer Communication Review*, *7*(3), 19–20. doi:10.1145/961268.961272

Lindgren, A., & Phanse, K. (2006). Evaluation of queueing policies and forwarding strategies for routing in intermittently connected networks. In *Proceedings of the First International Conference on COMmunication System softWAre and MiddlewaRE*, (pp. 1-10). IEEE.

Liu, B. (1996). Intelligent route finding: Combining knowledge, cases and an efficient search algorithm. In *Proceedings of the 12th European Conference on Artificial Intelligence,* (pp. 380-384). New York, NY: Wiley and Sons, Ltd.

Lochert, C., Scheuermann, B., & Mauve, M. (2007). Probabilistic aggregation for data dissemination in VANETs. In *Proceedings of the Fourth ACM International Workshop on Vehicular Ad Hoc Networks (VANET 2007),* (pp. 1-8). New York, NY: ACM.

Lochert, C., Scheuermann, B., Wewetzer, C., Luebke, A., & Mauve, M. (2008). Data aggregation and roadside unit placement for a vanet traffic information system. In *Proceedings of the Fifth ACM International Workshop on VehiculAr Inter-NETworking (VANET 2008),* (pp. 58-65). New York, NY: ACM.

MBTA. (2011). *Massachusetts bay transportation authority.* Retrieved from http://www.mbta.com/

Metro. (2011). *Companhia do metropolitano de São Paulo.* Retrieved from http://www.metro.sp.gov.br/

Metropolitano de Lisboa. (2011). *Metro de Lisboa reformula sistema de informação das estações.* Retrieved from http://www.metrolisboa.pt/Default.aspx?tabid=1063

Nadeem, T., Dashtinezhad, S., Liao, C., & Iftode, L. (2004). Trafficview: Traffic data dissemination using car-to-car communication. *ACM SIGMOBILE Mobile Computing and Communications Review, 8.*

Nzouonta, J., Rajgure, N., Wang, G., & Borcea, C. (2003). VANET routing on city roads using real-time vehicular traffic information. *IEEE Transactions on Vehicular Technology, 58*(7), 3609–3626. doi:10.1109/TVT.2009.2014455

Pereira, F., & Barreto, J. (2011). Easy-city: A route search system for public transport users. In *Proceedings of the Third International Workshop on Pervasive Mobile and Embedded Computing (M-MPAC 2011), ACM/IFIP/USENIX 12th International Middleware Conference Workshops.* Lisboa, Portugal: ACM Press.

Perkins, C., & Bhagwat, P. (1994). Highly dynamic destination-sequenced distance-vector routing (DSDV) for mobile computers. In *Proceedings of the Conference on Communications Architectures, Protocols and Applications (SIGCOMM 1994),* (pp. 234-244). New York, NY: ACM.

Perkins, C., & Royer, E. (1999). Ad-hoc on-demand distance vector routing. In *Proceedings of the Second IEEE Workshop on Mobile Computer Systems and Applications (WMCSA 1999).* IEEE Press.

Rajagopalan, R., & Varshney, P. (2006). Data aggregation techniques in sensor networks: A survey. *IEEE Communication Surveys & Tutorials, 8,* 48–63. doi:10.1109/COMST.2006.283821

RATP. (2010). *Ratp.fr – Accueil.* Retrieved from http://www.ratp.fr/

Spyropoulos, T., Psounis, K., & Raghavendra, C. (2005). Spray and wait: An efficient routing scheme for intermittently connected mobile networks. In *Proceedings of the 2005 ACM SIGCOMM Workshop on Delay-Tolerant Networking (WDTN 2005),* (pp. 252-259). New York, NY: ACM.

TFL. (2011). *Transport for London.* Retrieved from http://www.tfl.gov.uk/modalpages/2625.aspx

Vahdat, A., & Becker, D. (2000). *Epidemic routing for partially-connected ad hoc networks.* Technical Report CS-2000-06. Durham, NC: Duke University.

WMATA. (2011). *Washington metropolitan area transit authority*. Retrieved from http://www.wmata.com/

Ye, H., Chen, Z., Xia, Z., & Zhao, M. (2010). A data dissemination policy by using human mobility patterns for delay-tolerant networks. In *Proceedings of the International Conference on Communications and Mobile Computing,* (pp. 432-436). IEEE.

Yoneki, E., Hui, P., Chan, S., & Crowcroft, J. (2007). A socio-aware overlay for publish/subscribe communication in delay tolerant networks. In *Proceedings of the 10th ACM Symposium on Modeling, Analysis, and Simulation of Wireless and Mobile Systems (MSWiM 2007)*, (pp. 225-234). New York, NY: ACM.

Section 4
Information Dissemination

Chapter 11
A Survey on Information Dissemination in VANETs

Mahabaleshwar S. Kakkasageri
Basaveshwar Engineering College, India

Sunilkumar S. Manvi
REVA Institute of Technology and Management, India

ABSTRACT

Vehicular Ad Hoc Network (VANET) has become an active area of research, standardization, and development because next generation vehicles will be capable of sensing, computing, and communicating. Different components in a vehicle constantly exchange available information with other vehicles on the road and cooperate to ensure safety and comfort of users using VANET. In VANET, information like navigation, cooperative collision avoidance, lane changing, speed limit, accident, obstacle, or road condition warnings, location awareness services, etc. play a significant role in safety-related applications. Safety related information dissemination is challenging due to the delay-sensitive nature of safety services. In this chapter, the authors survey some of the ongoing recent research efforts in information dissemination in VANETs. They also outline some of the research challenges that still need to be addressed to enable efficient information dissemination in VANET.

INTRODUCTION

A Mobile Ad-Hoc Network (MANET) is comprised of a group of mobile nodes without fixed communication infrastructure. The network has the capability of self-organization in a decentralized fashion. A Vehicular Ad Hoc Network (VANET) is an example of a MANET where the mobile nodes are vehicles. Communication is possible between vehicles within each other's radio range as well as with fixed roadside infrastructure components. VANET concept is an integral part of the Intelligent Transportation System (ITS) architecture, which aims to improve road safety, optimize traffic flow, reduce congestion, and so on (Manvi, et al., 2008; Boukerche, et al., 2008).

The key differences of VANET as compared to MANET environment are as follows:

DOI: 10.4018/978-1-4666-2223-4.ch011

1. Components building the network are vehicles,
2. Restricted mobility constraints,
3. Extremely high mobility and time-varying vehicle traffic density,
4. Most of the vehicles provide sufficient computational and power resources, thus eliminating the need for introducing complicated energy-aware algorithms,
5. Vehicles will not be affected by the addition of extra weight for antennas and additional hardware.

VANET raises several interesting issues with regard to Media Access Control (MAC), Mobility management, Data aggregation, Data validation, Data dissemination, Routing, Network Congestion, Performance analysis, Privacy, and Security.

With the increase of portable devices as well as progress in wireless communication, VANET is gaining importance with the increasing number of widespread applications. Some of the important applications of VANETs are as follows:

1. Message and file delivery,
2. Providing location-dependent services like the location of the nearest facilities like fuel stations, parking zones, entertainment places, and restaurants, etc.,
3. Internet connectivity,
4. Information and warning functions,
5. Dissemination of road information (including incidents, congestion, surface condition, etc.) to vehicles distant from the subjected site,
6. Co-operative assistance systems,
7. Traffic monitoring and management services,
8. Other advanced services like interactions between VANET nodes and the road infrastructure, for example traffic calming measures (including automatic speed limiters), intelligent road signs, tolling (congestion charges for entering urban areas at peak times, cargo monitoring, etc.).

VANET architectures for vehicular communication may be classified into three types: purely ad hoc based, infrastructure based and hybrid type. In the purely ad hoc based VANET architecture, Vehicle to Vehicle (V2V) communication exists without the infrastructure. In the infrastructure based VANET, communication is possible in between vehicles using infrastructure (V2I) such as base stations or access points on the road. Combination of V2V and V2I architectures leads to the hybrid mode of VANET.

Data dissemination is an important feature of VANET. Vehicles must be able to communicate with each other so as to ensure that safety and traffic management applications can function successfully. In a hybrid VANET environment where heterogeneous access technologies are available, the manner in which information is propagated between the vehicles within short time is a major issue. The aim of data dissemination is to transport information to the specific vehicles while meeting a number of constraints. The information saturation time, lifetime of the data and reliability of its transportation across the vehicular system are some of the major considerations.

This chapter is organized as follows. The first section of the chapter explains the concept of data dissemination in VANETs and its importance and provide taxonomy for various dissemination methods. The following section presents various techniques for data dissemination in VANETs. Security and Privacy threats concerned to the information dissemination are subsequently discussed. The last section brings out future scope of research after highlighting the performance characteristics.

DATA DISSEMINATION IN VANETS

Data dissemination can be defined as broadcasting information about itself and the other vehicles.. Each time a vehicle receives information broadcast by another vehicle, it updates its stored information accordingly, and defers forwarding the information to the next broadcast period, at which time it broadcasts its updated information. The dissemination mechanism should be scalable, since the number of broadcast messages is limited, and they do not flood the network. VANET characteristics like high-speed node movement, frequent topology change, and short connection lifetime especially with multi-hop paths needs some typical data dissemination models for VANETs. This is because topological transmission range needs to maintain a path from the source to the destination, but the path expires quickly due to frequent topology changes.

A successful VANET data dissemination model needs to handle issues such as sparse network density, interfering environment, long path length, latency, etc. The transmission power signal level of a vehicle may be too strong or too weak during certain times of the day and in certain city environments. When the transmission range is too strong, it creates interference and lowers the system throughput. When transmission power signal level is too low, the vehicle cannot reach other vehicles. Smart algorithms for data dissemination that adjusts according to the transmission power signal level are needed.

The dissemination mechanisms can either broadcast information to vehicles in all directions, or perform a directed broadcast restricting information about a vehicle to vehicles behind it. Further, the communication could be relayed using only vehicles traveling in the same direction, vehicles traveling in the opposite direction, or vehicles traveling in both directions. In order to design a data dissemination model, we have to consider some of the following issues:

1. For one way and two way in the context of traffic, a system for scalable traffic data dissemination and visualization in VANETs is needed. Vehicles moving in both directions may yield the best performance. However, vehicles in the opposite direction needed better model to increase the data dissemination performance.

2. How to make efficient usage of available bandwidth consumed by each vehicle?

3. To limit the number of re-transmissions due to collisions.

4. In dense networks, such as cities or major highways with a large portion of equipped vehicles, the data load on the channel should be controlled in order not to exceed the limited wireless bandwidth. In contrast, in sparse networks, channel saturation is not a critical issue. Moreover, messages should be repeated since equipped vehicles are most likely out of wireless radio range of each other; vehicles inside the area of influence of a hazard, but not reachable at the time they are detected, should also be notified. Note that in case of experiencing a dense network; the forwarding strategy is required to be very efficient in terms of overhead while ensuring high reliability to priority messages with the most important payload, i.e., safety-of-life.

5. Safety information must be kept alive: Safety hazards can be associated with a time duration and geographical area while/where they can potentially affect vehicles safety state. The distribution of some state information will be repeated (e.g., periodically or at detection of a new neighboring vehicle) for a defined duration of time while being inside a specific geographical area. The specific strategy to optimize this repetition process is to be developed.

Data dissemination in transportation brings intelligence for vehicles, roadside systems, and individuals by creating a communications platform allowing vehicles and infrastructure to share information. Data dissemination techniques must address the following unique characteristics of the VANET:

1. **Geographically constrained topology:** Roads limit the network topology to actually one dimension, i.e., the road direction.

Except for crossroads or overlay bridges, roads are generally located far apart. Even in urban areas, where they are located close to each other, there exist obstacles, such as buildings and advertisement walls, which prevent wireless signals from traveling between roads. This implies that vehicles can be considered as points of the same line; a road can be approximated as a straight line, or a small-angled curve. This observation is quite important, because it affects the wireless technologies used for data dissemination that can be considered. For example, since the packet relays are almost all in the same one-directional deployment region, the use of directional antennas could be of great advantage.

2. **Partitioning and large-scale:** The probability of end-to-end connectivity decreases with distance. VANETs can extend in large areas, as far as there is road available. This artifact together with the one-dimensional deployment increases the above probability.

3. **Self-organization:** The vehicles in the network must be capable to detect each other and transmit packets, with or without the need for a base station.

4. **Unpredictability:** The vehicles constituting the network are highly mobile. Because of this reason, there is also a high degree of change in the number and distribution of the nodes currently in the network. The nodes must be constantly aware of the network status, keep track of the hosts associated with the network, detect broken links, and update their routing tables whenever necessary. Because vehicle mobility depends on the deployment scenario, the movement direction is predictable to some extent. In highways, vehicles often move at high speeds, while in urban areas they are slow. In addition, mobility is restricted by the road directions as well as by traffic regulations. Assuming that these regulations are obeyed, there are lower and upper speed bounds, and restriction signs that obligate drivers to move on specific roads and directions. Hence, mobility models can now include some level of predictability in movement patterns. Car manufacturing companies have already implemented such models for testing mechanical parts.

5. **Power consumption:** In traditional wireless networks, nodes are power limited and their life depends on their batteries—this is especially true for ad hoc networks. Vehicles however can provide continuous power to their computing and communication devices. As a result, routing protocols do not have to account for methodologies that try to prolong the battery life. Older network protocols include mechanisms such as battery-life reports for energy-efficient path selection, sleep-awake intervals, as well as advanced network/MAC cross-layer coordination algorithms. These schemes cannot offer any additional advantages to vehicular networks.

6. **Node reliability:** Vehicles may join and leave the network at any time and much more frequently than in other wireless networks. The arrival/departure rate of vehicles depends on their speed, the environment, as well as on the driver needs to be connected to the network. In case of ad hoc deployments, the communication does not easily depend on a single vehicle for packet forwarding. This occurs because of non-coverage of communication range between communicating vehicles. Thus, there is a need to take help of intermediate nodes for packet forwarding to destination vehicle. Intermediate nodes must be reliable to forward the packets efficiently.

7. **Channel capacity:** The channels in VANETs over which the terminals communicate are subjected to noise, fading, interference, multipath propagation, path loss, and has less bandwidth. So high bit-error rates are

common in VANETs. One end-to-end path can be shared by several sessions. In some scenarios, the path between any pair of users can traverse multiple wireless links and the link themselves can be heterogeneous. So smart algorithms are needed to fit for such kind of fluctuating link capacity networks.

8. **Vehicle density:** Multi-hop data delivery through vehicular ad hoc networks is complicated by the fact that vehicular networks are highly mobile and sometimes sparse. The network density is related to the traffic density, which is affected by the location and time. Although it is very difficult to find an end-to-end connection for a sparsely connected network, the high mobility of vehicular networks introduces opportunities for mobile vehicles to connect with each other intermittently during moving.

9. **Vehicle mobility:** Since the nodes are mobile, the network topology may change rapidly and unpredictably and the connectivity among the terminals may vary with time. VANET should adapt to the traffic and propagation conditions as well as the mobility patterns of the mobile network nodes. The mobile nodes in the network dynamically establish routing among themselves as they move about, forming their own network on the fly. Moreover, a user in the VANET may not only operate within the network, but may require access to a roadside infrastructure also. Hence there is a need of strong mobility patterns in VANETs.

Need for Data Dissemination in VANETs

Data is propagated in VANETs with the exchange of messages between the nodes. The restricted road topology in VANET forces a directional message flow. Also due to higher vehicle mobility and frequent connection and disconnection

between vehicles, it becomes necessary that data be transmitted in the most efficient ways and within short time. Basic purpose of data dissemination in VANETs is to disseminate safety and non-safety messages from vehicles and RSUs (Road Side Units). The aim of data dissemination is to enable dissemination of traffic information and road conditions as detected by independently moving vehicles and RSUs. Dissemination of data in VANETs is essential to improve the driving comfort in terms of safety, entertainment, time and distance. With efficient data dissemination techniques, we can safeguard vehicles, lives, and time by disseminating appropriate information to the driver or vehicle and RSUs. For example, if the vehicles are built with intelligent decision supporting systems and periodically provided with updated information regarding heavy traffic conditions on the road, helps to take right actions to avoid being trapped in heavy traffic jams. Intelligent decisions supporting systems means a situation in which vehicles intelligently choose the alternate free way. So data dissemination in VANETs plays important role for safety and non-safety applications. VANETs are based on short-range wireless communication. The Federal Communications Commission (FCC) has recently allocated 75 MHz in the 5.9 GHz band for licensed Dedicated Short Range Communication (DSRC).

To summarize, the basic need for data dissemination are as follows:

1. **Location Information:** Driving means changing constantly location. This means a constant demand for information on the current location and specifically for data on the surrounding traffic, routes and much more.

2. **Driver assistance and vehicle safety:** Includes many different things mostly based on sensor data from other cars like brake warning sent from preceding car, tailgate and collision warning, information about

road condition and maintenance, detailed regional weather forecast, premonition of traffic jams, caution to an accident behind the next bend, detailed information about an accident for the rescue team and many other things.

3. Local updates of the cars navigation systems or an assistant that helps to follow a friend's car.

4. **Infotainment services:** Infotainment for passengers. For example Internet access, chatting and interactive games between cars close to each other.

5. **Location awareness services:** Local information as next free parking space, detailed information about fuel stations, hospitals or just tourist information about sights.

6. Vehicle maintenance, for example online help from your car mechanic when your car breaks down or just simply service information.

Data Dissemination Techniques in VANETs

Vehicle communication in a VANET can be classified into three types:

1. Vehicle to Vehicle (V2V),
2. Vehicle to roadside Infrastructure (V2I),
3. Hybrid architecture combining both V2V and V2I.

Roadside infrastructure units (RSUs) are static nodes deployed along the road, which are used to improve connectivity and service provision. It is possible for roadside units to be connected to a core network or to the Internet. These concepts are illustrated in Figure 1. When a vehicle is far away from the service RSU, it may have to go through multiple hops over long distance to access the data on the roadside unit. But data access through multi hop is much more difficult because VANET is highly mobile and sometimes sparse or dense. It is difficult to find out the end-to-end connection for a sparsely connected network and free channels in a congested network.

The data dissemination approaches in VANETs are classified on the basis of V2I/I2V dissemination, V2V dissemination and in partitioned networks as shown in the Figure 2. V2I/I2V dissemination mechanisms are based on either push based or pull based. Flooding or Relaying are the mechanisms for V2V dissemination. Opportunistic forwarding, trajectory based forwarding and geographic forwarding are mechanisms for data

Figure 1. Architectures of VANET

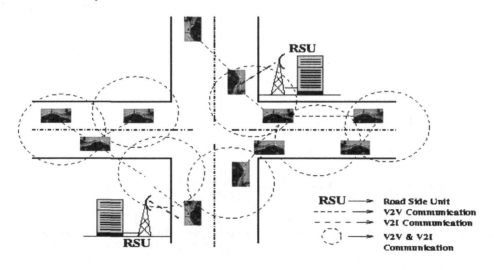

dissemination in partitioned networks. Network partitioning in a VANET is a technique that maximizes the benefits of network in terms of bandwidth, channels availability, connection to RSUs, etc.

Frequent network partitioning in VANETs require the "carry and forward" concept, where, if no direct connectivity exists, a packet is carried by a node until it could be forwarded to a node being closer to the destination.

Push-Based

In push based data dissemination, the data can be efficiently delivered from moving vehicles or RSU to another vehicle (as shown in Figure 3). In this scheme data is managed by data center (either vehicle or RSU) that collects the data and make it ready to deliver to the vehicles or RSU. Data center makes a list of the data items that have to be disseminated over network. It transmits this information on the road with header which stores all the necessary information like source id, source location, forwarding direction, packet generation time, etc. Data item also has two attributes:

- Dissemination zone in which packet can transmit, and
- Expiration time after which time the packet will expire.

Many of the applications built for VANETs will depend on the data push communication model, where information is disseminated to a group of vehicles. A formal model of data dissemination in VANETs and study how VANET characteristics, specifically the bidirectional mobility on well defined paths, affects the performance of data dissemination is discussed in Tamer, et al. (2006) along with a study of the data push model in the context of TrafficView. TrafficView is a system proposed to disseminate information about the vehicles on the road. Direction of the movement of the vehicles considered for Traffic data are vehicles moving on the same direction, vehicles moving in the opposite direction, or vehicles moving in both directions.

TrafficView is a system for traffic data dissemination and visualization in VANETs. The goal of TrafficView is to provide continuous updates to vehicles about traffic conditions, which can assist the driver in route planning as well as driving in adverse weather conditions when visibility is low. Mechanism of TrafficView system is as follows:

- A participating vehicle in TrafficView is equipped with a computing device, a short-range wireless interface, and a GPS receiver. An on-board diagnostics system (OBD) interface is used to acquire mechanical and electrical data from sensors installed in vehicles. The GPS receiver provides loca-

Figure 2. Taxonomy of data dissemination techniques in VANET

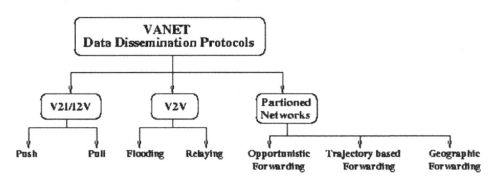

Figure 3. Push-based data dissemination in VANET

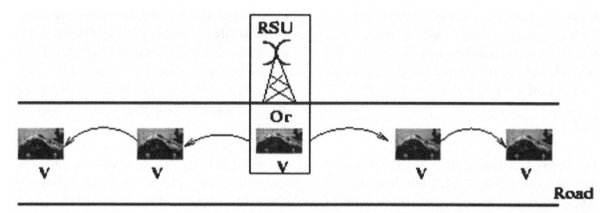

V : Vehicle   RSU: Road Side Unit

tion, speed, current time, and direction of the vehicle.

- The vehicle gathers and broadcasts information about itself and the other vehicles, in a peer-to-peer fashion.
- Gathered information is stored in local database records.
- A record consists of the vehicle identification, position in the form of latitude and longitude, current speed of the vehicle, direction, and timestamps corresponding to the time this record was first created and the time this record was received.
- An LCD touch-screen display fitted on the vehicle to show a map annotated with real-time traffic conditions on different roads as well as dynamic information about other vehicles, such as their location.
- Periodically broadcasting mechanism of stored data in a vehicle within a single packet is used in TrafficView. This scheme has three advantages:
  - It limits the bandwidth consumed by each vehicle,
  - It limits the number of re-transmissions due to collisions,
  - It avoids dealing with flow control, which would be necessary if data would be split in multiple packets.

Since the data stored at a vehicle is usually greater than the size of a packet, data aggregation techniques are applied. Data aggregation is based on the semantics of the data. For the aggregation mechanism, ratio based mechanism is used. In this mechanism, the road in front of a vehicle is divided into a number of regions. For each region, an aggregation ratio is assigned. The aggregation ratio is defined as the inverse of the number of individual records that would be aggregated in a single record. Each region is assigned a portion of the remaining free space in the broadcast message. The aggregation ratios and region portion values are assigned according to the importance of the regions and how accurate the broadcast information about the vehicles in that region is needed to be.

In TrafficView, the relative positions of vehicles are computed, using stored road maps by mapping the vehicle's latitude and longitude coordinates to points on the road in which the vehicle is driving. Using the relative positions of vehicles allows TrafficView to work in different road topologies. Driving vehicles in real traffic conditions does performance evaluation of the TrafficView. With this system, a driver can see the vehicles ahead of oneself using the TrafficView display component. The display consists of a first-person perspective view with visible vehicles as correspondingly colored 3D rectangles. Alternately, the driver can switch to a topological map view with roads colored according to traffic density. Additionally, drivers are warned of incidents like a vehicle in front pressing brakes by means of coloring the vehicle red.

Pull-Based

Pull based data dissemination is the type where any vehicle is enabled to query information about specific location or target. This is one form of request and response model as shown in Figure 4. In this type, enquiry about parking lot, nearby coffee shop etc. are the cases. This scheme is used by vehicles to query the data for the specific response from data center or from other vehicles. Pull based scheme is used by specific vehicles when there is a demand for specific information. When the vehicle needs any data, sends beacon message to find the list of neighbor vehicles. With the help of neighboring vehicles, the source vehicle collects (pulls) the required information.

The carry and forward mechanism is used to deliver the data in this approach. In this mechanism data packets are carried by the vehicles and when they found and other vehicle moving in the direction of destination in his range, it forward that packet to this vehicle. This mechanism takes some additional delay to transfer data to the destination as compared to the push approach. In this approach data packets are transferred using wireless channels but if the packet has to be transferred through the roads then those roads will be chosen for data transfer through which highly mobile vehicles are moving.

Since the VANETs are unpredictable in nature, so optimal path for successful routing cannot be computed before sending the packet. So the dynamic path selection is done through out the packet forwarding process. Since, pull based mechanism is generally used for making queries and receiving the response. Whole process is typically divided into two sub processes:

1.   Requesting data from moving vehicle to fixed location where packets are forwarded either in intersection mode or in straightway mode until it reaches to the destination,
2.   Receiving response from fixed location to moving vehicle.

In this process, usually the Global Positioning System (GPS) is used. Exact location of the vehicle the trajectory of vehicle is calculated and this trajectory could be included with the query

Figure 4. Pull-based data dissemination in VANET

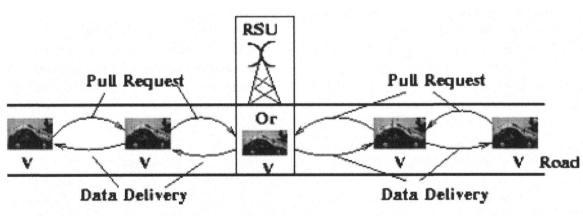

response packet and forward to the intermediate vehicles and these intermediate vehicles will calculate the destination position.

Vehicular Information Transfer Protocol (VITP), an application-layer communication protocol, which is designed to support the establishment of a distributed, ad-hoc service infrastructure over VANET is presented in Marios, et al. (2005). The VITP infrastructure is used to provide location based, traffic-oriented services to drivers, using information retrieved from vehicular sensors and taking advantage of onboard GPS navigation systems. VITP is an application-layer communication protocol specifies the syntax and the semantics of messages between VITP peers, i.e., the software components of service infrastructure. A VITP peer runs on the computing device of a vehicle, uses its inter-vehicle communication capabilities, and accesses the vehicle's sensors to retrieve useful information. VITP peers establish on-demand dynamic, ad-hoc groups, which collect, communicate, and combine information from the on-board sensors of different vehicles in order to resolve incoming requests.

VITP proposes the pull-based retrieval of traffic information, which can be triggered on-demand by location-sensitive queries issued from VITP-enabled vehicles. The pull mechanism of VITP can help drivers make adjustments to their path while driving to some destination on a given route; these adjustments can be based on information collected by VITP for shorter-term traffic conditions of nearby road segments. The pull-based mechanism of VITP can also provide time-sensitive information about services, such as the current value of gas in a nearby gas station, or the current number of free parking spaces in a nearby parking and so on.

Address Based Service Resolution Protocol (ABSRP) to discover services in VANETs is proposed in Mohandas, et al. (2008). ABSRP exploits the services provided by RSUs. Unique address is assigned to each service provider in order to discover a route to that service provider. Service

provider's address along with its servicing capabilities to other roadside units within a particular area is distributed. Each RSU will then utilize this information to service the request placed by the vehicles. If the service provider (destination node) is not reachable over the vehicular network, backbone network is used to provide to service requests. This approach is independent of the network layer routing protocol.

ABSRP scheme operates as follows. When a vehicle needs a service, it constructs a service request with the type of service and the area where the service is desired and transmits this service request to its current leader. The RSU unit after receiving this message will check if it has proactively learned about the service provider. If the RSU is aware of the service provider's IP address, it will forward the service request to the target service provider. If the RSU is not aware of the service provider, it will broadcast the service request destined to the target service provider over the backbone network. The target service provider, after receiving the service request, will construct a service response and will transmit the same to the request originator (vehicle). A RSU can transmit a service request to the target service provider over the VANET or backbone network.

VANETs are a compelling application of ad hoc networks, because of the potential to access specific context information (e.g. traffic conditions, service updates, route planning) and deliver multimedia services (Voice over IP, in-car entertainment, instant messaging, etc.). An agent based information dissemination model for VANETs is proposed in Manvi, et al. (2009). A two-tier agent architecture is employed in this work is comprised of 'lightweight,' network facing, mobile agents and 'heavyweight,' application-facing, norm-aware agents. This model provides flexibility, adaptability, and maintainability for traffic information dissemination in VANETs as well as supports robust and agile network management.

Cognitive agent based critical information gathering and dissemination in VANETs, which uses a set of static and mobile agents is proposed in Kakkasageri, et al. (2011). Static agent is an autonomous program, which executes on a host. Mobile agent is an itinerant agent consisting of program, data, and execution state information, which migrates from one host to another host in a heterogeneous network and executes at a remote host until it completes a given task. This scheme operates as follows:

1. Periodically sensed values from the environment through vehicle sensors are considered as belief sets of static agent VMA.
2. Belief sets lead to the generation of beliefs for static agent.
3. Static agent develops desire as push or pull.
4. If belief and desire are completely matched, intention is executed.
5. Otherwise modified desire is generated for an event.
6. This desire decides the intention to be executed (either push or pull).
7. Once intention is finalized, either for push or pull of an event is triggered.

Flooding

Basic idea in flooding is to broadcast the generated and received data to neighbor vehicles. In flooding, a node broadcasts the created data and receives data in vicinity (as shown in Figure 5). Generally, every vehicle participates in dissemination. Advantage of flooding scheme is easy to implement, but suffers from the broadcast storm problem. Flooding algorithm works in each vehicle of a network that receives a broadcast message for the first time, then rebroadcasts the message. A message sent to "n" vehicles results in the message-rebroadcast "n" times.

Broadcast storm problem can be characterized by redundant rebroadcasts, contention, and collisions. Firstly, when each vehicle rebroadcasts a message it is highly likely that the neighboring vehicles have already received the broadcast,

which results in the flooding creating a large number of redundant messages. Secondly, since all vehicles in the area try to rebroadcast the message at approximately the same time there will be a significant number of vehicles contending for access to the wireless channel. Thirdly, a high number of collisions will occur without the use of the (Request to Send/Clear to Send) RTS/CTS exchange, because the hidden terminal problem still exists. Another major advantage of flooding scheme is that it is suitable for delay sensitive applications. Major disadvantage is the high message overhead.

VANET applications such as traffic data dissemination are inherently flooding based and require communication protocols to be anonymous and scalable. Simple broadcast flooding satisfies these requirements, but its performance is highly dependent on network density and may lead to the broadcast storm problem. Stochastic broadcast as a solution for this problem in VANET is proposed in Michael, et al. (2010). Stochastic broadcast instructs nodes to rebroadcast messages according to a retransmit probability. This scheme has an undesirable dependency on vehicle density in the same manner as simple flooding. To solve this problem, the scheme is modeled as the link between the mathematical science of continuum percolation and stochastic broadcast. Critical percolation threshold in continuum percolation translates to the wireless broadcast context. Nodes tune the performance of the broadcast system to efficient levels by adjusting the retransmit probability so the apparent density of the network approaches the critical threshold.

In a pure flooding broadcast scheme, all nodes retransmit messages when they receive them. This algorithm is simple to implement and maximizes the likelihood of a message propagating through a network. However, it also can create a broadcast storm in which the medium is suffocated into uselessness. Pure flooding is analogous to continuum percolation. Stochastic broadcast directs each node to rebroadcast received messages with

Figure 5. Flooding-based data dissemination in VANET

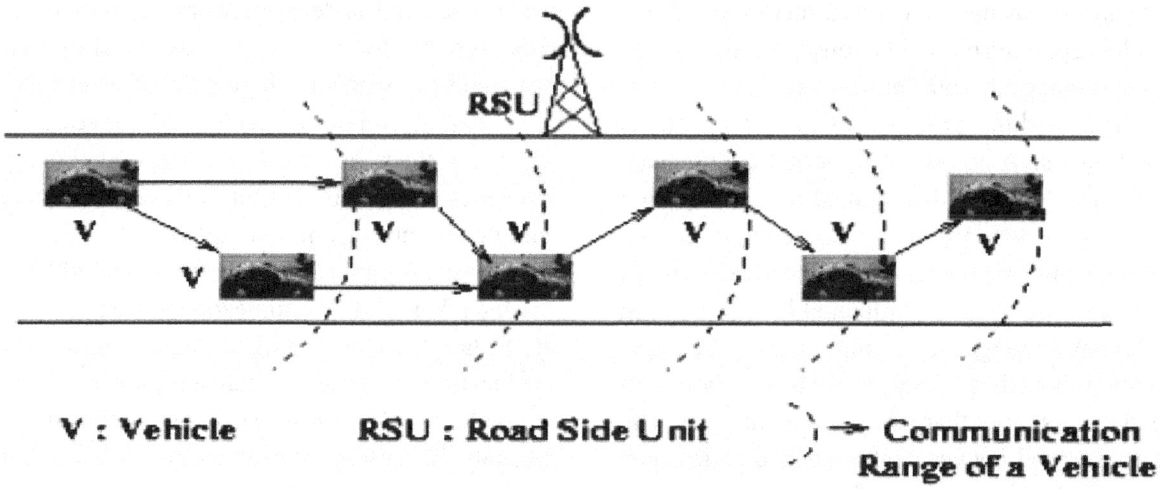

some probability. This probability may be fixed for all nodes or determined during runtime based on factors such distance from the last hop neighbor, distance from the broadcast origination, etc. No node identifiers are required to accomplish this so the scheme is private, and since all nodes make decisions independently using local information, it is scalable.

When nodes do not always rebroadcast a message, as in stochastic broadcast, the system is not precisely continuum percolation. In a stochastic broadcast system, if a node elects not to participate in the broadcast, it is the same as if the node were not there at all. Conceptually, this implies a stochastic broadcast network with constant retransmit probability should behave the same as the stochastic process reduces a pure flooding network except the density. In this scheme, two variations of stochastic broadcast are considered. First, all nodes are given a uniform and constant retransmission probability. Second, the retransmission probability is dynamically determined based on the distance between the receive node and the last hop (nodes that are farther from their last hop have a higher probability of retransmission).

Topology independent, scalable information dissemination algorithm for spatio-temporal traffic information such as parking place availability using VANET based on Wireless-LAN IEEE 802.11 is presented in Murat, et al. (2006). The algorithm uses periodic broadcasts for information dissemination. Broadcast redundancy is minimized by evaluation of application layer information and aggregation. Due to the spatio-temporal characteristics of parking place information, the spatial distribution of information is limited by utilizing techniques, which take the local relevance and age of information into account. This parking place search algorithm presents a solution to inform drivers about the parking place situation under urban traffic conditions. The algorithm exploits broadcasting techniques for information dissemination and takes the spatio-temporal character of parking places into account.

In this scheme, the information exchanged between vehicles and parking automats (parking automat is the German word for roadside parking fees payment terminal) are central elements, is categorized into atomic and aggregated information. Atomic information represents the availability of free parking places coordinated by one parking automat and aggregated information represents summarized information about an area covering more than one parking automat. The covered regions of aggregates are disjunct and hierarchically organized. Using the defined hierarchy allows building parking place situation reports for regions of variable geographic extensions.

The working principle of this algorithm is as follows. A pre-defined periodic broadcast interval is used to disseminate received atomic and aggregated information cached in a vehicle. Atomic information represents the availability of free parking places coordinated by one parking automat. Aggregated information provides information about the parking place situation in an area and covers more than one parking automat. The time interval between subsequent broadcasts is exploited to sort cached information and to generate new information for other vehicles. In this phase a vehicle replaces older entries with newer ones and builds aggregates for different spatial granularities termed in this chapter as aggregate levels. Each aggregate level represents a non-overlapping partitioning of the covered region. Using an overlay grid of a hierarchical quad-tree structure performs the aggregation.

Advantages of this scheme are as follows. Compared with broadcasting atomic information over the entire topology, bandwidth consumption is reduced. Second, aggregates about suitable parking areas are distributed over large distances, which could provide vehicles entering in a large area for an initial orientation to parking situation from a macro-perspective. Selecting a subset of all received information with specific attributes controls the distribution of atomic and aggregated information.

Relaying

Instead of flooding the network select a next hop (relay) which forwards the data to the next hop and so on. Relaying concept for data dissemination from source vehicle V5 to vehicle V1 is as shown in the Figure 6. Vehicles V3, V6, and V7 relays the data to deliver for vehicle V1. The main

advantage of this approach is it reduces congestion and it is scalable to dense networks. This is generally preferred for congested networks. However, the main problem of relaying is to select relay neighbors and reliability of the neighbor vehicles. Basically, the relay-based data dissemination approaches can be divided into two categories: 1) simple forwarding and 2) map-based forwarding (exploiting digital map information and GPS).

Inter-Vehicle Communication Systems rely on multi-hop broadcast to disseminate information to locations beyond the transmission range of individual nodes. Message dissemination is especially difficult in urban areas crowded with tall buildings because of the line-of-sight problem. IEEE 802.11 based multi-hop broadcast protocol to address the broadcast storm, hidden node, and reliability problems of multi-hop broadcast in urban areas are presented in Korkmaz, et al. (2004). Urban Multi-hop Broadcast protocol (UMB) protocol assigns the duty of forwarding and acknowledging the broadcast packet to only one vehicle by dividing the road portion inside the transmission range into segments and choosing the vehicle in the furthest non-empty segment without apriori topology information. When there is an intersection in the path of the message dissemination, new directional broadcasts are initiated by the repeaters located at the intersections.

UMB basically addresses three problems:

1. Broadcast storm,
2. Hidden node, and
3. Reliability problems in multi-hop broadcast.

The UMB protocol is composed of two phases, directional broadcast and intersection broadcast. In directional broadcast method, nodes try to select the furthest node in the broadcast direction to assign the duty of forwarding and acknowledging the packet without any a priori topology information i.e., sender selects the furthest node without knowing the ID or position of its neighbors. At

Figure 6. Relaying-based data dissemination in VANET

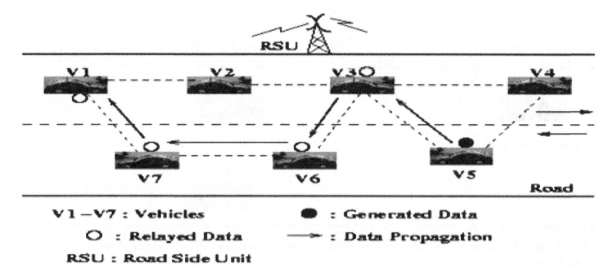

the intersection broadcast, repeaters are installed to forward the packet to all road segments.

Some of the advantages of UMB protocol are as follows:

1.   Avoiding collisions due to hidden nodes,
2.   Efficient usage of channel,
3.   Reliable broadcast communication, and
4.   Disseminating messages in all directions at an intersection.

To support VANET-based applications, it is necessary to disseminate data from an information source (data center) to many vehicles on the road. A data pouring and buffering scheme to address the data dissemination problem in VANET is proposed in Zhao, et al. (2007). In data pouring, data are periodically broadcast to vehicles on the road. As data are poured along the roads, they are delivered not only to the vehicles on these roads but also to the vehicles on the intersecting roads when they move across the intersections. At the intersection, data is poured from the source, buffered and rebroadcasts. This technique reduces the amount of data poured from the source by buffering and rebroadcast data at the intersection. Periodically pouring data on the road is

necessary since vehicles receiving the data may move away quickly, and vehicles coming later still need the data. With data pouring, the data are consistently available for vehicles crossing the dissemination area. In case there is a large amount of data from many information sources to disseminate, increase in the amount of data that can be disseminated on a given road is done. This scheme reliably disseminates the data, efficiently utilize the limited bandwidth, and maximize the dissemination capacity.

Opportunistic Forwarding

In VANET, when vehicles are not connected to network to forward the packet towards its destination, opportunistic forwarding scheme is used for data dissemination. The concept exploits mobility of the vehicles to forward packets across disconnected networks. Vehicles can store packets until they reach another vehicle to forward the packet store-and-forward/store-carry-forward. If no suitable forwarder vehicle is available, vehicles store the packet, carry the packet for some time, and forward the packet, when another vehicle is more suitable as next forwarder. The concept of opportunistic forwarding is shown in the Figure

Figure 7. Opportunistic forwarding in VANET

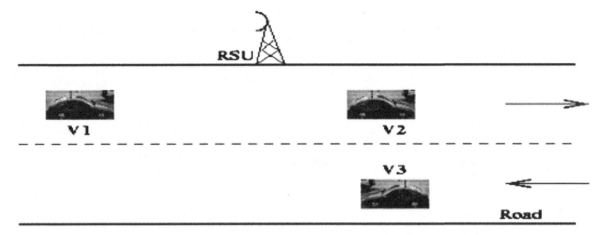

Vehicle V2 stores and carries the transmitted message from vehicle V1 –to vehicle V3.

7. Vehicle V2 stores transmitted message from vehicle V1 to vehicle V3.

This concept is suitable for sparse and partitioned VANETs, particularly important in deployment phase of V2V communications with low penetration rates. Packet forwarders and their connectivity are dynamic. Vehicle has to take the opportunity when it is available (opportunistic forwarding). Optimal node for store-and-forward has to be chosen based on the parameters like position, driving direction, roadmap, etc.

The concept of virtual "flea market" over VANET called FleaNet is proposed in Uichin, et al. (2006). In FleaNet, customers, either mobile (i.e., vehicles) or stationary (i.e., pedestrians, roadside shop owner), express their demands/offers, e.g., want to buy or sell an item, via radio queries. These queries are opportunistically disseminated exploiting in part the mobility of other customers in order to find the customer/vendor with matching needs/resources. Car communications system will not be used exclusively for mobile Internet access, but also as a distributed platform for the "opportunistic" cooperation among people with shared interests/goals. Exchanging safety messages among vehicles is a compelling example.

Stretching opportunistic cooperation well beyond safety messages is mainly pointed out in FleaNet.

In FleaNet mobility assisted query dissemination is proposed, where the query "originator" periodically advertises his query only to one-hop neighbors. Each neighbor then stores the advertisement (i.e., query) in its local database without any further relaying; thus, the query spreads only because of vehicle motion. Upon receiving a query, a node tries to resolve it locally in its database; in case of success, the originator will be automatically informed. A match only happens in its neighbors and thus, there is no redundant match notification. This match could lead to an actual transaction. FleaNet also provides a mechanism that routes the transaction request/reply by using Last Encounter Routing (LER). LER is based on geo-routing and combines location service and routing service. In FleaNet the query packet includes the originator geo-coordinates, and thus, LER does not incur any additional routing cost.

Ad hoc relay wireless networks over moving vehicles in highway scenario are proposed in Zong et al. (2001). Using motion of vehicles on a highway message delivery is done in this work. Messages are relayed/stored temporarily at moving vehicles and waiting for opportunities to be forwarded further. Using vehicle movement traces from a traffic micro simulator average message delivery time is measured. Advantage of this scheme is end-to-end transmission delay is improved as the vehicle motion increases.

Trajectory-Based Forwarding

This scheme uses the trajectory and the location of the last vehicle that forwarded the packet to forward a data packet from a source vehicle to a destination vehicle. The source vehicle defines the approximate trajectory, and each intermediate vehicle makes geographical forwarding along the trajectory. The source vehicle utilizes the digital map and GPS to define the trajectory of the message, i.e., choosing the proper road segments to constitute a shortest or fastest dissemination path. Trajectory based forwarding has less data packet overhead. Even there is no vehicle on one path, other paths can deliver message, and the message delivery is not confined to a single trajectory.

The concept of trajectory-based forwarding is shown in the Figure 8. Vehicle V1 has a data to forward to certain destination. There are two available vehicles for carrying the data; V2 and v3 are moving in opposite directions. Vehicle V1

has two choices on selecting the next hop for the data: V2 or V3. If Vehicle V2 is selected then it is geographically closer to V4 and can easily forward data to V4, whereas V3 could also be selected because by selecting V3 data will move in the direction of vehicle V4 as the vehicle V3 is moving in the direction of V4.

Trajectory-based forwarding along with applications are mentioned in Niculescu, et al. (2003). The operation sequence of the trajectory based forwarding scheme is as follows:

1. Each node in the network performs the start-up phase through the Hello packet exchange in order to get the information about its neighborhood; this phase permits the neighbor entry to be inserted and the neighbor table to be populated.
2. Acquisition of the local cell map where the mobile node is moving is done. This map can be requested from some map server disseminated in the VANET through some map distribution protocol.
3. After the acquisition of the cell map, registration on the Peer Server (called also Location Servers) needs to be performed. Peer Servers are distributed on a Grid basis.

Figure 8. Trajectory-based forwarding in VANET

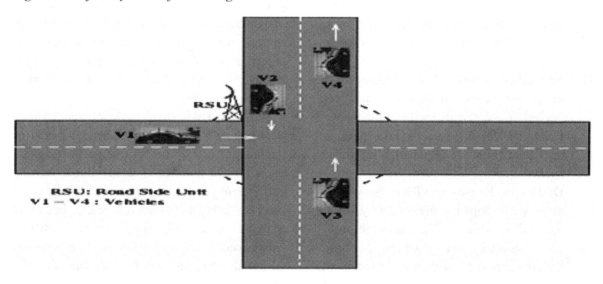

RSU: Road Side Unit
V1 – V4 : Vehicles

This procedure permits distribution of the node location information, so that after a query packet in the network, its exact location can be found.

4. The Peer Server, receiving the registration packet, will send back an acknowledgement packet.

5. Update packet to the sender node and will broadcast the registration packet to all its neighbor nodes in order to update their Client Table. This packet forwarding is important to guarantee a greater resilience to the Peer Server breakdown, because more nodes near the Server Point can be used as Peer Servers.

6. The registration phase will be completed with the reception of the acknowledgement packet.

7. Update packet of the sender, which will stop the timer at the source activated during the registration phase.

8. Each node that wants to communicate with the registered node can calculate the Server Point through the Hash function, which will receive the destination node identification as an input parameter.

9. Among the Server Points selected by the Hash Function, the nearest to the requesting node will be selected.

10. Thus, the requesting node will start a Location Discovery Phase to build the high-level trajectory up to the Server Point, in a way similar to the Registration/Update procedure.

11. This phase provides the forwarding of a destination request packet to some Peer Servers in the neighborhood of the Server Point that will send back the info stored in the Client Table in a Destination Response packet.

12. Destination Request and Response will be always sent applying the trajectory based forwarding strategy. The high-level cell-based trajectory will not be changed until the source and destination node moves in

the same cell, while the local trajectory can be dynamically changed on the traffic basis or on some other optimization criteria.

Two-Level Trajectory Based Routing (TTBR) protocol VANET environment of types Manhattan and the Freeway is proposed in De Rango, et al. (2009). Deterministic vehicles movement permits advantage to be taken of the map info to build a specific local trajectory to reach the destination node. Network scalability is offered with a high-level cell-based trajectory based on the coarse knowledge of the cell where the destination node is moving.

Geographic Forwarding

Geographic forwarding is a position based dissemination concept, that each vehicle knows its own location by using the GPS. When a source vehicle wants to send a packet to a destination vehicle, it uses the destination vehicle's location to find a neighbor vehicle that is closest in geographical distance to the destination vehicle, and closer than itself, and forwards the packet to that neighbor vehicle (as shown in Figure 9). The neighbor vehicle repeats the same procedure and until the packet makes it to the destination vehicle. The location of potential destination vehicles is assumed to be available via a location service. Geographical routes are quite stable due to the physical characteristics of the service area. This concept is useful for VANET where frequent topology changes that may cause route oscillation and path instability.

Fastest-Ferry Routing in Delay Tolerant Network enable VANET (FFRDV) is proposed in Danlei, et al. (2009). In this scheme, the message has a limited number of destinations, such as traffic management bureau, rescue headquarter, etc. The roads are divided into logical blocks of certain units. Initially, the first vehicle, which senses event, becomes the initial ferry. Afterward, the initial ferry compares the velocities of neigh-

Figure 9. Geographic forwarding in VANET

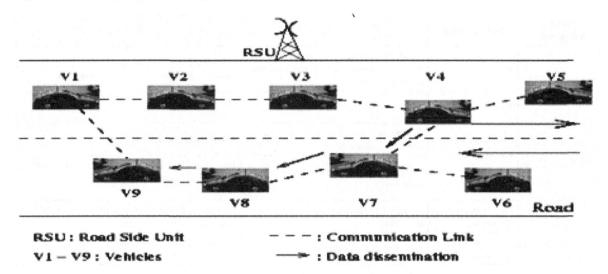

bors within one block, and chooses the fastest vehicle as the next ferry. The selection is performed, repeatedly block-by-block, until the bundles reach their destination. In FFRDV, velocities of vehicles are compared within one block. At the initialization of the network communication, every vehicle creates one state-report, which include the current position and velocity. In addition, the state report is updated periodically. The node (vehicle) is called message ferry only when it is carrying data. Once the bundles are forwarded and acknowledged, the ferry will discard the data and change to be normal mobile node. Within one block, the priority of vehicle selection is decided by maximum velocity.

In VANET for efficient opportunistic forwarding exploit on-board sensing, computing, and communication capabilities of vehicles MDDV, a mobility-centric approach for data dissemination in partitioned vehicular networks is proposed in Hao, et al. (2004). MDDV combines the idea of opportunistic forwarding, trajectory based forwarding and geographical forwarding. In V2V networks, opportunities to forward messages are created by vehicle movement, so it is natural to focus on vehicle mobility. A forwarding trajectory is specified extending from the source to the des-

tination (trajectory base forwarding) along which a message will be moved geographically closer to the destination (geographical forwarding). With an opportunistic forwarding approach, rules are defined to determine who is eligible to forward a message, when a copy of the message should be passed to another vehicle, and when a vehicle should hold/drop a message. For decision-making, a vehicle needs some approximate knowledge about the status of the dissemination.

Summarization of the advantages and disadvantages of the above mentioned data dissemination techniques are as shown in the Table 1.

SECURITY AND PRIVACY ISSUES FOR DATA DISSEMINATION IN VANETS

Like other wireless technologies security and privacy is a basic requirement for effective data dissemination techniques in VANETs. Disseminating message in a secure manner over relevant geographical area is a major challenge for VANET. VANET security issues have been studied well and there are several privacy and security issues are identified for VANET environment (Isaac, et

Table 1. Summary of advantages and disadvantages of data dissemination techniques

VANET Architecture	Dissemination	Advantages	Disadvantages
V2V/V2I	Push	Suitable for critical data applications, public interest data, Low contentions and collisions	Not suitable for delay tolerant applications, Everyone may not be interested in the same data
	Pull	Suitable for user demand data	Heavy interferences, Collisions, cross traffic problem
V2V	Flooding	Reliable and quick transmission of data, suitable for sparse networks	Not scalable for dense networks
	Relaying	Performance is good even in dense networks	Reliability is not guaranteed, Difficult to estimate rebroadcast interval, high overhead in dense networks.
Network Partitioned	Opportunistic forwarding	Suitable for network partitions for parse networks	Re-broadcast interval estimation is difficult, high overhead in dense networks
	Trajectory based forwarding	Less data packet overhead	Message delivery is not confined to a single trajectory
	Geographic forwarding	Suitable for dynamic topology and path change	High computational devices are required

al., 2010; Mahmoud, et al., 2009). Some of the security and privacy issues and attacks for data dissemination in VANETs are as follows:

- **Confidentiality:** In a vehicular safety message, dissemination system confidentiality is not an important issue, since messages distributed in the system are normally not confidential but meant to be received by all nodes, or at least by all nodes within a certain area. But for non-safety messages confidentiality is an important issue.

- **Integrity:** Regarding integrity, there are three immanent threats. All of these three concerns the content of distributed safety and non-safety messages. The first of these threats is having wrong or forged messages in the system. The second threat is messages being modified during distribution and the third is replayed messages. The threats have in common that they might lead to inappropriate warning messages being displayed to the driver and thereby in the worst case even provoke accidents.

- **Availability:** Threats against the availability of the disseminated messages are either the loss of single or multiple messages, or the system being not usable due to a denial of service attack.

- **Authenticity:** Authenticity of safety messages in VANETs is not required. For a vehicle receiving a warning message, it is not of interest to determine the identity of the message sender, but only that the message content should be reliable. But for non-safety messages authentication is a major concerned issue.

- **Bogus information dissemination:** Malicious vehicle in VANET can rebroadcast the received message with wrong information to other vehicles for its own advantage e.g. road clearance or any other objective. A faulty vehicle may attempt to disrupt the system stopping to respond, drop messages, or act arbitrarily.

- **Personal Information Tracing:** It is directly related to vehicle personal information like identity, location, etc. Malicious vehicle may use obtained private information for financial benefits or identity claim, etc.

- **Forging positions:** A forging position refers to a type of attack where the attacker misleads vehicle safety systems to display warnings to their drivers.

- **Privacy:** Privacy is one of the major security aims in intervehicle communication. Since most of the disseminated information is related to the driver and the respective vehicle, there is the threat of correlation of this data and driver identities by arbitrary third parties. This is due to the fact that data disseminated contains personal data such as speed and position, which could for instance be abused for driver profiling.

- **Roadside attacker:** This type of attacker is either an insider or outsider and he is acting intentional. The attacker is usually active in case he distributes forged messages. The attacker's motivation can also be both, malicious or profit oriented and he can act on his own or in collaboration with other attackers.

- **Vehicle (driver):** This represents clearly the case of an insider that is acting intentional or unintentional (e.g. vehicle with a defective warning system). He is active, malicious, or profit oriented.

- **Infrastructure-based attacker:** This type of attacker may be both, insider or outsider and acting intentionally for gaining the profit.

- **Sybil attack:** In Sybil attack, attacker broadcast messages with different fake identities for false information about road situation to alternate routes by sending wrong information, e.g. road break ahead.

- **Vehicle impersonation:** This type of attack is directly related to human safety where a vehicle can cause accidents among following vehicles by broadcasting message containing wrong information and deny from its own act.

- **Traffic analysis attacks:** In a traffic analysis attack, an attacker listens and/or compromises certain parts of the partitioned VANET to match a "message-disseminated sender" with the recipient. Malicious nodes in this attack redirects network traffic by altering control message fields or by forwarding routing messages with falsified values.

FUTURE RESEARCH DIRECTIONS

In this section, we address some of the emerging research issues that need to establish a new paradigm for information dissemination in VANETs are as follows:

- Almost all the data dissemination techniques are packet-based. A packet travels from a source to a destination untouched throughout the entire process. However, this packet-based paradigm no longer satisfies application requirements in VANET. First, for some applications, there is no definite source and destination, which is necessary for packet-based routing. Second, information is altered (or combined) throughout the forwarding process, and this is not a consideration of packet routing. In a traffic detection application, every vehicle may generate a traffic report that can be combined with other reports as it is disseminated. For all interested vehicles intended to be the recipients of these reports, there is no prior knowledge about how many, when, or where these vehicles might be. Hence, it is necessary to investigate a new paradigm for information dissemination. The new paradigm should enable information operations such as information generation, aggregation, dissemination, and invalidation.

- Main challenge of data dissemination lies in effectively representing, discovering, storing, and updating data throughout the network. Naming and addressing are central problems in vehicular networks. Data addressing from the physical world for efficient data storage and dissemination remains an unresolved problem. It is required that the addressing scheme should be hybrid, multi-level scheme, with context information. Another challenge is to dynamically map vehicle IDs to position-based addresses. This problem is particularly important for applications across the hybrid network architecture.

- Distributed data management is another challenging issue for VANET, impacting data replication, data elimination, and cache replacement. Traditional distributed data management assumes a network is connected with geographically distributed servers, which is no longer true for VANET. Essentially, VANET can be regarded as a large-scale distributed database in which each vehicle maintains a local part. Vehicles periodically exchange data to update this global database, and inconsistency cannot be avoided.

- Pull operation is limited to one hop at the initial stage, hence the efficient push strategies for data caching and aggregation must be taken into account.

- In VANETs, due to vehicle mobility, the network topology is highly dynamic and end-to-end connection is hard to maintain. Main problem for data dissemination is how to determine the appropriate relay selection strategy.

- Malicious vehicles: Most vehicles in the VANET could be trusted to follow the protocols specified by the application, some vehicles try to maximize their gains, regardless of the cost to the system. Efficient

algorithms are needed to identify and handle these malicious vehicles.

- Denial of Service (DoS): If the attacker can overwhelm a vehicle's resources or jam the communication channel used by the vehicular network, then he can prevent critical data from arriving. Hence, a mechanism for provoking the appropriate deceleration warnings is needed.

- Data suppression attacks: The adversary may use one or more vehicles to launch a data suppression attack by selectively dropping packets from the network. An attacker might suppress congestion alerts before selecting an alternate route, thus consigning subsequent vehicles to wait in traffic. Hence, some remedies are needed to overcome these data suppression attacks.

- Alteration Attacks. A particularly insidious attack in a vehicular network is to alter existing data. This includes deliberately delaying the transmission of information, replaying earlier transmissions or altering the individual entries within a transmission. So the algorithms are needed for authentication of both the source of the data and the data itself.

CONCLUSION

Vehicular ad hoc networks provide an exciting area of research at intersection of a number of disciplines and technologies. If there is an efficient data management technique exists in VANETs, there is a good future for applications of VANET, ranging from diagnostic, safety tools, information services, and traffic monitoring and management to in-car digital entertainment and business services. However, for these applications to become everyday reality, an array of technological challenges needs to be addressed. This chapter on data dissemination in VANET gives the concept and importance of information dissemination, security and privacy related issues, ongoing research works, and emerging research issues for information dissemination.

REFERENCES

Boukerche, A. (2008). Vehicular ad hoc networks: A new challenge for localization-based systems. *Computer Communications, 31*(12), 2838–2849. doi:10.1016/j.comcom.2007.12.004

Danlei, Y., & Bae Ko, Y. (2009). FFRDV: Fastest-ferry routing in DTN-enabled vehicular ad hoc networks. In *Proceedings of the 11th International Conference on Advanced Communication Technology*, (pp. 1410-1414). Piscataway, NJ: IEEE Press.

De Rango, F., Veltri, F., Fazio, P., & Marano, S. (2009). Two-level trajectory-based routing protocol for vehicular ad hoc networks in freeway and Manhattan environments. *Journal of Networks, 4*(9), 866–880.

Hao, W., Richard, F., Randall, G., & Michael, H. (2004). MDDV: A mobility-centric data dissemination algorithm for vehicular networks. In *Proceedings of the 1st ACM International Workshop on Vehicular Ad Hoc Networks,* (pp. 47-56). ACM Press.

Isaac, S. (2010). Security attacks and solutions for vehicular ad hoc networks. *IET Communications, 4*(7), 894–903. doi:10.1049/iet-com.2009.0191

Kakkasageri, M., & Manvi, S. (2011). Cognitive agent based framework for safety information dissemination in vehicular ad hoc networks. In *Proceedings of the First International Conference on Computer Science and Information Technology,* (pp. 254-264). Berlin, Germany: Springer Publishers.

Korkmaz, G., Ozguner, F., Ekici, E., & Ozguner, U. (2004). Urban multihop broadcast protocol for intervehicle communication systems. In *Proceedings of the 1st ACM International Workshop on Vehicular Ad Hoc Networks,* (pp. 76-85). ACM Press.

Mahmoud, A., Stephan, O., & Khaled, I. (2009). A secure and privacy aware data dissemination for the notification of traffic incidents. In *Proceedings of the Vehicular Technology Conference,* (pp. 1-5). IEEE.

Manvi, S., & Kakkasageri, M. (2008). Issues in mobile ad hoc networks for vehicular communication. *IETE Technical Review, 25*(2), 59–72.

Manvi, S., Kakkasageri, M., & Pitt, J. (2009). Multiagent based information dissemination in vehicular ad-hoc networks. *Mobile Information Systems, 5*(4), 363–389.

Marios, D., Saif, I., Tamer, N., & Liviu, I. (2005). VITP: An information transfer protocol for vehicular computing. In *Proceedings of the 2nd ACM International Workshop on Vehicular Ad Hoc Networks,* (pp. 30-39). ACM Press.

Michael, S., & Imad, M. (2010). Stochastic broadcast for VANET. In *Proceedings of the 7th IEEE Conference on Consumer Communications and Networking,* (pp. 13-18). IEEE Press.

Mohandas, B., Nayak, A., Naik, K., & Goel, N. (2008). ABSRP - A service discovery approach for vehicular ad-hoc network. In *Proceedings of the IEEE Asia-Pacific Services Computing Conference,* (pp. 1590-1594). IEEE Press.

Murat, C., Daniel, G., & Martin, M. (2006). Decentralized discovery of free parking places. In *Proceedings of the 3rd International Conference on Mobile Computing and Networking,* (pp. 30-39). IEEE.

Niculescu, D., & Nath, B. (2003). Trajectory based forwarding and its applications. In *Proceedings of the 9th International Conference on Mobile Computing and Networking*, (pp. 260-272). IEEE.

Tamer, N., Pravin, S., & Liviu, I. (2006). A comparative study of data dissemination models for VANETs. In *Proceedings of the Third Annual International Conference on Mobile and Ubiquitous Systems: Networking and Services*, (pp. 1-10). IEEE.

Uichin, L., Joon-Sang, P., Eyal, A., & Mario, G. (2006). FleaNet: A virtual market place on vehicular networks. In *Proceedings of the 3rd Annual International Conference on Mobile and Ubiquitous Systems*, (pp. 1-8). IEEE.

Zhao, J., Zhang, Y., & Cao, G. (2007). Data pouring and buffering on the road: A new data dissemination paradigm for vehicular ad hoc networks. *IEEE Transactions on Vehicular Technology*, *56*(6), 3266–3277. doi:10.1109/TVT.2007.906412

Zong, C., et al. (2001). Ad hoc relay wireless networks over moving vehicles on highways. In *Proceedings of the 2nd ACM International Symposium on Mobile Ad Hoc Networking & Computing*. ACM Press.

ADDITIONAL READING

David, C., & Jonathan, D. (2007). A vision for wireless access on the road network. In *Proceedings of the International Workshop on Intelligent Transportation*, (pp. 25-30). IEEE.

Hao, W., Mahesh, P., Richard, F., Jaesup, L., Joonho, K., Randall, G., & Michael, H. (2005). Vehicular networks in urban transportation systems. In *Proceedings of the Digital Government Conference*, (pp. 9- 10). Digital Government.

Josiane, N., & Cristian, B. (2006). *STEID: A protocol for emergency information dissemination in vehicular networks*. Newark, NJ: New Jersey Institute of Technology.

Junichiro, F. (2010). A probabilistic protocol for multihop routing in VANETs. *Journal of Electrical and Computer Engineering*, *57*(3), 1910–1922.

Kakkasageri, M., & Manvi, S. (2009). Push-pull based critical information gathering in VANETs: Multi agent system based approach. In *Proceedings of the IEEE International Conference in Vehicular Electronics and Safety*, (pp. 1-6). IEEE Press.

Kayhan, G., & Kamalrulnizam, B. (2010). Inter-vehicle communication protocols for multimedia transmission. In *Proceedings of the International MultiConference of Engineers and Computer Scientists*, (pp. 247-250). IEEE.

Kuong, C., Chyi, D., & Yi, L. (2008). HarpiaGrid: A reliable grid-based routing protocol for vehicular ad hoc networks. In *Proceedings of the 11th International IEEE Conference on Intelligent Transportation Systems*, (pp. 2491-2495). IEEE Press.

Linda, B., & Gunter, H. (2000). Role-based multicast in highly mobile but sparsely connected ad hoc networks. In *Proceedings of the First Annual Workshop on First Annual Workshop on Mobile and Ad Hoc Networking and Computing*, (pp. 45-50). IEEE.

Linda, B., Lorenz, S., & Gunter, H. (2000). Disseminating messages among highly mobile hosts based on inter-vehicle communication. In *Proceedings of the Intelligent Vehicles Symposium*, (pp. 522-527). IEEE.

Little, T., & Agarwal, A. (2005). A new information propagation scheme for vehicular networks. In *Proceedings of the 3rd International Conference on Mobile Systems, Applications and Services*, (pp. 1265-1275). IEEE.

Lochert, C., Scheuermann, B., & Mauve, M. (2007). Probabilistic aggregation for data dissemination in VANETs. In *Proceedings of the Fourth ACM International Workshop on Vehicular Ad Hoc Networks*, (pp. 1 - 8). ACM Press.

Manvi, S., & Kakkasageri, M. (2009). Emerging security issues in vehicular ad-hoc network for e – business. In Lee (Ed.), *Handbook of Research on Telecommunications Planning and Management for Business*, (pp. 599-614). Hershey, PA: IGI Global.

Manvi, S., & Kakkasageri, M. (2010). *Wireless and mobile network concepts and protocols*. New Delhi, India: Wiley India.

Manvi, S., Kakkasageri, M., & Pitt, J. (2007). Information search and access in vehicular ad-hoc networks: An agent based approach. In *Proceedings of the International Conference on Communication in Computing, The 2007 World Congress in Computer Science, Computer Engineering, & Applied Computing*, (pp. 23-29). IEEE.

Manvi, S., Kakkasageri, M., Pitt, J., & Alex, R. (2006). Multi-agent systems as a platform for VANETs. In *Proceedings of the Agents in Traffic and Transportation (ATT 2006), International Conference on Autonomous Agents and Multiagent Systems*, (pp. 35-42). ATT.

Marc, T. (2007). Inter-vehicle communications: Assessing information dissemination under safety constraints. In *Proceedings of the 4th Annual IEEE/IFIP Conference on Wireless On Demand Network Systems and Services*, (pp. 59-64). IEEE Press.

Marios, D., Andreas, F., Tamer, N., & Liviu, I. (2007). Location-aware services over vehicular ad-hoc networks using car-to-car communication. *IEEE Journal on Selected Areas in Communications*, *25*(8), 1590–1602. doi:10.1109/JSAC.2007.071008

Mooi Choo, C., & Fen, F. (2006). Performance study of robust data transfer protocol for VANETs. In *Proceedings of the Second International Conference Mobile Ad-Hoc and Sensor Networks*, (pp. 377-391). IEEE.

Olivia, B., Chong, S., Martin, K., Amir, T., & Dirk, P. (2007). A data dissemination strategy for cooperative vehicular systems. In *Proceedings of the 65th Vehicular Technology Conference*, (pp. 2501-2505). IEEE.

Ostermaier, B., Dotzer, F., & Strassberger, M. (2007). Enhancing the security of local danger warnings in VANETs - A simulative analysis of voting schemes. In *Proceedings of the Second International Conference on Availability, Reliability and Security*, (pp. 422-431). IEEE.

Ozan, T., Nawaporn, W., Fan, B., Priyantha, M., & Varsha, S. (2007). Broadcasting in VANET. In *Proceedings of the 2007 Mobile Networking for Vehicular Environments*, (pp. 7-12). IEEE.

Roberto, B., Carlos, B., & Maria, C. (2008). GeoSAC - Scalable address auto configuration for VANET using geographic networking concepts. In *Proceedings of the 19th IEEE International Symposium on Personal, Indoor and Mobile Radio Communications*, (pp. 1-7). IEEE Press.

Saleh, Y., Mahmoud, S., & Mahmood, F. (2006). Vehicular ad hoc networks: Challenges and perspectives. In *Proceedings of the 6th International Conference on ITS Telecommunications*. IEEE.

Sudarshan, C. (2006). Inter-vehicle data dissemination in sparse equipped traffic. In *Proceedings of the 9th IEEE International Conference on Intelligent Transportation Systems*, (pp. 273-280). IEEE Press.

Sudarshan, C. (2008). *Using dead drops to improve data dissemination in very sparse equipped traffic*. In IEEE Intelligent Vehicles Symposium. IEEE Press.

Tim, L., Elmar, S., Frank, K., & Christian, M. (2005). Influence of falsified position data on geographic ad-hoc routing. In *Proceedings of the Second European Workshop on Security and Privacy in Ad Hoc and Sensor Network,* (pp. 102-112). IEEE.

Tim, L., Robert, K., & Elmar, S. (2008). Modeling roadside attacker behavior in VANETs. In *Proceedings of the 3rd IEEE Workshop on Automotive Networking and Applications.* IEEE Press.

Vinod, K., Haitao, Z., Antony, R., & Ben, Z. (2010). On infostation density of vehicular networks. In *Proceedings of ACM Mobile Networking and Applications.* ACM Press.

Wegener, A., Hellbruck, H., Fischer, S., Schmidt, C., & Fekete, S. (2007). AutoCast: An adaptive data dissemination protocol for traffic information systems. In *Proceedings of VTC Fall 2007,* (pp. 1947-1951). VTC.

Zhou, W., & Chunxiao, C. (2007). Cooperation enhancement for message transmission in VANETs. *Wireless Personal Communications, 43,* 141–156. doi:10.1007/s11277-006-9235-2

KEY TERMS AND DEFINITIONS

Data Dissemination: Data dissemination can be defined as broadcasting information about itself and the other vehicles it knows about.

Flooding: Flooding is a process to broadcast the generated and received data to neighbor vehicles.

Forging Positions: A forging position refers to a type of attack where the attacker misleads vehicle safety systems to display warnings to their drivers.

Opportunistic Forwarding: Vehicles can store packets until they reach another vehicle to forward the packet store-and-forward/store-carry-forward. If no suitable forwarder vehicle is available, vehicles store the packet, carry the packet for some time, and forward the packet, when another vehicle is more suitable as next forwarder.

Pull: Pull-based data dissemination is the type where any vehicle is enabled to query information about specific location or target. This is one form of request and response model.

Push: Data can be efficiently delivered from moving vehicles or roadside unit to another vehicle.

Relaying: Relaying is a process to select a next hop (relay), which forwards the data to the next hop and so on.

Self-Organization: It is the capability of vehicles to detect each other and transmit packets, with or without the need for a base station.

Sybil Attack: In Sybil attack, attacker broadcast messages with different fake identities for false information about road situation to alternate routes by sending wrong information e.g. road break ahead.

Vehicle Impersonation: This type of attack is directly related to human safety where a vehicle can cause accidents among following vehicles by broadcasting message containing wrong information and deny from its own act.

Chapter 12
Information Dissemination in Urban VANETs:
Single-Hop or Multi-Hop?

Stefano Busanelli
Guglielmo Srl, Italy

Gianluigi Ferrari
University of Parma, Italy

Vito Andrea Giorgio
University of Parma, Italy

Nicola Iotti
Guglielmo Srl, Italy

ABSTRACT

In recent years, Vehicular Ad-hoc NETworks (VANETs) have experienced an intense development phase, driven by academia, industry, and public authorities. On the basis of the obtained results, it is reasonable to expect that VANETs will finally hit the market in the near future. In order to reach commercial success, VANETs must effectively operate during the first years of deployment, when the market penetration rate will be unavoidably low, and, consequently, only a small number of suitably equipped vehicles (VANET-enabled) will be present on the roads. Among the possible strategies to face the initial sparse VANET scenarios, the deployment of an auxiliary network constituted by fixed Road Side Units (RSUs), either Dissemination Points (DPs) or relays, is certainly one of the most promising. In order to maximize the benefits offered by this support infrastructure, the placement of RSUs needs to be carefully studied. In this chapter, the authors analyze, by means of numerical simulations, the performance of an application that leverages on a finite number of DPs for disseminating information to the transiting vehicles. The positions of the DPs are determined through a recently proposed family of optimal placement algorithms, on the basis of proper vehicular mobility traces. The analysis is carried out considering two realistic urban scenarios. In both cases, the performance improvement brought by the use of multi-hop broadcast protocols, with respect to classical single-hop communications with DPs, is investigated.

DOI: 10.4018/978-1-4666-2223-4.ch012

INTRODUCTION

Nowadays, most of the vehicles moving on our streets are powerful mobile computing devices, with sensorial, computational, and cognitive capabilities. Moreover, in the near future they will likely possess wireless communication capabilities as well, in order to exchange data with existing wide area networks (e.g., cellular networks) and to implement Dedicated Short-Range Communications (DSRCs) with the surrounding vehicles. The possibility of creating decentralized and self-organized vehicular networks, commonly denoted as Vehicular Ad-hoc NETworks (VANETs), is one of the most appealing applications which will be enabled by the exploitation of "smart vehicles."

It is widely recognized that the implementation of effective VANET-based services is a complex task, for several reasons:

1. The highly dynamic network topology, due to high vehicle mobility;
2. The severe fading that often characterizes the wireless communication channel;
3. The plethora of services with different requirements that may be supported in VANETs, ranging from safety-critical applications, with strict latency and reliability requirements, to bandwidth-consuming infotainment applications;
4. The large spectrum of traffic conditions that occurs in real roads, ranging from fluid traffic flow situations (as it happens in rural areas or during the night-hours) to jammed urban roads or congested freeways.

Historically, most of the research efforts have been focused on dense networks, with the aim of designing efficient and congestion-avoidance forwarding protocols. However, lack of connectivity in sparse networks will be the first critical issue to be addressed by VANET-based commercial communication systems. In fact, during the first years of deployment the market penetration rate of the inter-vehicular communications technologies will be unavoidably low, thus yielding to scenarios where VANETs will be typically sparse.

Among the possible approaches to avoid the lack of connectivity, the deployment of a complementary network infrastructure, constituted by fixed network nodes, is one of the first feasible solutions. These fixed nodes, denoted as Road Side Units (RSUs), are commonly equipped with the same communication technology of the vehicular mobile nodes. The RSUs can play different roles, acting as Disseminating Points (DPs) or relays. In the first case, we assume that a DP generates "new" information to be disseminated in a spatial region around itself—the size of this region depends on the communication strategy (either single-hop or multi-hop), as will be shown later. DPs are inter-connected by means of a backbone network constituted by either wireless or wired communication links. Since the backbone capacity is typically much higher than that of a VANET, it is reasonable to assume that a given information (generated by a control center) will be simultaneously available at every DP. In the second case, a relay actively participates to the forwarding process, by relaying the received packets a single time or by storing them for a certain finite time, periodically broadcasting them (store-and-forward). In this case, relays act as independent entities, without requiring to be connected to a backbone infrastructure.

On the basis of the considerations above, it emerges that RSUs will be highly instrumental to a successful commercial deployment of VANETs. In order to be cost-effective and to guarantee a significant improvement, in terms of Quality of Service (QoS), the number and the placement of the RSUs need to be properly optimized. However, despite the importance of this issue, to date a small number of works has addressed it.

In this chapter, we focus on the problem of optimizing the dissemination of information from a group of DPs to the vehicles in an urban scenario. We take into account a push transmission paradigm, where the DPs send data to all vehicles transiting in their neighborhoods, without the need of an explicit query. This approach is suitable for disseminating information of public interest, and, as shown in Kone, Zheng, Rowstron, and Zhao (2010), it is more efficient than a pull approach, in which the transiting vehicles have to explicitly query the desired data.

The goal of this chapter is two-fold:

1. To present the state-of-art approaches for the optimal placement of DPs;
2. To analyze, by means of numerical simulations, the performance of a dissemination application in realistic urban scenarios, by analyzing, from a comparative perspective, the performance with single-hop and multi-hop dissemination protocols.

BACKGROUND

The concept of drive-thru Internet—the idea of providing Internet connectivity to the vehicles by exploiting the existing roadside access points—was first introduced in Ott and Kutscher (2004). Subsequent experimental studies have confirmed the feasibility of WiFi-based vehicular Internet access, at least for non-interactive applications (Bychkovsky, Hull, Miu, Balakrishnan, & Madden, 2006; Eriksson, Balakrishnan, & Madden, 2008).

However, by only relying on the existing network infrastructure, it is difficult to guarantee a sufficiently high QoS. For this reason, in all scenarios with strict QoS requirements, the deployment of a network of dedicated RSUs is an unavoidable requirement. In order to reduce the economic and logistic burden caused by the deployment of a dedicated network of RSUs, it can be helpful to use a planning tool to optimize the number and placement of the RSUs.

A number of works in the literature has tackled the problem of planning the deployment of RSUs

for data dissemination in VANETs. Most of them merely propose heuristics for the deployment of the RSUs, thus relying on simulation analysis to validate the performance of the proposed approaches (Lochert, Scheuermann, Caliskan, & Mauve, 2007; Leontiadis, Costa, & Mascolo, 2009).

Theoretical frameworks have also been proposed to determine the quasi-optimal positions of the RSUs, on the basis of specific QoS criteria. For example, in Banerjee, Corner, Towsley, and Levine (2008), the authors propose an analytical model (also supported by experimental results) that offers significant insights on the tradeoffs, faced by a considered family of dissemination protocols, among the vehicle spatial density, the number of RSUs, and the roadside network architecture.

In Abdrabou and Zhuang (2011), the authors derive a relationship between the number of RSUs and the maximum end-to-end delay in a complementary (with respect to Banerjee, Corner, Towsley, & Levine, 2008) scenario, where the vehicles send data to the RSUs. In Zhao, Zhang, and Cao (2007), the authors present several dissemination protocols, whose parameters can be tuned in order to maximize the amount of data that can be disseminated in a given area.

In Zheng, Sinha, and Kumar (2009), the authors propose the concept of alpha-coverage, useful for characterizing a given DPs deployment, in terms of contacts between the DPs and the transiting vehicles. A more refined solution has been presented in Zheng, Lu, Sinha, and Kumar (2010), where the authors have introduced the concept of contact opportunity, which allows to characterize not only the number of contacts between the vehicles and the DPs, but also the fraction of time (or space) spent by a vehicle while connected with some DPs. They also present a DPs' deployment algorithm to maximize the worst-case contact opportunity, under some "budget" constraints—the budget is typically constituted by the total number of DPs. Similar metrics—with different names but approximately the same meaning—were considered in Trullols, Fiore, Casetti, Chiasserini, and Barcelo Ordinas (2010):

1. The coverage ratio, defined as the percentage of vehicles that have a contact with the DPs;
2. The coverage time, defined as the average sojourn time of the vehicles within the transmission range of the DPs.

In Trullols, Fiore, Casetti, Chiasserini, and Barcelo Ordinas (2010), the authors propose a method for the quasi-optimal placement of DPs, on the basis of a maximum coverage approach, in order to maximize either the coverage ratio or the coverage time.

While all the above-mentioned works are focused on single-hop communications, in Malandrino, Casetti, Chiasserini, and Fiore (2011) the authors consider the more general problem of the content downloading in vehicular networks. By following a graph-theoretic approach, the authors investigate various types of data dissemination: namely, direct transfer (e.g., single hop from the DPs), multi-hop forwarding (multihop unicast communications), and carry-and-forwards (vehicles store and carry the data).

A comparative investigation of single-hop and multi-hop communications, in the realm of wireless networking, is of interest. In fact, in a single-hop communication scenario, the concepts of coverage time and contact opportunity have a practical meaning, as the amount of data that can be transferred from the DPs to the passing vehicles can be estimating by simply considering the transmission rate of the DPs. On the contrary, when multi-hop (broadcast) dissemination protocols are used, this direct relationship no longer holds, since the amount of data that can be transferred depends on a broad range of parameters, including the vehicle spatial density, the vehicles' speed distribution, and the medium access protocol in use. Therefore, a direct comparison between single-hop and multi-hop communications in VANET-based

system is expected to shed light on the design and implementation of future urban wireless vehicular dissemination systems.

PHYSICAL CHANNEL CONSIDERATION

The Wireless Channel in VANETs

The statistical characterization of the physical channel of V2V communications is a challenging. First of all, a common reference scenario it is difficult to define, because of the wide variety of environments of interest for IVCs. Roads can run in a desert countryside, inside a tunnel, or in a "urban" canyon surraunded by with skyscrapers. Furthermore, because of its metallic nature, the density and the type of surrounding vehicles have a huge impact on the number of multi-path reflections experienced by the receiver. Moreover the antenna radiation pattern is highly influenced by its placement with respect to the vehicle (namely, inside or on the roof). The second, but not less important, reason is the consequent difficulty in deriving statistically accurate empirical models.

From the point of view of the network layer, a physical wireless channel behaves as an ON-OFF system, since the packet can be either successfully received or discarded. Typically, a checksum is used to determine the reception status of the channel (e.g., the FCS in the IEEE 802.11 model). In network simulator, a common approach consist in defining a hard threshold, the receiver sensitivity, denoted as RX_{TH} (dimension: [dB], such that a packet is successfully received, only and only if the received power P_r (dimension: [W] is higher then the sensitivity. On the other hand, the packet is discarded with probability 1 when $P_r < RX_{TH}$. Owning to this assumption, in order to know if a packet is correctly received or not, it is only necessary to derive P_r and compare it to RX_{TH}. Once the transmit power, denoted as P_t (dimension: [W]), has been fixed, the value of P_r

depends only on the inner characteristics of the wireless channel, and the distance between the transmitter and the receiver. There are two main families of physical channel models: deterministic and stochastic. With a deterministic path-loss model, such as Friis and Two Ray Ground (TRG) models, once the transmit power and the receiver sensitivity has been set, it is possible to compute the transmission range, defined in this work with the symbol z (dimension: [m]). When the distance is longer then the transmission range, the packet is never received, conversely it is always correctly detected for distance shorter than the transmission range. On the opposite, in stochastic models the instantaneous power is a random variable, and only the average received power can be computed. In this case, a finite transmission range cannot be defined, since it is not possible to a-priori predict, even knowing the distance from the source, if a packet will be successfully decoded. However, we will define the transmission range with respect to the average received power. Depending on the characteristic of the channel, there are several types of stochastic model, such as the shadowing, Rayleigh, or Nakagami.

The Friis model is valid in quite unrealistic scenarios, without any obstacles, while the TRG can be used where the transmitter and receivers antennas are near to the ground. In particular, according to the Friis model, the received power can be expressed as follows:

$$\mathrm{P_r}(d) = P_t G_t G_r \left(\frac{\lambda}{4\pi d} \right)^2,$$

where G_t and G_r denote the antenna gain of, respectively, the transmitter and the receiver, while λ (dimension: [m]) is the wavelength corresponding to the used the carrier frequency, denoted with f_c (dimension: [Hz]) (e.g., $\lambda = c/f_c$, where c represents the speed of light).

The TRG model is defined by the following equations:

$$P_r(d) = \begin{cases} P_t G_t G_r \left(\dfrac{\lambda}{4\pi d} \right)^2 & d \leq d^* \\[2em] P_t G_t G_r \left(\dfrac{h_t h_r}{4\pi d} \right)^2 & d > d^*, \end{cases}$$

where h_t and h_r are the heights of the transmitter and the receiver antenna, while d* is a threshold defined as:

$$d^* = \frac{4\pi h_t h_r}{\lambda}.$$

It is trivial to observe that in the interval [0, d^*] the Friis and the TRG models are identical.

According to a m-Nakagami distribution the signal amplitude is distributed as follows:

$$f_x(x) = \frac{2^m m^x 2^{m-1}}{\Gamma(m)\Omega(m)} \frac{y^{m-1}}{\Gamma(m)} \exp\left(-\frac{mx^2}{\Omega} \right),$$

$$x \geq 0, \Omega > 0, m > 0.5,$$

where m and Ω are suitable parameters—in particular Ω is the average received power.

The corresponding Probability Density Function (PDF) of the received power Pr it is therefore given by a gamma distribution of the following form:

$$f_Y(y) = \left(\frac{m}{\Omega} \right)^m \frac{y^{m-1}}{\Gamma(m)} \exp\left(-\frac{my}{\Omega} \right),$$

$$y \geq 0.$$

In order to use the Nakagami model it is necessary to specify the average received power (Γ). In Chen, Schmidt-Eisenlohr, Jiang, Torrent-Moreno, Delgrossi, and Hartenstein (2007), the authors define Ω (expressed in dB) as a piecewise constant function of d:

$$\Omega(d)[dB] = \begin{cases} 10\gamma_0 \log(d/d_{ref}) & 0 < d \le d_0^\gamma \\ 10\gamma_0 \log(d_0^\gamma/d_{ref}) + 10\gamma_1 \log(d/d_0^\gamma) & d_0^\gamma < d \le d_1^\gamma \\ 10\gamma_0 \log(d_0^\gamma/d_{ref}) + 10\gamma_1 \log(d_1^\gamma/d_0^\gamma) + 10\gamma_2 \log(d/d_1^\gamma) & d_1^\gamma < d, \end{cases}$$

where d_{ref} represents a reference distance that can be freely chosen (we set $d_{ref} = 1$ m), while $\gamma_0, \gamma_1, \gamma_2$, d_0, and d_1 have been set according to the empirical values obtained by measurements. Obviously, by setting $\gamma_i = 2$ for $i = 0, 1, 2$ in equation (2.4), we have the same attenuation of the Friis model.

The parameter m has a strong impact, since it determines the shape of the PDF. For instance: when $m = 1$ the Nakagami PDF coincides with a Rayleigh PDF; when $m < 1$ the Nakagami distribution determines a severe fading (worse than Rayleigh); while with $m > 1$ one obtains a Ricean model, less sever than Rayleigh (e.g., if $m \to \infty$ the Nakagami distribution reduces to deterministic model). In [113] the authors define m as a piecewise constant function of d:

$$m(d) = \begin{cases} m_0 \\ d < d_0^m \\ m_1 \\ d_0^m \le d < d_1^m \\ m_2 \\ d_1^m \le d, \end{cases}$$

where $m_0, m_1, m_2, d_0^m, d_1^m$ have been set according to the empirical values presented in Chen, Schmidt-Eisenlohr, Jiang, Torrent-Moreno, Delgrossi, and Hartenstein (2007) (see Table 1).

Basic IEEE 802.11 Mechanisms

As VANETs are characterized by the high speed of the nodes, a new communication standard, fit for this type of network, was required.

For this reason in 2003 the definition of a new communication standard for the Wireless Access

in Vehicular Enviromental (WAVE), the so called IEEE 802.11p, started.

The physical layer can rely on seven channel each one with a bandwith of 10 MHz and can use frequencies higher than 5 GHz.

The MAC layer in WAVE standard is equivalent to the IEEE 802.11e Enanched Distributed Channel Access (EDCA), introduced in the IEEE 802.11e amendment. The EDCA maintains the distributed approach of the CSMA/CA protocol as in legacy DCF, but introduces four Access Categories (ACs), each one defining a priority level for channel access and having a corresponding transmission queue at the MAC layer. Each AC in the queue behaves like a virtual station, and it follows its own DCF algorithm, independently contending with the others to obtain the channel access. Each *i-th* AC has a set of distinct channel access parameters, including Arbitration Inter-Frame Space (AIFS) duration and contention window size (CWmin[i] and CWmax[i]).

In Table 2, the more relevant parameters of the PHY and MAC layers of IEEE 802.11p are summarized, with the exception of the EDCA parameters which are listed in Table 3. From Table 2 we observe that IEEE 802.11p uses the same CWmin and CWmax values of the original IEEE 802.11e specification, but slightly modified

Table 1. Main parameters of Friis, TRG, and Nakagami propagation models

Parameters	Values
f_c	5.9 GHz
Gt, Gr	1
Ht, Hr	2 m
$\gamma 0, \gamma 1, \gamma 2$	1.9, 3.8, 3.8
$d_0^\gamma d_1^\gamma$	200, 500 m
m_0, m_1, m_2	1.5, 0.75, 0.75
$d_0^m d_1^m$	80, 200 m

Table 2. Main parameters of the IEEE 802.11p standard

Parameter	IEEE 802.11p
Carrier Frequency [GHz]	5.9
Bandwidth [MHz]	10
OFDM Guard Time [μs]	1.6
CWmin	See Table 3
CWmax	1023
TSLOT [μs]	13
TSIFS [μs]	32
Data rates [Mbit/s]	3, 4.5, 6, 9, 12, 18, 24, 27

Table 3. EDCA parameters of the IEEE 802.11p standard

AC	CWmin	CWmax	AIFSN
AC_BK	15	1023	9
AC_BE	15	1023	6
AC_VI	7	15	3
AC_VO	3	7	2

AIFSN values. While in standard WLAN the AC_VI and AC_VO means, respectively, Video and Voice, in the case of IEEE 802.11p, AC_VI and AC_VO have to interpreted as ACs reserved for prioritized messages (e.g., critical safety warnings) (see Figure 1).

REFERENCE SCENARIOS

Network Topology

In this work, we consider two urban scenarios: in the first, the roads form a symmetric Manhattan grid, while the second corresponds to a portion of a European-like city (namely, Parma, Italy), where the road structure is irregular. In both cases, the movements of the vehicles are generated using an open-source mobility simulator, called SUMO (Karnadi, Mo, & Lan, 2007) and freely available (SUMO Project). SUMO is a microscopic road traffic simulator that allows to create a scenario by converting an existing map or, alternatively, by using one of the external tool provided by the SUMO project itself (for example, NETGEN or NETCONVERT). Among the several vehicle mobility models supported by SUMO, we have employed a car-following dynamic model largely based on a physical model denoted as KWG from

the name of the authors that first proposed it in Krauss, Wagner, and Gawron (1997).

The regular scenario, represented in Figure 2(a), is a square-shaped sub-region, with an area equal to 1Km², of a Manhattan grid of infinite size. The considered region is constituted by 4 vertical (south-north) and 4 horizontal (east-west) roads, intersecting in uniformly-spaced junctions (the distance between two adjacent roads is equal to 200 m). Each road has a length equal to L_{road} (dimension: [m]) and is composed by two adjacent lanes: one reserved for the vehicles entering the network (inbound) and the other one reserved for the vehicles exiting the network (outbound). Each intersection is regulated by a Traffic Light (TL), with a deterministic and constant duty cycle. During its duty cycle, a TL stays green for $T_{green} = 55s$, red for $T_{red} = 60s$, and amber for $T_{amber} = 5s$. Obviously, the TLs lying in vertical roads have an orthogonal duty cycle with respect to those in the horizontal roads, under the assumption that the amber and green colors are orthogonal with respect to the red color. Moreover, in the presence of multiple intersections we assume that all TLs in the horizontal road are synchronized. An extension of this analysis to encompass the presence of roundabouts can be carried out by considering the approach presented in Busanelli, Ferrari, and Giorgio (2011).

The second scenario, shown in Figure 2(b), is based on a real urban map of a square-shaped portion of the city of Parma (Italy), with area equal to 1Km². The map has been retrieved from

Figure 1. Received power obtained with the Friis, TRG, and Nakagami propagation models, using the parameters summarized in Table 2, and Pt = 100mW

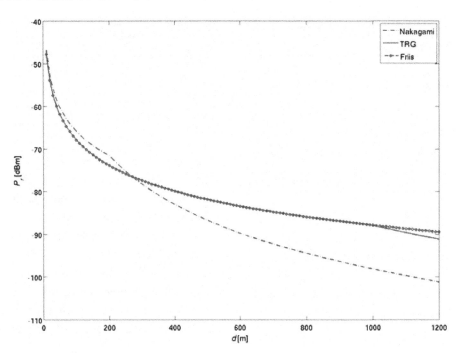

the website of the Open Street Map (OSM) project (Open Street Map). In this case, the roads are characterized by an irregular shape and there are junctions—note that the number of junctions is slightly higher than in the regular scenario.

In both scenarios, the vehicles' movements are generated as follows. The vehicular flow entering the considered spatial region is created according to a global (i.e., over all inbound lanes of the scenario at hand) time-domain Poisson process of parameter γ (dimension: [veh/s]). Once generated, each vehicle appears in one of the available inbound lanes and it then follows a random itinerary along the available roads, randomly determining its direction in correspondence to each junction. In the Manhattan scenario, we have assumed unbalanced probabilities of choosing the inbound lane, in order to generate a slightly asymmetric traffic pattern (e.g., some roads have a higher probability to be selected). Otherwise, due to the intrinsic symmetry of the scenario, every junction would have observed (on

average) the same traffic load, making useless the execution of the DPs placement algorithms (e.g., all the intersections would have been statistically identical). On the contrary, in the second (Parma) scenario, the probabilities of choosing the inbound lane are assumed to be uniform, since in this case this road topology is intrinsically asymmetric. The vehicle generation process stops as soon a pre-fixed number of vehicles, denoted as , have been generated. As shown in Figure 3, with the considered parameters' set ($\gamma = 0.5$ veh/s), the initial transitory phase ends after approximately 2000 s, while the generation process ends, on average, after approximately 14000 s.

Therefore, during the temporal window (2000 s, 13000 s) (with length equal to $T_{obs} = 11000s$), the network is stationary, in the sense that the number of entering vehicles is (on average) equal to the number of the exiting vehicles. In other words, in these conditions the global number of vehicles in the network varies little around its average.

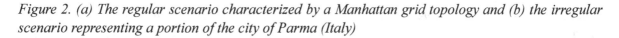

Figure 2. (a) The regular scenario characterized by a Manhattan grid topology and (b) the irregular scenario representing a portion of the city of Parma (Italy)

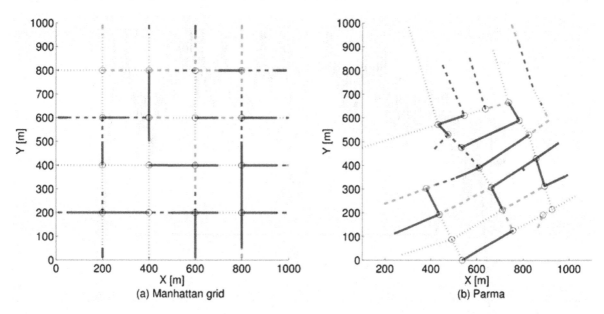

The average vehicular spatial density at a generic instant t of a generic road R, denoted as $\rho_s^R(t)$, is obtained by dividing the number of vehicles located within the road R, for the length of the road itself. By averaging over the simulation duration, it is possible to obtain the average per-road vehicular density denoted as ρ_s^R (dimension: [veh/m]).

Data Dissemination Paradigm

In this work, we consider a content distribution application in which the DPs broadcast public interest information to all the vehicles in a given spatial region. The contents to be broadcasted (e.g., the list of free parking places available in the city or the list of the currently congested streets) might be provided by some public authorities and periodically updated. Furthermore, it is reasonable to assume that the inter-update interval has a fixed length, denoted as T_I (dimension: [s]).The DPs are synchronized together by means of a backbone infrastructure: therefore, they send the same information at the same time. Each information block has a fixed size equal to $N_p P$ bytes, where N_p is the number of MAC-layer frames (note that in this section the words "frame" and "packet" are used interchangeably) that compose the block and P (dimension: [bytes]) denotes the fixed packet size. The packets are generated with a constant generation rate equal to λ (dimension: [pck/s]) and are transmitted according to a fixed datarate R (dimension: [Mbits/s]). The DPs continuously retransmit the information block for its entire "lifetime" (namely, T_I). The effective duration of an information block coincides with $\tau = \dfrac{N_P}{\lambda}$, while the number of the retransmissions, denoted as N_R, can be computed as $N_R = \dfrac{T_I}{\tau}$. Finally, we assume that the vehicles and the DPs have the same deterministic transmission range, denoted as (dimension: [m]).

By suitably choosing the parameters listed above, the proposed data dissemination paradigm

Figure 3. Overall number of vehicles in the Parma network, as a function of the time. The interval T_I and T_{obs} are also shown.

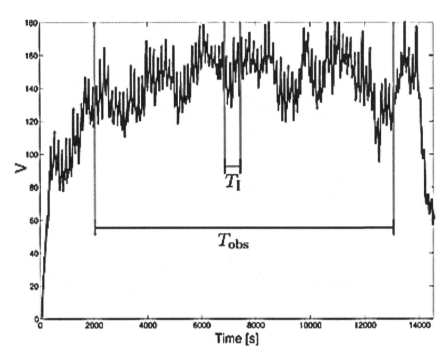

can encompass a wide array of applications, ranging from notifications, where the DPs disseminate a small amount of information (a few Kbytes), to media distribution applications, where the DPs disseminate a large amount of information (a few Mbytes). Regardless of the dimension of the information block, we consider a "best effort" transmission paradigm, based on a broadcast transmission protocol, without any feedback from the vehicles. Therefore, the vehicles send neither ACK nor NACK packets, but have no guarantee of receiving the distributed content.

We consider both single-hop and multi-hop broadcast protocols. The single-hop protocol, in the following denoted as SH, operates in a trivial manner: the DPs send a packet that is received by all the vehicles whose distance from the nearest DP is smaller than z. Besides the SH protocol, we also consider a multi-hop probabilistic protocol, denoted as Irresponsible Forwarding (IF) and previously introduced in Busanelli, Ferrari, and

Panichpapiboon (2009). In Figure 4 the propagation flows obtained by using, respectively, the SH and the IF broadcasting protocols, are shown.

The protocol is probabilistic in the sense that a vehicle decides if retransmit or not a packet in a probabilistic manner, according to a certain Probability Assignment Function (PAF), defined as follows:

$$p(d) = \exp\left(-\frac{\rho_s^v(t)(z-d)}{c}\right), \qquad (1)$$

where d is the distance between the last transmitter and the receiver of the packet; $c \geq 1$ is a tunable parameter which can be selected to "shape" the probability of rebroadcasting—the higher the value of c, the higher the probability of rebroadcasting at any position d—and $\rho_s^v(t)$ is the local vehicle spatial density, evaluated by each vehicle, independently from the other vehicles, at time t.

The local spatial density $\rho_s^v(t)$ can differ from the per-road vehicle spatial density $\rho_s^R(t)$, but they usually have the same order of magnitude. According to definition of PAF in Equation (1), it emerges that the retransmission probability is an increasing function of the distance from the last (re-)transmitter of the packet. In other words, the further is a node from the DP, the higher is its retransmission probability: it becomes 1 when z=d The inter-node distance can be estimated accurately under the assumption that the vehicles are equipped with a GPS receiver.

Without loss of generality, the operations of the IF protocol, with respect to a single DP, can be described as follows.

1. The DP sends a new frame.
2. The nodes within a distance z from the DP receive the packet and form the so-called 1-st transmission domain (as shown in Figure 4). If a node has already received a copy of the packet, it silently discards it without joining the 1-st transmission domain. This allows to prevent the formation of loops.
3. Every node in the 1-st transmission domain probabilistically computes the distance from the DP (i.e., d) and decides, according to the PAF in equation (1), to retransmit (or not) the packet.
4. The potential forwarders (i.e., the nodes of the 1-st transmission domain which have decided to retransmit) compete for channel access, by using the channel access mechanism of the underlying MAC protocol. As a consequence, a subset of the nodes within the first transmission domain may retransmit the packet.
5. Since the DP is placed in a road intersection, the re-broadcasters will likely belong to different roads. This implies that, at the second hop, there will a number of 2-nd transmission domains equal to the number of intersecting roads. In other words, the information

originated at the DP tends to propagate in all roads entering into the intersection.
6. The whole process (from step 1) is restarted at the 2-nd transmission domains (as shown in Figure 4). The only difference is constituted by the fact that the distance, required to evaluate the PAF, is measured with respect to the node from which a packet has been received, and not from the DP.
7. The propagation process is therefore constituted by multiple packet retransmissions, which continue at most till the end of the considered region—as will be clear in the following, with a probabilistic broadcasting protocol might stop the retransmission process might terminate before reaching the end of the network.

For more details about the IF protocol and its applications to urban junctions (with either traffic lights or roundabouts), the reader is referred to Busanelli, Ferrari, and Giorgio (2011).

OPTIMIZED PLACEMENT OF THE DISSEMINATION POINTS

In Trullols, Fiore, Casetti, Chiasserini, and Barcelo Ordinas (2010), the authors introduce a few algorithms that, on the basis of mobility traces, determine the optimal positions of a fixed number of DPs in a scenario constituted by a finite number of roads intersecting in a finite number of junctions. The algorithms only consider the road intersections as valid positions for the DPs, under the assumption that the number of DPs, denoted as k, is smaller than the number of the junctions. This assumption is clearly motivated in Trullols, Fiore, Casetti, Chiasserini, and Barcelo Ordinas (2010) and can be intuitively understood by observing that the vehicles spend (on average) a longer time in the proximity of intersections, rather than in the midst of a generic road segment.

Figure 4. The SH and IF propagation flows in the Parma scenario

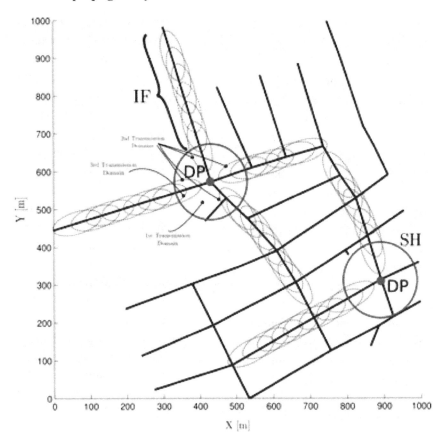

A mobility trace contains the discrete sequence of the movements of all the vehicles' transiting in the area of interest in a finite temporal interval. In order to have statistically meaningful information, a trace has to span a sufficiently long time interval. The mobility trace can be obtained either by means of experimental data or through numerical simulations, executed according to a statistically meaningful mobility model. In Trullols, Fiore, Casetti, Chiasserini, and Barcelo Ordinas (2010), the authors have used traces obtained from experimental traffic data. At the opposite, in our current work the mobility traces have been "artificially" generated using the SUMO simulator, in the manner described in the previous section.

In Trullols, Fiore, Casetti, Chiasserini, and Barcelo Ordinas (2010), the optimization of the DPs positions is performed in terms of two met-

rics, the coverage ratio and the coverage time. The former is defined as the ratio between the numbers of vehicles that experience at least one contact with a DP during the considered period, with respect to the number of vehicles in the scenario. From a communication viewpoint, as the coverage ratio increases, a larger number of vehicles is able to receive at least a packet from the DPs. The coverage time (dimension: [s]) is defined as the sojourn time of a vehicle within the transmission ranges of the DPs. The coverage time offers a rough estimation of the amount of information that can be transferred from the DPs to a certain vehicle. The actual amount of transferred data depends on a large series of factors (the fluctuations of the wireless channel, the data rate, the MAC protocol, the forwarding protocol), that has not been modeled in the framework. In order to assess the amount of transferred data, we introduce a suitable defined metric, improperly denoted as throughput, which is meaningful from a network-layer viewpoint. In fact, the throughput is defined as the ratio between the number of unique packets received by a given node, and the number of packets in the information block sent by the DPs (e.g., N_p).

The information offered by the considered mobility trace can be mapped in a couple of matrices. More specifically, denoting as V the number of vehicles contained in the input mobility trace, we introduce the following $N \times V$ matrix, denoted as $\mathbf{P}$, whose (i, j) element is defined as follows:

$$\mathbf{P}_{i,j} = \begin{cases} 1 \\ vehicle\_j\_crosses\_junction\_i \quad i = 1,...,V \quad j = 1,...,N \\ 0 \quad otherwise \end{cases}$$

Similarly, it is possible to introduce a $N \times V$ matrix, denoted as $\mathbf{T}$, whose (i, j) element represents the total time spent by the $j-$th vehicle under the coverage area of a DP hypothetically located at the intersection i.

In this work, we consider three of the algorithms originally introduced in Trullols, Fiore, Casetti, Chiasserini, and Barcelo Ordinas (2010), used to solve the following problems:

1. The Max Coverage Problem (MCP); and
2. The Knapsack Problem (KP) consist of the maximization of the number of contacts between the vehicles and at least a DP;
3. The Maximum Coverage with Time Threshold Problem (MCTTP) consists of the maximization of the number of vehicles that stay at least τ seconds in contact with a DP.

The algorithms used to solve the MCP and MCTTP assume to know the identity of the vehicles, while the algorithm used to solve the KP

is sub-optimal, since it needs to know only the number of vehicles that get in contact with the DPs, ignoring their identities. Given $\mathbf{T}$, $\mathbf{P}$, N, V, and τ, it is possible to solve the MCP, MCTTP, and KP by using the greedy approaches described in Trullols, Fiore, Casetti, Chiasserini, and Barcelo Ordinas (2010). With respect to the dissemination paradigm considered in our work, the minimum contact time τ considered in the MCTTP algorithm will be assumed to coincide with the duration of an information block.

In Figure 5, we show the optimized placement of the DPs obtained by executing, respectively, the MCP and the MCTTP algorithms in the Manhattan scenario, by considering $z = 100$m, several values of k (namely, 1, 4, 6, and 8), and two values of τ (namely, 3s and 30s). Obviously, the value of τ only affects the behavior of the MCTTP algorithm. It is interesting to observe that the MCTTP with $\tau = 3$s leads to the same DPs' configuration returned by the MCP algorithm. Figure 6 has been derived by considering the Parma scenario and the same set of parameters. In both scenarios, the width of a generic line is directly proportional to the average spatial vehicular density of the corresponding road (because of the internal structure of SUMO, the road between two junctions is typically composed by two distinct segments).

From Figure 5, it can be observed that the rightmost vertical roads and the upmost horizontal roads have a value of ρ_s^R significant higher than those of the other roads. For this reason, for small values of k, the MCP and MCTTP algorithms tend to concentrate in those roads the majority of the DPs. However, for increasing values of k the distribution of the DPs becomes "fairer." It can be also noted that the MCP and MCTTP algorithms lead to very different DPs architectures. From Figure 6, it can be observed that traffic tends to concentrate in a few, whereas most of the remaining roads tend to experience a limited vehicular traffic load. For this reason, in this scenario the differences between the MCP and MCTTP algorithms are less evident.

In order to evaluate the performance of the different DPs placement solutions, we first generate an independent mobility trace, with the same parameters of the SUMO simulator. In this case, we consider a shorter observation period with duration equal to $T_I = 60s$: this interval is selected in the center of the stationary region of the mobility trace, as shown in Figure 3. Then, we compute the approximated Cumulative Distribution Function (CDF) of the network coverage time, obtained by positioning the DPs according to the placements provided by the MCP, MCTTP, and KP algorithms, considering $z = 100m$, two values of τ (namely, 3s and 30s), and several values of k (namely, 1, 4, 6, and 8). The CDF of the coverage time can be derived in two easy step: (1) to collect in a histogram the coverage times experience by each vehicle transiting in the scenario during the interval T_I; (2) to normalize the histogram in order to obtain the PMF, and finally the CDF of the coverage time. The CDF of the throughput can be attained with a similar procedure.

The results obtained in the Manhattan scenario are shown in Figure 7, while those obtained in the Parma scenario are shown in Figure 8. As expected, in both scenarios the MCP and the MCTTP algorithms with $\tau = 3s$ lead to the same coverage time. In Figure 8, relative to the Parma scenario, there is a clear outcome: the MCP algorithm offers the best performance, the KP algorithm the worst (as expected), while the MCTTP algorithms with $\tau = 30s$ offers an intermediate performance level. In the Manhattan scenario, there is not a clear winner, especially in the case with a large value of k.

NUMERICAL ANALYSIS

IEEE 802.11 Implementation in ns-2

The last release of ns-2 (ns-2.34) contains two implementations of the IEEE standard, the default IEEE 802.11b module and a new IEEE 802.11p module, which differ in several aspects.

The default IEEE 802.11b module of ns-2 is not well coded and full of bugs. In particular, in, the authors have found several issues, not entirely fixed in the subsequent releases. In the current version there are still two main problems, both described in Schmidt-Eisenlohr, Letamendia-Murua, Torrent-Moreno, and Hartenstein (2006). The first is an incorrect management of the EIFS inter-frame after a collision, that leads to slightly better performance in congested networks. The second problem is related to the standard interpretation. As explained in Section 1.2.2, according to the IEEE 802.11 specifications a node should not enter in pre-backoff state if the channel is idle and it is sending the first frame of a burst or an isolated frame. The default IEEE 802.11b module of ns-2 acts differently. In particular, the senders always perform the pre-backoff wait even in sending an isolated packet and the channel is idle. This waste of time leads to slightly worse performance in non-congested scenarios, but it does not affect the saturated scenarios. On the other hand, it is beneficial in broadcast communications, since it avoids collisions in the first frames of the communication. We also remark that this approximation has been widely adopted in many theoretical studies (Oliveira, Bernardo, & Pinto, 2009).

The IEEE 802.11p module has been designed from scratch and simplements a completely revised architecture for the PHY and MAC modules (Chen, Schmidt-Eisenlohr, Jiang, Torrent-Moreno, Delgrossi, & Hartenstein, 2007). More precisely, the MAC layers models the basic DCF IEEE 802.11p mechanism, but without supporting the EDCA mechanism foresees by the IEEE 802.11p

Figure 5. The placement of the DPs in the Manhattan scenario, obtained by using the MCP and the MCTTP algorithms, by considering several values of k, namely, 1, 4, 6, and 8. The width of every line is proportional to the traffic density in the underlying road.

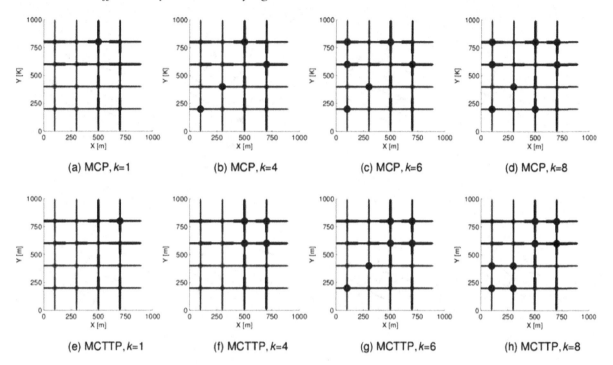

amendment. Therefore. using the IEEE 802.11p module the multi-channels features of the IEEE 802.11p/WAVE stack protocol cannot be simulated. We observe that in this implementation, the authors have correctly interpreted the standard, and hence, a node does non enter in the pre-backoff when sending the first frame of a burst. However, from the point of view of broadcast communications, the new implementation of the MAC behaves as the default IEEE 802.11 module. In fact, the reception of a frame is followed by a DIFS period, during which the receiver sees a busy channel. Therefore, in the case of a broadcast multihop protocol, all the retransmissions by the forwarder see a busy channel, and, hence, they always experience a pre-backoff. This happens as long the delay introduced by the higher layers is shorter than DIFS.

The PHY component of IEEE 802.11p module introduces a more advanced management of the interference, and of the phenomenon of "packet capturing." In particular, the PHY modules continuously tracks the cumulative received power comprehensive of both noise and signal(s), thus computing the Signal-to-Interference plus Noise Ratio (SINR) for every packet. A packet can be successfully decode if its SINR remains over a suitable threshold, associated to the used modulation format (i.e., 5 dB for Binary Phase Shift Keying, BPSK), for the entire packet duration. Unlike the standard module, the PHY module ignores the concept of receiving threshold, without assessing if the cumulative received power is over the carrier sense threshold, which is used to determine the status of the channel. done in the IEEE 802.11b module. We by-pass this problem by imposing that the carrier sense threshold value is identical to the sum of the modulation threshold (i.e., 5 dB for BPSK) and the noise power.

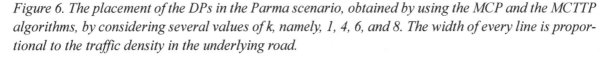

Figure 6. The placement of the DPs in the Parma scenario, obtained by using the MCP and the MCTTP algorithms, by considering several values of k, namely, 1, 4, 6, and 8. The width of every line is proportional to the traffic density in the underlying road.

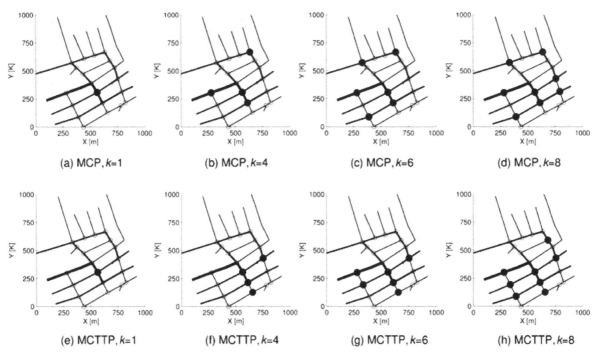

(a) MCP, *k*=1   (b) MCP, *k*=4   (c) MCP, *k*=6   (d) MCP, *k*=8

(e) MCTTP, *k*=1   (f) MCTTP, *k*=4   (g) MCTTP, *k*=6   (h) MCTTP, *k*=8

Simulation Setup

In this section, we analyze the performance of the considered urban scenarios, in terms of throughput and coverage ratio, by means of numerical simulations carried out with the ns-2 simulator (Network Simulator 2 [ns-2]). For the basic setup of simulations we assume that both the vehicles and the DPs are equipped with radio interfaces compliant with the IEEE 802.11b standard (IEEE, 2007), with a transmission range $z = 100$m, data rate $R = 1$Mbit/s, and different values of packet size $P = 10$, 100, 1000bytes. We set $T_1 = 60$s and we assume that each information block is constituted by 2.4Mbits. As a consequence of that, the number of packets for each information block is $N_p = 300$ packets.

In order to make the network simulation-based analysis more comprehensive, we made a comparison between IEEE 802.11b and IEEE 802.11p with Mac802_11Ext and WirelessPhy_Ext that are MAC and PHY layer extensions from IEEE 802.11a to IEEE 802.11p.

These extensions allows to correctly model the noise, the capture effect, the use of multiple modulation schemes.

It can be shown that when using a multihop broadcast protocol as IF, because of the contention of the channel and of the collisions due to the hidden terminal problem, the maximum sustainable data rate (e.g., with no packet losses) is approximately 80 Kbit/s. On the opposite, a SH protocol can support a much higher data rate (roughly equal to 800 Kbits/s) without packet losses.

Figure 7. CDF of the coverage time in the Manhattan scenario, obtained by considering the DPs placed according to the MCP, the MCTTP, and the KP algorithms, by considering different numbers of DPs, respectively, k=1, 4, 6, and 8, $z = 100$m, and two values of τ, respectively,3s and 30s

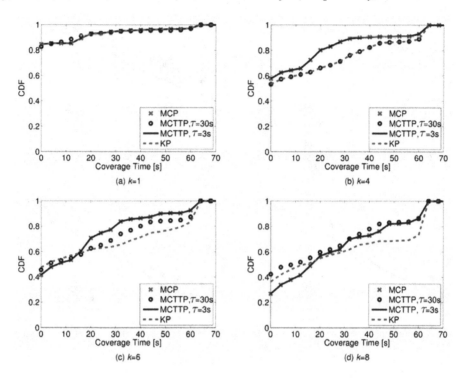

On the basis of the previous considerations, the simulations are carried out by considering 3 different parametric sets:

1. IF protocol with $\lambda = 10$ pck / s $(\tau = 30s)$,
2. SH protocol with $\lambda = 10$ pck / s $(\tau = 30s)$, and
3. SH protocol with $\lambda = 100$ pck / s $(\tau = 3s)$.

As previously explained, the identification of the DPs' optimized positions is based on a very long mobility trace, whereas the communication performance analysis is carried out by considering a portion of a (stable) mobility trace whose duration coincides with T_I. For this reason, in our ns-2 simulations we have considered the same mobility trace used in the previous section for deriving the CDF of the coverage time, with duration equal to $T_I = 60s$ and positioned in the

center of the steady region of a longer mobility trace, as shown in Figure 3.

Simulation Results

In Figure 9(a) and Figure 9(b), we show the coverage ratio obtained, respectively, in the Manhattan and Parma scenarios. It can be observed that in all cases the IF protocol offers a significantly higher throughput than the SH protocol. This is expected, as using probabilistic multi-hop forwarding around the "hot" (from a vehicular traffic perspective) junctions allows to reach a very large number of vehicles ("packed" around the junction). However, in both scenarios the coverage ratio with the IF protocol reaches a saturation value approximately at $k = 4$. This limit is almost equal to 1 in the Manhattan scenario, but it is much lower in the Parma scenario (roughly 0.75). This phenomenon can be interpreted as follows.

Figure 8. CDF of the coverage time in the Parma scenario, obtained by considering the DPs placed according to the MCP, the MCTTP, and the KP algorithms, by considering different numbers of DPs, respectively, k=1, 4, 6, and 8, $z = 100$m, and two values of τ, respectively, 3s and 30s

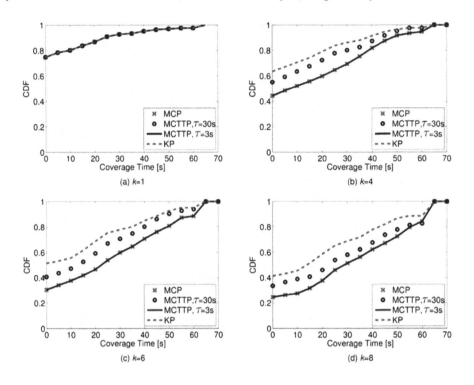

Figure 9. Coverage ratio as a function of k in the Parma scenario, obtained by considering the DPs placed according to the MCP, the MCTTP, and the KP algorithms, by considering different numbers of DPs, respectively, k=1, 4, 6, and 8, $z = 100$m, and two values of τ, respectively, 3s and 30s

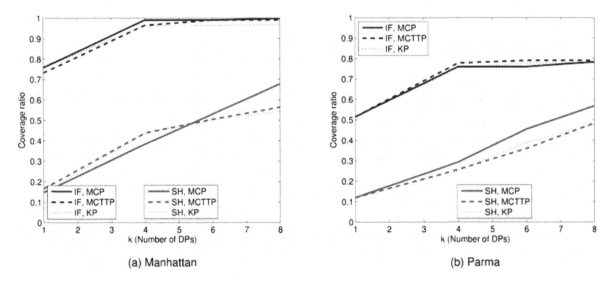

Figure 10. CDF of the throughput in the Manhattan scenario, obtained by considering the DPs placed according to the MCP and MCTTP algorithms, and by considering different numbers of DPs, respectively, k=1, 4, 6, and 8

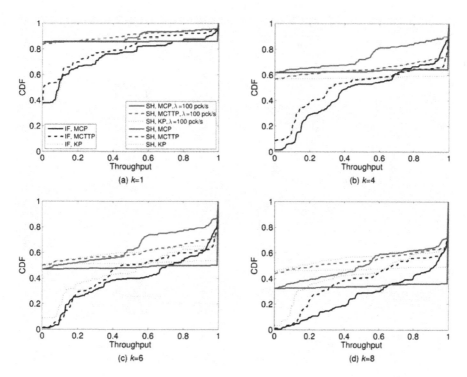

The Parma topology is irregular and, therefore, there is a significant number of roads with a small vehicular spatial density, which makes ineffective increasing the number of DPs, even under the use of multihop communication protocols. In other words, in the considered Parma scenario there are approximately 4 "hot" traffic junctions, whereas the remaining junctions do not experience a large vehicular flow: therefore, they contribute very little to information dissemination. In this case, the introduction of a fixed relays around the hot traffic junctions might represent a more effective solution to extend the coverage area guaranteed by the use of IF. It can be also observed that in the case of the SH protocol, the MCP algorithm tends to provide a higher coverage ratio in both scenarios, while when using the IF protocol the advantage is less significant. Finally, it is important to remark that the coverage ratio of the SH protocol is the same for both values of λ.

The coverage ratio gives an idea of the number of vehicles that get in contact with a DP at least once: as expected, the use of a multihop broadcast protocol is expedient to increase it. However, the coverage ratio does not provide any information concerning the quality of the connection between the DPs and the vehicles: in other words, it does not offer information about the effective amount of data that can be transferred. For this reason, we now move our attention to the throughput. In particular, in Figure 10 and Figure 11 we show the throughput obtained in the Manhattan and Parma scenarios, respectively, by considering the same parametric sets used in Figure 9.

From the results in Figure 10, the following considerations can be drawn.

• For a given value of λ, the IF protocol shows a significant advantage with respect to the SH protocol. However, if we con-

Figure 11. CDF of the throughput in the Parma scenario, obtained by considering the DPs placed according to the MCP, the MCTTP, and the KP algorithms, by considering different numbers of DPs, respectively, k=1, 4, 6, and 8, $z = 100$m, and two values of τ, respectively, 3s and 30s

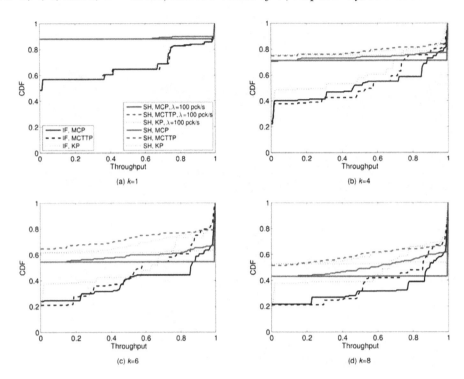

Figure 12. CDF of the throughput in the Parma scenario, obtained with the IF protocol and four DPs, with different values of packet size. Respectevely for the MCP and MCTTP algorithms, and a single value of τ 3s.

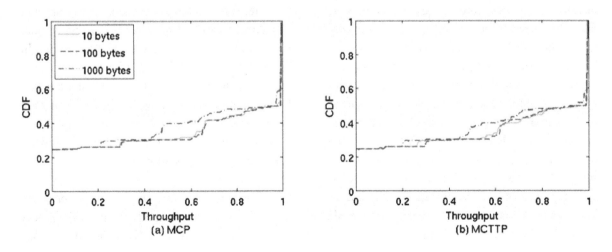

sider the SH protocol with a high value of λ (100 pck/s), the results change significantly. In fact, it turns out that the IF protocol allows to send at least a bit of information to almost all vehicles, but only a small fraction of them can receive the entire information content. On the contrary, the (SH, $\lambda = 100$ pck / s) configuration has a bi-stable behavior, in the sense that a vehicle is likely to receiver either no information at all or the entire information block. Therefore, depending on the application requirement, the SH solution could be preferable or vice-versa. For example, the (SH, $\lambda = 100$ pck / s) option is a better choice if the information block is a file, since all fragments are required. On the opposite, if the information block is associated to a media streaming, a small fraction of them can be sufficient, and IF is more appealing.

• As expected, in the SH configuration, the MCTTP is the algorithm providing (more or less) the best performance, while the KP offers the lowest throughput. On the contrary, when using the IF protocol, the MCP offers the best performance. This can

be easily justified by observing that the maximization of the coverage time by considering only SH communications, does not necessarily lead to the maximization of the coverage time by using multihop communications.

• Finally, by comparing the throughput CDFs obtained in the Parma and the Manhattan scenarios, it emerges that the former has a more irregular behavior, and this is due to the fact that the vehicles tend to be more clusterized than in the latter, where, instead, the vehicles distribution is slightly more homogeneous.

In Figure 12, we show the CDF of the throughput, for the Parma scenario in the case with 4 DPs, placed in according with the MCP and MCTTP algorithms—the KP case is similar to MCP case. We use different values of the packet size, namely 10, 100, and 1000 bytes. It can be observed that the performance, in both MCP and MCTTP cases, tends to remain similar regardless of the value of the packet size. Therefore, it can be concluded that the packet size has no influence on the network performance. This behavior is due to careful planning of the source position. The value of the

Figure 13. CDF of the throughput in the Parma scenario, obtained with the IF protocol and respectively for k=1 and 4 DPs, with a packet size P=1000bytes. For the MCP and MCTTP algorithms, and a single value of τ 3s.

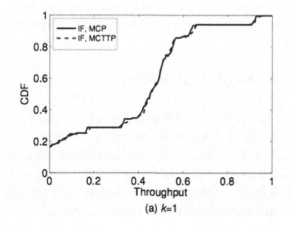

(a) *k*=1

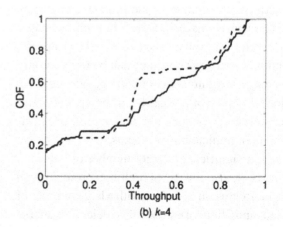

(b) *k*=4

packet size would have an impact if non-optimal sources placement was considered.

In the Figure 13, the CDF of the throughput is evaluated in the precence the Nakagami channel model, previously described. For this kind of simulation we used the same transmit power of the previous simulations, $P_{tx}=1$ mW. By comparing the performance of the Nakagami model with the Friis channel model, shown in Figure 11, it can be observed that the CDF in the Nakagami case increasis more rapidly than in the Friis case, even through the performances in both the scenarios are comparable.

The conclusion of the simulation analysis has shown that with optimized planning of the DPs the performance of the broadcast protocol, IF expecially with single hop communications, is not influenced by the choosen parameter and the channel model.

FUTURE RESEARCH DIRECTIONS

The problem of placing a fixed network of RSUs has been extensively analyzed in the domain of MANETs and cellular networks, but it still remains an open problem in VANETs, for the reasons illustrated in the following.

All the state-of-art DPs placement algorithms, including those considered in this work, tend to select the DPs positions in the proximity of intersections with a high traffic load, in order to maximize the number of the vehicles covered by SH transmissions of the DPs. While this technique is certainly optimal when using SH protocols, complete network coverage can be reached only placing a large number of DPs (e.g., one per junction). In this work, it has been shown that better results can be obtained by making use of multihop communications protocols, which allow to reach a significantly larger number of vehicles. However, also the use of multihop protocols can be ineffective in scenarios with a large number of roads and a limited number of vehicles (i.e., sparse

VANET scenarios). A possible countermeasure for coping with this problem consist in making use of some fixed relay nodes, not connected to the backbone network of the DPs and acting as bridges between different city areas connected by not sufficiently dense roads. According to these considerations, in the next future the algorithms currently available in the literature should be extended in order to encompass both the use of multihop broadcast protocols and the presence of fixed relay nodes. In fact, the optimized positions of relays tend to be typically different from the optimized DPs' positions.

CONCLUSION

In this book chapter, we have presented an overview of the approaches, recently proposed in the literature, for the identification of the optimal placement of strategy of fixed DPs in VANET-based urban communication scenarios. In particular, it has been shown that the approaches based on single-hop and multi-hop communications lead to very different performance. In particular, the SH approach guarantees a high QoS to a small number of vehicles, while the multihop approach offers a better average performance level. However in the latter case a very small number of vehicles experience a satisfactory dissemination service. The inclusion of fixed relay nodes, with intermediate characteristics between DPs and vehicles, is an appealing research direction for the design of efficient urban information dissemination systems.

ACKNOWLEDGMENT

The work of S. Busanelli is supported by the X-NETAD project sponsored by the Ministry of Foreign Affairs (Italy) and the Israeli Industry Center for R&D (Israel) under the "Israel-Italy Joint Innovation Program for Industrial, Scientific, and Technological Cooperation in R&D."

REFERENCES

Abdrabou, A., & Zhuang, W. (2011). Probabilistic delay control and road side unit placement for vehicular ad hoc networks with disrupted connectivity. *IEEE Journal on Selected Areas in Communications*, *29*, 129–139. doi:10.1109/JSAC.2011.110113

Banerjee, N., Corner, M. D., Towsley, D., & Levine, B. N. (2008). Relays, base stations, and meshes: Enhancing mobile networks with infrastructure. In *Proceedings of the ACM International Conference on Mobile Computing and Networking (MobiCom)*, (pp. 81-91). San Francisco, CA: ACM Press.

Busanelli, S., Ferrari, G., & Giorgio, V. A. (2011). I2V highway and urban vehicular networks: A comparative analysis of the impact of mobility on broadcast data dissemination. *The Journal of Communication*, *6*(1), 87–100.

Busanelli, S., Ferrari, G., & Panichpapiboon, S. (2009). Efficient broadcasting in IEEE 802.11 networks through irresponsible forwarding. In *Proceedings of the IEEE Global Telecommunications Conference (GLOBECOM)*, (pp. 1-6). Honolulu, HI: IEEE Press.

Bychkovsky, V., Hull, B., Miu, A., Balakrishnan, H., & Madden, S. (2006). A measurement study of vehicular internet access using in situ wi-fi networks. In *Proceedings of the International Conference on Mobile Computing and Networking (MobiCom)*, (pp. 50-61). San Francisco, CA: ACM Press.

Eriksson, J., Balakrishnan, H., & Madden, S. (2008). Cabernet: Vehicular content delivery using WiFi. In *Proceedings of the ACM International Conference on Mobile Computing and Networking (MobiCom)*, (pp. 199-210). San Francisco, CA: ACM Press.

IEEE. (2007). *IEEE Std 802.11TM-2007 part 11: Wireless LAN medium access control (MAC) and physical layer (PHY) specifications*. Washington, DC: IEEE Press.

Karnadi, F., Mo, Z. H., & Lan, K. C. (2007). Rapid generation of realistic mobility models for VANET. In *Proceedings of the IEEE Wireless Communications and Networking Conference (WCNC)*, (pp. 2506-2511). Hong Kong, China: IEEE Press.

Kone, V., Zheng, H., Rowstron, A., & Zhao, B. (2010). *The impact of infostation density on vehicular data dissemination*. Retrieved from http://www.cs.ucsb.edu/~ravenben/publications/pdf/vanet-monet10.pdf

Krauss, S., Wagner, P., & Gawron, C. (1997). Metastable states in a microscopic model of traffic flow. *Physical Review E: Statistical Physics, Plasmas, Fluids, and Related Interdisciplinary Topics*, *55*, 5597–5602. doi:10.1103/PhysRevE.55.5597

Leontiadis, I., Costa, P., & Mascolo, C. (2009). Persistent content-based information dissemination in hybrid vehicular networks. In *Proceedings on IEEE International Conference on Pervasive Computing and Communications*, (pp. 1-10). Galveston, TX: IEEE Press.

Lochert, C., Scheuermann, B., Caliskan, M., & Mauve, M. (2007). The feasibility of information dissemination in vehicular ad-hoc networks. In *Proceedings of the ACM International Conference on Wireless on Demand Network Systems*, (pp. 92-99). Obergurgl, Austria: ACM Press.

Malandrino, F., Casetti, C., Chiasserini, C.-F., & Fiore, M. (2011). Content downloading in vehicular networks: What really matters. In *Proceedings of the IEEE International Conference on Computer Communications (INFOCOM)*. Shangai, China: IEEE Press.

Network Simulator 2. (2011). *Website.* Retrieved from http://isi.edu/nsnam/ns/

Open Street Map. (2011). *Website.* Retrieved from http://www.openstreetmap.org

Ott, J., & Kutscher, D. (2004). Drive-thru internet: IEEE 802.11b for "automobile" users. In *Proceedings of the International Conference on Computer Communications (INFOCOM).* Hong Kong, China: IEEE Press.

SUMO Project. (2011). *Website.* Retrieved from http://sourceforge.net/projects/sumo/

Trullols, O., Fiore, M., Casetti, C., Chiasserini, C.-F., & Barcelo Ordinas, J. M. (2010). Planning roadside infrastructure for information dissemination in intelligent transportation systems. *Elsevier Computer Communications, 33,* 432–442.

Zhao, J., Zhang, Y., & Cao, G. (2007). Data pouring and buffering on the road: A new data dissemination paradigm for vehicular ad hoc networks. *IEEE Transactions on Vehicular Technology, 56,* 3266–3277. doi:10.1109/TVT.2007.906412

Zheng, Z., Lu, Z., Sinha, P., & Kumar, S. (2010). Maximizing the contact opportunity for vehicular internet access. In *Proceedings of the International Conference on Computer Communications (INFOCOM),* (pp. 1-9). San Diego, CA: IEEE Press.

Zheng, Z., Sinha, P., & Kumar, S. (2009). Alpha coverage: Bounding the interconnection gap for vehicular internet access. In *Proceedings of the International Conference on Computer Communications (INFOCOM),* (pp. 2831-2835). Rio de Janeiro, Brazil: IEEE Press.

ADDITIONAL READING

Barberis, C., & Malnati, G. (2011). Design and evaluation of a collaborative system for content diffusion and retrieval in vehicular networks. *IEEE Transactions on Consumer Electronics, 57,* 105–112. doi:10.1109/TCE.2011.5735489

Byers, J., Luby, M., & Mitzenmacher, M. (2002). A digital fountain approach to asynchronous reliable multicast. *IEEE Journal on Selected Areas in Communications, 20,* 1528–1540. doi:10.1109/JSAC.2002.803996

Cataldi, P., Tomatis, A., Grilli, G., & Gerla, M. (2009). CORP: Cooperative rateless code protocol for vehicular content dissemination. In *Proceedings of the IFIP Mediterranean Ad Hoc Networking Workshop (Med-Hoc-Net),* (pp. 1-7). Haifa, Israel: IEEE Press.

Cesana, M., Fratta, L., Gerla, M., Giordano, E., & Pau, G. (2010). C-VeT the UCLA campus vehicular testbed: Integration of VANET and mesh networks. In *Proceedings of the IEEE International Conference on European Wireless (EW),* (pp. 689-695). Lucca, Italy: IEEE Press.

Chaintreau, A., Mtibaa, A., Massoulie, L., & Diot, C. (2007). The diameter of opportunistic mobile networks. In *Proceedings of the ACM International Conference on Emerging Networking Experiments and Technologies,* (pp. 12:1-12:12). New York, NY: ACM Press.

Chen, B. B., & Chan, M. C. (2009). MobTorrent: A framework for mobile internet access from vehicles. In *Proceedings of the International Conference on Computer Communications (INFOCOM),* (pp. 1404-1412). Rio de Janeiro, Brazil: IEEE Press.

Conceicao, H., Ferreira, M., & Barros, J. (2008). On the urban connectivity of vehicular sensor networks. *Distributed Computing in Sensor Systems, 5067*, 112–125. doi:10.1007/978-3-540-69170-9_8

Dubey, B. B., Chauhan, N., & Awasthi, L. K. (2011). *NILDD: Nearest intersection location dependent dissemination of traffic information in VANETs*. New York, NY: ACM Press.

Fiore, M., & Harri, J. (2008). The networking shape of vehicular mobility. In *Proceedings of the ACM International Symposium on Mobile Ad Hoc Networks and Computers (MOBIHOC)*, (pp. 261-272). Hong Kong, China: ACM Press.

Gass, R., & Diot, C. (2010). Eliminating backhaul bottlenecks for opportunistically encountered wi-fi hotspots. In *Proceedings of IEEE International Conference on Vehicular Technology (VTC-Spring)*, (pp. 1-5). Taipei, Taiwan: IEEE Press.

Goodman, D., Borras, J., Mandayam, N., & Yates, R. (1997). Infostations: A new system model for data and messaging services. In *Proceedings of the IEEE Conference on Vehicular Technology (VTC)*, (pp. 969-973). Phoenix, AZ: IEEE Press.

Hartenstein, H., & Laberteaux, K. (2009). *VANET vehicular applications and inter-networking technologies*. New York, NY: John Wiley & Sons, Ltd.

Kone, V., Zheng, H., Rowstron, A., & Zhao, B. (2010). On infostation density of vehicular networks. In *Proceedings of the ICST Conference on Wireless Internet Conference (WICON)*, (pp. 1-9). Singapore, Singapore: IEEE Press.

Krohn, M., Daher, R., Arndt, M., & Tavangarian, D. (2009). Aspects of roadside backbone networks. In *Proceedings of IEEE International Conference on Wireless Communication, Vehicular Technology*, (pp. 788-792). Aalborg, Denmark: IEEE Press.

Lee, J., & Kim, C. (2010). A roadside unit placement scheme for vehicular telematics networks. *Advances in Computer Science and Information Technology, 6059*, 196–202. doi:10.1007/978-3-642-13577-4_17

Lee, J., Park, G., Kwak, H., Lee, S., & Kang, M. (2010). Design of a reliable wireless switch for the intersection area on vehicular telematics networks. In *Proceedings of the Advanced Communication and Networking Conference*, (pp. 1-8). IEEE Press.

Lee, S., Pan, G., Park, J., Gerla, M., & Lu, S. (2007). Secure incentives for commercial ad dissemination in vehicular networks. In *Proceedings of the ACM International Symposium on Mobile Ad Hoc Networking and Computing*, (pp. 150-159). Montreal, Canada: ACM Press.

Lochert, C., Scheuermann, B., Wewetzer, C., Luebke, A., & Mauve, M. (2008). Data aggregation and roadside unit placement for a vanet traffic information system. In *Proceedings of the ACM International Workshop on VehiculAr Inter-NETworking (VANET)*, (pp. 58-65). San Francisco, CA: ACM Press.

Mershad, K., & Artail, H. (2010). Using RSUs as delegates for pervasive access to services in vehicle ad hoc networks. In *Proceedings of the IEEE International Conference on Telecommunications (ICT)*, (pp. 790-797). Doha, Qatar: IEEE Press.

Nadeem, T., Dashtinezhad, S., Liao, C., & Iftode, L. (2004). TrafficView: Traffic data dissemination using car-to-car communication. *ACM SIGMOBILE Mobile Computing and Communications Review, 8*, 6–19. doi:10.1145/1031483.1031487

Nekovee, M. (2009). Epidemic algorithms for reliable and efficient information dissemination in vehicular ad hoc networks. *Intelligent Transport Systems, 3*, 104–110. doi:10.1049/iet-its:20070061

Pant, C. N. (2011). Effect of position of fixed infrastructure on data dissemination in VANETs. *International Journal of Research and Reviews in Computer Science, 2*, 482–486.

Sardari, M., Hendessi, F., & Fekri, F. (2009). Infocast: A new paradigm for collaborative content distribution from roadside units to vehicular networks. In *Proceedings of the IEEE Communications Society Conference on Sensor, Mesh*, (pp. 1-9). Rome, Italy: IEEE Press.

Sardari, M., Hendessi, F., & Fekri, F. (2010). DDRC: Data dissemination in vehicular networks using rateless codes. *Journal of Information Science and Engineering, 26*, 867–881.

Scheuermann, B., Lochert, C., Rybicki, J., & Mauve, M. (2009). A fundamental scalability criterion for data aggregation in VANETs. In *Proceedings of the ACM International Conference on Mobile Computing and Networking (MobiCom)*, (pp. 285-296). Beijing, China: ACM Press.

Schoch, E., Kargl, F., Weber, M., & Leinmuller, T. (2008). Communications patterns in VANETs. *Communication Magazine, 46*, 2–8.

Sollazzo, G., Musolesi, M., & Mascolo, C. (2007). TACO-DTN: A time-aware content-based dissemination system for delay tolerant networks. In *Proceedings of the International Workshop on Mobile Opportunistic Networking (MobiSys)*, (pp. 83-90). San Juan, Puerto Rico: ACM Press.

Stefanović, C. A. (2011). Urban infrastructure-to-vehicle traffic data dissemination using UEP rateless codes. *IEEE Journal on Selected Areas in Communications, 29*, 94–102. doi:10.1109/JSAC.2011.110110

Taheri, M., & Hendesi, F. (2011). Disseminating a large amount of data to vehicular network in an urban area. *International Journal of Vehicular Technology, 1*, 3.

Tan, W. L., Lau, W. C., Yue, O., & Hui, T. H. (2011). Analytical models and performance evaluation of drive-thru internet systems. *IEEE Journal on Selected Areas in Communications, 29*, 207–222. doi:10.1109/JSAC.2011.110120

Tomar, P., Chaurasia, B. K., & Tomar, G. S. (2010). State of the art of data dissemination in VANETs. *International Journal of Computer Theory and Engineering, 2*, 957–962.

Wang, T., Xing, G., Li, M., & Jia, W. (2010). Efficient wifi deployment algorithms based on realistic mobility characteristics. In *Proceedings of International Conference on Mobile Adhoc and Sensor Systems (MASS)*, (pp. 422-431). San Francisco, CA: IEEE Press.

Wischhof, L., Ebner, A., & Rohling, H. (2005). Information dissemination in self-organizing intervehicle networks. *IEEE Transactions on Intelligent Transportation Systems, 6*, 90–101. doi:10.1109/TITS.2004.842407

Wu, C., & Li, B. (2007). Outburst: Efficient overlay content distribution with rateless codes. *Networking 2007: Ad Hoc and Sensor Networks, Wireless Networks & Next Generation Internet, 4479*, 1208–1216.

Yi, C., Chuang, Y., Yeh, H., Tseng, Y., & Liu, P. (2010). Streetcast: An urban broadcast protocol for vehicular ad-hoc networks. In *Proceedings of IEEE International Conference on Vehicular Technology (VTC-Spring)*, (pp. 1-5). Taipei, Taiwan: IEEE Press.

Zhao, J., Arnold, T., Zhang, Y., & Cao, G. (2008). Extending drive-thru data access by vehicle-to-vehicle relay. In *Proceedings of the ACM International Workshop on VehiculAr InterNETworking (VANET)*, (pp. 66-75). San Francisco, CA: ACM Press.

Zhuang, Y., Pan, J., & Cai, L. (2010). A probabilistic model for message propagation in two-dimensional vehicular ad-hoc networks. In *Proceedings of the ACM International Workshop on VehiculAr InterNETworking (VANET),* (pp. 31-40). Chicago, IL: ACM Press.

KEY TERMS AND DEFINITIONS

Broadcast Protocol: A forwarding network protocol that allows transmitting information from a source to all the nodes of a given network, thus yielding to one-to-many communications. In this context, the definition of "network" is a broad concept that depends on the requirements of the applications of interest.

Coverage Ratio: The ratio between the number of vehicles that experience at least one contact with a DP (during the considered observation period) and the number of vehicles in the network.

Coverage Time: For a given observation period it is given by the time spent by a node under the coverage areas of all DPs during the considered observation period.

Dissemination Point (DP): A RSU in charge of disseminating information to the transiting vehicles in its proximity.

Mobility Simulator: Software that predicts the movements of a group of vehicles in a given environment, on the basis of approximate physical and behavioral models. The list of the generated movements can be saved in a database to be further analyzed or used by another (network) simulator.

Multi-Hop Broadcast Protocol: A broadcast protocol that foresees an active role for the network nodes that are supposed to forward to their neighbor, all received packet. In these protocols, the path covered by a packet is composed by multi-hop transmissions.

Network Simulator: A software that predicts the performance of a network (without an actual network being present), by considering an approximate behavioral model of the network nodes.

Probabilistic Broadcast Protocol: A multihop broadcast protocol, such that the network nodes probabilistically decide to participate to the forwarding process.

Relay: A RSU that does not generate information on its own, but that can only forward the received information.

Road Side Unit (RSU): A fixed network node, usually located beside a road infrastructure, which could coordinate or belong to a VANET.

Throughput: The ratio between the number of packets received by a given node and the number of packets in the information block sent by the DPs.

Vehicular Ad-Hoc NETwork (VANET): It is a particular type of mobile ad-hoc network, and its main feature is to provide communications among vehicles and between vehicles and fixed wireless nodes.

Chapter 13
Infrastructure Assisted Data Dissemination for Vehicular Sensor Networks in Metropolitan Areas

Ayşegül Tüysüz Erman
University of Twente, The Netherlands

Arta Dilo
University of Twente, The Netherlands

Ramon S. Schwartz
University of Twente, The Netherlands

Hans Scholten
University of Twente, The Netherlands

Paul Havinga
University of Twente, The Netherlands

ABSTRACT

Vehicular Sensor Networks (VSNs) are an emerging area of research that combines technologies developed in the domains of Intelligent Transport Systems (ITS) and Wireless Sensor Networks. Data dissemination is an important aspect of these networks. It enables vehicles to share relevant sensor data about accidents, traffic load, or pollution. Several protocols are proposed for Vehicle to Vehicle (V2V) communication, but they are prone to intermittent connectivity. In this chapter, the authors propose a roadside infrastructure to ensure stable connectivity by adding vehicle to infrastructure to the V2V communication. They introduce a data dissemination protocol, Hexagonal Cell-Based Data Dissemination, adapting it for VSNs within a metropolitan area. The virtual architecture of the proposed data dissemination protocol exploits the typical radial configuration of main roads in a city, and uses them as the basis for the communication infrastructure where data and queries are stored. The design of the communication infrastructure in accordance with the road infrastructure distributes the network data in locations that are close or easily reachable by most of the vehicles. The protocol performs a geographical routing and is suitable for highly dynamic networks, supporting a high number of mobile sources and destinations of data. It ensures reliable data delivery and fast response. The authors evaluate the performance of the proposed protocol in terms of data delivery ratio and data delivery delay. The simulation results show that HexDD significantly improves the data packet delivery ratio in VANETs.

DOI: 10.4018/978-1-4666-2223-4.ch013

INTRODUCTION

Traditionally, towns were built in a very specific fashion. In the center would be the church or town hall and a market square, surrounded by one or more circular roads. A number of radial roads would allow visitors to travel from the city gates in the outer wall to the center. Many modern European cities reflect this old city plan in their current street layout. And still the old circular and radial roads are the main traffic arteries in the city. Figure 1 shows the map of the city of Enschede in the Netherlands that clearly illustrates these characteristics. If one had to choose where to build a communication infrastructure in support of vehicular networks in metropolitan areas, these roads would be the prime candidates. As it is, potential support for such networks is scattered over the city in the form of GSM base stations, Wi-Fi hotspots, traffic light and the likes (see Figure 2). The result of this haphazard infrastructure is that some parts of the city have dense communication coverage while other parts have limited coverage or no coverage at all.

In the following, we propose a sensing and communication infrastructure, in support of a data dissemination protocol for Vehicular Sensor Networks (VSNs). The infrastructure consists of lampposts that are equipped with small transceivers and sensors, positioned along roads at roughly equal distances, in addition to the existing communication and traffic control infrastructure. Such implementation has many advantages. The lampposts are already in place and no new mechanical constructions to attach the radio nodes to are needed. Electricity is present in every lamppost and is available to power up the transceivers at minimal additional costs. Because existing utilities are used, disruptions during deployment are kept to a minimum.

These roadside wireless sensors form a typical static Wireless Sensor Network (WSN), which provides a full and stable coverage of a city area. This WSN has advantages compared to a vehicular network whose coverage depends on the traffic situation and is usually unevenly distributed over a city. Vehicles together with roadside sensor nodes form a hybrid network that can serve many ap-

Figure 1. OpenStreetMap of Enschede centre overlaid with a hexagonal tessellation of cell size around 70 meters

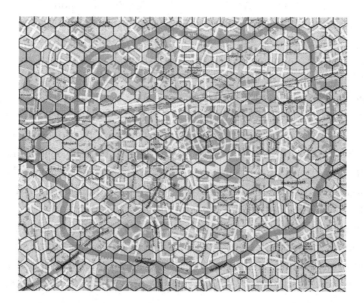

Figure 2. Virtual infrastructure of the hexagonal tessellation (white cells) overlaid on the existing infrastructure nodes; covered cells are shaded

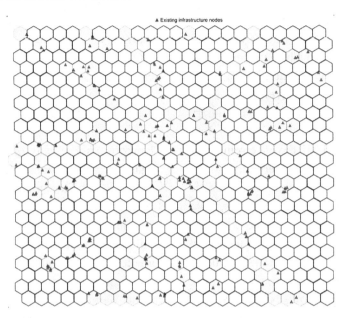

plications, such as traffic monitoring and control, environmental monitoring, and safety warning. The proposed data dissemination protocol, called Hexagonal cell-based Data Dissemination (Hex-DD), can be used by these applications.

HexDD protocol was originally created for mission critical WSN applications (Tuysuz-Erman, et al., 2010), and is suitable for highly dynamic networks. The protocol is built upon a virtual hexagonal tessellation of the network area (see Figure 1). The hexagonal tessellation creates a circular structure on the city, starting from the centre, and spreading with hexagonal rings to the end of the city. Three main diagonals crossing at the centre of the city partition its area into equal parts. These three virtual lines together with a hexagonal ring (see Figure 2) form the virtual infrastructure of the HexDD protocol. The layout of this virtual infrastructure is a close approximation of a city street layout, with the main diagonals being the (main) radial roads of the city and the hexagonal ring defined by the inner ring of the city. The HexDD protocol performs routing of data and query messages by exploiting the main roads

infrastructure as a communication infrastructure. The protocol provides for routing of messages, queries, or event data, without elaborating on different types or structure of information, neither on data aggregation.

We adapt the protocol for the hybrid WSN and vehicular network, and evaluate its performance in terms of latency and reliability of data delivery. The protocol is compared with a classical non-position-based ad hoc routing protocol, AODV (Perkins, Belding-Royer, & Das, 2003), and a position-based ad hoc routing protocol, GPSR (Karp & Kung, 2000).

The remainder of this chapter is organized as follows. Section 2 summarizes existing data dissemination protocols on vehicular sensor networks, together with other relevant work. The section 3 describes Vehicular Ad hoc NETworks (VANETs) applications that can benefit from the proposed protocol, followed by a realistic scenario. Section 4 elaborates further on the proposed sensing and communication infrastructure and its relation with the virtual infrastructure of the protocol. Section 5 explains the Hexagonal tessellation and Hexagonal cell-based Data Dissemination protocol. Finally, Section 6 shows the performance of the proposed data dissemination protocol, compared with other classical methods by simulations.

RELATED WORK

VANETs are a type of Mobile Ad Hoc Networks (MANETs) used for communication among vehicles and between vehicles and Roadside Units (RSUs). Since the operational principles of MANETs and VANETs resemble, most of the routing algorithms that were applicable to MANETs have been considered from VANETs, and modified for their high-speed mobility and the unpredictable nature of their movement. In a general context, routing protocols proposed for MANETs can be classified into two main categories: topology-based and geographical routing protocols (Misra, Woungang, & Misra, 2009). Topology-based routing protocols exploit topological connectivity information about the network links to establish and maintain source-destination paths. In this category, protocols are mostly classified as being either proactive or reactive.

In networks utilizing a proactive routing protocol, every node maintains one or more routing tables representing the entire topology of the network. These tables are updated regularly by means of data exchange between nodes to maintain up-to-date routing information. This process can lead to a high overhead on the network. One example of a proactive protocol is the Destination-Sequenced Distance-Vector routing (DSDV) (Perkins & Bhagwat, 1994). DSDV is based on the Bellman-Ford algorithm, however, with several modifications to make it suitable for a dynamic and self-starting network mechanism. In particular, it solves the routing loop problem. In the protocol, each entry in the routing table contains a sequence number generated by the destination, and the emitter needs to send out the

next update with this number. Routing information is distributed between nodes by sending full dumps infrequently, and smaller incremental updates more frequently.

In contrast, reactive routing protocols only initiate a route discovery process when a route to a destination is required. This leads to a higher latency compared with proactive protocols, however, with the benefit of a lower overhead. One example of protocols in this class is the Ad Hoc On-Demand Distance Vector Routing (AODV) (Perkins, Belding-Royer, & Das, 2003). In AODV, a route is created on demand when a source node wants to communicate with a destination node. The route creation involves flooding a route request message and establishing, at each hop, a backward pointer (the last transmitter of the request) to the source. A reply is unicast along this path by using the backward pointers while establishing forward pointers to the destination.

In the second class of MANET protocols are the geographical routing protocols. Geographical routing relies on the geographical position of nodes to forward a packet to its destination. Because only local information is required, they do not require the establishment or maintenance of end-to-end path. In this class is the Greedy Perimeter Stateless Routing (GPSR) (Karp & Kung, 2000). GPSR uses greedy geographical forwarding from the source node to the destination node. When a node cannot find a neighbor node that is closer to the destination position than itself, a recovery strategy based on planar graph traversal is applied.

Although VANETs are a special case of MANETs, the solutions proposed for MANETs do not take into account specific characteristics of vehicular environments such as intermittent connectivity and the high mobility of nodes. For these reasons, several data dissemination solutions have been proposed specifically for vehicular environments. In the remainder of this section, we review the current state-of-the-art of data dissemination protocols in VANETs by organizing recent works in two categories: infrastructure-less and infrastructure-assisted. The former comprises solutions that deal purely with Vehicle-to-Vehicle (V2V) communication while the latter includes solutions that make use of both vehicle-to-vehicle and Vehicle-to-Infrastructure (V2I) communication.

Infrastructure-Less

In the context of infrastructure-less protocols, various solutions aim to cope with message dissemination under different traffic conditions. In dense scenarios, suppression techniques have been proposed to address the so-called broadcast storm problem. For a given broadcast message, solutions for this problem consist in finding the minimum set of nodes capable of reaching all other nodes in the network. If only nodes in this set broadcast this message, redundancy is kept to a minimum. Current solutions in MANETs are generally not optimal for VANET scenarios, especially due to the intermittent connectivity present in VANETs. Therefore, a few suppression techniques have been proposed specifically for VANETs. In Wisitpongphan et al. (2007), three broadcast suppression techniques are proposed and used in the network layer. These techniques called as Persistence Broadcasting are either time-based or probabilistic, and seek to suppress redundant rebroadcasts.

In sparse networks, the Distributed Vehicular Broadcast (DV-CAST) protocol (Tonguz, Nawaporn Wisitpongphan, & Fan Bai, 2010), the Simple and Robust Dissemination Protocol (SRD) (Schwartz, Barbosa, Meratnia, Geert Heijenk, & Scholten, 2011) and the Acknowledged Parameterless Broadcast in Static to Highly Mobile (ackPBSM) (Ros, Ruiz, & Stojmenovic, 2009) present networking solutions based on the store-carry-forward principle. DV-CAST aims to adapt its mechanism to different traffic densities. Likewise, SRD is able to operate in both sparse and dense networks and outperforms DV-CAST in terms of delivery ratio and robustness. This is achieved by using an optimized suppression technique in dense scenarios and a robust store-carry-forward protocol in sparse networks. The ackPBSM protocol relies on the use of Connected Dominating Sets (CDS) to perform the broadcast. In contrast to a directional broadcast utilized by DV-CAST and SRD, it aims to spread messages to all the surrounding neighbors.

To further improve the delivery ratio, context information was used in Kosch, Adler, Eichler, Schroth, and Strassberger (2006) and Lee and Gerla (2010). The work in Kosch et al. (2006) presents a relevance-based, altruistic communication scheme, which helps achieve scalability by optimizing the application benefit and the bandwidth usage. The benefit refers to how useful the data is to neighboring nodes according to the application managing this data, and it is calculated by considering the current context and the content of the messages. In Lee and Gerla (2010), the use of opportunistic network concepts in vehicular environments is proposed. Authors examine their opportunistic geographical routing, GeoDTN+Nav, in two examples of opportunistic routing scenarios: delay tolerant geo-inspired routing, and real time video stream multicast. Emergency related multimedia reports are sent to vehicles in disconnected platoons using network coding.

Furthermore, various applications have been proposed with the use of data dissemination schemes in VANETs. The Abiding Geocast, described in Yu and Heijenk (2008), disseminates and keeps accident or congestion information to every vehicle passing through a warning zone during the event lifetime. In Schwartz et al. (2010), authors propose the Over-the-Horizon Awareness (OTHA) protocol that provides an extended view of the traffic ahead to Driver Support Systems (DSS). The protocol relies on periodic messages sent by each vehicle. These messages are disseminated in a multi-hop fashion to other vehicles located in the road upstream, and the speed profile of the current traffic is built collaboratively.

The work in Casteigts, Nayak, and Stojmenovic (2009) addresses the main aspects of vehicular communication such as the intelligent transportation system architecture, traffic models, and existing data dissemination protocols.

Infrastructure-Assisted

The quality of services relying on vehicle-to-vehicle communication will largely depend on the available network connectivity. Therefore, especially at an initial stage of vehicular technology deployment, infrastructure will play an important role in improving the delivery ratio in sparse networks. At the time of writing, just a few solutions have proposed the use of infrastructure to assist vehicular network protocols. In the following, we describe some of these efforts.

The use of infrastructure to improve reliability in multi-hop routing in vehicular networks was proposed in Borsetti and Gozalvez (2010), He, Rutagemwa, and Shen (2008), and Shrestha, Moh, Chung, and Choi (2010). The work presented in Borsetti and Gozalvez (2010) introduces a simple and new graph representation of the road-topology map. It takes into account the relaying capabilities of roadside units for multi-hop vehicular communications, and that can be applied to existing topology-aware routing protocols. Rather than proposing a routing protocol, authors focus on the assistance of geo-routing protocols by considering roadside units with high bandwidth, high transmission range, and all interconnected through a backbone. In He et al. (2008), two novel notions are introduced to cope with link failures in vehicular networks: virtual equivalent node and differentiated reliable path. These notions are used to design the on-demand Differentiated Reliable Routing (DRR) protocol. DRR relies on both roadside units and vehicle-to-vehicle communication to adaptively discover a sufficient number of link-disjoint paths to meet the application's specific reliability. To cope with frequent disconnections in vehicular networks, the work

in Shrestha et al. (2010) presents a multi-hop vehicle-to-infrastructure routing protocol, named Vertex-Based Predictive Greedy Routing (VPGR). VPGR predicts a sequence of valid vertices leveraging contextual information to forward data from a source vehicle to the infrastructure.

Also with the focus on routing, authors in Lim and Ko (2010), Peng, Abichar, and Chang (2006), and Piran (2010) aim to improve efficiency in terms of amount of data exchanged, overhead, and energy, respectively. In Lim and Ko (2010), authors propose the Multi-Hop Data Harvesting (MDH). MDH is a data-harvesting scheme that focuses on supporting applications that require multi-hop communication, such as real-time applications. In this scheme, vehicles make use of roadside sensors to send data requests and to receive data from multiple sensors. Furthermore, a data aggregation technique is used to cope with a high amount of data when using geocasting. In Peng et al. (2006), a novel routing approach, called RAR (Roadside-Aided Routing), is introduced. The proposed approach affiliates each vehicle to a sector, defined as the affiliation unit that is a road area bounded by neighboring RSUs. This can reduce significantly the affiliation overhead compared to other methods that use the concept of clusters. The protocol is also based on a single-phase routing scheme. Basically, two vehicles close to each other tend to communicate directly via ad hoc networks, whereas two vehicles close to RSUs or in different sectors tend to communicate via RSUs. The roadside units are assumed to be connected with each other by wired links or any links with high bandwidth, low delay, and low bit error rate. Therefore, the routing performance is improved by limiting ad hoc routing in a small scope, and utilizing a wired backbone network.

In contrast to routing, several works have been presented with solutions for disseminating data to multiple vehicles. In Zhao, Zhang, & Cao (2007), a data pouring and buffering paradigm for data dissemination in VANETs is proposed. Two schemes are introduced: Data Pouring (DP) and DP with Intersection Buffering (DP-IB). In DP, a data center in the infrastructure periodically broadcasts data to be disseminated and relayed by moving vehicles to pour the desired area. In DP-IB, the data poured from the source are buffered and rebroadcast at intersections. Authors in Trullols, Fiore, Casetti, Chiasserini, and Barcelo Ordinas (2010) consider the problem of deploying a given number of infrastructure nodes for disseminating information to vehicles in an urban area. The problem is formulated as a Maximum Coverage Problem (MCP) having as objective maximizing the number of vehicles in contact with infrastructure nodes. To provide a treatable solution, authors propose heuristic algorithms, which present different levels of complexity and knowledge.

To increase network connectivity in sparse networks, authors in Chawathe (2006) and Lok, Qazi, and Elmirghani (2009) proposed schemes with dropboxes. In Chawathe (2006), authors address the problem of disseminating data in sparse vehicular networks by using *dead drops* (dead letter boxes). Dead drops are wireless transceivers with storage capability that are not interconnected or connected to other network infrastructure. Such boxes, also known as dropboxes, can be used to both send and receive data to vehicles, in order to improve the overall network connectivity. This work presents a study of the optimum placement of dead drops in road intersections, and introduces an efficient greedy approximation algorithm called MCDD as a solution for such placement. The use of dropboxes is also discussed in Lok et al. (2009). Authors present a study of the impact of the following parameters when disseminating data with the help of dropboxes: end-to-end delay and Packet Dropping Probability (PDP), by varying the number of vehicles. In the same area of research, in Lochert, Scheuermann, Wewetzer, Luebke, and Mauve (2008) authors tackle both the problems of limited bandwidth and minimal initial deployment. An aggregation scheme is introduced to cope with the limited bandwidth. On the other hand,

by means of a genetic algorithm, the positions for placing static roadside units are identified.

A general discussion on using sensors in vehicular environments was presented in Lee and Gerla (2010) and Nekovee (2005). In Nekovee (2005), authors discuss unique features and challenges that distinguish vehicular sensor networks from other types of ad hoc sensor networks. In addition, possible applications of wireless grids in addressing data aggregation and processing challenges are considered. In Lee and Gerla (2010), authors survey the recent vehicular sensor network developments and identify new trends. Aspects such as how sensor information is collected, stored, and harvested are evaluated considering both uses of V2V and V2I communications.

Network architectures for VSNs were subject of study in Festag et al. (2008) and Gao et al. (2010). The use of a hybrid ITS safety architecture is proposed in Festag et al. (2008). The architecture combines both vehicle-to-vehicle and vehicle-to-infrastructure sensor communication. Roadside units are connected to wireless sensor networks, thereby reducing deployment costs compared to installing dedicated roadside units. Among potential services of the hybrid communication system, the work introduces accident prevention and post-accident investigation. In addition, the main components of the system, namely, radio, networking and services, and security are described. Likewise, in Gao et al. (2010), a similar architecture is proposed with sensor nodes deployed along the roadside to collect environmental data such as data on highway conditions (e.g. potholes, cracks on the road, ice on the road, and blind spots ahead). However, the focus is on a secure data collection of such data. To achieve security, a secure symmetric key-based protocol is designed and validated with real trace data through a real implementation. The work described in Salhi, Cherif, and Senouci (2008) focuses on an architecture where an ad hoc network is operated by a telecommunication provider. The goal is to combine non-valuable individual data sensed by each vehicle, in order to obtain an overview about road conditions in a certain geographical area. The aggregated information is then sent back to a roadside unit owned by the operator via a non-free frequency (WiMax or 2.5/3G). To reduce the use of high-cost links, authors present the Clustered Gathering Protocol (CGP).

With the goal of monitoring the condition of road networks, the work described in De Zoysa, Keppitiyagama, Seneviratne, and Shihan (2007) presents BusNet, which is a public transport system (i.e. buses) equipped with acceleration sensors to monitor the road surface. The same application is proposed in Eriksson et al. (2008). A system referred to as the Pothole Patrol (P2) exploits the mobility of vehicles to opportunistically gather data from vibration and GPS sensors, and process the data to assess road surface conditions. By using a machine-learning approach, authors study the viability of the system to identify potholes and other road surface anomalies from accelerometer data. Related to this works is the research presented in Wong, Chua, and Qingyun Li (2009). Authors use wireless vehicular sensor networks for environmental monitoring. Experiments carried out with a sensor platform for air-quality monitoring demonstrate an improved spatial coverage when using vehicular sensors over static sensors. In Murty et al. (2008), an open urban-scale testbed is introduced, in the effort to support novel research and application developments in wireless and vehicular sensor networks. The testbed called CitySense consists of several Linux-based embedded PCs outfitted with dual 802.11 a/b/g radios and various sensors, mounted on buildings and streetlights across the city of Cambridge.

Comparisons

Table 1 gives an overview of the abovementioned works that are more similar to our proposal in this chapter. From this overview, we can outline that existing approaches propose either a routing strategy or architecture for VANET applications. There is only one combined effort of routing and infrastructure (i.e. RAR) which assumes a wired link between RSUs of the backbone network. As it can be observed from the table, we can classify the routing protocols into three subclasses:

1. Broadcasting,
2. Geocasting, and
3. Unicasting.

In this chapter, we propose a unicast routing based on location information of the vehicles and RSUs.

The HexDD protocol has the following advantages over the existing works:

1. It proposes the use of an inexpensive network composed of small sensor nodes to be deployed in already existing infrastructure. Such approach can decrease deployment costs compared to installing a fixed powered roadside infrastructure as proposed, for example, in Borsetti and Gozalvez (2010) and Peng et al. (2006). Although the use of wireless sensor networks has been proposed in Festag et al. (2008) and Gao et al. (2010), these works have focused on different aspects, namely, architecture and security. In contrast, HexDD focuses on routing efficiency and robustness.

2. Considering the advantages of using an infrastructure-assisted approach, HexDD relies on a virtual infrastructure called 'hexagonal tessellation.' Due to its optimized topology, hexagonal tessellation allows for an efficient geographical routing of event messages to any vehicle in the network.

3. HexDD considers end-to-end wireless communication. RSUs also communicate wirelessly via sensors attached to them.

4. HexDD makes the system resistant to node failures in the virtual infrastructure and

supports quick routing around holes in the network.

5. HexDD has the unique feature of leveraging the original layout of the city to build its virtual infrastructure. This allows for an improved delivery ratio and end-to-end delay.

In particular, we consider in this work the case of European cities, where circular and radial roads surrounds the city center. This represents a very distinct approach when compared to other works in the current literature.

POSSIBLE APPLICATIONS

Vehicular sensor networks serve as means for effectively monitoring the physical world (Lee & Gerla, 2010). Vehicles continuously gather, process, and disseminate relevant sensor data. Such networks allow for the emergence of several new applications. Among potential applications are:

- **Traffic Monitoring and Control:** Sensors deployed in both vehicles and roadside units can be used to gather information such as the speed and position of vehicles to accurately estimate the current traffic condition. Such traffic information can be combined and sent to a central authority point such as the city hall whenever requested. In addition, traffic lights equipped with sensors nodes can request live traffic information from vehicles to control the time duration of each light adaptively to the current traffic.
- **Environment Monitoring:** A central point can send a query for data obtained from chemical sensors, installed both in vehicles and in roadside units. Such data, combined, can provide a global estimate of the level of pollution in different regions

of the city. Furthermore, sensors that are able to detect vibrations during the ride can generate estimates about the conditions of the road.
- **Safety Warnings:** Vehicle communication has the potential to complement internal on-board sensors (cameras or radars) to detect and warn drivers about hazardous situations when a vision beyond what sensors can provide is required. When a radio gap is present, roadside units can be used to store and later forward the corresponding data to potential interested vehicles and authorities.

Motivating Scenario

The scale of thousands of vehicles used as sensors collecting data is almost beyond imagination. Data is collected in places were previously no measurements were taken, thus broadening the scale and scope of information gathering considerably. Sharing and combining information collected by large numbers of cars will reveal patterns that were previously invisible. Acting on this newfound information, the city's stress (e.g. air pollution, traffic load and flow, noise) may be alleviated and thus improve quality of living. A vehicle sensor network alone has a drawback though. Dissemination of the sensor data is only possible when other cars are in communication range. If no car is in range, the data must be stored to be offloaded at a later time. The network becomes a delay tolerant network in which time between sensing the data and its dissemination can be considerable. During this period, the data can become stale and not valid anymore. The use of a fixed infrastructure to offload the data to—and to get the data from as well—will improve timeliness of data dissemination.

It is tempting to demonstrate the potential of infrastructure-assisted vehicular sensor networks and HexDD with an elaborate though realistic

Table 1. Overview of related works

Name of the work	Type	Goal
VANETs: infrastructure-less		
Persistence Broadcasting	Broadcasting	Broadcast suppression techniques
DV-CAST	Broadcasting	Directional broadcasting
SRD	Broadcasting	Directional broadcasting
ackPBSM	Broadcasting	Flooding
Kosch et al. (2006)	Broadcasting	Context-based flooding
OTHA	Broadcasting and Opportunistic sensing	Provide information of upcoming traffic
Abiding Geocast	Geocasting	Geocasting
GeoDTN+Nav	Unicast routing	Opportunistic geographical routing
VANETs: infrastructure-assisted		
DRR	Unicast routing	Multiple-path routing to meet services' reliability requirements
VPGR	Unicast routing	Context-based routing
MDH	Unicast routing and Geocasting	Data-harvesting to support applications' requirements, e.g., real-time
RAR	Unicast routing	Routing with reduced overhead by relying on a wired backbone network
DP and DP-IB	Geocasting	Dissemination to an area of interest
MCDD	Infrastructure deployment	Optimization of the placement of dead drops in road intersections
Festag et al. (2008)	Architecture	Connect roadside units to wireless sensor networks to reduce deployment costs
CGP	Architecture and data aggregation	Obtain an overview about road conditions in a certain geographical area
BusNet	Opportunistic sensing	Road surface monitoring
Pothole Patrol	Opportunistic sensing	Road surface monitoring

scenario taken from one of the application areas mentioned in the previous section. However, for the sake of clarity we will constrain ourselves in the following to a simple scenario where one vehicle provides data and another vehicle requests data.

THE INFRASTRUCTURE NETWORK WITH ROADSIDE UNITS

The vehicular sensor network that we consider is a hybrid between vehicular networks and WSNs. The network consists of static and mobile nodes. The static nodes are sensors located along the roads, attached to existing traffic signposts and other infrastructure, such as traffic lights, bus and tram stops, parking meters, railway stations, and buffer stops. Locating sensor nodes on this kind of road infrastructure will often result in a network that is not enough dense or not evenly distributed over a city. Figure 2 shows the existing infrastructure nodes, the blue triangles, in the same city area shown in Figure 1. The distribution of these nodes is not uniform over the whole area. It is dense in some parts of the city, and sparse in some others, creating also disconnected parts in the network. Additionally, we propose to deploy sensors on lampposts, assuming they are regularly positioned along roads in the city, e.g. every 100 meters. These nodes embedded on Roadside Units (RSUs) serve as sensor and relay nodes. The network formed by them gives a complete coverage of the city area. The static nodes may be powered or able to perform energy harvesting, e.g. from sun light, thus not depending only on battery power. Vehicles moving in the city are the mobile nodes in the network. They send the information collected by their possibly many sensors to the static nodes in the network. They also ask for information from the network. Vehicles may also serve as relay nodes, passing messages from one node to another in the network, but this is more a supporting role in case holes are created in the infrastructure network.

In this work, we propose to create a virtual regular tessellation over the network area. Cells of this regular tessellation are hexagons, whose size is calculated based on the communication range of the VSN nodes. The cell size is such that any node in a cell can communicate with every node in an adjacent cell. In Figure 1 is shown the centre of the city of Enschede, the Netherlands overlaid with a hexagonal tessellation assuming a communication range of 250m for RSUs. Figure 2 shows the hexagonal tessellation for the same city area, where the light blue cells show the coverage

that the exiting infrastructure nodes create for the virtual tessellation. The addition of the intelligent lampposts (iLPs) as RSUs ensures network connectivity and an acceptable sensor density, i.e. at least one sensor node per hexagonal cell. The yellow cells in Figure 2 show the virtual infrastructure defined by our protocol. This consists of three main diagonals of the tessellation and the n-hop ring around a centre cell (here the 3d-hop ring).

The virtual infrastructure is used by the data dissemination protocol for storing information produced by sensors in the network, e.g. detected events. Requests from vehicles are also sent to this infrastructure, making it a crucial element for the information exchange in the network. The virtual infrastructure is thus serving as a backbone for the communication. In a network where a major load of data and queries is coming from vehicles in the roads, it is reasonable to position the communication backbone in the major roads. These major roads have a strategic position for the transportation network, with most of the vehicles passing through them. The layout of our virtual infrastructure shows a strong similarity with the

Figure 3. Cell addressing in honeycomb tessellation and message data flow

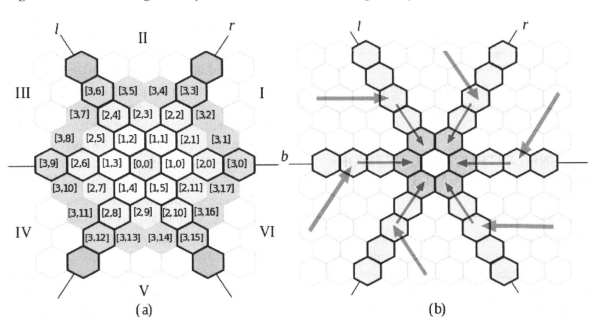

city street layout. This resemblance allows us to use the real road infrastructure as the communication backbone in our protocol. The approach presented in this chapter is built on the premise that there is a close fit between the street layout and the virtual infrastructure. When a main road deviates from our virtual infrastructure, we use roadside units that are within the virtual infrastructure instead of main road RSUs.

HEXAGONAL TESSELLATION FOR DATA DISSEMINATION IN VSN

Near real-time applications require a fast delivery of information, and for many of these applications, e.g. those related to safety, reliability of event data dissemination is an important concern. In this chapter, we propose a data dissemination protocol based on hexagonal tessellation for a V2I communication. Hexagonal tessellation, which is often used to model cellular networks, refers to a tessellation of the geographical area into hexagonal cells. It is important to point out that in our proposal we do not use the concept of cellular networks. In cellular networks, a land area is divided into hexagonal cells having a base station located in the middle to provide non-overlapping service to the entire network. Cellular networks use hexagonal cells to provide radio coverage over a wide geographic area and allow an efficient channel allocation. In our proposal, we do not assume a cluster head (i.e. data collector) at the middle of a cell. Here, we use hexagonal cells to reduce the position precision to what is needed for the geographical communication. In our approach, we use these addressable units for the purpose of geographical routing.

In this chapter, we focus on geographical (i.e. position-based) routing for the case of vehicular sensor networks in a city environment. Geographical routing is beneficial since no global route from source node to destination node need to be created and maintained. Two nodes (i.e. vehicles or

RSUs) can communicate when they are within a distance R of each other, called the communicable distance. Through periodic interactions (hello packets), a node can learn the location and cell of its neighbors. The data and query packets are sent without any map knowledge to the next hop neighbor, which is determined by our data dissemination protocol. In the rest of this section, we explain the creation of the hexagonal tessellation and its infrastructure followed by the hexagonal cell-based data dissemination, HexDD.

Construction of Virtual Infrastructure with Hexagonal Tessellation

Hexagonal tessellation construction is, which is done at the network setup phase, is the initial step of our proposal. A honeycomb tessellation is completely determined by one reference hexagon because, once one hexagon is known, the remaining hexagons can be easily positioned. As shown in Figure 4, if the center hexagon is fixed at the center of the city, the whole network is fixed. In the following discussion, we assume the network has a fixed cell size, r, and network orientation. A network with a fixed cell size and network orientation is solely determined by the position of one reference cell. In our previous works (Tuysuz-Erman, Dilo, & Havinga, 2010; Tuysuz-Erman & Havinga, 2010), it is shown how a node associates itself with a hexagonal cell where it is located in. For node-cell association, a node needs to know the edge length of the hexagon, r, and the center of the city. In order for all nodes in two adjacent cells to be able to communicate with each other, the longest distance between two adjacent cells, $l = \sqrt{13}r$ must satisfy $l = \sqrt{13}r \leq R,$ where R is the transmission range. Therefore, we choose the edge length of the hexagon, $r_{max} = R / \sqrt{13},$ such that sensors in adjacent cells are within communicable distance of each other. To let the other far infrastructure nodes know the center of the city, a static node deployed at the center of the city can broadcast its location over the city once at the network setup phase. All the RSUs receiving this information in the city can easily associate themselves with the hexagonal cell where they are located. When a vehicle starts to move in the city or enters into a new city, it asks the network settings (i.e. cell edge size, location of the center) of this city to the nearest RSU. After getting the settings, it will be able to calculate its cell address.

The hexagonal tessellation creates a circular structure on the city, starting from the center, and spreading with hexagonal rings to the end of the city. We use a kind of polar coordinate system to address the cells of the tessellation. Figure 3 shows the cell addressing used in hexagonal tessellation. We assign addresses of the form *[H, I]* to each sensor in the same cell, where H is the shortest cell-count of the node from the origin cell and I denotes the index of the hop-H hexagonal cell. The index starts at the right side of line b in Fig-

ure 3(a) and increases in the counter-clockwise direction. Hence, the nodes in the first-hop cells are addressed as [1, 0], [1, 1],..., [1, 5]. Observe that nodes of the form *[H,.]* are all located on the same hexagonal ring at distance H form the center cell. Since the number of cells on H^{th} hop hexagonal ring is $6 \times H$, the cell addresses range from $[H, 0]$ to $[H, 6H-1]$. This addressing scheme serves as a positioning (coordinate) system that is rougher than the coordinates of the wireless nodes, with a precision appropriate for transmission range. Wireless nodes are associated with cell 'coordinates' based on their locations. The geographical routing that HexDD performs is based on cell addresses.

In hexagonal tessellation, we classify the wireless nodes into three groups:

1. Border nodes,
2. Ring nodes, and

Figure 4. Hexagonal tessellation overlaid on city area (assuming g =1) and data-query dissemination

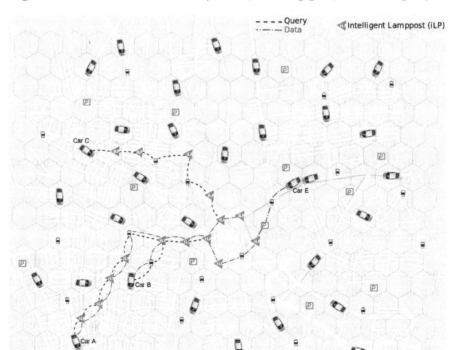

3. Regular nodes, according to their position on the hexagonal tessellation.

The ring cells are selected according to the position of the most inner ring of the city. If the inner ring road of the city is covered by the hexagonal ring, g, then every node on ring g becomes a 'ring node.' In Figure 3(b), dark yellow cells are the ring cells assuming $g = 1$. The cells addressed as *[H, I]* are 'border cells' if $I = (k - 1)xH$, where $H > g$ and $k \in \{1, ..., 6\}$. The nodes associated with border cells, which are shown by yellow cells in Figure 3(b), are called 'border nodes.' The virtual tessellation is partitioned from border cells into different parts, called city zones, which are the white regions in Figure 3(b). All the other nodes located in city zones are called 'regular nodes.'

The virtual tessellation is partitioned from the main road-lines running through the city center into different parts (i.e. city zones) as shown in Figure 4. These main lines (yellow lines in Figure 4) together with a hexagonal ring (the most inner ring in a city) constitute the infrastructure for our protocol. They serve as a storage place for data and a meeting point for data and queries coming from cars moving in the city.

Lines *l*, *r*, and *s* are called as "diagonal lines" and half of these lines are called "border lines." A city is indeed split into zones with these borderlines. Each borderline caches information coming from the representative zone according to the forwarding directions shown in Figure 3(b). Finally, the central ring caches the information coming from all city zones.

Hexagonal Cell-Based Data Dissemination

In the context of vehicular sensor networks, the network we envision consists of vehicles and wireless nodes located on the fixed infrastructure on the roadside. Vehicles are the mobile sources (see Car E in Figure 4), reporting information from collected or processed data from their pos-

sibly many sensors. They are at the same time the mobile destinations (see Car A in Figure 4), asking information that the driver/owner considers important. Wireless nodes embedded on roadside units (iLP, parking places [P], and bus stops in Figure 4) serve as sensor and relay nodes.

In the rest of this section, we explain the main features of our data dissemination protocol: (1) data and query forwarding between sources, destinations and border/ring nodes, (2) Fault tolerance mechanism, and, (3) Mobility Management.

(Event) Data and Query Forwarding

Data and queries coming from each part of the city are sent to one of the main roads (i.e. borderline) bordering it, according to the predefined directions shown in Figure 3(b). The data is then sent towards the central ring, which has therefore knowledge about the whole city. The data is cached on every cell of the central ring. In our data dissemination protocol, we assume a pull based approach, which is a form of request and response model. In pull based data dissemination, any vehicle is enabled to query information about a specific type and/or location. Once a query is issued from a car (Car A and C in Figure 4), it is sent to the main road assigned to the part of the city where the car is. The query is sent along the main line towards the central ring to search for the required data. When the data is found, it is sent to the car that issued the query. While the data is being forwarded towards a destination node along the border cells, border nodes receiving data also cache it. If the data is already in that main line (assume Car B sends a query after Car A gets the data from central ring), it is sent back to the car without its query is being forwarded to the central ring. The HexDD protocol performs this routing of data and query messages by exploiting the road infrastructure as a communication infrastructure. The strategic position of the road infrastructure allows for fast communication routes, assuring fast response and at the same time efficient data dissemination.

The following algorithm shows how a node finds the next hop cell based on cell addressing used in hexagonal tessellation. In the first part, it calculates the next hop cell of a node in one of the city zones towards the central ring via border cells. This part is used for data and query dissemination towards the central ring. The second part shows the calculation of the opposite path from central ring towards a cell in one of the city zones via border cells.

Algorithm 1: Hexagonal Cell-Based Data Dissemination

- Input
  - $[H, I]$, address of the current cell
  - $[H_s, I_s]$, address of the destination vehicle's current cell
  - g, H of the central ring
- Output
  - $[H, I]$, address of the next hop cell
- Find next hop cell towards central ring
  - $k = \lceil I / H \rceil$
  - *If $H < g$ then*
  - $[H, I] \Leftarrow [H - 1, I - 1]$
  - *else if $H == g$ then*
  - *Circulate packet in the ring*
  - *end if*
- Find next hop cell towards destination vehicle
  - $k = \left\lceil I_s / H_s \right\rceil$
  - $H \Leftarrow H + 1$
  - *If $H \leq kH_s - I_s$ then*
  - $I \Leftarrow I + k - 1 //$ *in the border line*
  - *else*
  - $I \Leftarrow I + k //$ *within a city zone*
  - *end if*

Fault Tolerance

The proposed data dissemination protocol assumes that there is at least one node (preferably a RSU) which performs multi-hop routing within each cell. However, this may not be always the case. Some nodes may be temporarily unavailable. Therefore, holes are created where there is a group of cells that do not have any active RSU inside. To handle this problem, we propose a hole detection and bypassing mechanism, which is an important feature that shows how to maintain the honeycomb tessellation even if a part of the infrastructure is missing.

A vehicle or RSU can easily detect the hole region by checking its neighbor table, which is updated by periodic beacon packets. If the node has no neighbor on the next 2-hop cells in its transmission range, it concludes that there is a hole at that part of the city. We can divide hole bypassing mechanism into two parts:

1. **Route recovery when sending packets (data or query) from a vehicle on a city zone towards the central ring:** To find an alternative path, the node, which wants to forward its packet towards the central ring, checks its neighbors and chooses the neighbor having the smallest H. By sending the packet to the neighbor node having the smallest H, the node tries to get as much as close to the central ring. Having a smaller H than the others means that this node has a smaller hop count to the central ring.

2. **Route recovery when sending data packets from the central ring towards a destination vehicle on a city zone:** The easiest ways to establish the path from the central ring to a destination vehicle moving on a city zone is storing the reverse path in the query. Since sink sends a new query whenever it changes its cell, it is an efficient approach. The reverse path in the query packet recovers the holes at the path back to the sink because when the query is being sent towards the central ring, the alternative path is calculated and stored in the query. It is also possible to calculate

the reverse path from the cell address of the destination vehicle.

Algorithm 2 gives the details of HexDD with route recovery. For simplicity, we only give the details of route recovery when sending packets from a vehicle on a city zone towards the central ring. The opposite path recovery uses a similar approach to calculate the next hop to recover holes. Figure 5 illustrates the fault tolerance mechanism in HexDD.

Algorithm 2: Hexagonal cell-based data dissemination with route recovery

- Input
  - $[H, I]$, address of the current cell
  - g, H of the central ring
  - $N = \{n_1, ..., n_m\}$, list of neighbors
  - $N_a = \{[H_1, I_1], ..., [H_m, I_m]\}$, list of cell addresses of neighbors, where node n_m is in cell $[H_m, I_m]$
- Output
  - n, next hop neighbor to forward packet
- Find next hop neighbor towards central ring
  - $[H_c, I_c] \Leftarrow$ *find next hop cell towards central ring (Algorithm 1.I)*
  - *If* $[H_c, I_c] == [H_i, I_i] \in N_a$ *then*
  - $n \Leftarrow n_i$ // *forward data to a neighbor in the next cell*
  - *else* // *there is a hole, enter route recovery*
  - $n \Leftarrow n_j$ *with* H_j *the smallest* H *in* N_a *where* $j \leq g$
  - *end if*

Mobility Management

In the motivating VANET scenario, both the source and destination vehicles are mobile entities of the network. The impact of destination and source mobility on the dissemination scheme is very small because when destination or source

Figure 5. Route recovery mechanism in HexDD

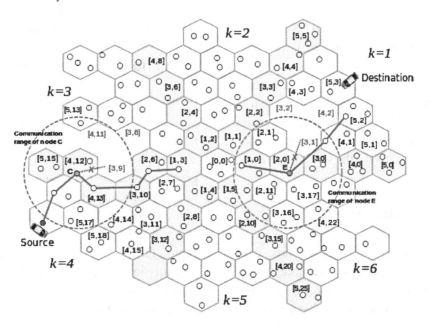

vehicle moves to another cell, it only changes its connection point to the static infrastructure. When a source vehicle moves to another cell, it sends its data to the nearest RSU to become connected to the infrastructure. When destination vehicles move between cells, they need to send a new query message towards the central ring to inform the ring nodes about their new cells. If there is no direct communication exists between a destination/source node and a RSU, another vehicle in the next hop cell can be used as next hop until reaching a RSU. Another option is that the packet is carried by the destination/source vehicle until it could be forwarded to a node which will be a RSU if any exits in the communication range or a vehicle. This 'carry and forward' concept (Zhao & Cao, 2008) can be easily combined with our geographic forwarding protocol, HexDD.

PERFORMANCE EVALUATION

In order to evaluate the performance of our data dissemination protocol described above, we used the open source network simulator NS-2 (Mc-Canne, Floyd, Fall, & Varadhan, 1997) version 2.33 as it is widely used for research in vehicular ad hoc networks. We have added a new data dissemination agent (i.e. HexDD) into NS-2 over the currently implemented network stack and added our logic as a routing agent.

In the following, we provide first a description of the simulation environment and scenarios characteristics and then present the evaluation methodology, the metrics for comparing the protocols. Finally, we analyze the simulation results we obtained.

Simulation Environment

In our VANET simulation we use three main components: a network component, capable of simulating the behavior of a wireless network, a vehicular traffic component, able to provide an accurate mobility model for the nodes of a VANET, and a map component, capable of creating and providing free geographic data such as street maps. The vehicular mobility and wireless network models are incorporated in different simulation tools. SUMO – Simulation of Urban MObility (Krajzewicz, Hertkorn, Rössel, & Wagner, 2002) implements complex validated vehicular traffic mobility models. It is used for simulating a traffic scenario and generating an output file with vehicular mobility traces. The trace generated by SUMO is a mobility log for vehicles moving based on traffic regulations. It is possible to import different maps to SUMO to generate different test cases. Realistic urban areas (i.e. Enschede, the Netherlands) extracted from actual street maps are imported to SUMO. These maps are extracted from free maps available in OpenStreetMap (Haklay & Weber, 2008). After generation of mobility traces, they are fed into the network simulator, NS-2, as mobility scenario. In addition, static road infrastructure points, e.g. traffic lights, transportation points, and parking meters, obtained from OpenStreetMap are used as Road Side infrastructure Units (RSUs) in NS-2. We also generated iLP nodes in NS-2. The simulation is performed by NS-2 to obtain the final simulation results with the given inputs. Figure 6 shows the general view of the simulation environment.

Scenario Characteristics

In this chapter, we consider an urban area of $3500 \times 4000 m^2$ that is the downtown and residential area of the city Enschede in the Netherlands. Vehicles are able to move freely on the urban graph respecting roads and intersection rules, more specifically, speed limitations and stops. Vehicles are able to communicate with each other using the IEEE 802.11 DCF MAC layer (Chen, Jiang, Taliwal, & Delgrossi, 2006). The radio transmission range has been deliberately over-evaluated and set to 250m for VANETs as we wanted to avoid biased performance evaluations

Figure 6. Simulation environment

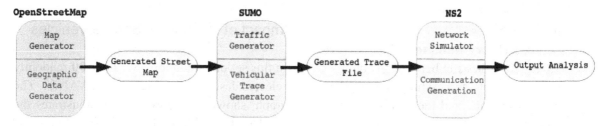

due to disconnected networks. The simulation parameters are given in Table 2.

Evaluation Methodology

We compare the performance of the HexDD protocol with representatives from two main classes of ad hoc routing protocols:

1. AODV (Perkins, Belding-Royer, & Das, 2003), which is a MANET reactive routing protocol,
2. GPSR (Karp & Kung, 2000), which is a MANET geographical routing protocol.

Since only a limited work has been done on infrastructure-assisted data dissemination for vehicular sensor networks inside the city environment, we have chosen two MANET protocols for comparison. Although the operations of VANET and MANET are the same, due to the difference in high-speed mobility of vehicles, VANET communication requires suitable modification in the predefined routing protocols. Some efforts on improving classical MANET routing protocols to operate efficiently in VANET can be found in Abedi, Fathy, and Taghiloo (2008) and Wu, Wang, and Lee (2010). Since we have no intention of coding these improvements in NS-2 from scratch due to time constraints, we use AODV and GPSR implementations in NS-2.33. These protocols are served as the benchmark to judge the performance of our proposed HexDD.

HexDD, AODV, and GPSR protocols are based on only local knowledge (i.e. one-hop neighbors). Vehicles do not use any global knowledge such as a digital map of the region to forward their data packets (Lochert, et al., 2003). In HexDD, AODV, and GPSR, we make use of periodic "hello" messages to get information from the one-hop neighbors of vehicles and RSUs.

Metrics

The performance of the routing protocols has been evaluated by varying the number of destination and source vehicles. We have measured several significant metrics for data dissemination in VSNs:

*   **Packet Delivery Ratio to Destinations (PDR$_D$):** It is the ratio between the number of data packets successfully delivered

Table 2. NS2 simulation parameters

Simulation time	300s
Simulation Area	3500x4000m²
Transmission Range	250m
Number of RSUs	800
Number of vehicles	300
Vehicle mobility	v_{min}=0km/h, v_{max}=100km/h
Source/Destination selection	Random
Number of source vehicles	1, 5, 10, 15, 20
Number of destination vehicles	10, 20, 30, 40, 50
MAC Protocol	IEEE 802.11 DFC
Hello Interval	1s
Data Interval	1s

281

at destination vehicles and the number of data requests (i.e. queries) sent by the destination vehicles.

- **Packet Delivery Ratio to Infrastructure (PDR$_I$):** It is the ratio between the number of data packets successfully delivered at the infrastructure and the number of data packets sent by the source vehicles. The average packet delivery ratios *(PDR$_D$)* and *(PDR$_I$)* show together the ability of the routing protocol to successfully transfer data on an end-to-end basis.

- **End-to-End Delay (E2E):** It measures the average end-to-end transmission delay by taking into account only the successfully received packets. The average delay characterizes the latency that the routing approach generated.

- **Response Time (RT):** It is the average time between sending the request and getting the data for each vehicle.

Simulation Results

Impact of Number of Source Vehicles

In this set of simulations, we have 30 randomly selected destination vehicles in the VANET. The graph, shown in Figure 7(a), demonstrates the good performance of the proposed HexDD in terms of higher PDR$_D$, compared to the other two protocols, and that is for varying number of vehicular sources in the VANET. This is an expected result of using roadside network for vehicular communication. The graph indicates that regardless of the underlying protocol, PDR$_D$ generally tends to decrease along with increase in the number of sources. Indeed, when the number of sources increases, the packet drops subsequently increase. Since only HexDD proposes a virtual infrastructure in VANET, we have calculated PDR$_I$ only for HexDD in the simualtions. The data packet delivery ratio to infrastructure is also very high in HexDD protocol. Results prove that the use of RSUs and virtual infrastructure in order to cache the data coming from different sources improves the performance of data dissemination in terms of data delivery ratio. Figure 7(b) shows end to

Figure 7. Performance of three protocols in terms of (a) data packet delivery and (b) average delay for different numbers of vehicular sources

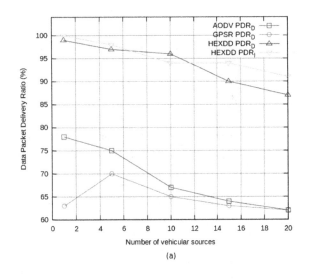

(a)

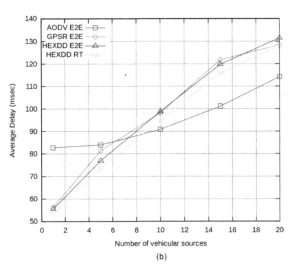

(b)

end delay for three protocols and response time for HexDD. Since we use a pull-based approach in HexDD, we have also defined and measured RT, which is the time elapsed between when a destination vehicle sends a query and when it receives the data coming from the central ring. As show in the Figure 7(b), RT of HexDD is smaller than E2E delay of the HexDD. The E2E delay of HexDD and GPSR are very close to each other. The E2E delay of AODV is the smallest when we have 10 or more sources in the network. The AODV protocol is able to keep the average delay of the transmitted packet in an implicit control by dropping packets for which it does not have a route.

Impact of Number of Destination Vehicles

Figure 8 shows the comparison of three protocols in terms of data delivery ratio and average delay for varying number of destinations when we have 20 randomly selected vehicular sources in the VANET. In Figure 8(a), when there are 10 sources in the network, PDR_D and PDR_I of HexDD are very close to 100%. Both PDR_D and PDR_I of HexDD decrease when we increase the number of destinations. However, decrease in PDR_D of HexDD is bigger than decrease in PDR_I of HexDD. On the other hand, AODV and GPSR show the most drastic drops in their delivery ratios, with a 20-24% decrease from the 10 destinations simulation to the 50 destinations simulation. Figure 8(b) plots the average data delivery delay for all protocols and also response time for HexDD. E2E delay of AODV is less sensitive to the added destinations than the other protocols. Since GPSR and HexDD are based on geographic routing, their E2E delays are close to each other. Both have route recovery phases when a packet reaches to a dead end. The planar graph traversal strategy of GPSR can not always guarantee to recover the route to the destination; therefore, its data delivery ratio is much smaller than HexDD. However, although the data delivery ratio of GPSR is much smaller

than HexDD, its E2E delay for successfully received packets at destination vehicles is close to HexDD. This is due to the fact that the route recovery strategy of GPSR also results in longer paths than recovery strategy of HexDD.

FUTURE RESEARCH DIRECTIONS

The protocol we propose takes care only of the routing of messages, leaving aside related topics like data aggregation through the route, neither any kind of data processing. The communication infrastructure that we use takes over the storing of network data. This makes it a good candidate where information processing can take place. This could be supported by deploying powerful RSU nodes in the infrastructure.

The HexDD protocol does not put attention on the kind of information that is flown in the network. Indeed, different sensors can be deployed on roadside units and many others are available on cars. This richness of data collected by the different sensors need to be properly handled, in terms of storage, intelligent processing, and transmission.

In this work, we did not put much attention to the fitting of virtual infrastructure with the read road infrastructure. A best fit can be reached via transformation of the tessellation, e.g. rotation, directional scaling, etc. Such transformation would require an adaptation of the addressing scheme, i.e. the association of a node with the virtual hexagonal cell. The routing of messages remains the same, requiring no changes.

CONCLUSION

In this chapter, we proposed a data dissemination protocol for VSNs. The network we envision consists of vehicles and roadside units. The RSUs are the lampposts equipped with small transceivers and sensors, positioned along roads at roughly equal distances, in addition to the existing com-

Figure 8. Performance of three protocols in terms of (a) data packet delivery and (b) average delay for different numbers of vehicular destinations

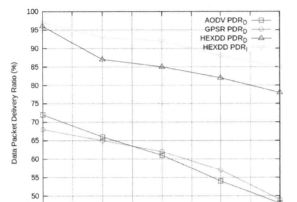
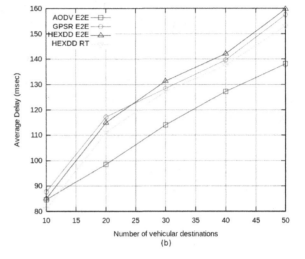

munication and traffic control infrastructure. This fixed network is inexpensive, and it provides a full and stable coverage of a city area. This VSN has advantages compared to a vehicular network whose coverage depends on the traffic situation and is usually unevenly distributed over a city.

The proposed data dissemination protocol, HexDD, is built upon a virtual tessellation of the city area. The cell size of a hexagon is such that any two nodes in adjacent cells can communicate with each other. The hexagonal tessellation creates a circular structure on the city, starting from the centre, and spreading with hexagonal rings to the end of the city. The main diagonals of the hexagonal tessellation together with a hexagonal ring constitute the infrastructure for our protocol. We use a kind of polar coordinate system to address the cells of the tessellation. This addressing scheme serves as a positioning (coordinate) system that is rougher than the coordinates of the wireless nodes, with a precision appropriate for

the transition range. Wireless nodes are associated with cell 'coordinates' based on their location. The geographical routing that HexDD performs is based on cell addresses.

This virtual infrastructure fits with main radial roads of the inner ring of a city that become the communication backbone for the protocol. They serve as a storage place for data and queries coming from cars moving in the city. Data and queries coming from each part of the city are sent to one of the main roads bordering it. The data is then sent towards the central ring, which has therefore knowledge about the whole city. Using main radial roads and the inner ring as rendezvous areas for data and queries, and employing roadside network for vehicular communication help to improve data delivery ratio while providing fast response in VANETs as shown in the simulations. The protocol can serve many applications of a VSN, such as traffic monitoring and control, environmental monitoring, and safety warning.

REFERENCES

Abedi, O., Fathy, M., & Taghiloo, J. (2008). Enhancing AODV routing protocol using mobility parameters in VANET. In *Proceedings of the 2008 IEEE/ACS International Conference on Computer Systems and Applications,* (pp. 229-235). IEEE Press.

Borsetti, D., & Gozalvez, J. (2010). Infrastructure-assisted geo-routing for cooperative vehicular networks. In *Proceedings of the 2010 IEEE Vehicular Networking Conference,* (pp. 255-262). IEEE Press.

Casteigts, A., Nayak, A., & Stojmenovic, I. (2009). Communication protocols for vehicular ad hoc networks. In *Wireless Communications and Mobile Computing.* New York, NY: John Wiley & Sons. doi:10.1002/wcm.879

Chawathe, S. S. (2006). Inter-vehicle data dissemination in sparse equipped traffic. In *Proceedings of the 2006 IEEE Intelligent Transportation Systems Conference,* (pp. 273-280). IEEE Press.

Chen, Q., Jiang, D., Taliwal, V., & Delgrossi, L. (2006). IEEE 802.11 based vehicular communication simulation design for NS-2. In *Proceedings of the 3rd International Workshop on Vehicular Ad Hoc Networks,* (p. 50–56). New York, NY: ACM Press.

De Zoysa, K., Keppitiyagama, C., Seneviratne, G. P., & Shihan, W. W. A. T. (2007). A public transport system based sensor network for road surface condition monitoring. In *Proceedings of the 2007 Workshop on Networked Systems for Developing Regions - NSDR 2007,* (p. 1). New York, NY: ACM Press.

Eriksson, J., Girod, L., Hull, B., Newton, R., Madden, S., & Balakrishnan, H. (2008). The pothole patrol. In *Proceeding of the 6th International Conference on Mobile Systems, Applications, and Services - MobiSys 2008,* (p. 29). New York, NY: ACM Press.

Festag, A., Hessler, A., Baldessari, R., Le, L., Zhang, W., & Westhoff, D. (2008). Vehicle-to-vehicle and road-side sensor communication for enhanced road safety. In *Proceedings of the 9th International Conference on Intelligent Tutoring Systems (ITS 2008).* IEEE Press.

Gao, H., Utecht, S., Patrick, G., Hsieh, G., Xu, F., & Wang, H. (2010). High speed data routing in vehicular sensor networks. *The Journal of Communication, 5*(3), 181–188.

Haklay, M., & Weber, P. (2008). OpenStreetMap: User-generated street maps. *IEEE Pervasive Computing / IEEE Computer Society [and] IEEE Communications Society, 7*(4), 12–18. doi:10.1109/MPRV.2008.80

He, R., Rutagemwa, H., & Shen, X. (2008). Differentiated reliable routing in hybrid vehicular ad-hoc networks. In *Proceedings of the 2008 IEEE International Conference on Communications,* (pp. 2353-2358). IEEE Press.

Karp, B., & Kung, H. T. (2000). GPSR: Greedy perimeter stateless routing for wireless networks. In *Proceedings of the 6th Annual International Conference on Mobile Computing and Networking,* (pp. 243–254). ACM Press.

Kosch, T., Adler, C., Eichler, S., Schroth, C., & Strassberger, M. (2006). The scalability problem of vehicular ad hoc networks and how to solve it. *IEEE Wireless Communications, 13*(5), 22–28. doi:10.1109/WC-M.2006.250354

Krajzewicz, D., Hertkorn, G., Rössel, C., & Wagner, P. (2002). SUMO (simulation of urban mobility)-An open-source traffic simulation. In *Proceedings of the 4th Middle East Symposium on Simulation and Modelling (MESM 2002),* (pp. 183–187). MESM.

Lee, K. C., & Gerla, M. (2010). Opportunistic vehicular routing. In *Proceedings of the 2010 European Wireless Conference (EW),* (pp. 873-880). Lucca, Italy: IEEE Press.

Lee, U., & Gerla, M. (2010). A survey of urban vehicular sensing platforms. *Computer Networks, 54*(4), 527–544. doi:10.1016/j.comnet.2009.07.011

Lim, K. W., & Ko, Y.-B. (2010). Multi-hop data harvesting in vehicular sensor networks. *IET Communications, 4*(7), 768. doi:10.1049/iet-com.2009.0075

Lochert, C., Hartenstein, H., Tian, J., Fussler, H., Hermann, D., & Mauve, M. (2003). A routing strategy for vehicular ad hoc networks in city environments. In *Proceedings of the Intelligent Vehicles Symposium, 2003,* (Vol. 2000, pp. 156–161). IEEE Press.

Lochert, C., Scheuermann, B., Wewetzer, C., Luebke, A., & Mauve, M. (2008). Data aggregation and roadside unit placement for a vanet traffic information system. In *Proceedings of the Fifth ACM International Workshop on VehiculAr InterNETworking,* (pp. 58–65). ACM Press.

Lok, M. J., Qazi, B. R., & Elmirghani, J. M. H. (2009). Data dissemination with drop boxes. In *Proceedings of the 2009 International Conference on Advanced Information Networking and Applications,* (pp. 451-455). IEEE Press.

McCanne, S., Floyd, S., Fall, K., Varadhan, K., et al. (1997). *Network simulator ns-2.*

Misra, S., Woungang, I., & Misra, S. C. (2009). *Guide to wireless ad hoc networks.* New York, NY: Springer-Verlag. doi:10.1007/978-1-84800-328-6

Murty, R. N., Mainland, G., Rose, I., Chowdhury, A. R., Gosain, A., Bers, J., et al. (2008). CitySense: An urban-scale wireless sensor network and testbed. In *Proceedings of the 2008 IEEE Conference on Technologies for Homeland Security,* (pp. 583-588). IEEE Press.

Nekovee, M. (2005). *Sensor networks on the road: The promises and challenges of vehicular ad hoc networks and grids.* Paper presented at the Workshop on Ubiquitous Computing and e-Research. Edinburgh, UK.

Peng, Y., Abichar, Z., & Chang, J. (2006). Roadside-aided routing (RAR) in vehicular networks. In *Proceedings of the 2006 IEEE International Conference on Communications,* (pp. 3602-3607). IEEE Press.

Perkins, C., Belding-Royer, E., & Das, S. (2003). *RFC3561: Ad hoc on-demand distance vector (AODV) routing.* Retrieved from http://www.ietf.org/rfc/rfc3561.txt

Perkins, C. E., & Bhagwat, P. (1994). Highly dynamic destination-sequenced distance-vector routing (DSDV) for mobile computers. *ACM SIGCOMM Computer Communication Review, 24,* 234–244. doi:10.1145/190809.190336

Piran, M. J. (2010). A novel routing algorithm for vehicular sensor networks. *Wireless Sensor Network, 2*(12), 919–923. doi:10.4236/wsn.2010.212110

Ros, F. J., Ruiz, P. M., & Stojmenovic, I. (2009). Reliable and efficient broadcasting in vehicular ad hoc networks. In *Proceedings of the 69th IEEE Vehicular Technology Conference, 2009,* (pp. 1-5). IEEE Press.

Salhi, I., Cherif, M., & Senouci, S. M. (2008). *Data collection in vehicular networks.* Paper presented at the Autonomous and Spontaneous Networks Symposium. Paris, France.

Schwartz, R. S., Barbosa, R. R., Meratnia, N., Heijenk, G., & Scholten, H. (2011). *A directional data dissemination protocol for vehicular environments.* In Computer Communications. London, UK: Elsevier. doi:10.1016/j.comcom.2011.03.007

Schwartz, R. S., & Eenennaam, M. van, Karagi-annis, G., Heijenk, G., Klein Wolterink, W., & Scholten, H. (2010). Using V2V communication to create over-the-horizon awareness in multiple-lane highway scenarios. In *Proceedings of the 2010 IEEE Intelligent Vehicles Symposium,* (pp. 998-1005). IEEE Press.

Shrestha, R. K., Moh, S., Chung, I., & Choi, D. (2010). Vertex-based multihop vehicle-to-infrastructure routing for vehicular ad hoc networks. In *Proceedings of the 2010 43rd Hawaii International Conference on System Sciences,* (pp. 1-7). IEEE Press.

Tonguz, O., Wisitpongphan, N., & Bai, F. (2010). DV-CAST: A distributed vehicular broadcast protocol for vehicular ad hoc networks. *IEEE Wireless Communications, 17*(2), 47–57. doi:10.1109/MWC.2010.5450660

Trullols, O., Fiore, M., Casetti, C., Chiasserini, C. F., & Barcelo Ordinas, J. M. (2010). Planning roadside infrastructure for information dissemination in intelligent transportation systems. *Computer Communications, 33*(4), 432–442. doi:10.1016/j.comcom.2009.11.021

Tuysuz-Erman, A., Dilo, A., & Havinga, P. (2010). A fault-tolerant data dissemination based on honeycomb architecture for mobile multi-sink wireless sensor networks. In *Proceedings of the Intelligent Sensors, Sensor Networks and Information Processing (ISSNIP),* (p. 97–102). IEEE Press.

Tuysuz-Erman, A., & Havinga, P. (2010). Data dissemination of emergency messages in mobile multi-sink wireless sensor networks. In *Proceedings of the 2010 9th IFIP Annual Mediterranean Ad Hoc Networking Workshop (Med-Hoc-Net),* (p. 1–8). IEEE Press.

Wisitpongphan, N., Tonguz, O. K., Parikh, J. S., Mudalige, P., Bai, F., & Sadekar, V. (2007). Broadcast storm mitigation techniques in vehicular ad hoc networks. *IEEE Wireless Communications, 14*(6), 84–94. doi:10.1109/MWC.2007.4407231

Wong, K.-J., Chua, C.-C., & Li, Q. (2009). Environmental monitoring using wireless vehicular sensor networks. In *Proceedings of the 2009 5th International Conference on Wireless Communications, Networking and Mobile Computing,* (pp. 1-4). IEEE Press.

Wu, T. Y., Wang, Y. B., & Lee, W. T. (2010). Mixing greedy and predictive approaches to improve geographic routing for VANET. In *Wireless Communications and Mobile Computing.* New York, NY: Wiley. doi:10.1002/wcm.1033

Yu, Q., & Heijenk, G. (2008). Abiding geocast for warning message dissemination in vehicular ad hoc networks. In *Proceedings of the ICC Workshops - 2008 IEEE International Conference on Communications Workshops,* (pp. 400-404). IEEE Press.

Zhao, J., & Cao, G. (2008). VADD: Vehicle-assisted data delivery in vehicular ad hoc networks. In *Proceedings IEEE INFOCOM 2006,* (Vol. 57, pp. 1-12). IEEE Press.

Zhao, J., Zhang, Y., & Cao, G. (2007). Data Pouring and buffering on the road: A new data dissemination paradigm for vehicular networks. *IEEE Transactions on Vehicular Technology, 56*(6), 3266–3277. doi:10.1109/TVT.2007.906412

Compilation of References

Abdrabou, A., & Zhuang, W. (2011). Probabilistic delay control and road side unit placement for vehicular ad hoc networks with disrupted connectivity. *IEEE Journal on Selected Areas in Communications*, *29*, 129–139. doi:10.1109/JSAC.2011.110113

Abedi, O., Fathy, M., & Taghiloo, J. (2008). Enhancing AODV routing protocol using mobility parameters in VANET. In *Proceedings of the 2008 IEEE/ACS International Conference on Computer Systems and Applications*, (pp. 229-235). IEEE Press.

Ageev, A. A., & Sviridenko, M. I. (1999). Approximation algorithms for maximum coverage and max cut with given sizes of parts. *Lecture Notes in Computer Science*, *1610*, 17–30. doi:10.1007/3-540-48777-8_2

Aguiar, R. L., Tavares, A., Cura, J. L., de Vasconcelos, E., Alves, L. N., Valadas, R., & Santos, D. M. (1999). Considerations on the design of transceivers for wireless optical LANs. In Proceedings of the IEE Electronics & Communications, Colloquium on Optical Wireless Communications. London, UK: IEE.

Ahmed, S., & Kanhere, S. (2009). HUBCODE: Message forwarding using hub-based network coding in delay tolerant networks. In *Proceedings of the 12th ACM International Conference on Modeling, Analysis and Simulation of Wireless and Mobile Systems (MSWiM 2009)*, (pp. 288-296). New York, NY: ACM Press.

Ahn, J., Krishnamachari, B., Bai, F., & Zhang, L. (2011). *Optimizing content dissemination in heterogeneous vehicular networks*. Technical Report. Retrieved from http://ceng.usc.edu/assets/002/69415.pdf

Ahn, K., Rakha, H., Trani, A., & Van Aerde, M. (2002). Estimating vehicle fuel consumption and emissions based on instantaneous speed and acceleration levels. *Journal of Transportation Engineering*, *128*(2), 182–190. doi:10.1061/(ASCE)0733-947X(2002)128:2(182)

Aidouni, F., Latapy, M., & Magnien, C. (2009). Ten weeks in the life of an eDonkey server. In *Proceedings of the Sixth International Workshop on Hot Topics in Peer-to-Peer Systems (Hot-P2P 2009)*. Rome, Italy: Hot-P2P.

Akanegawa, M., Tanaka, Y., & Nakagawa, M. (2001). Basic study on traffic information systems using LED traffic lights. *IEEE Transactions on Intelligent Transportation Systems*, *2*, 197–203. doi:10.1109/6979.969365

Aktiv CoCar Project. (2009). *Website.* Retrieved from http://www.aktiv-online.org/english/aktiv-cocar.html

Akyildiz, F., Su, W., Sankarasubramaniam, Y., & Cayirci, E. (2002). Wireless sensor networks: A survey. *Computer Networks Journal*, *38*(4), 393–422. doi:10.1016/S1389-1286(01)00302-4

Akyildiz, I. F., Wang, X., & Wang, W. (2005). Wireless mesh networks: A survey. *Computer Networks*, *47*(3), 445–487. doi:10.1016/j.comnet.2004.12.001

Alcaraz, J., Vales-Alonso, J., & Garcia-Haro, J. (2009). Control-based scheduling with QoS support for vehicle to infrastructure communications. *Wireless Communications*, *16*, 32–39. doi:10.1109/MWC.2009.5361176

Alshaer, H., & Elmirghani, J. M. H. (2009). Road safety based on efficient vehicular communications. In *Proceedings of the IEEE Intelligent Vehicle Symposium*. XI' an, China: IEEE Press.

Alshaer, H., Ernst, T., & Fortelle, A. D. L. (2012). An integrated architecture for multi-homed vehicle-to-infrastructure communications. In *Proceedings of the 13th IEEE/IFIP Network Operations and Management Symposium (NOMS)*, (pp. 1042—1047). IEEE Press.

Alshaer, H., Ernst, T., & Fortelle, A. D. L. (2012). A QoS architecture for provisioning high quality in intelligent transportation services. In *Proceedings of the 13th IEEE/IFIP Network Operations and Management Symposium (NOMS)*, (pp. 595—598). IEEE Press.

Alshaer, H., & Elmirghani, J. M. H. (2009). Fourth-generation (4G) wireless networks: Applications and innovations. In *An End-to-End QoS Framework for Vehicular Mobile Networks*. Hershey, PA: IGI Global.

Andrews, J., Ghosh, A., & Muhamed, R. (2007). *Fundamentals of WiMAX: Understanding broadband wireless networking*. Upper Saddle River, NJ: Prentice Hall.

Annese, S., Casetti, C., Chiasserini, C. F., Di Maio, N., Ghittino, A., & Reineri, M. (2011). Seamless connectivity and routing in vehicular networks with infrastructure. *IEEE Journal on Selected Areas in Communications*, *29*(3), 501–514. doi:10.1109/JSAC.2011.110302

Bai, B., Chen, W., Letaief, K., & Cao, Z. (2011). Low complexity outage optimal distributed channel allocation for vehicle-to-vehicle communications. *IEEE Journal on Selected Areas in Communications*, *29*(1), 161–172. doi:10.1109/JSAC.2011.110116

Bakhouya, M., Gaber, J., & Wack, M. (2009). Performance evaluation of dream protocol for inter-vehicle communication. In *Proceedings of the International Conference on Wireless Communication, Vehicular Technology, Information Theory and Aerospace Electronic Systems Technology*, (pp. 289 –293). IEEE.

Balasubramanian, A., Levine, B., & Venkataramani, A. (2007). DTN routing as a resource allocation problem. *SIGCOMM Computer Communication Review*, *37*(4), 373–384. doi:10.1145/1282427.1282422

Banerjee, N., Corner, M. D., Towsley, D., & Levine, B. N. (2008). Relays, base stations, and meshes: Enhancing mobile networks with infrastructure. In *Proceedings of the ACM International Conference on Mobile Computing and Networking (MobiCom)*, (pp. 81-91). San Francisco, CA: ACM Press.

Barry, J. R. (1994). *Infrared communications*. Dordrecht, The Netherlands: Kluwer Academic Publishers. doi:10.1007/978-1-4615-2700-8

Bates, T., & Rekhter, Y. (1998). *Scalable support for multihomed multi-provider connectivity*. RFC 2260. Retrieved from http://tools.ietf.org/html/rfc2260

Bazzi, A., Masini, B. M., & Andrisano, O. (2010). On the impact of real time data acquisition from vehicles through UMTS. In *Proceedings of the IEEE International Symposium on Personal, Indoor and Mobile Radio Communications, PIMRC*. Istanbul, Turkey: IEEE Press.

Bazzi, A., Pasolini, G., & Gambetti, C. (2006). SHINE: Simulation platform for heterogeneous interworking networks. In *Proceedings of the IEEE International Conference on Communications*, (vol. 12, pp. 5534-5539). IEEE Press.

Blum, J., Eskandarian, A., & Hoffmman, L. (2004). Challenges of inter-vehicle ad-hoc networks. *IEEE Transactions on Intelligent Transportation Systems*, *5*(4), 347–351. doi:10.1109/TITS.2004.838218

Boneh, D., & Boyen, X. (2004). Short signatures without random oracles. In C. Cachin & J. Camenisch (Eds.), *Eurocrypt 2004 Conference*, (pp. 56–73). Eurocrypt.

Boneh, D., Boyen, X., & Shacham, H. (2004). Short group signatures. *Lecture Notes in Computer Science*, *3152*, 41–55. doi:10.1007/978-3-540-28628-8_3

Borsetti, D., & Gozalvez, J. (2010). Infrastructure-assisted geo-routing for cooperative vehicular networks. In *Proceedings of the 2010 IEEE Vehicular Networking Conference*, (pp. 255-262). IEEE Press.

Boukerche, A. (2008). Vehicular ad hoc networks: A new challenge for localization-based systems. *Computer Communications, 31*(12), 2838–2849. doi:10.1016/j.comcom.2007.12.004

Boynton, T. (2006). *General motors computerized vehicle control systems: A short history.* Retrieved from http://tomboynton.com/GMnetworks.pdf

Brahmi, N., Boukhatem, L., Boukhatem, N., Boussedjra, M., Nuy, N., Dau Labiod, H., & Mouzna, J. (2010). End-to-end routing through a hybrid ad hoc architecture for V2V and V2I communications. In *Proceedings of the 9th IFIP Annual Mediterranean Ad Hoc Networking Workshop*, (pp. 1-8). IFIP.

Burgess, J., Gallagher, B., Jensen, D., & Levine, B. (2006). MaxProp: Routing for vehicle-based disruption-tolerant networks. In *Proceedings IEEE INFOCOM 2006, 25TH IEEE International Conference on Computer Communications*, (pp. 1-11). IEEE Press.

Busanelli, S., Ferrari, G., & Panichpapiboon, S. (2009). Efficient broadcasting in IEEE 802.11 networks through irresponsible forwarding. In *Proceedings of the IEEE Global Telecommunications Conference (GLOBECOM)*, (pp. 1-6). Honolulu, HI: IEEE Press.

Busanelli, S., Ferrari, G., & Giorgio, V. A. (2011). I2V highway and urban vehicular networks: A comparative analysis of the impact of mobility on broadcast data dissemination. *The Journal of Communication, 6*(1), 87–100.

Busse, M., Haenselmann, T., & Effelsberg, W. (2006). TECA: A topology and energy control algorithm for wireless sensor networks. In *Proceedings of ACM Modeling Analysis and Simulation of Wireless and Mobile Systems*, (pp. 317-321). ACM Press.

Bychkovsky, V., Hull, B., Miu, A. K., Balakrishnan, H., & Madden, S. (2006). A measurement study of vehicular internet access using in situ wi-fi networks. In *Proceedings of the ACM/IEEE International Conference on Mobile Computing and Networking (MobiCom).* Los Angeles, CA: ACM/IEEE.

Cai, H., & Lin, Y. (2005). Design of a roadside seamless wireless communication system for intelligent highway. In *Proceedings of the IEEE Network Sensors Control*, (pp. 342–347). IEEE Press.

Calandriello, G., Papadimitratos, P., Hubaux, J.-P., & Lioy, A. (2007). Efficient and robust pseudonymous authentication in VANET. In *Proceedings of the Fourth ACM International Workshop on Vehicular Ad Hoc Networks*, (pp. 19–28). ACM.

California Air Resources Board. (1992). *On-board diagnostics (OBD-II)*. Sacramento, CA: California Air Resources Board.

CALM Forum Ltd. (2006). *The CALM handbook.* Retrieved from http://www.isotc204wg16.org/pubdocs

Campolo, C., & Molinaro, A. (2010). Vehicle-to-roadside multihop data delivery in 802.11p/WAVE vehicular ad hoc networks. In *Proceedings of the GLOBECOM, IEEE Global Telecommunications Conference*, (pp. 1–5). IEEE Press.

Car 2 Car Communication Consortium. (2007). *The car 2 car communication consortium manifesto.* Retrieved from http://www.car-to-car.org

Carris. (2010). *Transportes públicos Lisboa.* Retrieved from from http://www.carris.pt/

Casteigts, A., Nayak, A., & Stojmenovic, I. (2009). Communication protocols for vehicular ad hoc networks. In *Wireless Communications and Mobile Computing.* New York, NY: John Wiley & Sons. doi:10.1002/wcm.879

Cencioni, P., & Di Pietro, R. (2007). VIPER: A vehicle-to-infrastructure communication privacy enforcement protocol. In *Proceedings of the IEEE International Conference on Mobile Adhoc and Sensor Systems*, (pp. 1-6). IEEE.

Ceriotti, M., Corrà, M., Orazio, L. D., Doriguzzi, R., Facchin, D., & Jesi, G. P. … Torghele, C. (2011). Is there light at the ends of the tunnel? Wireless sensor net works for adaptive lighting in road tunnels. In *Proceedings of ACM/IEEE International Conference on Information Processing in Sensor Networks.* Chicago, IL: ACM/IEEE.

Cesana, M., Fratta, L., Gerla, M., Giordano, E., & Pau, G. (2010). C-VeT the UCLA campus vehicular testbed: Integration of VANET and mesh networks. In *Proceedings of European Wireless Conference*. Lucca, Italy: IEEE.

Cetin, N., Burri, A., & Nagel, K. (2003). A large-scale multi-agent traffic microsimulation based on queue model. In *Proceedings of the Swiss Conference on Transport Research (STRC)*. Ascona, Switzerland: STRC.

Chang, C.-J., Cheng, R.-G., Shih, H.-T., & Chen, Y.-S. (2007). Maximum freedom last scheduling algorithm for downlinks of DSRC networks. *IEEE Transactions on Intelligent Transportation Systems*, 8(2), 223–232. doi:10.1109/TITS.2006.889440

Charette, R. N. (2009). This car runs on code. *IEEE Spectrum*. Retrieved from http://spectrum.ieee.org/green-tech/advanced-cars/this-car-runs-on-code/0

Chawathe, S. S. (2006). Inter-vehicle data dissemination in sparse equipped traffic. In *Proceedings of the 2006 IEEE Intelligent Transportation Systems Conference*, (pp. 273-280). IEEE Press.

Chen, Q., Jiang, D., Taliwal, V., & Delgrossi, L. (2006). IEEE 802.11 based vehicular communication simulation design for NS-2. In *Proceedings of the 3rd International Workshop on Vehicular Ad Hoc Networks*, (p. 50–56). New York, NY: ACM Press.

Chen, W., Guha, R., Kwon, T. J., Lee, J., & Hsu, I. (2008). A survey and challenges in routing and data dissemination in vehicular ad-hoc networks. In *Proceedings of the IEEE International Conference on Vehicular Electronics and Safety*, (pp. 328 –333). IEEE Press.

Chen, Y., & Son, S. H. (2005). A fault tolerant topology control in wireless sensor networks. In *Proceedings of ACM/IEEE International Conference on Computer Systems and Applications*, (pp. 57-64). ACM/IEEE.

Chen, Y., Xiang, Z., Jian, W., & Jiang, W. (2009). A cross-layer AOMDV routing protocol for v2v communication in urban vanet. In *Proceedings of the IEEE International Conference on Mobile Ad-Hoc and Sensor Networks*, (pp. 353 –359). IEEE Press.

Cheng, H. T., Shan, H., & Zhuang, W. (2012). Infotainment and road safety service support in vehicular networking: From a communication perspective. *Mechanical Systems and Signal Processing Journal*. Retrieved from http://bbcr.uwaterloo.ca/~wzhuang/papers/MSSP_vanet_survey_2010.pdf

Cheng, L., Henty, B. E., Stancil, D. D., Bai, F., & Mudalige, P. (2007). Mobile vehicle-to-vehicle narrow-band channel measurement and characterization of the 5.9 GHz dedicated short range communication (DSRC) frequency band. *IEEE Journal on Selected Areas in Communications*, 25(8), 1501–1516. doi:10.1109/JSAC.2007.071002

Chen, H.-H., & Guizani, M. (2006). *Next generation wireless systems and networks*. New York, NY: John Wiley and Sons Ltd. doi:10.1002/0470024569

Chen, W., Delgrossi, L., Kosch, T., & Saito, T. (2009). Topics in automotive networking. *IEEE Communications Magazine*, 47(11), 82–83. doi:10.1109/MCOM.2009.5307470

Chicago Transit Authority. (2010). *Website*. Retrieved from http://www.transitchicago.com/

Chou, H., & DeWitt, D. (1985). An evaluation of buffer management strategies for relational database systems. In *Proceedings of the 11th International Conference on Very Large Data Bases (VLDB 1985)*, (vol 11, pp. 27-141). VLDB Endowment.

Chung, Y., & Cho, D.-H. (2003). Performance evaluation of soft handoff for multimedia services in intelligent transportation systems based on CDMA. *IEEE Transactions on Intelligent Transportation Systems*, 4, 189–197. doi:10.1109/TITS.2003.821343

Cicconetti, C., Lenzini, L., & Mingozzi, E. (2008). Scheduling and dynamic relocation for IEEE 802.11s mesh deterministic access. In *Proceedings of the Annual IEEE Communications Society Conference on Sensor, Mesh and Ad Hoc Communications and Networks*, (pp. 19–27). IEEE Press.

Cicconetti, C., Erta, A., Lenzini, L., & Mingozzi, E. (2007). Performance evaluation of the IEEE 802.16 MAC for QoS support. *IEEE Transactions on Mobile Computing*, 6(1), 26–38. doi:10.1109/TMC.2007.250669

Cisco Systems. (2006). *Optimized edge routing*. Retrieved from http://www.cisco.com/en/US/products/ps6628/products_ios_protocol_option_home.html

COMeSafety. (2010). *Communication for esafety*. Retreived Jul. 2010 from http://www.comesafety.org/

Conti, A., Bazzi, A., Masini, B. M., & Andrisano, O. (2009). *Vehicular networks: Techniques, standards, and applications*. Boca Raton, FL: Auerbach Publications.

Costlow, T. (2008). VII (vehicle infrastructure integration) highway communication system gains momentum. *Automotive Engineering International, 116*, 44–45.

Cottingham, D. N., Wassell, I. J., & Harle, R. K. (2007). Performance of IEEE 802.11a in vehicular contexts. In *Proceedings of IEEE Vehicular Technology Conference.* Dublin, Ireland: IEEE Press.

Dahlman, E., Parkvall, S., Skold, J., & Berning, P. (2008). *3G evolution: HSPA and LTE for mobile broadband*. Boston, MA: Academic Press. doi:10.1587/transcom.E92.B.1432

Danlei, Y., & Bae Ko, Y. (2009). FFRDV: Fastest-ferry routing in DTN-enabled vehicular ad hoc networks. In *Proceedings of the 11ᵗʰ International Conference on Advanced Communication Technology*, (pp. 1410-1414). Piscataway, NJ: IEEE Press.

Daoud, R. M., El-Dakroury, M. A., Amer, H. H., Elsayed, H. M., & El-Soudani, M. (2007). *WiFi architecture for traffic control using MIPv6*. Paper presented at the IEEE Mediterranean Conference on Control & Automation MED. Athens, Greece.

Daoud, R. M., El-Dakroury, M. A., Amer, H. H., Elsayed, H. M., El-Soudani, M., & Sallez, Y. (2006). *Wireless vehicle communication for traffic control in urban areas.* Paper presented at the 32nd Annual Conference of the IEEE Industrial Electronics Society IECON. Paris, France.

De Rango, F., Veltri, F., Fazio, P., & Marano, S. (2009). Two-level trajectory-based routing protocol for vehicular ad hoc networks in freeway and Manhattan environments. *Journal of Networks, 4*(9), 866–880.

De Zoysa, K., Keppitiyagama, C., Seneviratne, G. P., & Shihan, W. W. A. T. (2007). A public transport system based sensor network for road surface condition monitoring. In *Proceedings of the 2007 Workshop on Networked Systems for Developing Regions - NSDR 2007,* (p. 1). New York, NY: ACM Press.

Devarapalli, V., Wakikawa, R., Petrescu, A., & Thubert, P. (2005). *Network mobility (NEMO) basic support protocol*. IETF RFC3963. Retrieved from http://www.ietf.org/rfc/rfc3963.txt

Dhurandher, S. K., Obaidat, M. S., Jaiswal, A., Tiwari, A., & Tyagi, A. (2010). Securing vehicular networks: A reputation and plausibility checks-based approach. In *Proceedings of the GLOBECOM Workshops*, (pp. 1550-1554). GLOBECOM.

Ding, Y., Wang, C., & Xiao, L. (2007). A static-node assisted adaptive routing protocol in vehicular networks. In *Proceedings of the ACM International Workshop on Vehicular Ad Hoc Networks (VANET)*. Montreal, Canada: ACM Press.

Document, I. T. U. 5D/469-E. (2009). *Guidelines for using IMT-Advanced channel models*. Retrieved August 6, 2009, from http://projects.celtic-initiative.org/winner+/WINNER+%20and%20ITU-R%20EG%20documents/R07-WP5D-C-0469!!MSW-E%20%28Guidelines%20Finland%29.pdf

Dötzer, F. (2005). Privacy issues in vehicular ad hoc networks. In *Proceedings of the Workshop on Privacy Enhancing Technologies (PET)*. ACM Press.

DTNRG. (2010). *Delay tolerant networking research group*. Retrieved from http://www.dtnrg.org/

Du, K., Wu, J., & Zhou, D. (2003). Chain-based protocols for data broadcasting and gathering in sensor networks. In *Proceedings of the International Parallel and Distributed Processing Symposium,* (pp. 260-267). International Parallel and Distributed Processing.

Eichler, S. (2007). Performance evaluation of the IEEE 802.11p WAVE communication standard. In *Proceedings of the Vehicular Technology Conference*, (pp. 2199–2203). IEEE Press.

El-Dakroury, M. A., Zekry, A. H., Amer, H. H., & Daoud, R. M. (2010). *Traffic control using WiMAX with dual trigger handover*. Paper presented at the 6th International Engineering conference on Computer Engineering ICENCO. Cairo, Egypt.

Eriksson, J., Balakrishnan, H., & Madden, S. (2008). Cabernet: Vehicular content delivery using WiFi. In *Proceedings of the ACM International Conference on Mobile Computing and Networking (MobiCom)*, (pp. 199-210). San Francisco, CA: ACM Press.

Eriksson, J., Girod, L., Hull, B., Newton, R., Madden, S., & Balakrishnan, H. (2008). The pothole patrol. In *Proceeding of the 6th International Conference on Mobile Systems, Applications, and Services - MobiSys 2008*, (p. 29). New York, NY: ACM Press.

Ernst, T., Nebehaj, V., & Srasen, R. (2009). CVIS: CALM proof of concept preliminary results. In *Proceedings of International Conference on Intelligent Transport Systems Telecommunications*. Lille, France: IEEE.

ETSI. (2011). *ETSI technical committee on intelligent transport systems*. Retrieved from http://www.etsi.org/website/Technologies/IntelligentTransportSystems.asp

European Parliament. (2010). Directive 2010/40/EU on the framework for the deployment of intelligent transport systems in the field of road transport and for interfaces with other modes of transport. *Official Journal of European Union*. Lyon, France: European Parliament.

Evensen, K. (2010). Intelligent transport systems, European standardization for ITS: WG2 architecture. In *Proceedings of the ETSI TC ITS Workshop*. ETSI.

Fan, Z., & Zhou, H. (2007). A scalable power-efficient data gathering protocol with delay guaranty for wireless sensor networks. *Lecture Notes in Computer Science*, *4864*, 221–232. doi:10.1007/978-3-540-77024-4_22

Farsi, M., Ratcliff, K., & Barbosa, M. (1999). An overview of controller area network. *Computing & Control Engineering Journal*, *10*(3), 113–120. doi:10.1049/cce:19990304

Ferreira, N., Meireles, T., & Fonseca, J. A. (2009). An RSU coordination scheme for WAVE safety services support. In *Proceedings of the IEEE Conference on Emerging Technologies & Factory Automation*, (pp. 1-4). IEEE.

Festag, A., Hessler, A., Baldessari, R., Le, L., Zhang, W., & Westhoff, D. (2008). Vehicle-to-vehicle and road-side sensor communication for enhanced road safety. In *Proceedings of the 9th International Conference on Intelligent Tutoring Systems (ITS 2008)*. IEEE Press.

Fiore, M., & Barcelo-Ordinas, J. M. (2009). Cooperative download in urban vehicular networks. In *Proceedings of the IEEE International Conference on Mobile Adhoc and Sensor Systems (MASS)*. Macau, China: IEEE Press.

Freudiger, J., Raya, M., Félegyházi, M., Papadimitratos, P., & Hubaux, J.-P. (2007). *Mix-zones for location privacy in vehicular networks*. Paper presented at the 1st International Workshop on Wireless Networking for Intelligent Transportation Systems. Vancouver, Canada.

Friedman, R., Gavidia, D., Rodrigues, L., Viana, A., & Voulgaris, S. (2007). Gossiping on MANETs: The beauty and the beast. *SIGOPS Operating Systems Review*, *41*(5), 237–288.

Gao, W., & Cao, G. (2011). User-centric data dissemination in disruption tolerant networks. In *Proceedings of INFOCOM*. IEEE.

Gao, H., Utecht, S., Patrick, G., Hsieh, G., Xu, F., & Wang, H. (2010). High speed data routing in vehicular sensor networks. *The Journal of Communication*, *5*(3), 181–188.

GeoNET. (2010). *Geographic addressing and routing for vehicular communications*. Retreived Nov. 2010 from http://www.geonet-project.eu/

Ghassemlooy, Z., & Boucouvalas, A. C. (2005). Indoor optical wireless communications systems and networks. *International Journal of Communication Systems*, *18*, 191–193. doi:10.1002/dac.698

Giordano, S., Lenzarini, D., Puiatti, A., Kulig, M., Nguyen, H. A., & Vanini, S. (2006). Demonstrating seamless handover of multi-hop networks. In *Proceedings of International Workshop on Multi-Hop Ad Hoc Networks: From Theory to Reality*. Florence, Italy: IEEE.

Gomez Marmol, F., & Martinez Perez, G. (2011). TRIP: A trust and reputation infrastructure-based proposal for vehicular ad hoc networks. *Network and Computer Applications Journal*. Retrieved from http://people.stfx.ca/x2010/x2010qfo/HONOR_THESIS/TRMSIM_RESOURCES/TRIP,%20a%20trust%20and%20reputation%20infrastructure-based%20proposal%20for%20vehicular%20and%20Ad%20Hoc%20Network.pdf

Google. (2011). *Map data & Europa technologies, INEGI*. Retrieved from http://maps.google.com/

Gu, B., Jung, J., Kim, K., Heo, J., Park, N., Jeon, G., & Cho, Y. (2010). SWICOM: An SDR-based wireless communication gateway for vehicles. *IEEE Transactions on Vehicular Technology*, *59*, 1593–1605. doi:10.1109/TVT.2009.2040004

Gukhool, B., & Cherkaoui, S. (2008). IEEE 802.11p modeling in ns-2. In *Proceedings of the 33rd IEEE Conference on Local Computer Networks, LCN*, (pp. 622–626). IEEE Press.

Guo, H., & Wu, Y. (2009). An integrated embedded solution for vehicle communication & control. In *Proceedings of International Conference on Robotics, Informatics, Intelligence Control System Technologies*. Bangkok, Thailand: IEEE.

Guo, J., Baugh, J. P., & Wang, S. (2007). A group signature based secure and privacy-preserving vehicular communication framework. In *Proceedings of the Mobile Networking for Vehicular Environments Conference*, (pp. 103-108). IEEE.

Guo, M., Ammar, M.-H., & Zegura, E. W. (2005). V3: A vehicle-to-vehicle live video streaming architecture. In *Proceedings of IEEE International Conference on PerCom*, (pp. 171–180). IEEE Press.

Gupta, A., Chaudhary, V., Kumar, V., Nishad, B., & Tapaswi, S. (2010). VD4: Vehicular density-dependent data delivery model in vehicular ad hoc networks. In *Proceedings of the Sixth Advanced International Conference on Telecommunications*, (pp. 286-291). IEEE.

Haas, J. J., Hu, Y.-C., & Laberteaux, K. P. (2010). The impact of key assignment on VANET privacy. In *Proceedings of 1st International Workshop on Security and Communication Networks*, (vol 3, pp. 233-249). New York, NY: John Wiley & Sons, Ltd.

Haas, Z., Halpern, J., & Li, L. (2006). Gossip-based ad hoc routing. *IEEE/ACM Transactions on Networking*, *14*(3), 479–491. doi:10.1109/TNET.2006.876186

Haenselmann, T. (2006). *GFDL wireless sensor network textbook*. GFDL.

Haklay, M., & Weber, P. (2008). OpenStreetMap: User-generated street maps. *IEEE Pervasive Computing / IEEE Computer Society [and] IEEE Communications Society*, *7*(4), 12–18. doi:10.1109/MPRV.2008.80

Hao, W., Richard, F., Randall, G., & Michael, H. (2004). MDDV: A mobility-centric data dissemination algorithm for vehicular networks. In *Proceedings of the 1st ACM International Workshop on Vehicular Ad Hoc Networks*, (pp. 47-56). ACM Press.

He, R., Rutagemwa, H., & Shen, X. (2008). Differentiated reliable routing in hybrid vehicular ad hoc networks. In *Proceedings of the IEEE International Conference on Communications*, (pp. 2353-2358). IEEE.

Heinzelman, W., Chandrakasan, A., & Balakrishnan, H. (2000). Energy efficient communication protocol for wireless micro sensor networks. In *Proceedings of the 33rd Annual Hawaii International Conference on System Sciences*, (pp. 3005-3014). Hawaii, HI: IEEE.

Heinzelman, W., Chandrakasan, A., & Balakrishnan, H. (2002). An application-specific protocol architecture for wireless microsensor networks. *IEEE Transactions on Wireless Communications*, *1*, 660–670. doi:10.1109/TWC.2002.804190

Hiertz, G., Denteneer, D., Max, S., Taori, R., Cardona, J., Berlemann, L., & Walke, W. (2010). IEEE 802.11s: The WLAN mesh standard. *IEEE Wireless Communications*, *17*(1), 104–111. doi:10.1109/MWC.2010.5416357

Hightower, J., & Borriello, G. (2001). Location systems for ubiquitous computing. *Computer, 34*(8), 57–66. doi:10.1109/2.940014

Holma, H., & Toskala, A. (2004). *WCDMA for UMTS - Radio access for third generation mobile communications* (4th ed.). New York, NY: Wiley.

Hossain, I., & Mahmud, S. M. (2007). Analysis of a secure software upload technique in advanced vehicles using wireless links. [IEEE Press.]. *Proceedings of IEEE ITS, C*, 1010–1015.

Hsiao, P., Hwang, A., Kung, H. T., & Vlah, D. (2001). Load balancing routing for wireless access network. []. Cambridge, MA: INFOCOM.]. *Proceedings of INFO-COM, 2*, 986–995.

Huang, L., Matsuura, K., Yamane, H., & Sezaki, K. (2005). Enhancing wireless location privacy using silent period. In *Proceedings of the Wireless Communications and Networking Conference*, (pp. 1187-1192). IEEE.

Hubaux, J. P., Capkun, S., & Luo, J. (2004). The security and privacy of smart vehicles. *IEEE Security & Privacy, 2*, 49–55. doi:10.1109/MSP.2004.26

Hui, P., Crowcroft, J., & Yoneki, E. (2008). Bubble rap: Social-based forwarding in delay tolerant networks. In *Proceedings of the 9th ACM International Symposium on Mobile Ad Hoc Networking and Computing (MobiHoc 2008)*, (pp. 241-250). New York, NY: ACM.

Hu, Y., Xue, Y., Li, Q., Liu, F., Keung, G. Y., & Li, B. (2009). The sink node placement and performance implication in mobile sensor networks. [MONET]. *Journal on Mobile Networks and Applications, 14*, 230–240. doi:10.1007/s11036-009-0158-5

IEEE 802.11p. (2010). *Standard for information technology- Telecommunications and information exchange between systems- Local and metropolitan area networks- Specific requirements part 11 - Amendment 6: Wireless access in vehicular environment*. Washington, DC: IEEE.

IEEE 802.11p. (2010). *Website*. Retrieved July 2010, from http://www.ieee802.org/11/Reports/tgp update.htm

IEEE 802.15.7. (2010). *Website*. Retrieved March 2010 from http://www.ieee802.org/15/pub/TG7.html

IEEE Standard 802.16e-2005. (2006). *Amendment to IEEE standard for local and metropolitan area networks – Part 16: Air interface for fixed broadband wireless access systems – Physical and medium access control layers for combined fixed and mobile operation in licensed bands*. Retrieved Feb 15, 2009, from http://ieee802.org/16/pubs/80216e.html

IEEE. (2007). *IEEE standards association, IEEE P1609.1—Standard for wireless access in vehicular environments (WAVE)—Resource manager, IEEE P1609.2—Standard for wireless access in vehicular environments (WAVE)—Security services for applications and management messages, IEEE P1609.3—Standard for wireless access in vehicular environments (WAVE)—Networking services, IEEE P1609.4— Standard for wireless access in vehicular environments (WAVE)—Multi-channel operations, adopted for trial-use in 2007*. Piscataway, NJ: IEEE Press.

IEEE. (2007). *IEEE Std 802.11TM-2007 part 11: Wireless LAN medium access control (MAC) and physical layer (PHY) specifications*. Washington, DC: IEEE Press.

IEEE. (2010). IEEE standard for information technology--Telecommunications and information exchange between systems--Local and metropolitan area networks--Specific requirements part 11: Wireless LAN medium access control (MAC) and physical layer (PHY) specifications amendment 6: Wireless access in vehicular environments. In *IEEE Std 802.11p-2010 (Amendment to IEEE Std 802.11-2007 as amended by IEEE Std 802.11k-2008, IEEE Std 802.11r-2008, IEEE Std 802.11y-2008, IEEE Std 802.11n-2009, and IEEE Std 802.11w-2009)*, (pp. 1-51). Washington, DC: IEEE Press.

IEEE. Computer Society. (2003). *Wireless medium access control (MAC) and physical layer (PHY) specifications for low-rate wireless personal area networks (LR- WPAN)*. Washington, DC: IEEE Computer Society.

IEEE. Computer Society. (2010). *802.11p-2010 - IEEE standard for local and metropolitan area networks - Specific requirements part 11: Wireless LAN medium access control (MAC) and physical layer (PHY) specifications amendment 6: Wireless access in vehicular environments*. Washington, DC: IEEE Computer Society.

Iera, A., Molinaro, A., Polito, S., & Ruggeri, G. (2008). A multi-layer cooperation framework for QoS-aware internet access in Vanets. *Ubiquitous Computing and Communication Journal, 10*(4), 10–19.

Isaac, S. (2010). Security attacks and solutions for vehicular ad hoc networks. *IET Communications, 4*(7), 894–903. doi:10.1049/iet-com.2009.0191

ISO TC 204 WG 16. (2011). *Communications access for land mobiles (CALM)*. Retrieved from http://www.isotc204wg16.org

ISOTC204WG16. (2009). *Communication access for land mobile*. Retreived Aug. 2009 from http://www.isotc204wg16.org/concept

ISOTC204WG16. (2010). *Communication access for land mobile*. Retrieved from http://www.isotc204wg16.org/concept

ITS. (2010). *Website*. Retrieved from http://www.its.dot.gov/research.htm

ITU-R M.1225 Recommendation for IMT-2000 Radio Interfaces. (1997). *Guidelines for evaluation of radio transmission technologies for IMT-2000*. Retrieved June 6, 2009, from http://www.itu.int/dms_pubrec/itu-r/rec/m/R-REC-M.1225-0-199702-I!!PDF-E.pdf

Iwasaki, S., Wada, M., Endo, T., Fujii, T., & Tanimoto, M. (2007). Basic Experiments on parallel wireless optical communication for ITS. In *Proceedings of the IEEE Intelligent Vehicles Symposium*, (pp. 321-326). IEEE Press.

Japan Ministry of Land. (2007). *Infrastructure and transport, road bureau, smartway 2007 public road test*. Retrieved from http://www.its.go.jp/ITS/topindex/topindex_sw2007.html

Jenhui, C., Chih-Chieh, W., & Jiann-Der, L. (2007). *Pre-coordination mechanism for fast handover in WiMAX networks*. Paper presented at the 2nd International Conference on Wireless Broadband and Ultra Wideband Communications (AusWireless). Sydney, Australia.

Jerbi, M., Senouci, S.-M., Rasheed, T., & Ghamri-Doudane, Y. (2009). Towards efficient geographic routing in urban vehicular networks. *IEEE Transactions on Vehicular Technology, 58*(9), 5048–5059. doi:10.1109/TVT.2009.2024341

Jiang, D., & Delgrossi, L. (2008). IEEE 802.11p: Towards an international standard for wireless access in vehicular environments. In *Proceedings of the Vehicular Technology Conference, VTC Spring*, (pp. 2036–2040). IEEE Press.

Johnson, D., Perkins, C., & Arkko, J. (2004). *Mobility support in IPv6*. RFC 3775. Retrieved from http://www.ietf.org/rfc/rfc3775.txt

Johnson, D., & Maltz, D. (1996). Dynamic source routing in ad hoc wireless networks. In Imielinski, T., & Korth, H. F. (Eds.), *Mobile Computing* (pp. 153–181). Dordrecht, The Netherlands: Kluwer International. doi:10.1007/978-0-585-29603-6_5

Journey Planner. (2011). *Transport for London*. Retrieved from http://journeyplanner.tfl.gov.uk/

Jung, W. S., Lim, K. W., Ko, Y. B., & Park, S. J. (2009). A hybrid approach for clustering-based data aggregation in wireless sensor networks. In *Proceedings of the Third International Conference on Digital Society*, (pp. 112-117). IEEE.

Jungum, N. V., Doomun, R. M., Ghurbhurrun, S. D., & Pudaruth, S. (2008). Collaborative driving support system in mobile pervasive environments. In *Proceedings of ICWMC*, (pp. 358–363). ICWMC.

Kakkasageri, M., & Manvi, S. (2011). Cognitive agent based framework for safety information dissemination in vehicular ad hoc networks. In *Proceedings of the First International Conference on Computer Science and Information Technology*, (pp. 254-264). Berlin, Germany: Springer Publishers.

Kamini, & Kumar, R. (2010). VANET parameters and applications: A review. *Global Journal of Computer Science and Technology, 10*(7), 72-77.

Karedal, J., Czink, N., Paier, A., Tufvesson, F., & Molisch, A. F. (2011). Path loss modeling for vehicle-to-vehicle communications. *IEEE Transactions on Vehicular Technology, 60*, 323–328. doi:10.1109/TVT.2010.2094632

Karnadi, F., Mo, Z. H., & Lan, K. C. (2007). Rapid generation of realistic mobility models for VANET. In *Proceedings of the IEEE Wireless Communications and Networking Conference (WCNC)*, (pp. 2506-2511). Hong Kong, China: IEEE Press.

Karp, B., & Kung, H. T. (2000). GPSR: Greedy perimeter stateless routing for wireless networks. In *Proceedings of the 6th Annual International Conference on Mobile Computing and Networking*, (pp. 243–254). ACM Press.

Karp, B. N. (2000). *Geographic routing for wireless networks*. Boston, MA: Harvard University.

Khan, J. M., & Barry, J. R. (1997). Wireless infrared communications. *Proceedings of the IEEE, 85*, 265–298. doi:10.1109/5.554222

Kim, H. S., & Han, K. J. (2005). A power efficient routing protocol based on balanced tree in the WSN. In *Proceedings of the 1st International Conference on Distributed Framework for Multimedia Applications*, (pp. 138-143). IEEE.

Kim, H., Seok, Y., Choi, N., Choi, Y., & Kwon, T. (2005). Optimal multi-sink positioning and energy-efficient routing in wireless sensor networks. In *Proceedings of the International Conference on Information Networking (ICOIN)*. Jeju Island, Korea: ICOIN.

Kiokes, G., Amditis, A., & Uzunoglu, N. K. (2009). Simulation-based performance analysis and improvement of orthogonal frequency division multiplexing – 802.11p system for vehicular communications. In *Proceedings of the IET Intelligent Transport Systems*, (pp. 429–436). IET.

Kitano, S., Haruyama, S., & Nakagawa, M. (2003). LED road illumination communication system. In *Proceedings of the IEEE Vehicular Technology Conference*, (vol. 5, pp. 3346-3350). IEEE Press.

Kone, V., Zheng, H., Rowstron, A., & Zhao, B. (2010). *The impact of infostation density on vehicular data dissemination*. Retrieved from http://www.cs.ucsb.edu/~ravenben/publications/pdf/vanet-monet10.pdf

Korkmaz, G., Ekici, E., & Ozguner, F. (2006). Internet access protocol providing QoS in vehicular networks with infrastructure support. In *Proceedings of the Intelligent Transportation Systems Conference ITSC*, (pp. 1412-1417). IEEE.

Korkmaz, G., Ozguner, F., Ekici, E., & Ozguner, U. (2004). Urban multihop broadcast protocol for intervehicle communication systems. In *Proceedings of the 1st ACM International Workshop on Vehicular Ad Hoc Networks*, (pp. 76-85). ACM Press.

Kosch, T., Adler, C., Eichler, S., Schroth, C., & Strassberger, M. (2006). The scalability problem of vehicular ad hoc networks and how to solve it. *IEEE Wireless Communications, 13*(5), 22–28. doi:10.1109/WC-M.2006.250354

Krajzewicz, D., Hertkorn, G., Rössel, C., & Wagner, P. (2002). SUMO (simulation of urban mobility)-An open-source traffic simulation. In *Proceedings of the 4th Middle East Symposium on Simulation and Modelling (MESM 2002)*, (pp. 183–187). MESM.

Krauss, S., Wagner, P., & Gawron, C. (1997). Metastable states in a microscopic model of traffic flow. *Physical Review E: Statistical Physics, Plasmas, Fluids, and Related Interdisciplinary Topics, 55*, 5597–5602. doi:10.1103/PhysRevE.55.5597

Krumke, S. O., Marathe, M. V., Poensgen, D., Ravi, S. S., & Wirth, H.-C. (2002). Budgeted maximum graph coverage. *Lecture Notes in Computer Science, 2573*, 321–332. doi:10.1007/3-540-36379-3_28

Kruskal, J. B. (1956). On the shortest spanning subtree of a graph and the traveling salesman problem. *Proceedings of the American Mathematical Society, 7*(1), 48–50. doi:10.1090/S0002-9939-1956-0078686-7

Ksentini, A., Tounsi, H., & Frikha, M. (2010). A proxy-based framework for QoS-enabled internet access in VANETS. In *Proceedings of the Second International Conference on Communications and Networking*, (pp. 1-8). IEEE.

Kumar, N., Alves, L. N., & Aguiar, R. L. (2011). Performance study of direct sequence spread spectrum based visible light communication systems for traffic information transmission. Unpublished.

Kumar, N., Terra, D., Lourenço, N., Alves, L. N., & Aguiar, R. L. (2011). *Visible light communication for intelligent transportation in road safety application*. Paper presented at 7th International Wireless Communications and Mobile Computing Conference. Istanbul, Turkey.

Kumar, V., & Chand, N. (2010). Data scheduling in VANETs: A review. *International Journal of Computer Science & Communication, 1*(2), 399–403.

Lai, K. K., & Jimmy, W. M. C. (1997). Developing a simulated annealing algorithm for the cutting stock problem. *Pergamon Press, 32*, 115-127.

Lal, S., & Panwar, D. K. (2007). *Coverage analysis of handoff algorithm with adaptive hysteresis margin.* Paper presented at the 10th International Conference on Information Technology ICIT. Rourkela, India.

Langley, C., Lucas, R., & Fu, H. (2008). Key management in vehicular ad-hoc networks. In *Proceedings of International Conference on Electro/Information Technology,* (pp. 223-226). IEEE.

Lee, K. C., & Gerla, M. (2010). Opportunistic vehicular routing. In *Proceedings of the 2010 European Wireless Conference (EW),* (pp. 873-880). Lucca, Italy: IEEE Press.

Lee, U., Park, J.-S., Amir, E., & Gerla, M. (2006). Fleanet: A virtual market place on vehicular networks. In *Proceedings of the International Conference on Mobile Ubiquitous Systems Workshops,* (pp. 1–8). IEEE.

Lee, U., & Gerla, M. (2010). A survey of urban vehicular sensing platforms. *Computer Networks, 54*(4), 527–544. doi:10.1016/j.comnet.2009.07.011

Lenzini, L., & Mingozzi, E. (2001). Performance evaluation of capacity request and allocation mechanisms for HiperLAN/2 wireless LANs. *Computer Networks, 37*(1), 5–15. doi:10.1016/S1389-1286(01)00194-3

Leontiadis, I., Costa, P., & Mascolo, C. (2009). Persistent content-based information dissemination in hybrid vehicular networks. In *Proceedings on IEEE International Conference on Pervasive Computing and Communications,* (pp. 1-10). Galveston, TX: IEEE Press.

Li, F., & Wang, Y. (2007). Routing in vehicular ad hoc networks: A survey. *IEEE Vehicular Technology Magazine, 2*(2), 12–22. doi:10.1109/MVT.2007.912927

Lim, K. W., & Ko, Y.-B. (2010). Multi-hop data harvesting in vehicular sensor networks. *IET Communications, 4*(7), 768. doi:10.1049/iet-com.2009.0075

Lindgren, A., & Phanse, K. (2006). Evaluation of queueing policies and forwarding strategies for routing in intermittently connected networks. In *Proceedings of the First International Conference on COMmunication System softWAre and MiddlewaRE,* (pp. 1-10). IEEE.

Lindgren, A., Doria, A., & Schelén, O. (2003). Probabilistic routing in intermittently connected networks. *SIGMOBILE Mobile Computer Communication Review, 7*(3), 19–20. doi:10.1145/961268.961272

Lindsey, S., & Raghavendra, C. S. (2002). PEGASIS: Power-efficient gathering in sensor information systems. In *Proceedings of IEEE Aerospace Conference,* (vol 3, pp. 1125-1130). IEEE Press.

Lin, Y.-B., Lai, W.-R., & Chen, J.-J. (2003). Effects of cache mechanism on wireless data access. *IEEE Transactions on Wireless Communications, 2,* 1247–1258. doi:10.1109/TWC.2003.819019

Li, R., & Jia, L. (2009). On the layout of fixed urban traffic detectors: An application study. *IEEE Intelligent Transportation Systems Magazine, 1*(2), 6–12. doi:10.1109/MITS.2009.933858

Liu, B. (1996). Intelligent route finding: Combining knowledge, cases and an efficient search algorithm. In *Proceedings of the 12th European Conference on Artificial Intelligence,* (pp. 380-384). New York, NY: Wiley and Sons, Ltd.

Liu, B., Zhong, Y., & Zhang, S. (2007). Probabilistic isolation of malicious vehicles in pseudonym changing VANETS. In *Proceedings of the 7th IEEE International Conference on Computer and Information Technology,* (pp. 967-972). IEEE.

Liu, Y., Bi, J., & Yang, J. (2009). Research on vehicular ad hoc networks. In *Proceedings of the Control and Decision Conference, CCDC 2009,* (pp. 4430-4435). CCDC.

Lo, N.-W., & Tsai, H.-C. (2007). Illusion attack on VANET applications - A message plausibility problem. In *Proceedings of the 2nd IEEE Workshop on Automotive Networking and Applications (AutoNet 2007),* (pp. 1-8, 26-30). IEEE.

Lochert, C., Hartenstein, H., Tian, J., Fussler, H., Hermann, D., & Mauve, M. (2003). A routing strategy for vehicular ad hoc networks in city environments. In *Proceedings of the Intelligent Vehicles Symposium, 2003,* (Vol. 2000, pp. 156–161). IEEE Press.

Lochert, C., Scheuermann, B., & Mauve, M. (2007). Probabilistic aggregation for data dissemination in VANETs. In *Proceedings of the Fourth ACM International Workshop on Vehicular Ad Hoc Networks (VANET 2007)*, (pp. 1-8). New York, NY: ACM.

Lochert, C., Scheuermann, B., Caliskan, M., & Mauve, M. (2007). The feasibility of information dissemination in vehicular ad-hoc networks. In *Proceedings of the ACM International Conference on Wireless on Demand Network Systems*, (pp. 92-99). Obergurgl, Austria: ACM Press.

Lochert, C., Scheuermann, B., Wewetzer, C., Luebke, A., & Mauve, M. (2008). Data aggregation and roadside unit placement for a VANET traffic information system. In *Proceedings of the ACM International Workshop on Vehicular Ad Hoc Networks (VANET)*. San Francisco, CA: ACM Press.

Lochert, C., Scheuermann, B., Wewetzer, C., Luebke, A., & Mauve, M. (2008). Data aggregation and roadside unit placement for a vanet traffic information system. In *Proceedings of the Fifth ACM International Workshop on VehiculAr Inter-NETworking*, (pp. 58–65). ACM Press.

Lok, M. J., Qazi, B. R., & Elmirghani, J. M. H. (2009). Data dissemination with drop boxes. In *Proceedings of the 2009 International Conference on Advanced Information Networking and Applications*, (pp. 451-455). IEEE Press.

Mahmoud, A., Stephan, O., & Khaled, I. (2009). A secure and privacy aware data dissemination for the notification of traffic incidents. In *Proceedings of the Vehicular Technology Conference*, (pp. 1-5). IEEE.

Majanen, M., Perala, P. H. J., Casey, T., Nurmi, J., & Veselinovic, N. (2009). *Mobile WiMAX handover performance evaluation*. Paper presented at the IEEE Fifth International Conference on Networking and Services ICNS. Valencia, Spain.

Malandrino, F., Casetti, C., Chiasserini, C.-F., & Fiore, M. (2011). Content downloading in vehicular networks: What really matters. In *Proceedings of the IEEE International Conference on Computer Communications (INFOCOM)*. Shangai, China: IEEE Press.

Mambrini, R., Rossi, A., Pagano, P., Ancilotti, P., Salvetti, O., & Bertolino, A. … Costalli, L. (2011). IPERMOB: Towards an information system to handle urban mobility data. In *Proceedings of Models and Technologies for ITS*. Leuven, Belgium: ITS.

Mancuso, V., & Bianchi, G. (2004). Streaming for vehicular users via elastic proxy buffer management. *IEEE Communications Magazine, 42*, 144–152. doi:10.1109/MCOM.2004.1362558

Manvi, S., & Kakkasageri, M. (2008). Issues in mobile ad hoc networks for vehicular communication. *IETE Technical Review, 25*(2), 59–72.

Manvi, S., Kakkasageri, M., & Pitt, J. (2009). Multiagent based information dissemination in vehicular ad-hoc networks. *Mobile Information Systems, 5*(4), 363–389.

Marfia, G., Pau, G., Giordano, E., De Sena, E., & Gerla, M. (2007). Evaluating vehicle network strategies for downtown Portland: Opportunistic infrastructure and importance of realistic mobility models. In *Proceedings of the ACM International Workshop on Mobile Opportunistic Networking (MobiOpp)*. San Juan, Puerto Rico: ACM Press.

Marios, D., Saif, I., Tamer, N., & Liviu, I. (2005). VITP: An information transfer protocol for vehicular computing. In *Proceedings of the 2nd ACM International Workshop on Vehicular Ad Hoc Networks*, (pp. 30-39). ACM Press.

Mariyasagayam, M. N., Menouar, H., & Lenardi, M. (2008). *GeoNet: A project enabling active safety and IPv6 vehicular applications*. Paper presented at IEEE International Conference on Vehicular Electronics and Safety (ICVES). Columbus, OH.

Martelli, F., Renda, M. E., & Santi, P. (2011). Measuring IEEE 802.11p performance for active safety applications in cooperative vehicular systems. In *Proceedings of IEEE Vehicular Technology Conference*. Budapest, Hungary: IEEE Press.

Martinez, F., Toh, C.-K., Cano, J.-C., Calafate, C., & Manzoni, P. (2009). Realistic radio propagation models (rpms) for VANET simulations. In *Proceedings of the Wireless Communications and Networking Conference, WCNC*, (pp. 1–6). IEEE Press.

Martinez, F., Toh, C.-K., Cano, J.-C., Calafate, C., & Manzoni, P. (2010). Emergency services in future intelligent transportation systems based on vehicular communication networks. *IEEE Intelligent Transportation Systems Magazine, 2*(2), 6–20. doi:10.1109/MITS.2010.938166

Masini, B. M., Fontana, C., & Verdone, R. (2004). Provision of an emergency warning service through GPRS: Performance evaluation. In *Proceedings. The 7th International IEEE Conference on Intelligent Transportation Systems*, (pp. 1098-1102). IEEE Press.

Masini, B. M., Zuliani, L., & Andrisano, O. (2006). On the effectiveness of a GPRS based intelligent transportation system in a realistic scenario. In *Proceedings of the IEEE Vehicular Technology Conference, VTC*, (vol. 6, pp. 2997-3001). IEEE Press.

MBTA. (2011). *Massachusetts bay transportation authority*. Retrieved from http://www.mbta.com/

McCanne, S., Floyd, S., Fall, K., Varadhan, K., et al. (1997). *Network simulator ns-2.*

Menouar, H., Filali, F., & Lenardi, M. (2006). A survey and qualitative analysis of MAC protocols for vehicular ad hoc networks. *IEEE Wireless Communication, 13*, 30–35. doi:10.1109/WC-M.2006.250355

Metro. (2011). *Companhia do metropolitano de São Paulo*. Retrieved from http://www.metro.sp.gov.br/

Metropolitano de Lisboa. (2011). *Metro de Lisboa reformula sistema de informação das estações*. Retrieved from http://www.metrolisboa.pt/Default.aspx?tabid=1063

Michael, S., & Imad, M. (2010). Stochastic broadcast for VANET. In *Proceedings of the 7th IEEE Conference on Consumer Communications and Networking*, (pp. 13-18). IEEE Press.

Miller, J. (2012). Vehicle-to-vehicle-to-infrastructure (V2V2I) intelligent transportation system architecture. In *Proceedings of the IEEE Intelligent Vehicles Symposium*, (pp. 715 –720). IEEE Press.

Misra, S., Woungang, I., & Misra, S. C. (2009). *Guide to wireless ad hoc networks*. New York, NY: Springer-Verlag. doi:10.1007/978-1-84800-328-6

Mobile WiMAX – Part 1. (2007). *A technical overview and performance evaluation*. Retrieved August 27, 2008, from http://www.wimaxforum.org/technology/downloads/Mobile_WiMAX_Part1_Overview_and_Performance.pdf

Modeler Key Features, O. P. N. E. T. (2009). *OPNET modeler official website*. Retrieved January 15, 2010, from http://www.opnet.com/solutions/network_rd/modeler.html

Mohandas, B. K., Liscano, R., & Yang, O. (2009). *Vehicle traffic congestion management in vehicular ad-hoc networks*. Paper presented at the IEEE 34th Conference on Local Computer Networks LCN. Zürich, Switzerland.

Mohandas, B., Nayak, A., Naik, K., & Goel, N. (2008). ABSRP - A service discovery approach for vehicular ad-hoc network. In *Proceedings of the IEEE Asia-Pacific Services Computing Conference*, (pp. 1590-1594). IEEE Press.

Motorola Wi4 WiMAX Access Service Network ASN Gateway Data Sheet. (2008). *Website*. Retrieved April 6, 2010, from http://www.motorola.com/web/Business/Products/WirelessBroadbanNetworks/WiMAX/WiMAX-AccessPoints/WAP600/_Documents/Static_files/wi4_WiMAX_Access_Service_Network_ASN_Gateway_Data_Sheet_Copy.pdf

Motsinger, C., & Hubbing, T. (2007). *A review of vehicle-to-vehicle and vehicle-to-infrastructure initiatives*. Clemson, SC: University of Clemson.

Moustafa, H., & Zhang, Y. (Eds.). (2009). *Vehicular networks techniques: Standards and applications*. Boca Raton, FL: CRC Press. doi:10.1201/9781420085723

Murat, C., Daniel, G., & Martin, M. (2006). Decentralized discovery of free parking places. In *Proceedings of the 3rd International Conference on Mobile Computing and Networking*, (pp. 30-39). IEEE.

Murty, R. N., Mainland, G., Rose, I., Chowdhury, A. R., Gosain, A., Bers, J., et al. (2008). CitySense: An urbanscale wireless sensor network and testbed. In *Proceedings of the 2008 IEEE Conference on Technologies for Homeland Security*, (pp. 583-588). IEEE Press.

Nadeem, T., Dashtinezhad, S., Liao, C., & Iftode, L. (2004). Trafficview: Traffic data dissemination using car-to-car communication. *ACM SIGMOBILE Mobile Computing and Communications Review, 8.*

National Marine Electronics Association. (1993). *NMEA 0183: Standard for interfacing marine eletronic devices.* Severna Park, MD: NMEA.

Naumov, V. (2011). *Realistic vehicular traces.* Retrieved April 6, 2011, from http://lst.inf.ethz.ch/ad-hoc/car-traces

Nekovee, M. (2005). *Sensor networks on the road: The promises and challenges of vehicular adhoc networks and vehicular grids.* Paper presented at the Workshop on Ubiquitous Computing and e-Research. Edinburgh, UK.

Network Simulator 2. (2011). *Website.* Retrieved from http://isi.edu/nsnam/ns/

Ng, C., Ernst, T., Paik, E., & Bagnulo, M. (2007). *Analysis of multihomming in network mobility support.* RFC 4980. Retrieved from http://ietfreport.isoc.org/idref/rfc4980/

Niculescu, D., & Nath, B. (2003). Trajectory based forwarding and its applications. In *Proceedings of the 9th International Conference on Mobile Computing and Networking,* (pp. 260-272). IEEE.

Nzouonta, J., Rajgure, N., Wang, G., & Borcea, C. (2003). VANET routing on city roads using real-time vehicular traffic information. *IEEE Transactions on Vehicular Technology, 58*(7), 3609–3626. doi:10.1109/TVT.2009.2014455

Ohmori, S., Yamao, Y., & Nakajima, N. (2000). The future generations of mobile communications based on broadband access technologies. *IEEE Communications Magazine, 38*(12), 134–142. doi:10.1109/35.888267

Olariu, S., & Weigle, C. M. (Eds.). (2009). *Vehicular networks from theory to practice.* Boca Raton, FL: CRC Press. doi:10.1201/9781420085891

Open Street Map. (2011). *Website.* Retrieved from http://www.openstreetmap.org

Ott, J., & Kutscher, D. (2004). Drive-thru internet: IEEE 802.11b for "automobile" users. In *Proceedings of the International Conference on Computer Communications (INFOCOM).* Hong Kong, China: IEEE Press.

Oyama, S. (2008). *Vehicle safety communications: Progresses in Japan.* Paper presented at the IEEE International Conference on Vehicular Electronics and Safety ICVES. Columbus, OH.

Oyman, E. I., & Ersoy, C. (2004). Multiple sink network design problem in large scale wireless networks. In *Proceedings of the IEEE International Conference on Communications (ICC).* Paris, France: IEEE Press.

Pagano, P., Petracca, M., Alessandrelli, D., & Nastasi, C. (2011). Enabling technologies and reference architecture for a EU-wide distributed intelligent transport system. In *Proceedings of ITS European Congress.* Lyon, France: ITS.

Palazzo, S., Cuomo, F., & Galluccio, L. (2009). Data aggregation in wireless sensor networks: A multifaceted perspective. In Ferrari, G. (Ed.), *Sensor Networks: Where Technology Meets Practice* (pp. 103–143). Berlin, Germany: Springer. doi:10.1007/978-3-642-01341-6_6

Papadimitratos, P., Buttyan, L., Hubaux, J.-P., Kargl, F., Kung, A., & Raya, M. (2007). Architecture for secure and private vehicular communications. In *Proceedings of ITST 2007, 7th International Conference on ITS Telecommunications,* (pp. 1-6). ITST.

Papadimitratos, P., Gligor, V., & Hubaux, J.-P. (2006). Securing vehicular communications - Assumptions, requirements, and principles. In *Proccedings of Workshop on Embedded Security in Cars.* IEEE.

Papadimitratos, P., Buttyan, L., Holczer, T., Schoch, E., Freudiger, J., & Raya, M. (2008). Secure vehicular communication systems: Design and architecture. *IEEE Communications, 46,* 100–109. doi:10.1109/MCOM.2008.4689252

Papadimitratos, P., La Fortelle, A., Evenssen, K., Brignolo, R., & Cosenza, S. (2009). Vehicular communication systems: Enabling technologies, applications, and future outlook on intelligent transportation. *IEEE Communications Magazine, 47*(11), 84–95. doi:10.1109/MCOM.2009.5307471

Park, S., Aslam, B., Turgut, D., & Zou, C. C. (2009). Defense against Sybil attack in vehicular ad hoc network based on roadside unit support. In *Proceedings of the Military Communications Conference,* (pp. 1-7). IEEE.

Peng, Y., Abichar, Z., & Chang, J. M. (2006). Roadside-aided routing (RAR) in vehicular networks. In *Proceedings of the IEEE International Conference on Communications*, (pp. 3602-3607). IEEE.

Pereira, F., & Barreto, J. (2011). Easy-city: A route search system for public transport users. In *Proceedings of the Third International Workshop on Pervasive Mobile and Embedded Computing (M-MPAC 2011), ACM/IFIP/USENIX 12th International Middleware Conference Workshops*. Lisboa, Portugal: ACM Press.

Perkins, C., & Bhagwat, P. (1994). Highly dynamic destination-sequenced distance-vector routing (DSDV) for mobile computers. In *Proceedings of the Conference on Communications Architectures, Protocols and Applications (SIGCOMM 1994)*, (pp. 234-244). New York, NY: ACM.

Perkins, C., & Royer, E. (1999). Ad-hoc on-demand distance vector routing. In *Proceedings of the Second IEEE Workshop on Mobile Computer Systems and Applications (WMCSA 1999)*. IEEE Press.

Perkins, C., Belding-Royer, E., & Das, S. (2003). *RFC3561: Ad hoc on-demand distance vector (AODV) routing*. Retrieved from http://www.ietf.org/rfc/rfc3561.txt

Perkins, C. E., & Bhagwat, P. (1994). Highly dynamic destination-sequenced distance-vector routing (DSDV) for mobile computers. *ACM SIGCOMM Computer Communication Review*, *24*, 234–244. doi:10.1145/190809.190336

Perrig, A., Canetti, R., Tygar, J., & Song, D. (2002). The TESLA broadcast authentication protocol. *RSA CryptoBytes Newsletter*, *5*, 2–13.

Persone, V. N., & Grassi, V. (2003). Performance analysis of caching and prefetching strategies for palmtop-based navigational tools. *IEEE Transactions on Intelligent Transportation Systems*, *4*(1), 23–34. doi:10.1109/TITS.2002.808416

Piran, M. J. (2010). A novel routing algorithm for vehicular sensor networks. *Wireless Sensor Network*, *2*(12), 919–923. doi:10.4236/wsn.2010.212110

Pisinger, D. (2004). Where are the hard knapsack problems? *Computers & Operations Research*, *32*, 2271–2284. doi:10.1016/j.cor.2004.03.002

Poe, W. Y., & Schmitt, J. B. (2007). *Minimizing the maximum delay in wireless sensor networks by intelligent sink placement*. Technical Report 362/07. Kaiserlautern, Germany: University of Kaiserslautern.

Popescu-Zeletin, R., Radusch, I., & Rigani, M. A. (2010). *Vehicular-2-X communication*. Berlin, Germany: Springer. doi:10.1007/978-3-540-77143-2

PreDRIVE C2X. (2010). *Preparation for driving implementation and evaluation of car 2 X communication technology*. Retrieved Jul. 2010 from http://www.pre-drive-c2x.eu/index.dhtml/444d919dde59571535mo/-/deDE/-/CS/-/

Prevent, I. P. (2010). *Website*. Retrieved from http://www.prevent-ip.org/

Ptolemy Team. (2008). *Visualsens*. Retrieved from http://ptolemy.berkeley.edu/visualsense/

Qian, Y., & Moayery, N. (2009). Medium access control protocols for vehicular networks. In Moustafa, H., & Zhang, Y. (Eds.), *Vehicular Networks Techniques, Standards, and Applications* (pp. 41–62). Boca Raton, FL: CRC Press. doi:10.1201/9781420085723.ch3

Qiu, L., Chandra, R., Jain, K., & Mahdian, M. (2004). Optimizing the placement of integration points in multi-hop wireless networks. In *Proceedings of the IEEE International Conference on Network Protocols (ICNP)*. Berlin, Germany: IEEE Press.

Rajagopalan, R., & Varshney, P. (2006). Data aggregation techniques in sensor networks: A survey. *IEEE Communication Surveys & Tutorials*, *8*, 48–63. doi:10.1109/COMST.2006.283821

Raleigh, G. G., & Cioffi, J. M. (1998). Spatio-temporal coding for wireless communication. *IEEE Transactions on Communications*, *46*(3), 357–366. doi:10.1109/26.662641

Ramadan, R. (2009). Agent based multipath routing in wireless sensor networks. In *Proceedings of IEEE Symposium Series on Computational Intelligence*, (pp. 1548-1551). IEEE Press.

Ramirez, C. L., & Veiga, M. F. (2007). QoS in vehicular and intelligent transport networks using multicast routing. In *Proceedings of the IEEE International Symposium on Industrial Electronics*, (pp. 2556–2561). IEEE.

RATP. (2010). *Ratp.fr – Accueil.* Retrieved from http://www.ratp.fr/

Rawat, D. B. Treeumnuk, D., Popescu, D. C., Abuelela, M., & Olariu, S. (2008). Challenges and perspectives in the implementation of NOTICE architecture for vehicular communications. In *Proceedings of the 5th IEEE International Conference on Mobile Ad Hoc and Sensor Systems,* (pp. 707-711). IEEE.

Raya, M., Papadimitratos, P., Aad, I., Jungels, D., & Hubaux, J.-P. (2007). Eviction of misbehaving and faulty nodes in vehicular networks. *IEEE Journal on Selected Areas in Communications, 25*(8), 1557–1568. doi:10.1109/JSAC.2007.071006

RFC3775. (2004). *Website.* Retrieved from http://www.ietf.org/rfc/rfc3775.txt

RFC4260. (2005). *Website.* Retrieved from http://ietfreport.isoc.org/idref/rfc4260/

Ribeiro, C. (2005). *Bringing wireless access to the automobile: A comparison of Wi-Fi, WiMAX, MBWA, and 3G.* Paper presented at the 21st Computer Science Seminar. Troy, NY.

Romer, K., & Mattern, F. (2004). The design space of wireless sensor networks. *IEEE Wireless Communications, 11*(6), 54–61. doi:10.1109/MWC.2004.1368897

Ros, F. J., Ruiz, P. M., & Stojmenovic, I. (2009). Reliable and efficient broadcasting in vehicular ad hoc networks. In *Proceedings of the 69th IEEE Vehicular Technology Conference, 2009,* (pp. 1-5). IEEE Press.

Saleet, H., Langar, R., Basir, O., & Boutaba, R. (2009). Adaptive message routing with QoS support in vehicular ad hoc networks. In *Proceedings of the Global Telecommunications Conference,* (pp. 1-6). IEEE.

Saleet, H., Langar, R., Naik, S., Boutaba, R., Nayak, A., & Goel, N. (2010). QoS support in delay tolerant vehicular ad hoc networks. In *Proceedings of the IEEE Global Telecommunications Conference,* (pp. 1-10). IEEE.

Salhi, I., Cherif, M., & Senouci, S. M. (2008). *Data collection in vehicular networks.* Paper presented at the Autonomous and Spontaneous Networks Symposium. Paris, France.

Sallez, Y., Berger, T., & Tahon, C. (2005). *Stigmergic approach and potential field based method for intelligent routing in FMS.* Paper presented at the International Conference on Industrial Engineering and Systems Management IESM. Marrakech, Morocco.

Sampigethaya, K., Huang, L., Li, M., Poovendran, R., Matsuura, K., & Sezaki, K. (2005). CARAVAN: Providing location privacy for VANET. In *Proceedings of the Workshop on Embedded Security in Cars.* Embedded Security in Cars.

Schwartz, R. S., & Eenennaam, M. van, Karagiannis, G., Heijenk, G., Klein Wolterink, W., & Scholten, H. (2010). Using V2V communication to create over-the-horizon awareness in multiple-lane highway scenarios. In *Proceedings of the 2010 IEEE Intelligent Vehicles Symposium,* (pp. 998-1005). IEEE Press.

Schwartz, R. S., Barbosa, R. R., Meratnia, N., Heijenk, G., & Scholten, H. (2011). A directional data dissemination protocol for vehicular environments. In *Computer Communications.* London, UK: Elsevier. doi:10.1016/j.comcom.2011.03.007

Sen, I., & Matolak, D. (2008). Vehicle-vehicle channel models for the 5-Ghz band. *IEEE Transactions on Intelligent Transportation Systems, 9*(2), 235–245. doi:10.1109/TITS.2008.922881

Serna, J., Luna, J., & Medina, M. (2008). Geolocation-based trust for Vanet's privacy. In *Proceedings of the Fourth International Conference on Information Assurance and Security,* (pp. 287-290). IEEE.

SeVeCom. (2010). *Secure vehicle communication.* Retreived Nov. 2010 from http://www.sevecom.org/

Shin, J., & Suh, C. (2008). Energy efficient chain topology in ubiquitous sensor network. In *Proceeding of the 10th International Conference on Advanced Communication Technology,* (pp. 1688-1693). IEEE.

Shi, W., Wu, J., Zhou, S., Zhang, L., Tang, Z., & Yin, Y. (2009). Variable message sign and dynamic regional traffic guidance. *IEEE Intelligent Transportation Systems Magazine, 1*(3), 15–21. doi:10.1109/MITS.2009.934642

Shrestha, R. K., Moh, S., Chung, I., & Choi, D. (2010). Vertex-based multihop vehicle-to-infrastructure routing for vehicular ad hoc networks. In *Proceedings of the 2010 43rd Hawaii International Conference on System Sciences,* (pp. 1-7). IEEE Press.

Sichitiu, M. L., & Kihl, M. (2008). Inter-vehicle communication systems: A survey. *Communications Surveys & Tutorials, 10*(2), 88–105. doi:10.1109/COMST.2008.4564481

Sikdar, B. (2008). Design and analysis of a MAC protocol for vehicle to roadside networks. In *Proceedings of the Wireless Communications and Networking Conference,* (pp. 1525-3511). IEEE.

Sim, S., Han, S., Park, J., & Lee, S. (2009). Seamless IP mobility support for flat architecture mobile WiMAX networks. *IEEE Communications Magazine, 47*(6), 142–148. doi:10.1109/MCOM.2009.5116811

Soldo, F., Cigno, R. L., & Gerla, M. (2008). Cooperative synchronous broadcasting in infrastructure-to-vehicles networks. In *Proceedings of Conference WONS,* (pp. 125–132). WONS.

Spyropoulos, T., Psounis, K., & Raghavendra, C. (2005). Spray and wait: An efficient routing scheme for intermittently connected mobile networks. In *Proceedings of the 2005 ACM SIGCOMM Workshop on Delay-Tolerant Networking (WDTN 2005),* (pp. 252-259). New York, NY: ACM.

Stampoulis, A., & Chai, Z. (2007). *Survey of security in vehicular networks.* Project CPSC 534. Retrieved from http://zoo.cs.yale.edu/~ams257/projects/wireless-survey.pdf

Stephanie, L., Cauligi, R., & Krishna, M. S. (2002). Data gathering algorithms in sensor networks using energy metrics. *IEEE Transactions on Parallel and Distributed Systems, 13*(9), 924–935. doi:10.1109/TPDS.2002.1036066

Stibor, L., Zang, Y., & Reumerman, H.-J. (2007). Evaluation of communication distance of broadcast messages in a vehicular ad-hoc network using IEEE 802.11p. In *Proceedings of the IEEE Wireless Communications and Networking Conference, WCNC,* (pp. 254–257). IEEE Press.

Studer, A., Bai, F., Bellur, B., & Perrig, A. (2008). Flexible, extensible, and efficient VANET authentication. In *Proceedings of 6th Annual Conference on Embedded Security in Cars.* Embedded Security in Cars.

Studer, A., Shi, E., Fan, B., & Perrig, A. (2009). TACKing together efficient authentication, revocation, and privacy in VANETs. In *Proceedings of 6th Annual IEEE Communications Society Conference on Sensor, Mesh and Ad Hoc Communications and Networks,* (pp. 1-9). IEEE.

SUMO Project. (2011). *Website.* Retrieved from http://sourceforge.net/projects/sumo/

Sun, W., Yamaguchi, H., Yukimasa, K., & Kusumoto, S. (2006). GVGrid: A QoS routing protocol for vehicular ad hoc networks. In *Proceedings of the 14th IEEE International Workshop on Quality of Service,* (pp. 130-139). IEEE.

Sun, X., Lin, X., & Ho, P.-H. (2007). Secure vehicular communications based on group signature and ID-based signature scheme. In *Proceedings of the IEEE International Conference on Communications,* (pp. 1539-1545). IEEE Press.

Tabassum, N., Ehsanul, Q., Mamun, K., & Urano, Y. (2006). COSEN: A chain oriented sensor network for efficient data collection. In *Proceedings of the Third International Conference on Information Technology,* (pp. 260-267). IEEE.

Taghikhaki, Z., Meratnia, N., & Havinga, P. J. M. (2011). Energy-efficient trust-based aggregation in wireless sensor networks. In *Proceedings of the 3rd International Workshop on Wireless Sensor, Actuator and Robot Networks (WiSARN), In Conjunction with IEEE InfoCom,* (pp. 10-15). IEEE.

Takagi, H., & Kleinrock, L. (1984). Optimal transmission ranges for randomly distributed packet radio terminals. *IEEE Transactions on Communications, 32*(3), 246–257. doi:10.1109/TCOM.1984.1096061

Takayuki, T., & Ryuji, K. (2000). Inter-Vehicle communication protocol using common spreading code. In *Proceedings of the IEEE Intelligent Vehicles Symposium.* IEEE Press.

Tamer, N., Pravin, S., & Liviu, I. (2006). A comparative study of data dissemination models for VANETs. In *Proceedings of the Third Annual International Conference on Mobile and Ubiquitous Systems: Networking and Services*, (pp. 1-10). IEEE.

Tan, H. O., & Korpeoglu, I. (2003). Power efficient data gathering and aggregation in wireless sensor networks. *Proceedings of ACM International Conference Management of Data, 32*(4), 66-71.

Taniuchi, K., Ohba, Y., Fajardo, V., Das, S., Tauil, M., & Cheng, Y.-H. (2009). IEEE 802.21: Media independent handover: Features, applicability, and realization. *IEEE Communications Magazine, 47*(1), 112–120. doi:10.1109/MCOM.2009.4752687

Tao, S., Xu, K., Xu, Y., Fei, T., Gao, L., & Guerin, R. … Towsley, D. (2004). Exploring the performance benefits of end-to-end path switching. In *Proceedings of the ICNP*. ICNP.

Tele Atlas. (2010). *Web site*. Retrieved from http://www.teleatlas.com

TFL. (2011). *Transport for London*. Retrieved from http://www.tfl.gov.uk/modalpages/2625.aspx

Thaler, D., & Hopps, C. (2000). *Multipath issues in unicast and multicast next-hop selection*. RFC. Retrieved from http://www.ietf.org

Thaler, D., & Ravishankar, C. V. (1998). Using name-based mappings to increase hit rates. *IEEE/ACM Transactions on Networking, 6*, 1–14. doi:10.1109/90.663936

Tonguz, O., Wisitpongphan, N., & Bai, F. (2010). DV-CAST: A distributed vehicular broadcast protocol for vehicular ad hoc networks. *IEEE Wireless Communications, 17*(2), 47–57. doi:10.1109/MWC.2010.5450660

Toor, Y., Muhlethaler, P., & Laouiti, A. (2008). Vehicle ad hoc networks: Applications and related technical issues. *IEEE Communications Surveys & Tutorials, 10*, 74–88. doi:10.1109/COMST.2008.4625806

Toppan, A., Bazzi, A., Toppan, P., Masini, B. M., & Andrisano, O. (2010). Architecture of a simulation platform for the smart navigation service investigation. In *Proceedings of the 16th International Conference on Wireless and Mobile Computing, Networking and Communications (WiMob)*, (pp. 548–554). IEEE Press.

Toshiki, H., Shinya, I., Tomohiro, Y., Toshiaki, F., & Masayuki, T. (2007). A new receiving system of visible light communication for ITS. In *Proceedings of the 2007 IEEE Intelligent Vehicles Symposium.* Istanbul, Turkey: IEEE Press.

Toulminet, G., Boussuge, J., & Laurgeau, C. (2008). *Comparative synthesis of the 3 main European projects dealing with cooperative systems (CVIS, SAFESPOT, and COOPERS) and description of COOPERS demonstration site 4.* Paper presented at the 11th International IEEE Conference on Intelligent Transportation Systems ITSC. Maastricht, The Netherlands.

Trullols, O., Fiore, M., Casetti, C., Chiasserini, C.-F., & Barcelo Ordinas, J. M. (2010). Planning roadside infrastructure for information dissemination in intelligent transportation systems. *Elsevier Computer Communications, 33*, 432–442.

Tsugawa, S. (2005). Issues and recent trends in vehicle safety communication systems: IATSS research. *Journal of International Association of Traffic and Safety Sciences, 29*(1), 7–15.

Tuysuz-Erman, A., & Havinga, P. (2010). Data dissemination of emergency messages in mobile multi-sink wireless sensor networks. In *Proceedings of the 2010 9th IFIP Annual Mediterranean Ad Hoc Networking Workshop (Med-Hoc-Net)*, (p. 1–8). IEEE Press.

Tuysuz-Erman, A., Dilo, A., & Havinga, P. (2010). A fault-tolerant data dissemination based on honeycomb architecture for mobile multi-sink wireless sensor networks. In *Proceedings of the Intelligent Sensors, Sensor Networks and Information Processing (ISSNIP)*, (p. 97–102). IEEE Press.

Uichin, L., Joon-Sang, P., Eyal, A., & Mario, G. (2006). FleaNet: A virtual market place on vehicular networks. In *Proceedings of the 3rd Annual International Conference on Mobile and Ubiquitous Systems*, (pp. 1-8). IEEE.

Uzcategui, R., & Acosta-Marum, G. (2009). WAVE: A tutorial. *IEEE Communications Magazine, 47*(5), 126–133. doi:10.1109/MCOM.2009.4939288

Vahdat, A., & Becker, D. (2000). *Epidemic routing for partially-connected ad hoc networks*. Technical Report CS-2000-06. Durham, NC: Duke University.

Van Mierlo, J., Maggetto, G., Van de Burgwal, E., & Gense, R. (2004). Driving style and traffic measures-influence on vehicle emissions and fuel consumption. *Journal of Automobile Engineering, 218*(1), 43–50. doi:10.1243/095440704322829155

Vidhyapriya, R., & Vanathi, P. (2007). Energy efficient adaptive multipath routing for wireless sensor networks. *International Journal of Computer Science, 34*(1).

Villeforceix, B., & Petti, S. (2011). Communications in ITS for cooperative systems deployment. In *Proceedings of the Fully Networked Car Workshop*. Geneva, Switzerland: IEEE.

Vissim. (2009). *Website.* Retrieved from http://www.ptvamerica.com/software/ptv-vision/vissim/

Vivo, G., Dalmasso, P., & Vernacchia, F. (2007). The European integrated project SAFESPOT: How ADAS applications co-operate for the driving safety. In *Proceedings of Intelligent Transportation Systems Conference*. Seattle, WA: IEEE.

Wada, M., Yendo, T., Fujii, T., & Tanimoto, M. (2005). Road-to-vehicle communication using LED traffic light. In *Proceedings of the 2005 IEEE Intelligent Vehicles Symposium*, (pp. 601- 606). IEEE Press.

Wahl, R., Tørset, T., & Vaa, T. (2008). Large scale introduction of automated transport which legal and administrative barriers are present? *ITS World 2008*. Retrieved March 13, 2010, from http://www.citymobil-project.eu

Wan, S., Tang, J., & Wolff, R. S. (2008). Reliable routing for roadside to vehicle communications in rural areas. In *Proceedings of the IEEE International Conference on Communications*, (pp. 3017-3021). IEEE.

Wang, H., Xie, H., Qi, L., Siberschatz, A., & Yang, Y. R. (2005). Optimal ISP subscription for internet multihoming: Algorithm design and implication analysis. In *Proceedings of the IEEE Infocom*. IEEE Press.

Wang, Y., Ahmed, A., Krishnamachari, B., & Psounis, K. (2008). IEEE 802.11p performance evaluation and protocol enhancement. *ICVES IEEE International Conference on Vehicular Electronics and Safety*, (pp. 317-322). IEEE Press.

Wang, X., Georgios, B., Giannakis, A., & Marques, G. (2007). A unified approach to QoS guaranteed scheduling for channel-adaptive wireless networks. *Proceedings of the IEEE Journal, 95*(12), 2410–2431. doi:10.1109/JPROC.2007.907120

Wasef, A., & Shen, X. (2009). ASIC: Aggregate signatures and certificates verification scheme for vehicular networks. In *Proceedings of Global Telecommunications Conference*, (pp. 1-6). IEEE.

Wasef, A., & Shen, X. (2009). MAAC: Message authentication acceleration protocol for vehicular ad hoc networks. In *Proceedings of Global Telecommunications Conference*, (pp. 1-6). IEEE.

WAVE. (2006). *IEEE trial-use standard for wireless access in vehicular environments (WAVE) - Multi-channel operation, standard*. Washington, DC: IEEE.

Weil, T. (2009). *Service management for ITS using WAVE (1609.3) networking.* Paper presented at the IEEE GLOBECOM Workshops. Hawaii, HI.

Weissenberger, S. (1998). *Why its projects should be small, local and private*. Research Report UCB-ITS-PRR-98-23. Berkeley, CA: University of California.

Werner, W., & Lars, R. (2010). C2X communications overview. In *Proceedings of the URSI International Symposium on Electromagnetic Theory*, (pp. 868-871). URSI.

Wex, P., Breuer, J., Held, A., Leinmuller, T., & Delgrossi, L. (2008). Trust issues for vehicular ad hoc networks. In *Proceedings of the Vehicular Technology Conference*, (pp. 2800-2804). IEEE.

Whitaker, R. M., Raisanen, L., & Hurley, S. (2005). The infrastructure efficiency of cellular wireless networks. *Elsevier Computer Networks, 48*(6), 941–959. doi:10.1016/j.comnet.2004.11.014

Whitbeck, J., Lopez, Y., Leguay, J., Conan, V., & Dias de Amorim, M. (2011). Relieving the wireless infrastructure: When opportunistic networks meet guaranteed delays. In *Proceedings of the IEEE International Symposium on a World of Wireless, Mobile and Multimedia Networks (WoWMoM)*. Lucca, Italy: IEEE Press.

Wisitpongphan, N., Tonguz, O. K., Parikh, J. S., Mudalige, P., Bai, F., & Sadekar, V. (2007). Broadcast storm mitigation techniques in vehicular ad hoc networks. *IEEE Wireless Communications, 14*(6), 84–94. doi:10.1109/MWC.2007.4407231

WMATA. (2011). *Washington metropolitan area transit authority*. Retrieved from http://www.wmata.com/

Wohlmacher, P. (2000). Digital certificates: A survey of revocation methods. In *Proceedings of the ACM Workshop,* (pp. 111–114). ACM Press.

Wong, K.-J., Chua, C.-C., & Li, Q. (2009). Environmental monitoring using wireless vehicular sensor networks. In *Proceedings of the 2009 5th International Conference on Wireless Communications, Networking and Mobile Computing,* (pp. 1-4). IEEE Press.

World Health Organization. (2008). *The top ten causes of death. Fact sheet No. 310*. Geneva, Switzerland: WHO.

Wu, T. Y., Wang, Y. B., & Lee, W. T. (2010). Mixing greedy and predictive approaches to improve geographic routing for VANET. In *Wireless Communications and Mobile Computing*. New York, NY: Wiley. doi:10.1002/wcm.1033

Xie, F., Hua, K. A., Wang, W., & Ho, Y. (2007). Performance study of live video streaming over highway vehicular ad hoc networks. In *Proceedings of IEEE VTC Spring,* (pp. 2121–2125). IEEE Press.

Xie, J., & Narayanan, U. (2010). Performance analysis of mobility support in IPv4/IPv6 mixed wireless networks. *IEEE Transactions on Vehicular Technology, 59,* 962–973. doi:10.1109/TVT.2009.2034668

Yan, G., Olariu, S., & Weigle, M. C. (2008). Providing VANET security through active position detection. *Computer Communications, 31,* 2883–2897. doi:10.1016/j.comcom.2008.01.009

Yang, K., Ou, S., Chen, H.-H., & He, J. (2007). A multihop peer-communication protocol with fairness guarantee for IEEE 802.16-based vehicular networks. *IEEE Transactions on Vehicular Technology, 56,* 3358–3370. doi:10.1109/TVT.2007.906875

Ye, H., Chen, Z., Xia, Z., & Zhao, M. (2010). A data dissemination policy by using human mobility patterns for delay-tolerant networks. In *Proceedings of the International Conference on Communications and Mobile Computing,* (pp. 432-436). IEEE.

Yoneki, E., Hui, P., Chan, S., & Crowcroft, J. (2007). A socio-aware overlay for publish/subscribe communication in delay tolerant networks. In *Proceedings of the 10th ACM Symposium on Modeling, Analysis, and Simulation of Wireless and Mobile Systems (MSWiM 2007),* (pp. 225-234). New York, NY: ACM.

Yoon, S., Ngo, H. Q., & Qiao, C. (2007). On "shooting" a moving vehicle with data flows. In *Proceedings of the IEEE Workshop on Mobile Networks for Vehicular Environments (MOVE)*. Anchorage, AK: IEEE Press.

Yu, Q., & Heijenk, G. (2008). Abiding geocast for warning message dissemination in vehicular ad hoc networks. In *Proceedings of the ICC Workshops - 2008 IEEE International Conference on Communications Workshops,* (pp. 400-404). IEEE Press.

Yuen, A., & Chung, T. (2007). *Traffic engineering for multi-homed mobile networks*. (PhD Thesis). The University of New South Wales. Sydney, Australia.

Zhang, C., Lin, X., Lu, R., & Ho, P.-H. (2008). RAISE: An efficient RSU-aided message authentication scheme in vehicular communication networks. In *Proceedings of the IEEE International Conference on Communications,* (pp. 1451-1457). IEEE.

Zhang, Y., Zhao, J., & Cao, G. (2007). On scheduling vehicle-roadside data access. *ACM International Workshop on VehiculAr Inter-NETworking ACM VANET,* (pp. 10–19). ACM Press.

Zhao, J., & Cao, G. (2008). VADD: Vehicle-assisted data delivery in vehicular ad hoc networks. In *Proceedings IEEE INFOCOM 2006,* (Vol. 57, pp. 1-12). IEEE Press.

Zhao, J., & Cao, G. (2008). VADD: Vehicle-assisted data delivery in vehicular ad hoc networks. *IEEE Transactions on Vehicular Technology, 57*(3), 1910–1922. doi:10.1109/TVT.2007.901869

Zhao, J., Zhang, Y., & Cao, G. (2007). Data Pouring and buffering on the road: A new data dissemination paradigm for vehicular networks. *IEEE Transactions on Vehicular Technology*, *56*(6), 3266–3277. doi:10.1109/TVT.2007.906412

Zheng, Z., Lu, Z., Sinha, P., & Kumar, S. (2010). Maximizing the contact opportunity for vehicular internet access. In *Proceedings of the International Conference on Computer Communications (INFOCOM)*, (pp. 1-9). San Diego, CA: IEEE Press.

Zheng, Z., Sinha, P., & Kumar, S. (2009). Alpha coverage: Bounding the interconnection gap for vehicular internet access. In *Proceedings of the IEEE International Conference on Computer Communications (INFOCOM)*. Rio de Janeiro, Brasil: IEEE Press.

Zong, C., et al. (2001). Ad hoc relay wireless networks over moving vehicles on highways. In *Proceedings of the 2nd ACM International Symposium on Mobile Ad Hoc Networking & Computing*. ACM Press.

About the Contributors

Robil Daher is a Scientific Assistant at the Department of Computer Architecture at the University of Rostock (Germany). He received his B.Sc. degree in Electronic Engineering from Tishreen University (Syria) in 1996, and his Ph.D. from Rostock University in 2007 in the field of Load Balancing and QoS for Wireless Networks. In 1997, he was awarded a certificate and prize by the Ministry of Higher Education (Syria) for excellent achievements and also for being the best student among the graduates. His research interests include vehicular communication networks, wireless ad hoc networks, heterogeneous wireless networks, resource and mobility management, QoS and load balancing, and routing protocols. He is also interested in inter-planetary communication networks and bionic-inspired solutions for performance enhancement of wireless networks. He is organiser of several workshops and author/ co-author of several scientific publications. He is a member of several scientific organizations and has recently established the community "Routing Lexicon" for studying and classification of routing mechanisms and protocols of different technologies. He is the Head of the workgroup Wireless Networks at the Department of Computer Architecture and currently works as a Team Manager in the project Wi-Roads (Wireless Infrastructure Networks for High-Speed Roads). Additionally, He is currently working on his next book, *Theory of Load Distribution*.

Alexey Vinel received the B.S. (Hons.) and M.S. (Hons.) degrees in Information Systems from Saint Petersburg State University of Aerospace Instrumentation, St. Petersburg, Russia, in 2003 and 2005, respectively, and the Ph.D. (Candidate of Science) degree in Technical Sciences from the Institute for Information Transmission Problems, Russian Academy of Sciences, Moscow, Russia, in 2007. He is currently a Researcher with the Department of Communications Engineering, Tampere University of Technology, Tampere, Finland. He has published over 50 papers in peer-reviewed international journals (including top-rated journals in telecommunications, such as IEEE JSAC, IEEE TVT, etc.) and conference proceedings. His research interests include multiple-access protocols and intelligent transportation systems. He has been a Fellow of the Alexander von Humboldt Foundation since 2008 and a member of organizing and technical committees of many international conferences. He has been a Senior Member of IEEE and Associate Editor for *IEEE Communications Letters* since 2012.

* * *

Rui L. Aguiar received a Ph.D. degree in Electrical Engineering in 2001 from the University of Aveiro. He is currently an Associate Professor with "Agregação" at the University of Aveiro, where he is responsible for networking subjects. He is leading ATNOG, a research team at the Institute of Telecommunications, on next-generation network architectures and protocols. He has more than 300 published papers in those areas. He has served as technical and general chair of several conferences, such as ICNS 2005, ICT 2006, ISCC 2007, and Monami 2011, and has been invited to keynote lectures in multiple fora. Prof. Aguiar is currently Associate Editor of Wileys' ETT, a Senior Member of IEEE, and a Member of ACM.

Hamada Alshaer (M 2004) is currently a Senior Researcher in the Etisalat BT Innovation Center (EBTIC), Khalifa University, Abu Dhabi, UAE. He received a BEng degree in Electrical Engineering and Computer Science from Birzeit University, Palestine, in 2001, an MS (DEA) degree in Information Technology and Systems (ITS) from Compiegne University of Technology, France, in 2002, and a PhD degree in Computer Science and Telecommunications from Pierre et Marie Curie University, France, in 2005. He then joined the Electronic and Electrical Engineering Department at Brunel University, in West London, as a Postdoctoral Research Fellow. He later worked as a Research Scientist at INRIA, France. Between November 2007 and September 2009, he worked as a Research Fellow in the School of Electronic and Electrical Engineering at the University of Leeds, UK. His research interests include QoS, optical communications and networking, wireless sensor networks, and intelligent transportation. He has served on the technical program committee of various IEEE conferences, including the Intelligent Vehicles Symposium, Vehicular Technology Conference, Globecom, ICC, and WCNC, and chaired some of their sessions. He is the recipient of the 2009 Royal Academy of Engineering Travel Award, as well as scholarships from UNRWA, the French Government and Pierre et Marie Curie University for academic distinctions.

Luis Nero Alves received his Licenciatura, MsC, and PhD degrees from the University of Aveiro in the years of 1997, 2001, and 2008, respectively. He is Professor at the Electronics Telecommunications and Informatics Department from the University of Aveiro since 2003, where he teaches several electronic related disciplines. He is leading a research team at the Institute of Telecommunications, Aveiro, on Integrated Circuits and Systems Design. His current research interests are mainly focused on analogue integrated electronic system design, with application to free space optical signal reception.

Hassanein H. Amer is a Professor and the Founding Chair of the Electronics Engineering Department, American University, Cairo, Egypt. He received his B.Sc. in Electronics Engineering from Cairo University in 1978 and his M.Sc. and PhD degrees in Electrical Engineering from Stanford University, CA, USA in 1983 and 1987, respectively. He founded the SEAD research group in 2003. He is a Member of the IEEE Reliability Society since 1985, a Member of the Industrial Relations Committee for the IEEE SMC Society, a Member of the IEEE Industrial Electronics Society, and an Honorary Member of the International Society for Advanced Research. His research interests include the reliability and testing of digital and mixed-signal circuits, reliability modeling, fault modeling in VLSI, self-checking circuits, analysis of temporary failures, cache memory systems, networked control systems, wireless sensor networks, and wireless communications.

Jose M. Barcelo-Ordinas is Associate Professor at Universitat Politecnica de Catalunya (UPC). He earned his Telecommunication Engineering degree in 1991 and his PhD in Telecommunication Engineering in 1998 at UPC. He joined the CompNet Research Group in 1993. He has participated in several European projects such as EXPLOIT, BAF, EXPERT, NETPERF, MOEBIUS, WIDENS projects, and

EuroNGI, EuroNFI, and EuroNF (VII FP) Networks of Excellence (NoE). His currently research areas are wireless and mobile networks, focusing in delay/disruptive tolerant networks, VANETs, and wireless sensor networks. He is a member of the IEEE.

Joao Barreto is an Assistant Professor at the Computer and Information Systems Department at the Technical University of Lisbon (Instituto Superior Tecnico – IST/UTL), Portugal. He received his Ph.D. degree in Computer Science in 2009, from IST/UTL, the same university where he completed his M.Sc. (2004) and Bs.E.E. (2002). He is a Researcher at INESC-ID since 2001, as a member of the Distributed Systems Group. His research interests are distributed systems and operating systems, in particular: transactional memory, optimistic replication in mobile, pervasive, and ubiquitous environments, and distributed data deduplication. He has participated in a number of international projects and is author or co-author of over 20 peer-reviewed scientific communications. He is a member of ACM and IEEE.

Alessandro Bazzi received the Dr. Ing. degree (with honors) and the Ph.D. degree in Telecommunications Engineering both from the University of Bologna, Italy, in 2002 and 2006, respectively. Since 2002, he joined the Research Unit of Bologna of the Institute for Electronics and for Information and Telecommunications Engineering (IEIIT), Research Unit of Bologna, of the National Research Council (CNR). His research interests include performance investigation of wireless systems including WLANs, WiMax, cellular technologies, and heterogeneous networks, with focus ranging from physical level to medium access control and radio resource management. His studies also include wireless technologies applied to Intelligent Transportation Systems (ITS). He is author of several publications in international conferences proceedings, journals, and book chapters, and he served as a reviewer and TPC member for various IEEE journals and conferences. Since the academic year 2006/2007, he has the appointment of Professor in courses at the University of Bologna and the University of Ferrara, Italy.

Stefano Busanelli was born in Castelnovo né Monti, Italy, in 1982. He received his "Laurea," "Laurea Specialistica," and PhD degrees, in 2004, 2007, and 2011, respectively, from University of Parma, Italy. From June 2008 to October 2008, he was an intern at Thales Communications (Colombes, France), working on cooperative wireless communications. Since March 2012, he leads the R&D Department of Guglielmo Srl (Pilastro di Langhirano, Italy). As of today, he has published more than 20 papers in leading international journals and conferences. His research interests include wireless ad hoc and sensor networking, vehicular ad-hoc networks, digital signal processing, and vertical handover in heterogeneous networks. He participates in several research projects funded by public and private bodies. Dr. Busanelli is a co-recipient of an award for the outstanding technical contributions at ITST-2011 and a member of the WASNLab team that won the first Body Sensor Network (BSN) contest, held in conjunction with BSN 2011. He acts as a frequent reviewer for many international journals and conferences.

Claudio Casetti graduated in Electrical Engineering from Politecnico di Torino in 1992 and received his PhD in Electronic Engineering from the same institution in 1997. He is an Assistant Professor at the Dipartimento di Elettronica of Politecnico di Torino. He has coauthored more than 130 journal and conference papers in the fields of networking and holds three patents. His interests focus on ad hoc wireless networks and vehicular networks.

Periklis Chatzimisios is currently an Assistant Professor with the Computing Systems, Security, and Networks (CSSN) Research Lab of the Department of Informatics at the Alexander TEI of Thessaloniki, Greece. He presently participates in several European and national research projects acting in several research and management positions. Dr. Chatzimisios also serves as a Member in the IEEE Communication Society (ComSoc) Standards Board. He is the author of 8 books and more than 60 peer-reviewed papers and book chapters in the areas of multimedia communications (mainly quality of service and quality of experience), wireless communications (mainly in IEEE 802.11 and 802.16 protocols), and security. His published research work has received more than 500 citations by other researchers.

Carla-Fabiana Chiasserini received her Ph.D. from Politecnico di Torino in 2000. She has worked as a Visiting Researcher at UCSD in 1998-2003, and she is currently an Associate Professor at Politecnico di Torino. Her research interests include architectures, protocols, and performance analysis of wireless networks. Dr. Chiasserini has published over 200 papers in prestigious journals and leading international conferences, and she serves as associated editor of several journals.

Claudio Cicconetti holds a PhD in Information Engineering from the University of Pisa (2007), where he also received his Laurea degree (5 years) in Computer Science Engineering in 2003. He has been working in Intecs since 2009, where he is the R&D Manager for Telecommunications. He has been actively involved in many R&D projects both European (SANDRA – FP7, EuQoS – FP6, Celtic – Eureka) and Italian (QuaSAR, NADIR, IPERMOB). He is on the editorial board of Computer Networks (Elsevier) and has served as a member of the organization committee of several international conferences (WoWMoM, ISCC, WiOpt, European Wireless, SIMUTools, Valuetools, QoSim, NSTools). He co-authored 40+ papers published in international journals, peer-reviewed conference proceedings, and book chapters, and two international patents. He has an Erdös Number 3. He is the ETSI official contact for Intecs.

Ramèz M. Daoud (S 2000, M 2009) received his B.Sc. and M.Sc. in Control Engineering in 2000 and 2004, respectively, from Cairo University, Egypt, and his D.Sc. in Control and Industrial Informatics with High Honors from Universite de Valenciennes, France, in 2008. He is a founding member of the SEAD research group at AUC. He received the IEEE SMCia/05 "Best Industrial Application Certificate" in 2005 from the IEEE SMC Society and is a Member of the Industrial Relations Committee for the IEEE SMC Society. He also received the "Best Student Presentation Award" of the IEEE ConTel in 2007. He is an honorary member of the International Society for Advanced Research and an Associate Editor of the *International Journal of Systems, Control, and Communications*. He is an IEEE Member of the Control Society, Communications Society, Industrial Electronics Society, Intelligent Transportation Systems Society, Vehicular Technology Society and Computer Society, Systems, Man, and Cybernetics Society, since 2000. His research interests include digital circuit design, wireless communications, automotive control, vehicular technology, car automation, real-time systems, networked control systems, and industrial automation and informatics.

Arnaud de La Fortelle is both director of the Mines ParisTech Robotics Lab (CAOR) and of the Joint Research Unit LaRA. He has a Ph.D. in Applied Mathematics and Engineer degrees for the French Ecole Polytechnique and Ecole des Ponts et Chaussées. He managed for LaRA several French and European projects (Puvame, Prevent/Intersafe, REACT, COM2REACT…) and has been coordinator of the European project GeoNet and of the French project AROS. He has been elected to the Board of Governors of IEEE ITSS (Intelligent Transportation System Society). Arnaud de La Fortelle first studied theoretical properties of probability distributions (large deviations) with application to queuing networks (1997-2003). He then applied this knowledge to vehicle networks with a special focus for cyber cars (2003-2005). At the same time, he began to manage projects at INRIA; then he managed part of the team IMARA at INRIA and then also at Mines ParisTech. He became Director of the Joint Research Unit LaRA (the automated road) between INRIA and Mines ParisTech in 2006. He moved to Mines ParisTech in 2006 (keeping managerial responsibilities at INRIA) where he became Director of the Robotics Lab (CAOR) in 2008. During that period, he investigated communications for cooperative systems and the architecture needed in distributed systems. While keeping some fundamental research in probability theory, his main topic of interest is now cooperative systems (data distribution, control, mathematical certification) and their applications (e.g. cyber cars, collective taxis).

Arta Dilo received a Master degree in Applied Mathematics from the University of Tirana, Albania, and an MSc and PhD degree in Geo-Informatics from the International Institute for Geo-Information Science and Earth Observation (ITC) and Wageningen University, The Netherlands. She is currently a Researcher in the Pervasive Systems Group at the University of Twente. Previously, she has held researcher positions at Delft University of Technology and ITC, The Netherlands, and the Institute of Informatics and Applied Mathematics, Albania, and as Assistant Professor at the University of Tirana. She has participated in several European and national projects, and serves as reviewer for several journals and programme committee member for international conferences. She has published more than 25 papers in journals and conferences. Her current research interests are on routing and optimization over wireless sensor networks, and (spatial) data modelling and processing.

Mohamed A. El-Dakroury received his B.S. degrees from Ain Shams University, Cairo, Egypt, in July 2000, and the M.S. degree in Data Application over WiFi in November 2004, respectively. He joined Vodafone Egypt in 2005. He is currently supervising data and Internet services in Vodafone Egypt. He is a member of the Vodafone Egypt R&D team. He is leading research projects sponsored by Vodafone Egypt. He is also a Research Assistant at the American University in Egypt. He is a member of SEAD research group since 2006. He is leading multiple projects concerning real time applications over WiFi and WiMAX.

Ayşegül Tüysüz Erman is currently an Assistant Professor in the Computer Science and Engineering Department of the Isik University, Turkey. She received her Ph.D. in Computer Science from the University of Twente, The Netherlands, in September 2011. Her dissertation focused on efficient and reliable data routing in mobile wireless sensor networks and was titled "Multi-Sink Mobile Wireless Sensor Networks: Dissemination Protocols, Design, and Evaluation." She received her BSc degree in Computer Engineering from Yeditepe University, Turkey, in 2004 and her MSc degree in Computer Engineering from the Bogazici University, Turkey, in 2006. She was also an affiliated researcher at the

Satellite Networks Research Laboratory, at the Boğaziçi University in 2005 – 2006. Her research interests are in the design and analysis of algorithms/protocols for wireless mobile networks, particularly for sensor networks and vehicular sensor networks, and in the performance evaluation of communication networks.

Thierry Ernst holds a PhD in Networking from University Joseph Fourier in Grenoble, obtained in October 2001 and performed within the PLANETE project-team at INRIA in association with Motorola Labs. He is internationally recognized in the field of IPv6 mobility particularly in the Network Mobility (NEMO) research topic he launched. During his 4-year long non-tenure researcher position at Keio University, Japan, he founded and chaired the Nautilus6 working group within the WIDE organization, and the NEMO and MonAmi6 working groups within the IETF. His research work on IPv6 mobility has then led him to focus on Cooperative ITS (Cooperative Intelligent Transport Systems or C-ITS). Back to France in 2006, he then took the leadership of a 5-6 person strong research and development group specialized in IPv6 communications for Cooperative ITS within LaRA (La Route Automatique – The Automated Road), a Joint-Research Unit between INRIA (IMARA project-team) and Mines ParisTech (CAOR robotic lab). As such, he has setup and ensured the technical coordination of the FP7 GeoNet project, which aimed at specifying and developing the IPv6 multicast distribution of messages to vehicles located in a geographic area (IPv6 GeoNetworking). He is now coordinating the recently started FP7 ITSSv6 project (IPv6 stack for ITS stations) and is involved in field operational tests of cooperative ITS (FP7 DRIVE-C2X and SCOREF in France). He is also heavily involved in cooperative ITS standardization activities (ITS station reference architecture set of standards) at ISO TC204 (CALM), CEN TC278 WG16 / ISO TC204 WG18 (Cooperative ITS), and ETSI TC ITS, and is member of the French national delegation in these groups. He is currently serving as co-chair of ETSI TC ITS WG3.

Gianluigi Ferrari was born in Parma, Italy, in 1974. He received his "Laurea" and PhD degrees from the University of Parma, Italy, in 1998 and 2002, respectively. Since 2002, he has been with the University Parma, where he currently is an Associate Professor of Telecommunications. He was a Visiting Researcher at USC (Los Angeles, CA, USA, 2000-2001), CMU (Pittsburgh, PA, USA, 2002-2004), KMITL (Bangkok, Thailand, 2007), and ULB (Bruxelles, Belgium, 2010). Since 2006, he has been the Coordinator of the Wireless Ad-Hoc and Sensor Networks (WASN) Lab (http://wasnlab.tlc.unipr.it/) in the Department of Information Engineering of the University of Parma. As of today, he has published more than 160 papers in leading international journals and conferences, and more than 10 book chapters. He is coauthor of 7 books, including *Detection Algorithms for Wireless Communications with Applications to Wired and Storage Systems* (Wiley: 2004), *Ad Hoc Wireless Networks: A Communication-Theoretic Perspective* (Wiley: 2006-technical best seller), *LDPC Coded Modulations* (Springer: 2009), and *Sensor Networks with IEEE 802.15.4 Systems: Distributed Processing, MAC, and Connectivity* (Springer: 2011). He edited the book S*ensor Networks: Where Theory Meets Practice* (Springer: 2010). His research interests include digital communication systems analysis and design, wireless ad hoc and sensor networking, adaptive digital signal processing. He participates in several research projects funded by public and private bodies. Prof. Ferrari is a co-recipient of a best student paper award at IWWAN 2006; a best paper award at EMERGING 2010; an award for the outstanding technical contributions at ITST-2011; the best paper award at SENSORNETS 2012. The WASNLab team won the first Body Sensor Network (BSN) contest, held in conjunction with BSN 2011. He acts as a frequent reviewer for many international journals and conferences. He acts also as a technical program member for many international conferences. He currently serves on the editorial boards of several international journals. He was a Guest Editor of the 2010 EURASIP JWCN Special Issue on "Dynamic Spectrum Access: From the Concept to the Implementation" and is the Lead Guest Editor of the 2012 JCNC Special Issue on "The Internet of Wireless Things."

Marco Fiore is a tenured Assistant Professor at INSA Lyon since 2009, and an INRIA researcher within the UrbaNet team hosted by the CITI Lab since 2011. He received his PhD from Politecnico di Torino, in 2008, and M.Sc degrees from University of Illinois and Politecnico di Torino, in 2003 and 2004, respectively. He has been a Visiting Researcher at Rice University, in 2006 and 2007, and Universitat Politecnica de Catalunya, in 2008. His research interests are in the field of mobile networking, with focuses on vehicular networks, mobility modeling and analysis, opportunistic communication, and security. He is a member of the IEEE.

Marco Ghibaudi received the M.S. degree in Computer Science Engineering, Factory Automation, from the University of Pavia in 2009. Since November 2010, he is a Ph.D. student in Innovation Technologies (curriculum Embedded System) at the Scuola Superiore Sant'Anna, Pisa, Italy. He is co-author of papers focusing on wireless sensor networks and intelligent transport systems.

Vito Andrea Giorgio was born in Acquaviva Delle Fonti (Ba), Italy, in 1982. He received the "Laurea" (3-year program) and "Laurea Magistrale" (2-year program) degrees in Telecommunications Engineering from the University of Parma in 2005 and 2010, respectively. In 2010, he held a Spinner scholarship for the design of efficient information dissemination systems in urban vehicular networks. Since January 2011, he has been a Ph.D. student in "Information Technologies" at the Department of Information Engineering at the University of Parma. His research interests include the design of efficient communication protocols for ad-hoc and vehicular networking.

Paul J. M. Havinga is Full Professor and Chair of the Pervasive Systems Research Group at the Computer Science Department at the University of Twente in The Netherlands. He received his PhD at the University of Twente on the thesis titled "Mobile Multimedia Systems" in 2000, and was awarded with the "DOW Dissertation Energy Award" for this work. His research themes are focused on wireless sensor networks, large-scale distributed systems, and energy-efficient wireless communication.

Nicola Iotti was born in Reggio Emilia (RE), Italy, in August 1972. He received the 5-year degree "Laurea" in Electronic Engineering, with specialization in Communication and Networking, on February 2001 from the University of Parma, Italy. He is certified Cisco CCNA and Cisco Instructor CCAI. He has about ten years of working experience in ITC field and he is one of the founders of the Guglielmo S.r.l., one of the most important wireless Internet service providers in Italy. He is Chief Technical Officier (CTO) and Executive Director of the research projects for Guglielmo S.r.l. Nicola Iotti is co-author of papers about vertical handover and vehicular networks. He was also speaker at the Future Generation Communication and Networking Conference (FGCN 2010) and is currently an editorial board member of the *International Journal of Energy, Information and Communications.*

George Kadas holds a B.Sc. degree in Informatics from Alexander Technological Educational Institute of Thessaloniki (Greece) in 2011. He is currently a Research Assistant with the Computing Systems, Security, and Networks (CSSN) Research Lab of the Department of Informatics at the Alexander TEI of Thessaloniki, Greece. His current research interests are mainly focused on vehicular ad-hoc networks and wireless communication protocols.

Mahabaleshwar S. Kakkasageri completed his B. E in Electronics and Communication Engineering from Karnatak University Dharwad, India, and M.Tech from Visvesvaraya Technological University Belgaum, India. He has submitted his Ph.D thesis on "Multiagent System-Based Safety Information Gathering, Aggregation, and Dissemination in Vehicular Ad Hoc Networks." Presently, he is working as Faculty in Department of Electronics and Communication Engineering, Basaveshwar Engineering College, Bagalkot, Karnataka, India. He has published 18 national and international conference papers and 6 national and international journal articles. Recently, he has coauthored a book on *Wireless and Mobile Networks: Concepts and Protocols*, published by Wiley-India. His area of interest is a wireless network, especially vehicular ad hoc networks, and sensor networks. He is a member of IETE India and student member of IEEE USA.

Navin Kumar received degree in Electronics and Telecommunication from IETE, New Delhi in 1995-96 and ME/M Tech in 2000 from Motilal Nehru National Institute of Technology, Allahabad, India, and Ph.D in 2011 in Telecommunication from Universities of Aveiro Minho and Porto of Portugal. He has served in Indian Air Force as Graduate Engineer and has worked as expatriate teaching faculty at Addis Ababa University Ethiopia from 2003 to 2007. Currently, he is continuing his research at Institute of Telecommunication, Aveiro. His research interests include intelligent transportation systems, optical wireless, access networks, and vehicular communication and networks. He is member of IEEE, IET(UK), IAENG(Hong Kong), IETE, IE(India).

Raffaella Mambrini received her MS degree in Telecommunications Engineering in 1998 from the University of Pisa. She is currently the Telecommunications and ITS Business Units Leader at Intecs S.p.a., Italy. She is a member of Verification and Validation and Model Driven Engineering Intecs Excellence Teams. She has been involved in leading roles in many national and European R&D projects (currently: IPERMOB, SANDRA). Her last research interests include short- and long-range wireless networks, next generation network, Software Defined Radio (SDR), and applications for Intelligent Transportation Systems (ITS). She has 13 years working experience in many industrial projects related to development of safety critical embedded systems in railway, automotive, and telecommunications domains as a software engineer, then as a project manager, and finally, as head of 2 business units (TLC and ITS) of about 30 people.

Sunilkumar S. Manvi received M.E. degree in Electronics from the University of Visvesvaraya College of Engineering, Bangalore, and Ph.D degree in Electrical Communication Engineering, Indian Institute of Science, Bangalore, India. He is currently working as Dean (R&D), Professor and Head of Department of Electronics and Communication Engineering, Reva Institute of Technology and Management, Bangalore, India. He is involved in research of agent-based applications in multimedia communications, grid computing, vehicular ad-hoc networks, e-commerce, and mobile computing. He has published about 130 papers in national and international conferences and 70 papers in national and international journals. He has published 3 books. He is a Fellow IETE (FIETE, India), Fellow IE (FIE, India), and Member ISTE (MISTE, India), Member of IEEE (MIEEE, USA). He has been listed in Marqui's Whos Who in the World.

Barbara M. Masini received the Dr. Ing. degree (with honors) and the Ph.D. degree in Telecommunications Engineering both from the University of Bologna, Italy, in 2001 and 2005, respectively. Since 2004, she is with the Institute for Electronics and for Information and Telecommunications Engineering (IEIIT), Research Unit of Bologna, of the National Research Council (CNR) of Italy, working as Researcher on Wireless Communication Systems. Her research interests are mainly focused on physical layer aspects, including short-range wireless communications systems and their coexistence, multi-carrier transmission techniques, and cooperative networks. She also deals with Intelligent Transportation Systems (ITS), especially applying wireless technology to mobile environments to improve safety and efficiency in transportation. She is a member of IEEE, an author of several publications on international journals, conferences, and books chapters, and she acts as a reviewer for numerous IEEE journals and as TPC for IEEE conferences. She also has the appointment of Professor of Telecommunications Courses at the University of Bologna.

Nirvana Meratnia is Assistant Professor in the Pervasive System group at the University of Twente. Her research interests are in the area of distributed data management and reasoning in wireless sensor networks, smart and collaborative objects, ambient intelligence, and context-aware applications.

Christian Nastasi was born in 1982. He received his B.D. in Computer and Telecommunication Engineering from the University of Messina in 2005 and his M.D. in Computer Engineering from the University of Pisa in 2008. Since November 2008, he is PhD student at the RetisLab, Scuola Superiore Sant'Anna, in Pisa, with a research project on distributed vision systems for wireless sensor networks.

Paolo Pagano received his M.S. degree in Physics in 1999 from Trieste University (I). In 2003, he received his Ph.D. degree in High Energy Physics from Trieste University having worked for the COM-PASS collaboration at CERN (CH). In 2004, he was hired by HISKP at Bonn University (D). In 2006, he received a Master in Computer Science from Scuola Superiore Sant'Anna in Pisa (I). In the same year, he joined the REal-TIme System (RETIS) laboratory of the Scuola. Since 2009, he has been with the CNIT (National Inter-University Consortium for Telecommunications). He is leading the real-time wireless networks team at Sant'Anna University in Pisa. His research activities have a specific focus on wireless sensor networks applied to traffic monitoring. He is responsible of public and private research grants in the domain of intelligent transport systems. He co-authored about 50 peer-reviewed papers to international journals and conferences.

Gianni Pasolini received the Dr. Ing. degree in Telecommunications Engineering and the Ph.D. degree in Electronic Engineering and Computer Science from the University of Bologna, Italy, in 1999 and 2003, respectively. In May 1999, he joined the CSITE (Centre for Studies in Computer Science and Telecommunication Systems) of the Italian National Research Council (CNR), which became, in Nov. 2002, the Research Unit of Bologna of the IEIIT (CNR Institute for Electronics and for Information and Telecommunications Engineering). Since 2006, he is a Researcher at the University of Bologna where he has the appointment of Professor of Electrical Communications. His research interests include wireless communication systems, with particular reference to WLANs, WPANs, WiMax, UMTS, digital signal processing, and Intelligent Transportation Systems (ITS). He is author of several publications on international conferences proceedings, journals, and book chapters, and he served as a reviewer and TPC member for various IEEE journals and conferences.

Riccardo Pelliccia was born in 1983, he received his M.S. degree con laude in Electronic Engineering at the Università Politecnica delle Marche in February 2011. Since November 2011, he is a Ph.D. student in Innovation Technologies (curriculum Embedded System) at the Scuola Superiore Sant'Anna, Pisa, Italy.

Fabio Pereira is a former student from Information Systems and Computer Engineering course at Technical University of Lisbon (Instituto Superior Tecnico – IST/UTL), Portugal. Fabio received his Master degree in Information Systems and Computer Engineering in 2011. Currently, he is a Technical Assistant at Maksen, a consulting services provider company. His personal research interests are distributed systems and computer networks, more specifically: P2P systems, ubiquitous computing, parallel computing and networks, and computers security.

Matteo Petracca received the M.S. degree in Telecommunication Engineering in 2003 and the Ph.D. degree in Information and System Engineering in 2007, both from the Politecnico di Torino, Turin, Italy. From April 2007 to November 2009, he was a post-doc researcher at the Politecnico di Torino working on multimedia processing and transmission over packet networks. In 2009, he joined the Scuola Superiore Sant'Anna in Pisa, Italy, and in the 2011, the CNIT (National Inter-University Consortium for Telecommunications) as Researcher. Dr. Petracca has been actively involved in many R&D projects in US (UTMOST, UTDRIVE) in collaboration with the University of Texas at Dallas, and in Italy (VICSUM, IPERMOB). He was the leader of the Work Package related to WSN implementation in the IPERMOB project. He is co-author of papers published in international journals, peer-reviewed conference proceedings, and book chapters.

Massimo Reineri received his Master degree from Politecnico di Torino, in 2009. From February to December 2009, he worked as a Research Assistant with the Dipartimento di Elettronica of Politecnico di Torino. In 2010, he joined the Telecommunication Networks Group at the Dipartimento di Elettronica of Politecnico di Torino as a Ph.D student. In 2011, he won a Fulbright grant, and from September 2011 to April 2012, he has been a Visiting Scholar at the University of California, Los Angeles. His research activities are focused on testbed, content downloading, routing, and channel assignment in wireless mesh and vehicular networks.

Alessandro Rossi holds a degree in Electronic Engineering and he has been in Intecs for 9 years, working in SW verification and validation and development for railway, TLC, and automotive systems. He is now a Project Manager within the Intelligent Transportation System Business Unit of the Automotive and Telecommunications Division.

Claudio Salvadori was born in Arezzo, Italy, in 1978. He received the Laurea degree in Telecommunication Engineering in 2006 from the Universitá degli Studi di Siena, Italy. Since November 2009, he is a Ph.D. student in Wireless Sensor Network at Scuola Superiore Sant'Anna, Pisa, Italy.

Hans Scholten is a Researcher in the Pervasive Systems Group at the University of Twente. He has published over 80 papers in journals and conferences. He is a reviewer and member of the editorial board of several journals, and he has acted as program chair and member of the program committee of international conferences. He has been coordinator of and participates in several national and European projects, like At Home Anywhere (NWO), TEAHA (FP6), Smart Surroundings (BSIK), iLand (Artemis), and SenSafety (Commit). Hans Scholten teaches courses in Computer Architecture, Ubiquitous Computing, and Opportunistic Sensing and Communication. His current research interests are smart environments, vehicular and wireless sensor networks, opportunistic sensing, and delay tolerant networks.

Ramon S. Schwartz received his M.Sc. in Telematics from the University of Twente, The Netherlands, in 2009. Currently, he is a Research Assistant working toward a Ph.D. degree in Computer Science at the Pervasive Systems Group, University of Twente. He regularly serves as reviewer for international conferences and journals in the area of vehicular networks including Vehicular Technology Conference (VTC) and *Vehicular Technology Magazine*. His main research interests are in the area of mobile and wireless networks, in particular, data dissemination in vehicular environments.

Zahra Taghikhaki is currently a PhD student at the Pervasive System Research Group of the University of Twente. She holds her MSc degree from Iran University of Science and Technology with emphasis on Wireless Sensor Networks. Her research is currently focused on in-network data processing, collaborative event detection, and situation awareness in WSN.

Oscar Trullols-Cruces received both the BSc and MSc degrees in Computer Engineering from the Universitat Polite`cnica de Catalunya, Barcelona, Spain, in July 2008. He joined the Computer Networking Research Group in July 2007, where he is working toward the PhD degree. He visited the Royal Institute of Technology (KTH), Stockholm, Sweden, during the spring semester in 2009. His research interests include vehicular networks, delay tolerant networks, and mobility modeling. He is a student member of the IEEE.

Abdelhalim Zekry (M 1994) was born in Menofia, Egypt, on August 8, 1946. He received the B.Sc. and M.Sc. degrees from Cairo University, Cairo, Egypt, in 1969 and 1973, respectively, and the Dr.Ing. degree from the Technical University of Berlin, Berlin, Germany, in 1981. He joined the Institute of Electrical Materials, Technical University of Berlin, in 1975, as a Scientific Coworker. In 1982, he became an Assistant Professor in the Department of Electronics and Computers, Faculty of Engineering, Ain-Shams University, Cairo. In 1988, he moved to King Saud University, Riadh, Saudi Arabia, as an Associate Professor. In August 1992, he became a Professor of Electronics at the same university. In 1996, he returned to Ain-Shams University, where he is currently active. His main research activities are devoted to solid-state devices and circuits for power electronics and communications. He authored two university textbooks on electronic devices and has published more than 100+ publications and research reports. He has a main contribution in the telecommunication research in Ain Shams University. Dr. Zekry was awarded the Best Research Prize of Ain-Shams University in 1987, the State Prize in 1992, and the Decoration of Art and Science in 1996. He was included in the 16th edition of Who's Who in the World.

Yang Zhang is currently a Post-Doctoral Researcher at the Pervasive Systems Group in the University of Twente, The Netherlands. He received his MSc and PhD degrees in Computer Science from this same group in 2006 and 2010. His research interests include wireless sensor networks, data mining, machine learning, and outlier and event detection. He has been involved in several European research projects, i.e., e-SENSE, SENSEI, and GENESI, focusing on distributed data processing in wireless sensor networks. He has published many high-level scientific articles and been invited as reviewer for international journals and conferences.

Index